Lecture Notes in Computer Science 3853

Commenced Publication in 1973
Founding and Former Series Editors:
Gerhard Goos, Juris Hartmanis, and Jan van Leeuwen

Auke Jan Ijspeert   Toshimitsu Masuzawa
Shinji Kusumoto (Eds.)

Biologically Inspired Approaches to Advanced Information Technology

Second International Workshop, BioADIT 2006
Osaka, Japan, January 26-27, 2006
Proceedings

 Springer

Volume Editors

Auke Jan Ijspeert
Swiss Federal Institute of Technology (EPFL)
School of Computer and Communication Sciences
1015 Lausanne, Switzerland
E-mail: auke.ijspeert@epfl.ch

Toshimitsu Masuzawa
Shinji Kusumoto
Osaka University
Graduate School of Information Science and Technology
1-3 Machikaneyama, Toyonaka, Osaka 560-8531, Japan
E-mail: {masuzawa,kusumoto}@ist.osaka-u.ac.jp

Library of Congress Control Number: 2005938022

CR Subject Classification (1998): F.1, C.2, H.4, I.2, F.2, I.4

ISSN   0302-9743
ISBN-10   3-540-31253-6 Springer Berlin Heidelberg New York
ISBN-13   978-3-540-31253-6 Springer Berlin Heidelberg New York

Springer is a part of Springer Science+Business Media

springer.com

© Springer-Verlag Berlin Heidelberg 2006
Printed in Germany

Typesetting: Camera-ready by author, data conversion by Scientific Publishing Services, Chennai, India
Printed on acid-free paper   SPIN: 11613022   06/3142   5 4 3 2 1 0

Preface

This book contains 30 articles and three abstracts of invited talks presented at The Second International Workshop on Biologically Inspired Approaches for Advanced Information Technology (Bio-ADIT 2006) held at Senri Life Science Center, Osaka, Japan, on January 26–27, 2006. Bio-ADIT 2006 follows the success of the first workshop Bio-ADIT 2004, held at the Swiss Federal Institute of Technology, Lausanne (EPFL), Switzerland, in January 2004. The workshop is intended to provide an effective forum for original research results in the field of bio-inspired approaches to advanced information technologies. It also serves to foster the connection between biological paradigms and solutions to building the next-generation information systems. In particular, the aim of the workshop is to explore and discuss how biologically inspired approaches can help in designing the next generation of information systems which, like their biological counterparts, will be capable of adaptation, self-organization, replication, and self-repair.

We were honored to have the participation as invited speakers of three leading researchers in this field: James C. Liao, Rolf Pfeifer, and Toshio Yanagida. The invited talks dealt with the very interesting subjects of bio-inspired approaches to information systems, and provided stimulating ideas to the workshop attendees to pursue further research in this exciting field.

The articles cover a large range of topics including networking, robotics, evolutionary computation, neural computation, biochemical networks, reconfigurable hardware, and machine vision. The contributions range from basic research in biology and in information technology, to more application-oriented developments in software and in hardware. To ensure the content quality, each paper was carefully reviewed by two or three reviewers, and revised according to the reviewers' comments. The papers are divided into 22 oral presentations and 8 poster presentations. The articles published in this book underline the international importance of this field of research, with contributions from China, Germany, India, Japan, Norway, Spain, Sweden, Switzerland, United Kingdom, and USA. It strongly indicates the importance and world-wide impact of the field.

We wish to express our appreciation of the efforts of all the authors who helped to make this book happen. We also gratefully acknowledge the extensive reviewing work carried out by the Technical Program Committee members and additional reviewers. We are indebted to Daniel Mange and Shojiro Nishio, General Co-chairs, for managing the workshop. We would also like to again acknowledge the financial support from the 21st Century Center of Excellence Program of the Ministry of Education, Culture, Sports, Science and Technology

(MEXT) of Japan under the program "New Information Technologies for Building a Networked Symbiosis Environment". We would like to acknowledge the technical support from IEEE ComSom Japan Chapter.

January 2006

Auke Jan Ijspeert
Toshimitsu Masuzawa
Technical Program Committee Co-chairs
Bio-ADIT 2006

Organization

Executive Committee

General Co-chairs	Daniel Mange (EPFL, Switzerland)
	Shojiro Nishio (Osaka University, Japan)
Technical Program	Auke Jan Ijspeert (EPFL, Switzerland)
Committee Co-chairs	Toshimitsu Masuzawa (Osaka University, Japan)
Special Session Program Chair	Hiroshi Shimizu (Osaka University, Japan)
Finance Chair	Toru Fujiwara (Osaka University, Japan)
Publicity Co-chairs	Christof Teuscher (UCSD, USA)
	Yoshinori Takeuchi (Osaka University, Japan)
Internet Chair	Hideki Tode (Osaka University, Japan)
Publications Chair	Shinji Kusumoto (Osaka University, Japan)
Local Arrangement Chair	Tatsuhiro Tsuchiya (Osaka University, Japan)

Technical Program Committee

Co-chairs	Auke Jan Ijspeert (EPFL - Ecole Polytechnique Fédérale de Lausanne, Switzerland)
	Toshimitsu Masuzawa (Osaka University, Japan)
Members	Luc Berthouze (Neuroscience Research Institute (AIST), Japan)
	Giovanna Di Marzo Serugendo (University of Geneva, Switzerland)
	Ezequiel Di Paolo (University of Sussex, UK)
	Marco Dorigo (IRIDIA - Université Libre de Bruxelles, Belgium)
	Raphael Holzer (EPFL - Ecole Polytechnique Fédérale de Lausanne, Switzerland)
	Koh Hosoda (Osaka University, Japan)
	Katsuro Inoue (Osaka University, Japan)
	Laurent Itti (University of Southern California, USA)
	Satoshi Kurihara (Osaka University, Japan)
	Anders Lansner (Stockholm University and Royal Institute of Technology, Sweden)

Vincent Lepetit (EPFL - Ecole Polytechnique Fédérale de
Lausanne, Switzerland)
James Liao (University of California, Los Angeles, USA)
Wolfgang Maass (Graz University of Technology, Austria)
Masayuki Murata (Osaka University, Japan)
Alberto Montresor (University of Bologna, Italy)
Mitsuyuki Nakao (Tohoku University, Japan)
Chrystopher Nehaniv (University of Hertforsdshire, UK)
Masahiro Okamoto (Kyushu University, Japan)
Takao Onoye (Osaka University, Japan)
Rolf Pfeifer (University of Zurich, Switzerland)
Hiroshi Shimizu (Osaka University, Japan)
Gregory   Stephanopoulos   (Massachusetts   Institute   of
Technology, USA)
Tim Taylor (Timberpost Ltd. Edinburgh, UK)
Gianluca Tempesti (EPFL - Ecole Polytechnique Fédérale de
Lausanne, Switzerland)
Daniel Thalmann (EPFL - Ecole Polytechnique Fédérale de
Lausanne, Switzerland)
Tatsuhiro Tsuchiya (Osaka University, Japan)
Sethu Vijayakumar (University of Edinburgh, UK)
Koichi Wada (Nagoya Institute of Technology, Japan)
Naoki Wakamiya (Osaka University, Japan)
Hans   Westerhoff   (Vrije   Universiteit   Amsterdam,
Netherlands)
Masafumi Yamashita (Kyushu University, Japan)
Xin Yao (University of Birmingham, UK)
Tom Ziemke (University of Skovde, Sweden)

Additional Reviewers

Stefano Arteconi
Jonas Buchli
Wei Chen
Peter Eggenberger
Miriam Fend
Julia Handl

Wan Ching Ho
Nobuhiro Inuzuka
Gian Paolo Jesi
Yoshiaki Katayama
Takio Kurita
Dominik Langer

Kenji Leibnitz
Lukas Lichtensteiger
Hiroshi Matsuo
Lars Olsson

Bio-ADIT Steering Committee

Chair   Hideo Miyahara (Osaka University, Japan)
Members   Albert-Laszlo Barabasi (University of Notre
Dame, USA)

Auke Jan Ijspeert (EPFL, Switzerland)
Daniel Mange (EPFL, Switzerland)
Masayuki Murata (Osaka University, Japan)
Shojiro Nishio (Osaka University, Japan)
Hiroshi Shimizu (Osaka University, Japan)
Hans V. Westerhoff (Vrije Universiteit
    Amsterdam, Netherlands)

Sponsoring Institutions

Graduate School of Information Science and Technology, Osaka University
Cybermedia Center, Osaka University
(Under The 21st Century Center of Excellence Program of the Ministry of Education, Culture, Sports, Science and Technology (MEXT), Japan, titled "New Information Technologies for Building a Networked Symbiosis Environment.")
IEEE ComSom Japan Chapter (Technical Co-sponsorship)

Table of Contents

Self-organization

Evolutionary Computation

Modeling and Imaging

Networking II

Posters

Design of Synthetic Gene-Metabolic Circuits

James C. Liao

Department of Chemical and Biomolecular Engineering,
University of California, Los Angeles

The design approach in engineering has created industrial revolution and modern civilization. The basis of design is the understanding of key principles underlying the system of interest. Such an approach has not been explored in biology until recently. While much remained unknown in the cell, key functional paradigms and many molecular components have been extensively characterized. The design approach can now be used in the cell to explore possible applications of biological components beyond their natural configurations, much like the design of analog computers using well characterized modules. In addition, the design approach provides an alternative method to explore design principles used by nature.

However, application of complex design scenarios in the cell has proved challenging, with the perturbation of cellular networks remaining a concern. Recently, several synthetic circuits, such as oscillators, toggle switches and feedback loops were designed and implemented experimentally to function independently from cellular metabolism and physiology. To enhance control capabilities and create novel functionalities, another dimension can be added to the synthetic circuit architecture by integrating both transcriptional and metabolic controls. Implementation of such a design would require extensive knowledge of an organism's physiology. To this end, we chose *E. coli* as the host due to the extensive knowledge of its metabolic pathways, metabolic control and transcriptional regulation. We have engineered an intracellular dynamic feedback controller that senses metabolic state and allows separation of growth phase and metabolite production phase to improve lycopene production; we have constructed a gene-metabolic network for artificial cell-cell communication using acetate as the signalling molecule, thus enabling coordinated population level control. Recently, we have built a synthetic gene metabolic oscillator that creates autonomous oscillation between two pools of metabolites. The success of these circuits demonstrated that the key features in physiological regulation were correctly captured in the design considerations.

A.J. Ijspeert et al. (Eds.): BioADIT 2006, LNCS 3853, p. 1, 2006.

Morphological Computation: Connecting Brain, Body, and Environment

Rolf Pfeifer

Artificial Intelligence Laboratory, Department of Informatics,
University of Zurich, Andreasstrasse 15,
CH-8050 Zurich, Switzerland
pfeifer@ifi.unizh.ch

Traditionally, in robotics, artificial intelligence, and neuroscience, there has been a focus on the study of the control or the neural system itself. Recently there has been an increasing interest into the notion of embodiment not only in robotics and artificial intelligence, but also in the neurosciences, psychology, and philosophy. In this paper, we introduce the notion of morphological computation and demonstrate how it can be exploited on the one hand for designing intelligent, adaptive robotic systems, and on the other for understanding natural systems. While embodiment has often been used in its trivial meaning, i.e. "intelligence requires a body", the concept has deeper and more important implications, concerned with the relation between physical and information (neural, control) processes. Behavior is not the result of brain processes only, but there is a "task distribution" among brain processes (control), morphology, and materials. For example, the positioning of the sensors on the agent, the particular morphology (the anatomy), and the material properties of the muscle-tendon system (the biomechanical constraints) can be exploited for generating adaptive behavior. Morphological computation is about connecting brain, body, and environment (e.g. Pfeifer, et al., 2005, Pfeifer and Gomez, 2005, and Pfeifer and Bongard, 2005).

A number of case studies are presented to illustrate the concept: For sensor morphology, the Eyebot (Fig. 1), for body morphology and materials, the "Yokoi hand" (Fig. 2), and for exploitation of the interaction with the environment, the robot fish "Wanda" (Fig. 3). So, some of the processing is performed not by the brain, but

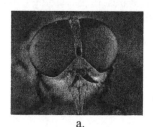 

a.   b.

Fig. 1. Morphological computation through sensor morphology - the Eyebot. The specific non-homogeneous arrangement of the facets compensates for motion parallax, thereby facilitating neural processing. (a) Insect eye. (b) picture of the Eyebot.

A.J. Ijspeert et al. (Eds.): BioADIT 2006, LNCS 3853, pp. 2 – 3, 2006.
© Springer-Verlag Berlin Heidelberg 2006

by the morphology, by the materials, and the interaction with the environment. If we are to understand how behavior in natural systems comes about, and how we should design artificial systems, it is not sufficient to deal with control. In order to comprehend the function of the brain, we must not only look at the brain itself, but at how the brain is embedded in the physical organism, what the properties of this organism are, and what specific interactions the agent is engaged in. Similarly, in order to design good robots, one cannot only program the controller, but all the other aspects must be designed at the same time.

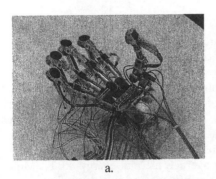 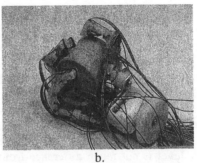

a.   b.

Fig. 2. The "Yokoi hand". (a) The robot hand. (b) Grasping an object; through the particular shape of the hand, the deformable materials and the elastic tendons it self-adapts to a large variety of different bjects without a priori knowledge about their shapes.

a.   b.

Fig. 3. The robot fish W0anda". (a) View from above. (b) sideview while swimming. By exploiting the interaction with the environment, "Wanda" can reach any point in 3D space with just one degree of freedom of actuation (wiggling its tail fin).

References

Pfeifer, R., Iida, F., and Bongard, J. (2005). *New robotics: design principles for intelligent systems*. Artificial Life, January 2005, vol. 11, no. 1-2, 99-120.

Pfeifer, R. and Gomez, G. (2005). Interacting with the real world: design principles for intelligent systems. Artificial life and Robotics. Vol 9. Issue 1. pp. 1-6.

Pfeifer, R. and Bongard, J. (In press). *How the Body Shapes the Way We Think: A New View of Intelligence*. MIT Press.

Single Molecule Nano-Bioscience

Toshio Yanagida

Formation of soft nano-machines CREST, JST, and
Graduate School of Frontier Bioscience, Osaka University Medical School
http://www.phys1.med.osaka-u.ac.jp/

Biomolecules assemble to form molecular machines such as molecular motors, cell signal processors, DNA transcription processors and protein synthesizers to fulfill their functions. Their collaboration allows the activity of biological systems. The reactions and behaviors of molecular machines vary flexibly while responding to their surroundings. This flexibility is essential for biological organisms. The underlying mechanism of molecular machines is not as simple as that expected from analogy with man-made machines. Since molecular machines are only nanometers in size and has a flexible structure, it is very prone to thermal agitation. Furthermore, the input energy level is not much difference from average thermal energy, kBT. Molecular machines can thus operate under the strong influence of this thermal noise, with a high efficiency of energy conversion. They would not overcome thermal noise but effectively use it for their functions. This is in sharp contrast to man-made machines that operate at energies much higher than the thermal noise. In recent years, the single molecule detection (SMD) and nano-technologies have rapidly been expanding to include a wide range of life science. The dynamic properties of biomolecules and the unique operations of molecular machines, which were previously hidden in averaged ensemble measurements, have now been unveiled. The aim of our research is to approach the engineering principle of adaptive biological system by uncovering the unique operation of biological molecular machines. I survey our SMD experiments designed to investigate molecular motors, enzyme reactions, protein dynamics, DNA transcription and cell signaling.

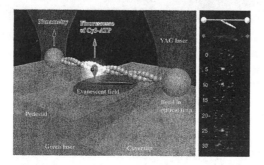

Fig. 1. Single molecule imaging and nano-manipulation of an actomyosin molecular motor. The position and chemical (ATPase) reaction of a myosin molecule are observed by evanescence-based fluorescence microscopy and individual mechanical events due to actin and myosin interaction are detected by optical trapping nanometry.

A.J. Ijspeert et al. (Eds.): BioADIT 2006, LNCS 3853, p. 4, 2006.
© Springer-Verlag Berlin Heidelberg 2006

Evolving the Walking Behaviour of a 12 DOF Quadruped Using a Distributed Neural Architecture

Ricardo A. Téllez, Cecilio Angulo, and Diego E. Pardo

GREC Research Group at Technical University of Catalonia, Spain

Abstract. This paper describes how a distributed neural architecture for the general control of robots has been applied for the generation of a walking behaviour in the Aibo robotic dog. The architecture described has been already demonstrated useful for the generation of more simple behaviours like standing or standing up. This paper describes specifically how it has been applied to the generation of a walking pattern in a quadruped with twelve degrees of freedom, in both simulator and real robot.

The main target of this paper is to show that our distributed architecture can be applied to complex dynamic tasks like walking. Nevertheless, by showing this, we also show how a completely neural and distributed controller can be obtained for a robot as complex as Aibo on a task as complex as walking. This second result is by itself a new and interesting one since, to our extent, there are no other completely neural controllers for quadruped with so many DOF that allow the robot to walk.

Bio-inspiration is used in three ways: first we use the concept of central pattern generators in animals to obtain the desired walking robot. Second we apply evolutionary processes to obtain the neural controllers. Third, we seek limitations in how real dogs do walk in order to apply them to our controller and limit the search space.

1   Introduction

The generation of a walking behaviour in a quadruped as complex as Aibo is a hard task. The robot has many degrees of freedom (twelve) and the coordination of all them to obtain a walking pattern becomes very difficult. In this paper, we evolve a neural controller for the Aibo robot only using neural networks distributed all over the robot. We base our design in the creation and utilisation of Central Pattern Generators (CPGs). Biological CPGs are composed of groups of neurons, capables of producing oscillatory signals without oscillatory inputs. It has been discovered that walking movements of cats and dogs are governed by those elements, and it is thought that humans too behave in the same way [1]. We will implement artificial CPGs using artificial neural networks (ANNs).

CPGs have been already employed by other researchers in the generation of gaits for robots, like for example by Ijspeert on lamprey [2] and salamander simulations [3], Kimura et al. on quadrupeds [4,5] or Collins and Richmon in quadrupeds too [6]. Our work follows the research line taken by Ijspeert with

A.J. Ijspeert et al. (Eds.): BioADIT 2006, LNCS 3853, pp. 5–19, 2006.

their results in the generation of gaits for the lamprey and the salamander, but we try to slightly improve his results in several points: first, we use a more complex robot (every leg has three degrees of freedom that must coordinate); second, we apply it to a real robot; and third, we introduce a general architecture made of standard blocks (see our previous work [7]).

Previously to the present work, we developed a completely distributed architecture for the general control of autonomous robots. Our architecture provides a mechanism for the creation of controllers for autonomous robots in a modular and distributed way, and the architecture is completely based on neural networks. It has already been tested on other simpler tasks like standing up or standing [8], but not in such a complex task like walking. Walking requires special considerations since it contains a special dynamic that has to be taken into account (the robot movement has dependency on previous movement states). We say that while standing or standing up are static tasks (in the sense that for each sensory pattern there is a unique motor answer), walking requires the acquisition of the dynamics of the system, and for each sensory pattern, different motor answers could be applied, depending on the state of the movement (is not the same situation having the leg going than having the leg coming, even the sensory pattern at a specified position is the same).

To overcome the problem of capturing the dynamics of the system, we have used continuous time recurrent neural networks (CTRNNs), instead of using simple feed-forward neural nets like in our previous works. These are neural networks with internal states that allow the capture of the dynamics of a system and have already successfully been applied to the generation of walking patterns in other robots [9, 10].

In order to obtain the correct weights for the neural networks for the task we use neuro-evolution [11]. All the evolutionary process is performed under simulation using the Webots software [12], and once the simulation has the complete walking behaviour, we transfer the resulting ANNs to the real robot to test its validity on real life.

This paper is organised as follows: first we describe the architecture used for the experiments. Then the neural model used is described, followed by a description of the implementation of the architecture in the problem of walking generation is exposed in three stages. Last section discuss the results and points towards future work.

2   Architecture Description

The architecture is based on several uniform modules, composed of ANNs, where each module is in charge of one sensor or actuator of the robot. Through the use of a neuro-evolutionary algorithm, modules learn how to cooperate between them and how to control its associated element, allowing the whole robot to accomplish the task at hands (in this case, generate a walking pattern). All the architecture description has been highly inspired by the concepts of *society of mind* of Minsky [13] and *massive modularity of mind* [14].

2.1   Hardware

We define the Intelligent Hardware Unit (IHU) as a module created around a physical device of the robot (sensor or actuator). Every IHU is composed by a sensor or an actuator and a micro-controller implementing an ANN that processes the information of its associated device (received sensor information for sensors, commands sent to the actuator for actuators). We say that the ANN is in charge of its sensor/actuator. This means that is the neural net the one that decides which commands must be sent to the actuator, or how a value received from a sensor must be interpreted. All IHUs are interconnected to each other in order to be aware of what the other IHUs are doing. So in some sense, the net is also in charge of deciding what to say to the other elements as well as to interpret what the others are saying. The structure of a IHU can be seen in figure 1, and figure 2 shows a neural controller for a simple robotic system with two sensors and two actuators.

It should be stated that when put several IHU together on a control task, each element has its own particular vision of the situation because each one is in charge of its own sensor or actuator. This leads to a situation where each unit knows what the others are doing but needs to select an action for its controller

Intelligent Hardware Unit

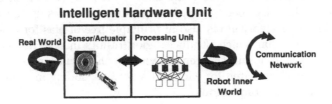

Fig. 1. Schematics of an IHU

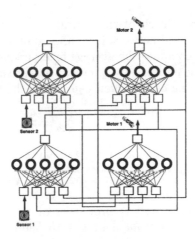

Fig. 2. Connection schema of four ANNs from four IHUs controlling a simple robot composed of two sensors and two actuators

or sensor output, and based on its knowledge of the global situation and that of its particular device, decides what the next action will be.

Even though in the original definition a microprocessor was required for any IHU element, on the experiments presented here it has been simulated the existence of the micro-controllers linked to each device by allocating some processing time in the robot central processor for each IHU, since it was not physically possible to have one dedicated micro-controller for each IHU, neither in the simulations, nor in the real robot tests. It will be assumed that the results are not very different from the original idea.

2.2 Neuro-evolutionary Algorithm

To teach the networks the coordination required for the task a neuro-evolutionary approach has been selected. For the co-evolution of the different networks and due to the necessity of evolving different ANNs for different roles on a common task, a co-evolutionary algorithm is required. By using such kind of algorithm it is possible to teach to the networks how they must cooperate to achieve a common goal, when every network has its own an different vision of the whole system.

The algorithm selected to evolve the nets is the ESP (Enforced Sub-Popula tions) [15][16], which has been proved to produce good results on distributed controllers [11]. This algorithm is also in principle free of bias for a special task. It is a general algorithm which produces good results in systems where several parts must interact to obtain the general view of the situation.

A chromosome is generated for each IHUs network coding in a direct way the weights of the network connections.

3 Neuronal Model

For the implementation of each of the neural elements of the IHUs we use a CTRNN. This type of neural network is composed of a set of neurons modelled as *leaky integrator* that compute the average firing frequency of the neuron [17]. All hidden neurons in one network are interconnected to each other (see figure 3).

The equations governing each hidden neuron are the following:

$$\tau_i \frac{dm_i}{dt} = -m_i + \sum w_{ij} x_j$$

$$x_i = (1 + e^{(m_i + \theta_i)})^{-1}$$

where m_i represents the mean membrane potential of neuron i, x_i is the short-term average firing frequency of neuron i, θ_i is the neuron bias, τ_i is a time constant associated with the passive properties of the neuron's membrane, and w_{ij} is the connection weight from neuron j to neuron i. Calculation of each neuron output is performed using the Euler method for solving differential equations with a step of 96 ms. More complicated models for the hidden neurons are

Output

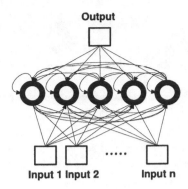

Input 1 Input 2   **Input n**

Fig. 3. Schematics of the CTRNN used in the walking controller

available and have been demonstrated quite useful in the evolution of gaits for quadrupeds [18], but they require higher computational resources that we try to avoid in order to make the robot as autonomous as possible.

For each neural element of the IHUs we use a neural net like the one showed in the figure 3, where the number of inputs depends on the stage of the evolution (see next section), the number of hidden units is five, and the number of output units is one.

For each network it is necessary to evolve the weights, the neuron bias and the time constant of each hidden neuron. However, as we will see in the next section, inter-neuron weights, bias and time constant are only evolved in the first stage (that is the stage that creates the CPGs). Later stages only evolve the interconnections between different CPGs.

4   Staged Evolution of the Walking Behaviour

For the generation of the walking behaviour we implement the explained architecture of section 2. We do not try to indicate that this may be the neural architecture on real dogs, but to show that our architecture is capable of performing the required behaviour.

We implement with our architecture what has been shown to be the way animals perform rhythmic movements like walking, and it is by implementing CPGs on each of its joints. In real animals, there is a CPG for each joint and they are interconnected only with the nearer CPGs. In our case, Aibo's joints are composed of a sensor (that obtains the position of the joint at every moment) and an actuator (that moves the joint). Since our architecture indicates that there must be an IHU for each sensor and actuator, we implement a CPG for each joint by the coupling of a neural net for the joint sensor and a neural net for the joint actuator (see figure 5).

Another difference between real CPGs and our architecture is that in real, only contiguous CPGs are connected to each other. In our case, as the architecture specifies, all IHUs must be connected to all IHUs. Then, all CPGs are connected

Fig. 4. Simulations used for the first and second stages. From left to right: evolving one leg joints, evolving two leg joints, evolving four leg joints.

to all CPGs. Nevertheless, all connections are not evolved at the same time, since, if that was the case, the search space for the evolutionary algorithm would be too high and the required walking solution never be found. For this reason, a staged evolution should be performed, in order to guide the evolutionary process a little bit to the correct solution. The different stages for the generation of the walking are: generation of the CPG oscillator, where a segmental oscillator is evolved for each type of joint, generation of a layer of joints of the same type that oscillate in counter phase by using the previously generated CPGs, and coupling of the three layers to obtain the final walking behaviour.

A very important point is that the generation of the oscillatory patterns is not performed aside of the robot, it is, we have not evolved an isolated oscillator unrelated to the robot. We evolve the oscillatory pattern over the robot itself (in the simulation). This allows the neural nets to capture the dynamics of the (simulated) robot, producing an oscillatory signal that takes into account inertias, decelerations, etc. All these features are important for a robot of the size of Aibo.

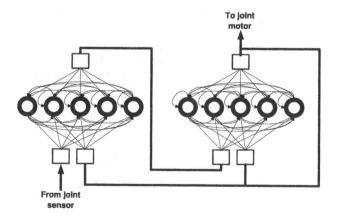

Fig. 5. Schematics of the coupling between two neural nets of a joint. This represents the coupling between the IHU of the joint sensor and the IHU of the joint motor.

4.1   First Stage: Generation of the CPG Oscillatory Pattern

At this stage we must obtain an oscillator capable of generate an oscillatory pattern for each type of joint of the robot. Joints in the robot legs are of three different types that we will call J1, J2 and J3. J1 is in charge of the rotatory movement, J2 of the lateral movement and J3 of the knee movement. Each joint is physically implemented using different PID controllers. Also their movement limits are different. For this reason, we must implement a different type of CPG for each type of joint (this is, three types of CPGs). Nevertheless, the process for the generation of each type is exactly the same, been the limitation of movements the only difference between them.

For each joint, we implement each CPG by the coupling of two CTRNN networks one for the sensor of the joint and another for the actuator (the motor). It is like we apply the architecture described in section 2 to a unique joint.

Both nets are interconnected as the architecture specify but each one is in charge of a different element (the sensor net is in charge of the sensor, and the motor net is in charge of the motor). At each step of the evolutionary process, the value of the sensor is read and entered in the sensor IHU. Then the output is computed and given to the actuator IHU. The output of the actuator IHU specifies the velocity that has to be applied to the motor, and, after escalation, it is directly applied to it. The evolution of the oscillatory movement is then performed over the robot, allowing this to include in the networks the effects of inertias and general dynamics of the robot leg (see figure 6).

The weights of the nets are evolved using the ESP algorithm and a fitness function that rewards the production of an oscillatory pattern in the motor joint. We do not specify the type of pattern to obtain but only that has to be periodic and between some oscillatory limits. Aibo joints can oscillate between very large limits, but those are too large for an appropriate walking behaviour. We limit then here the limits of oscillation by looking at the limits of real dogs and how

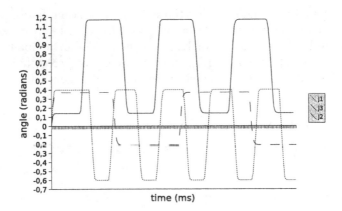

Fig. 6. Oscillatory patterns obtained for all three types of joints. Every joint has its own range of oscillation.

Table 1. Limits for Aibo joints based on real dogs movements when walking

Joint	Max	Min	Mean
J1, fore	0.3936	-0.5837	-0.0982
J2, fore	0.3702	-0.2163	0.0904
J3, fore	1.1732	0.1435	0.6305
J1, hind	0.0059	-0.7848	-0.4200
J2, hind	0.4215	-0.2163	0.1034
J3, hind	1.6599	0.9907	1.2499

do they perform when walking and making a scale conversion to our robotic dog [19]. From that gathered data we obtain the limits indicated in table 1.

The fitness function applied to the neuro-evolution algorithm is defined to reward regular oscillations within the limits of each joint. We want the system to generate a joint movement around the mean value of the table, and maximal variance within the limits of each joint. The fitness function is then:

$$fitness = [V - (A - M)] * C^2$$

been V the variance of the position of the joint during the 200 steps, A its average value, M the mean value of the joint obtained from table 1, and C the number of crossings that the joint performed through the mean position value.

Results: For each type of joint we carried ten runs starting with different initial random populations (weight values between -6 and 6). Each run was composed of 200 simulation steps of 96 ms on a first stage. After 13 generations all runs converged to networks capable of maintained oscillations within the range specified, and the number of steps was augmented to 400 for other ten generations, and later to 800 steps for five generations more. After this final stage, the networks were capable of a continuous oscillatory pattern on an unlimited amount of time.

As an additional note, indicate that the same oscillatory mechanism was obtained in some evolutionary test we performed where the CPGs were only composed of the actuator IHU, it is, no sensor IHU was included and the joint sensor was directly connected to the motor IHU. However we decided to include the sensor IHU for architecture's coherence, and having in mind future benefits. This will be more discussed in section 5.

4.2   Second Stage: Generation of Three Layers

From previous stage we obtained a group of different CPGs each one for a type of joint (three types). In this stage we are going to replicate the CPG of each type in the two fore legs in a first step, and for the four joints in all legs in a second step.

What we do in this case is to duplicate for each joint the CPG formed by the couple of two IHUs from one leg to the other. Duplication and new evolution is performed for one type of joint at a time. Once we have an IHU couple controlling

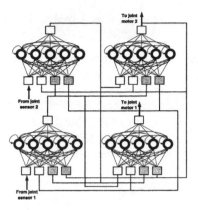

Fig. 7. Connections between four IHUs corresponding to two joints of the same type

each leg, then we apply again the architecture definition, that indicates how all IHUs must be interconnected between them. This implies that each neural net will have to add two more inputs coming from the outputs of the other two neural nets duplicated (see figure 7). The evolutionary process will only evolve the new connections between IHUs, but not the internal connections of the neurons obtained from the previous stage. Since the oscillation has already been obtained in the previous stage, this stage will not have to evolve it, but the synchronisation between the two CPGs. The type of synchronisation to evolve will depend on the type of gait required.

In this case, since we want the robot to implement a simple walking gait, we need a phase relation between those two legs of 180° (in all types of joints). The fitness function will be then that which punctuates the phase difference between the legs that is close to those 180° and rewards a continuous movement of both legs. To implement this function we divided it in three parts: two parts are the fitness function of the first stage for each leg. The third part is the one that measures the variance between the movements of both legs, and tries to maximise it.

$$O_i = [V_i - (A_i - M_i)] * C_i^2$$

$$VL = \frac{1}{N} \sum (diff_j - AvDiff)^2$$

$$fitness = O_1 * O_2 * VL$$

where O_i, V_i, A_i, M_i and C are the variance of the position of the joint during the N steps, the average value, the mean value of the joint obtained from table 1, and the number of crossings that the joint performed through the mean position value, respectively, for each joint i. VL is the variance between legs trajectories, N the number of steps, $diff_j$ is the difference of positions between legs for each evaluation step j, and $AvDiff$ is the average of difference positions between legs.

Results: For each type of joint we carried ten runs to evolve only the connections between CPGs. Each run was composed of 400 simulation steps of 96 ms. After

14 generations, 90% of the networks were capable of a counter-phase oscillatory pattern.

Once we have this two legs oscillatory coupling, we replicated it to the rear legs, and repeated the evolutionary process to evolve only the weights of the new connections between the new IHUs. In this case, we needed to evolve 4 connections per network, having a total number of IHUs of 8 per type of joint. We evolved the whole group by imposing that the oscillations from the fore legs must have a 90° phase difference with the oscillations from the rear legs. To impose this condition, we calculated the difference of positions between fore legs ($diff\_F$) and the difference of positions between rear legs ($diff\_R$), in the same way as was done for the oscillation of two legs. Then we calculated the difference between the differences:

$$totalDiff = diff\_F - diff\_R$$

So finally the fitness to obtain the coordination was composed of five parts: one part for each leg that express the necessity of oscillation, one part that express the necessity of maximal variance between the fore legs, and one last part that express the necessity of maximal variance between differences fore-rear.

This is specified in the following fitness function.

$$O_i = [V_i - (A_i - M_i)] * C_i^2$$

$$VL = \frac{1}{N} \sum (diff_j - AvDiff)^2$$

$$varF\_R = \frac{1}{N} \sum (diffF\_R_j - AvDiffF\_R)^2$$

$$fitness = O_1 * O_2 * O_3 * O_4 * VL * varF\_R$$

where $diffF\_R_j$ is the difference between the difference of positions for fore legs and the difference of positions of rear legs for each evaluation step j, and

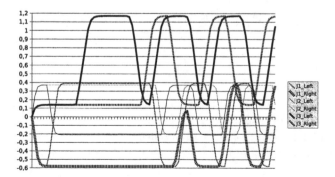

Fig. 8. Oscillations obtained for each type of joint when two joints are evolved

$AvDiffF\_R$ is the average value of such differences. varF_R measures the variance between fore and rear legs.

Results: We carried ten runs for each type of joint. Each run was composed of 400 simulation steps of 96 ms each. After 26 generations, 90% of the networks

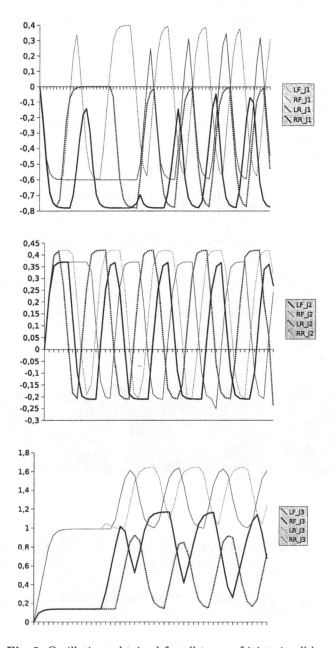

Fig. 9. Oscillations obtained for all types of joints in all legs

were capable of the typical oscillatory walking pattern 0°, 180°, 90°, 270° (for the legs sequence fore_left, fore_right, rear_left, rear_right). The oscillatory patterns obtained can be seen in figure 8.

4.3   Third Stage: Coupling Between Layers

Last stage is the coupling between layers of joints. From previous stage we have three different layers, one per type of joint, of four joints of the same type oscillating together with a *walking* phase relation. Now we need to connect the three layers between them in order to have the complete architecture finished. We will have then to evolve the connections between layers to finally obtain the whole robot walking with the full architecture completed. The connection between layers should bring coordination at walking between the different types of joints that have been evolved separately.

For this stage the fitness function is only the distance d walked by the robot, when the robot does not fall. Zero otherwise.

$$fitness = \begin{cases} d & when\ final\ height > 0 \\ 0 & otherwise \end{cases}$$

Results: A walking behaviour was obtained after 37 generations for about 88% of the populations. A sequence of the walking obtained is shown in figure 9.

The resulting ANN based controller was then transferred to the real robot using the Webots simulator cross-compilation feature that we have collaborated to develop with Cyberbotics. This cross-compilation process takes the exact controller developed in the simulator (the best of the evolved ones), and automatically translates it to Aibo OPEN-R code that is executed on the real robot.

Fig. 10. Simulated Aibo walking sequence

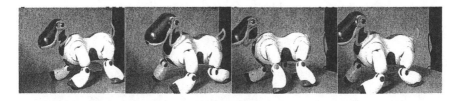

Fig. 11. Real Aibo walking sequence

The result was an Aibo robot that walks in the same manner as the simulated robot with some minor differences. A sequence of the walking obtained is shown in figure 10.

5 Discussion

The present paper shows how a distributed architecture can be used for the generation of gaits in a very complex robot. It also shows that a completely neural network based controller is possible for the generation of a walking behaviour in a quadruped of 12 degrees of freedom. Both of them are new results in the area of autonomous robots and intelligent control systems.

We have implemented each CPG by using two neural nets, one in charge of the sensor and one in charge of the actuator. In a formal way, the implementation of a CPG does not require the use of sensor inputs, but the introduction of the sensor networks could provide the system with a reflex system that may be helpful in front of unpredicted circumstances [20]. Our architecture does integrate already the sensor's feedback into the CPG, but its benefits have not been studied yet and is part of our future work. In particular, this reflex system would be integrated into the own CPG walking structure, not being a separated system, and could benefit the walking style in front of irregular terrain with small obstacles, allowing the robot to adapt to them and keep walking.

When developing the sequence of actions that would lead us to obtain a walking controller, we found that it was impossible to obtain a walking controller if the architecture was directly applied and all the nets (24) were evolved at the same time. The evolutionary algorithm always found an easier and useless solution other than walk in order to go forward. This is due to the complexity of the search space, that makes useless to perform a brute force search. This is the reason why an evolution by stages was required. But the evolution by stages has the drawback that a previous knowledge of the situation is required by the engineer in order to find the best way to implement the stages and find the good fitness functions, and this is one of the main criticisms against the evolutionary robotics methods. That is why, neuro evolutionary roboticists try to avoid as much as possible to introduce their knowledge of the situation, allowing the robot to find their own solution and not biasing the search of it. However, we do bet for the use of the engineer knowledge in the application of the evolutionary process, in order to reduce the search space. We do think it is necessary because, at difference at how real evolution did, we do have to evolve the robot controller on an already made robot, meanwhile real evolution evolved at the same time the structure of the living system and its controller. This puts us on disadvantage when compared to evolution, and that disadvantage needs to be overcome by our analysis and knowledge of the situation. This analysis of the situation should lead to an engineered evolutionary process with some engineer defined fitness functions, resulting on an equilibred evolutionary process that should restrict the search space enough but, at the same time, give space enough to the evolutionary process to explore for the solution. Other approaches are also possible, like for example, to imitate real evolution and evolve at the same time body and controller as some recent works try to implement[21].

Acknowledgements

The authors would like to specially thank Professor Auke J. Ijspeert for insightful comments on the necessity of division of the search space in order to be able to find a good solution, and Dr. Olivier Michel for his support on the use of the simulator.

References

1. Grillner, S.: Neurobiological bases of rhythmic motor acts in vertebrates. Science **228** (1985) 143–149
2. Hallam, J., Ijspeert, A.: 4. In: Using evolutionary methods to parametrize neural models: a study of the lamprey central pattern generator. Physica-Verlag (2003) 119–142
3. Ijspeert, A.J.: A connectionist central pattern generator for the aquatic and terrestrial gaits of a simulated salamander. Biological Cybernetics **84** (2001) 331–348
4. Hiroshi Kimura, S.A., Sakurama, K.: Realization of dinamic walking and running of the quadruped using neural oscillator. Autonomous Robots **7**(3) (1999) 247–258
5. Hiroshi Kimura, Y.F., Konaga, K.: Adaptive dynamic walking of a quadruped robot by using neural system model. Advanced Robot **15** (2001) 859–876
6. Collins, J., Richmond, S.: Hard-wired central pattern generators for quadrupedal locomotion. Biological Cybernetics **71** (1994) 375–385
7. Téllez, R., Angulo, C.: Evolving cooperation of simple agents for the control of an autonomous robot. In: Proceedings of the 5th IFAC Symposium on Intelligent Autonomous Vehicles. (2004)
8. Téllez, R., Angulo, C., Pardo, D.: Highly modular architecture for the general control of autonomous robots. In: Proceedings of the 8th International Work-Conference on Artificial Neural Networks. (2005)
9. Seys, C.W., Beer, R.D.: Evolving walking: the anatomy of an evolutionary search. In: From Animals to Animats: Proceedings of the eighth international conference on simulation of adaptive behavior. Volume 8. (2004)
10. Mathayomchan, B., Beer, R.: Center-crossing recurrent neural networks for the evolution of rhythmic behavior. Neural Computation **14** (2002) 2043–2051
11. Yong, H., Miikkulainen, R.: Cooperative coevolution of multiagent systems. Technical Report AI01-287, Department of computer sciences, University of Texas (2001)
12. Michel, O.: Webots: Professional mobile robot simulation. Journal of Advanced Robotics Systems **1**(1) (2004) 39–42
13. Minsky, M.: The Society of Mind. Touchtone Books (1988)
14. Carruthers, P.: The case for massively modular models of mind. In: Contemporary Debates in Cognitive Science. Blackwell (2005)
15. Gómez, F., Miikkulainen, R.: Solving non-markovian control tasks with neuroevolution. In: Proceedings of the IJCAI99. (1999)
16. Gomez, F., Miikkulainen, R.: Incremental evolution of complex general behavior. Technical Report AI96-248, University of Texas (1996)

17. Hopfield, J.: Neurons with graded response properties have collective computational properties like those of two-state neurons. In: Proc. National Academy of Sciences USA. Volume 81. (1984) 3088–3092
18. Reeve, R.: Generating walking behaviours in legged robots. PhD thesis, University of Edinburgh (1999)
19. Nunamaker, D.M., Blauner, P.: Normal and abnormal gait. In: Textbook of small animal orthopaedics. International veterinary information service, USA (1985)
20. Ijspeert, A.: Locomotion, vertebrate. The handbook of brain theory and neural networks, second edition (2002) 649–654
21. Pollack, J. B., H.G.S.L.H., Funes, P.: Computer creativity in the automatic design of robots. LEONARDO **36**(2) (2003) 115–121

Robot Control:
From Silicon Circuitry to Cells

Soichiro Tsuda[1,*], Klaus-Peter Zauner[2], and Yukio-Pegio Gunji[1]

[1] Graduate School of Science and Technology,
Kobe University Nada, Kobe 657-8501, Japan
Fax: +81-78-803-5759
026d874n@y04.kobe-u.ac.jp, yukio@kobe-u.ac.jp
[2] School of Electronics and Computer Science,
University of Southampton, SO17 1BJ, United Kingdom
Fax: +44-23-8059-2865
kpz@ecs.soton.ac.uk

Abstract. Life-like adaptive behaviour is so far an illusive goal in robot control. A capability to act successfully in a complex, ambiguous, and harsh environment would vastly increase the application domain of robotic devices. Established methods for robot control run up against a complexity barrier, yet living organisms amply demonstrate that this barrier is not a fundamental limitation. To gain an understanding of how the nimble behaviour of organisms can be duplicated in made-for-purpose devices we are exploring the use of biological cells in robot control. This paper describes an experimental setup that interfaces an amoeboid plasmodium of *Physarum polycephalum* with an omnidirectional hexapod robot to realise an interaction loop between environment and plasticity in control. Through this bio-electronic hybrid architecture the continuous negotiation process between local intracellular reconfiguration on the micro-physical scale and global behaviour of the cell in a macroscale environment can be studied in a device setting.

1 The Biological Paradigm

Information processing is essential for life. From the very outset living matter had to defend its organisation against the onslaught of entropy. Subsequently the need to compete with rivalling life forms required evermore refined information processing. As a consequence organisms exhibit an intriguing sophistication in overcoming computationally difficult challenges. In the area of robotics, where restrictions in power consumption and size collide with real-time processing requirements for complex data streams, the discrepancy between technology and nature is particularly apparent.

Although competent artificial autonomous systems capable of successfully acting in an unknown and unbounded dynamic environment are not in sight, directing attention on biological systems has brought several issues to the fore.

---

* Corresponding author.

A.J. Ijspeert et al. (Eds.): BioADIT 2006, LNCS 3853, pp. 20–32, 2006.

It is well known that organisms employ a pragmatic tailoring of sensory information for their specific needs [1]. Conversely, it has been shown that apparently complex behaviour requires only relatively simple control structures [2]. Central to a reduction in computational requirements for control is the task specific adaptation of sensors and actuators [3]. In fact the conceptual separation between sensing, coordinating, and acting may not be tenable for such systems. Mechanical components of a robot's structure can become part of the information processing architecture [4] and thus behaviour is not reflecting the direct actions of a controller but emerges from the interaction of control, body and environment [5, 6].

After what has been stated it may seem that such an approach achieves efficiency by trading away versatility. Yet, clearly, organisms exhibit an enviable capability for coping with unknown situations. How can they achieve efficiency without compromising versatility? Arguably, the key lies in the plasticity of the architecture that allows for the dynamic formation of sensory, computational, and effector structures in reciprocation with the environment [7, 8].

The paradigms outlined above have in common that they go beyond the remit of formal computation by drawing on specific properties of the computing substrate and even extending the latter to include the environment of the robotic device. Hybrid architectures that interface nature's computing substrates with artificial devices open up a path to investigate these paradigms. In the present context the coupling of biological tissue or whole organisms with robotic devices is of interest. Some of the research in this area is motivated by potential applications in prosthetics. It has been demonstrated, for instance, that simultaneous recordings from populations of neurons can enable rats to control a robotic arm [9]. Other approaches focus on the the computational properties of the neural tissue. DeMarse et al. have interfaced cultured rat neurons with a computer simulated environment to study the effect of closed loop feedback to the neuronal network [10]. In a similar vein Reger et al. extracted the brain stem of a fish larva and stimulated it with signals derived from light sensors mounted on a mobile robot. Neural activity in two regions of the brain stem was used to control the robot's movements. We must not omit to mention here the art installations of Ken Rinaldo. He built a number of different robots that are controlled by the position to which a fish swims in its tank and he has implemented what is likely to be the first interaction among robots controlled by organisms (other than humans) [11].

The direction of the work presented in this paper differs from the aforementioned in its focus on robot technology. Here the robot does not serve as a tool for the organism that is in control, nor is it purely a research tool in the study of biological information processing. The long-term objective of the line of research described here is the integration of, potentially modified, cells into made-for-purpose robotic devices.

In the following we first consider the self-organisation and information processing properties of single cells, next focus on a specific cell, the plasmodia of *Physarum polycephalum*, and then describe a hybrid approach in which a plasmodium is integrated into a robot controller to import the plasticity and adaptability of a living organism into a device architecture.

2   Cellular Information Processing

Single cells cannot take recourse to specialised tissues such as a nervous system for their information processing needs. Nonetheless, even bacteria possess elaborate signal processing capabilities [12]. Single cell organisms, by necessity, implement sensors, information processing, and effectors on the molecular level. In examining what is known about nature's molecular level computing it becomes evident that matter is used in a markedly different way than in conventional computing architectures. Information processing mechanisms are tightly coupled to physiochemical properties of the materials rather than being narrowly constraint to enact a rigid formalism [13].

Rothstein speculated that living matter has a large amount of information coded in its structure and used the term 'instructions' for the constraints the system structure imposes on the physicochemical dynamics [14]. This viewpoint is supported by experimental findings. If cells are cooled to very low temperatures all molecules in the cell come almost to a halt. During warming the linear and angular momenta of the molecules in the cell are randomised. This procedure erases the dynamic state information of the cell. Nevertheless cells survive and the cell's static structure is able to revive the dynamics of the living state after warming [15]. Instructions in the sense of Rothstein, however, should not be misconstrued with the careful state preparation required in programming conventional computing devices which depend crucially on the initial state for correct operation. On the contrary, indeed, it is found, for instance, that physicochemical dynamics is able to recreate the intracellular infrastructure even after the spatial arrangement of practically all enzymes has significantly been altered by ultracentrifugation [16]. In combination these observations point to an organisational principle in which cell structure and cell dynamics mutually maintain each other. Prerequisite for such an organisation is, what may be called structure-function self-consistency. Not only does the structure self-organise, as for example in protein folding or virus self-assembly, but also the functional dynamics arises directly from the physical interaction of the components following a course determined by free-energy minimisation. This principle is very different from established information processing technology where the course of a computation is critically dependent on the precise preparation of an initial machine state. It does not only contribute to the robustness and resilience of natural information processors, but, moreover, allows for more efficient implementations. This is the case, because a smaller fraction of the architecture is required to establish constraints and the system state does not need to be tightly constraint with high energy barriers [17].

We will now turn to the the plasmodium of the true slime mold *Physarum polycephalum*, to discuss a specific example of a self-organising, robust information processing architecture that exhibits the aforementioned properties.

3   Characteristics of *Physarum* Plasmodia

The plasmodial stage of *Physarum polycephalum* is a single, giant, multi-nuclear cell. It moves like a large amoeba and is feeding on bacteria. The size of this amorphous organism ranges from several tens of micrometers to a few meters. Figure 1 shows the typical organisation of cytoplasm in a plasmodium. An external membrane encloses a possibly large mass of cytoplasm. Small cells often rely on diffusion to communicate materials and signals internal to the cell. For the giant cells of *Physarum polycephalum*, however, diffusion among distant parts of the cell would be exceedingly slow. An active mechanism is therefore required to coordinate behaviour across the whole organism. A network of tubes spans the plasmodium and connects to its flat border zone. Cytoplasm oscillates forward and backward within the tubes. This, so called shuttle streaming, is driven by hydrostatic pressure gradients along the tubes. The tubes themselves apparently consist of gelled cytoplasm and tubes are formed, interconnected, resized, and disassembled to adapt to changes in the environment as well as to growth [18].

Fig. 1. Part of a plasmodium of *Physarum polycephalum* in developed form. Sheet-like fringe areas (upper part of the photograph) are connected by a network of tubular structures (lower part of the photograph). The section shown is 30 mm wide.

3.1   Distributed Information Processing

The dynamic tubular network provides the necessary infrastructure to integrate information from peripheral zones of the plasmodium and enables this primitive motile system to respond to local stimuli with a coordinated movement of the whole organism. If the plasmodium locally touches a food source, it will gather around it and than cover it. Conversely if an area of the plasmodium comes into contact with a chemical it finds repulsive (NaCl for instance), the entire plasmodium will collectively move away from the stimulated region.

The plasmodium shows chemotaxis, phototaxis, thermotaxis and prefers humid over dry locations. Yet, it does not possess a central processing system for sensory signals. It relies on distributed information processing and communication through the shuttle streaming mechanism to generate the appropriate response to stimuli. The rhythm of the shuttle streaming is known to be synchronised with intracellular chemical oscillation, such as ATP and Ca^{2+} concentration [19]. A local attractive stimulus (e.g., glucose or warmth) is first converted to an increase in frequency of the local protoplasm oscillations and similarly a repellent (e.g., blue light) will lead to a reduced local frequency. The local oscillations are then communicated through the tubular network to couple to oscillations modulated by stimuli received at other regions of the cell [20]. Finally the overall oscillatory pattern of the cytoplasmic streaming gives rise to an approaching or escaping movement. This signal processing mechanism has been modelled with a reaction-diffusion system [21] and shown to be size-invariant [22].

Numerous observations have confirmed the versatility of the distributed processing implemented by the *Physarum polycephalum* plasmodium. Nakagaki and coworkers, for example, showed that the plasmodium can find the shortest path in a maze [23] and that it can solve small instances of optimisation problems [24]. Aono recently constructed a novel neural network system driven by a plasmodium [25]. Some of us implemented self-repairing logic gates with plasmodia [26], which leads to another aspect of *Physarum polycephalum* that is of interest with regard to robot control.

3.2   Self-repair and Robust Behaviour

Among the most enviable features of natural information processing systems is their robustness. Typically they exhibit both, robust function in face of component variation or failure, and robust behaviour in face of unanticipated or paradoxical situations. Both are difficult to achieve with established robot control technology. With progressing miniaturisation of robotic devices these features will become increasingly important. The former because detailed prescriptive control in fabrication will become economically, if not physically, infeasible [27] and the latter because the potential application areas for miniaturised robotic devices call for a high degree of autonomy.

The self-maintenance principle of cells discussed in section 2 in combination with the distributed organisation described in the previous section endows the plasmodium with functional robustness. If a tube of a plasmodium is severed, cytoplasm pumped through the tube will leak into the area surrounding the cut and gel to seal the tube. This sol-gel state transition of the cytoplasm together with the fact that a plasmodium typically contains numerous nuclei allows for much more drastic damage to be overcome. A plasmoidum can be physically taken apart into small pieces, each of which will seal itself up and survive as a smaller, individual, fully functional plasmodium. But, moreover, if two plasmodia get in contact, they can fuse into a single cell and act as one plasmodium after the fusion. This feature has been exploited by Takamatsu et al. to construct coupled nonlinear oscillator circuits [28] and the robot control architecture described below builds on their technique.

As to the phenomena of behavioural robustness in the face of contradictory stimuli, Nomura observed that a plasmodium surrounded by a repellent chemical will eventually move towards the repulsive stimuli and break out of the trap [29]. Further studies are needed to establish whether this is the result of random errors in the information processing cascade that occur with low probability and thus, after a period of exploration, cause the escape, or whether a more sophisticated mechanism gives rise to the approach of the repellent. Studies with multiple attractants also indicate a graceful response of the plasmodium [24].

3.3 Plasmodium Properties Used in the Robot Controller

The cell-based robot controller described in the following section draws on many of the features mentioned so far. A few additional facts are pertinent to the construction and function of the bio-hybrid control architecture. Plasmodia can be grown in a desired geometry by means of a negative plastic mask. A disk-shaped area with a diameter that is small compared to the spatial wavelength of the shuttle-streaming oscillations will be in synchrony and can be assumed to be a single oscillator. And, furthermore, if two such areas are connected by a channel in the mask, the phase wave of an oscillator is propagated only through tube structures formed in the channel [28].

The cytoplasm flow of the shuttle-streaming leads to oscillations in the local thickness of the plasmodium cell. Because plasmodia are not sensitive to light near 600 nm the shuttle-streaming can be monitored through the change in light absorbance concomitant with the thickness variation. To blue light, however, the plasmodia show negative phototaxis and blue or white light can therefore be used as stimuli [30]. In combination these two facts allow for an optical interface to the plasmodium.

4   Robot Control with *Physarum* Circuits

In contrast to conventional information processing architectures, the infrastructure of a cell is in a continual state of flow. This dynamic replacement of components serves maintenance and facilitates structural reorganisation. Self-modification is thus inherent in cells. It would be very difficult to capture even part of this adaptive aspect in a purely artificial device based on current technology. By taking a hybrid approach that integrates a cell into a robot control architecture, however, we can experimentally investigate the interaction of a device that comprises autonomous, self-modifying, and self-maintaining components with its environment.

The design of the architecture is illustrated in Fig. 2. Local shuttle streaming oscillations of a plasmodium are measured and used to affect the phase and

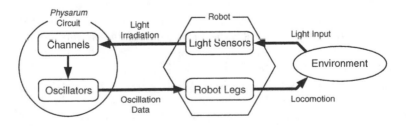

Fig. 2. Physarum-Robot-Environment Interaction Loop

frequency of leg swing in a six-legged robot. The combined action of the legs results in a motion of the robot through its environment which is structured by light sources. Signals from light sensors mounted on the robot are transduced to white light stimuli for a plasmodium. These stimuli in turn affect the shuttle streaming and consequently alter the motion of the robot. However, the cell will respond also with structural reconfiguration. Conrad suggested that in such a self-modifying system structural improvements are possible if errors destabilise the structure and termed this process 'adaptive self-stabilisation' [31]. We adapt a similar perspective, which briefly put, can be pictured as follows. A signal from the environment impinging on the cell gives rise to a local perturbation. As a consequence, locally, the cell state is not aligned with the global state of the cell. The cell will strive to reestablish a self-consistent state by updating its sensory, computational, and effector structures. These structures are of course highly interdependent and pursuing a self-consistent state may involve a lengthy cascade of self-modifications, a process here referred to as *negotiation* between the local and the global. From the structural changes that accompany the local-global negotiation process, an altered global behaviour of the cell emerges. For a formal model of this process see [32].

4.1   The Making of a Cell Circuit

To control the six legs of a hexapod robot we use the star shaped circuit shown in Fig.3. Each of the six circular wells acts as a nonlinear oscillator and all oscillators are coupled through the channels that meet at a single central point. The plasmodium is patterned by letting it grow into the open parts of a mask cut from plastic film that is placed on a 3–5 mm layer of 1.5 % agar in a Petri dish. To fabricate the plastic mask, the circuit pattern with $\approx$ 1.5 mm diameter wells and 0.5 mm wide channels is printed with a laser printer on an overhead projector foil. The wells are cut out with a 1/16" hand punch (www.fiskars.com) and the channels are cut with a sharp blade under a stereo-microscope. The distance from the centre of a well to the junction of the six channels is 3.75 mm.

When the mask is placed on the agar plate it leaves a moist agar region in the desired geometry exposed and confines this area with the dry plastic surface. The plasmodium preferentially grows on a moist surface and usually does not migrate over a dry region. The fact, above mentioned, that plasmodia can be cut into pieces and will fuse into a single cell allows for a cut-and-paste approach in filling the mask. Plasmodia are cultured on 1.5 % agar gel plates that are sprinkled with oat flakes to supply bacteria as food for the plasmodium. A tip of a plasmodium culture is cut off and placed on the exposed agar gel inside each well so that it covers the well region (Fig. 3B). The Petri dish with the developing circuit is then incubated at about 20°C in the dark for 10 hours. During incubation the six plasmodia in the wells grow along the exposed agar surface in the channels (Fig. 3C) and upon meeting in the centre fuse into a single plasmodium. Approximately four hours after fusion tube structures have been formed in the channels (Fig. 3D) and the circuit is ready for use.

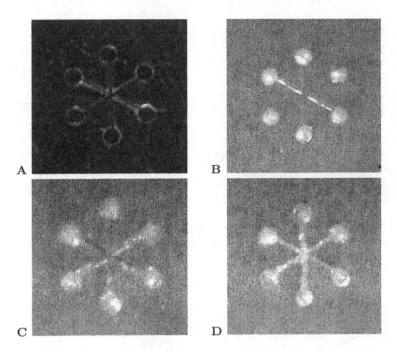

Fig. 3. *Physarum* circuit. The plasmodium is patterned as six oscillators with star coupling by means of a negative plastic mask (A). Panel (B) to (D) show snapshots of the plasmodia growth. Shortly after preparation (B), 5 hours after preparation (C), and the fully developed circuit 10 hours after preparation (D).

4.2   The Robotic Platform and Cell-Robot Interface

A simple six-legged robot with a hexagonal body and radial leg swing provides a platform with excellent static stability. There is no possibility for mechanical interference among the actuators, even if every leg performs random motions and on a flat surface the robot will not tip over. This robot, depicted in Fig. 4, can move and sense omnidirectional and offers numerous possible gate patterns with only a single degree of freedom per leg. If groups of legs are driven in anti-phase the robot exhibits directional movement. The legs of the robot are driven by six servos controlled through a serial interface with a PC. The robot is equipped with six light sensors that feed into six channels of a sound card in the PC. A flexible wire bundle connects the robot with the PC.

Now, to implement the interaction loop shown in Fig. 2, the robot needs to be bi-directionally interfaced with the *Physarum* circuit. The thickness variation of the plasmodium on the one side and its phototactic response on the other side allow for an all-optical interface. Figure 5 shows the overall architecture, the software for which was implemented in Tcl/Tk (cf., wiki.tcl.tk) using the Snack library (www.speech.kth.se/snack/).

One direction will transmit signals received by the robot's sensors to the plasmodium. The signals that arrive at the sound card of the PC are interpreted

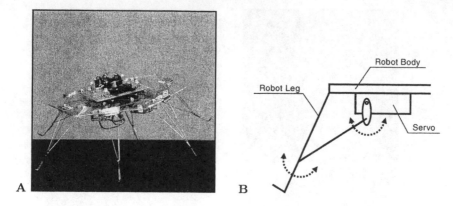

Fig. 4. A tethered hexapod robot (A) is used for its stance stability and gait flexibility. Each leg has only one degree of freedom and swings radial to the body (B). Whether a leg is in contact with the ground during its move will depend on the position of the other legs.

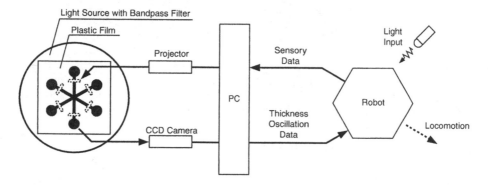

Fig. 5. Cellular robot controller. See text for details.

by the PC and translated into an entry from a fixed image table. Each image in the table has a different white pattern on black background. The image selected from the table is projected with a data projector onto the *Physarum* circuit in such a way that the white patterns (indicated by dashed rectangular boxes in the left of Fig. 5) fall on the channels that connect the wells in the circuit and thus locally stimulate the circuit. Each light sensor on the robot has a corresponding white bar in the projected pattern.

The other direction of the cell-robot interface will transmit the response of the plasmodium to the actuators of the robot. To this end the Petri dish with the fully developed circuit is placed on a cold light source which is bandpass filtered (NT46-152, www.edmundoptics.com) to the spectral region near 600 nm. A CCD camera mounted above the Petri dish detects the red light transmitted through the *Physarum* circuit. For each well the 8-bit brightness values of pixels from the central region are averaged and used to calculate an amplitude signal for the oscillator comprised by the part of the plasmodium in that well. To suppress camera noise, a moving average over a window of 15 samples is used as final output signal of the well. The signal from the six oscillators typically have a period of one to two minutes—too long to be ideal for directly driving the legs of the robot. The plasmodial oscillators, however can be coupled to software oscillators that drive the six robot legs at a higher frequency, yet preserve the phase relationship of the physarum circuit wells. This form of coupling also compensates for the typical variations in amplitude of the signals measured from different wells. The phase relationships among the six legs determine the locomotion of the robot and as a consequence lead to changes in the light levels received by the robot's sensors and accordingly the white light stimulation received by the circuit—thus closing the interaction loop.

4.3 *Physarum* Oscillatory Behaviour

Experiments with a model of coupled nonlinear oscillators confirmed that the robotic platform is capable of directed motion and of direction change when the legs are driven by the oscillators. These experiments showed that changes in the phase relationship among the legs are sufficient to switch between different gait modes.

Our current experiments focus therefore on the phase relationship of the wells in the six-oscillator configuration described in section 4.1. The plasmoidum is known to be active even without food over several days and will go into a dormant state if starved longer. Measurements over extended time periods are therefore possible. We generally conduct experiments with the circuits for 5–10 hours. A typical behaviour of this circuit is shown in Fig. 6. The transitions among phase patterns that are visible in the figure are spontaneous, no stimulus has been applied over the time period depicted.

Stable global in-phase, anti-phase, and rotational oscillations have been observed. Brief periods of unstable oscillations also occur. These oscillations are inherent to the physiology of the plasmodium and occur even without external stimulation. Preliminary experiments with light stimulation indicate that local stimuli can affect the global circuit mode. For instance, we have observed two oscillators located directly opposite each other change from in-phase to anti-phase oscillation immediately after a light stimulus was removed. At present, however, we do not have enough data to establish the nature of this phenomenon. To further investigate the effect of local stimuli on the global oscillation patterns, we have recently modified the experimental procedure to also irradiate the wells with white light (interrupting the stimulus briefly to permit the measurement of transmitted red light).

As noted above, anti-phase oscillations are effective to generate one-directional movement of the robot. Conversely unstable oscillatory patterns typically result in a change of orientation of the robot. As a consequence, despite the robot's morphological symmetry, it will move in a different direction after a phase of unstable oscillations, even if the plasmodium returns to the previous anti-phase pattern.

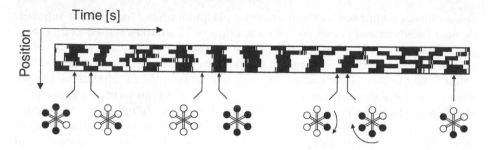

Fig. 6. Spontaneous change in phase relation among the six oscillators of the circuit shown in Fig.3. The graph represents the binarised thickness oscillation rhythm for the oscillators. No stimulus was applied. The six horizontal bands from top to bottom correspond to oscillator wells 1–6, numbered counterclockwise from the upper right (one-a-clock) position. Black lines represent an increase and white vertical lines a decrease in thickness. The horizontal axis represents time with the total length of the graph corresponding to 1000s. Several spontaneous transitions among synchronisation patterns are observed over this time period.

5   Discussion and Perspective

Purposeful operation in a complex ambiguous environment requires versatility rather than controllability. With the current information technology paradigm finding more complex or efficient behavioural strategies is paraphrased as a problem of proper tuning of system parameters and components. But for a system that is required to operate in an ill-defined real world environment, the established concept does not work. The set of key parameters to be considered is bound to be vague and one cannot predetermine all of the possibilities at one's disposal. Nature evolved information processors that are up to this challenge. The plasticity that is a prerequisite for evolutionary progress at the same time opens a path to continual self-adaptation. The architecture of such a system is a response to the current and past interaction with the environment and does in general not have a fixed organisation. The system structure is in a perpetual state of change while local alterations to sensors and signal processing cascades affect the global behaviour which in turn requires a re-alignment of local structure. This local-global negotiation process replaces the tuning of parameters in a conventional system which is necessarily as much ad hoc as it is a priori. This crucial difference between natural and artificial information processors has received considerable attention in the theoretical literature (for pointers see the citations in sections 1, 2, and 4). An experimental approach from an information processing perspective, however, has been difficult.

Although our experiments are at an early stage, we expect that the bio-hybrid architecture presented above will open a path in this direction. From our experience so far, we conclude that the plasmodium of *Physarum polycephalum* is well suited to study device architectures based on autonomous components. At this stage many questions are open. We currently study the effect of the light input signals on circuits to gain a better understanding of what the determinants of the observed transitions in the phase patterns are. We are also investigating how the repertoire of phase patterns relates to circuit topology.

On a longer perspective, we expect robust biological cells such as those of molds and thermophilic bacteria to become an integral part of technological devices. We believe that the efficient and quality controlled nano-fabrication offered by biological cells may turn out to be a suitable way of obtaining highly integrated, robust information processors, at least for niche applications.

Acknowledgements

The authors thank Masashi Aono for helpful discussions. The research reported here was supported in part by the Science and Technology Agency of Japan through the Center of Excellence (COE) program.

References

1. J. Y. Lettvin, H. R. Maturana, W. S. McCulloch, and W. H. Pitts. What the frog's eye tells the frog's brain. *Proc. Inst. Radio Engr.*, 47:1940–1951, 1959. Reprinted in The Mind: Biological Approaches to its Functions, W. C. Corning and M. Balaban, (Eds.), 1968, pp. 233–258.
2. V. Braitenberg. *Experiments in Synthetic Psychology*. MIT Press, Cambridge, MA, 1984.
3. B. Webb. View from the boundary. *Biological Bulletin*, 200(2):184–189, 2001.
4. B. Hasslacher and M. W. Tilden. Living machines. *Robotics and Autonomous Systems*, pages 143–169, 1995.
5. R. D. Beer. *Intelligence as Adaptive Behavior, an Experiment in Computational Neuroethology*. Academic Press, 1990.
6. H. J. Chiel and R. D. Beer. The brain has a body: adaptive behavior emerges from interaction of nervous system, body and environment. *Trends In Neuroscience*, 12:553–557, 1997.
7. H. R. Maturana and F. J. Varela. *Autopoiesis and Cognition: The Realization of the Living*, volume 42 of *Boston Studies in the Philosophy of Science*. D. Reidel Publishing, Dordecht, Holland, 1980.
8. P. Cariani. Some epistemological implications of devices which construct their own sensors and effectors. In F. J. Varela and P. Bourgine, editors, *Toward a Practice of Autonomous Systems: Proceedings of the First European Conference on Artificial Life*, pages 484–493, Cambridge, MA, 1992. MIT Press.
9. J. K. Chapin, K. A. Moxon, R. S. Markowitz, and M. A. L. Nicolelis. Real-time control of a robot arm using simultaneously recorded neurons in the motor cortex. *Nature neuroscience*, 2(7):664–670, 1999.
10. T. B. DeMarse, D. A. Wagenaar, A. W. Blau, and S. M. Potter. The neurally controlled animat: Biological brains acting with simulated bodies. *Autonomous Robots*, 11:305–310, 2001.
11. K. Rinaldo. Augmented fish reality. ARS Electronica Center, Linz, 2004. See also: http://accad.osu.edu/~rinaldo/works/augmented/.
12. J. Adler and W.-W. Tso. "Decision"-making in bacteria: Chemotactic response of Escherichia coli to conflicting stimuli. *Science*, 184:1292–1294, 1974.

13. K.-P. Zauner. Molecular information technology. *Critical Reviews in Solid State and Material Sciences*, 30(1):33–69, 2005.
14. J. Rothstein. Information, measurement, and quantum mechanics. Reprinted in: H. S. Leff and A. F. Rex (Eds.), Maxwell's Demon—Entropy, Information, Computing, pp. 104–108, Bristol: Adam Hilger, 1990, 1951.
15. A. I. Skoultchi and H. J. Morowitz. Information storage and survival of biological systems at temperatures near absolute zero. *Yale J. Biol. Med.*, 37:158–163, 1964.
16. H. Kondo, M. Yamamoto, and M. Watanabe. Reversible intracellular displacement of the cytoskeletal protein and organelles by ultracentrifugation of the sympathetic ganglion. *J. Submicrosc. Cytol. Pathol.*, 24:241–250, 1992.
17. Michael Conrad. The price of programmability. *The Universal Turing Machine: A Half-Century Survey*, pages 285–307, 1988.
18. W. Korohoda, L. Rakoczy, and T. Walczak. On the control mechanism of protoplasmic streamings in the plasmodia of *Myxomycetes*. *Acta Protozoologica*, VII(29):363–373, 1970.
19. T. Ueda, K. Matsumoto, and Y. Kobatake. Spatial and temporal organization of intracellular adenine nucleotides and cyclic nucleotides in relation to rhythmic motility in physarum plasmodium. *Experimental Cell Research*, 162(2):486–494, February 1986.
20. A. C. H. Durham and E. B. Ridgway. Control of chemotaxis in *physarum polycephalum*. *The Journal of Cell Biology*, 69:218–223, 1976.
21. H. Miura and M. Yano. A model of organization of size invariant positional information in taxis of physarum plasmodium. *Progress of Theoretical Physics*, 100(2):235–251, 1998.
22. Y. Miyake, S. Tabata, H. Murakami, M. Yano, and H. Shimizu. Environmental-dependent self-organization of positional information field in chemotaxis of *physarum* plasmodium. *Journal of Theoretical Biology*, 178:341–353, 1996.
23. T. Nakagaki, H. Yamada, and A. Toth. Intelligence: Maze-solving by an amoeboid organism. *Nature*, 407:470, 2000.
24. T. Nakagaki, R. Kobayashi, Y. Nishiura, and T. Ueda. Obtaining multiple separate food sources: behavioural intelligence in the physarum plasmodium. *R. Soc. Proc.: Biol. Sci.*, 271(1554):2305–2310, 2004.
25. M. Aono. Personal communication, 2004.
26. S. Tsuda, M. Aono, and Y.-P. Gunji. Robust and emergent physarum logical-computing. *BioSystems*, 73:45–55, 2004.
27. K.-P. Zauner. From prescriptive programming of solid-state devices to orchestrated self-organisation of informed matter. In J.-P. Banâtre, J.-L. Giavitto, P. Fradet, and O. Michel, editors, *Proceedings of UPP 2004, Unconventional Programming Paradigms, 15–17 September, Le Mont Saint-Michel, France*, volume 3566 of *LNCS*, pages 47–55. Springer, 2005.
28. A. Takamtsu, T. Fujii, and I. Endo. Control of interaction strength in a network of the true slime mold by a microfabricated structure. *BioSystems*, 55:33–38, 2000.
29. S. Nomura. *Symbolization of an object and its freedom in biological systems*. PhD thesis, Kobe University, 2001.
30. T. Ueda, Y. Mori, T. Nakagaki, and Y. Kobatake. Action spectra for superoxide generation and UV and visible light photoavoidance in plasmodia of *physarum polycephalum*. *Photochemistry and Photobiology*, 48:705–709, 1988.
31. M. Conrad. Emergent computation through self-assembly. *Nanobiology*, 2:5–30, 1993.
32. Y.-P. Gunji, T. Takahashi, and M. Aono. Dynamical infomorphism: form of endo-perspective. *Chaos, Solitons and Fractals*, 22:1077–1101, 2004.

Proposal and Evaluation of a Cooperative Mechanism for Pure P2P File Sharing Networks

Junjiro Konishi, Naoki Wakamiya, and Masayuki Murata

Graduate School of Information Science and Technology, Osaka University,
1–5 Yamadaoka, Suita-shi, Osaka 565–0871, Japan
{j-konisi, wakamiya, murata}@ist.osaka-u.ac.jp

Abstract. To provide application-oriented network services, a variety of overlay networks are deployed over physical IP networks. Since they share and compete for the same physical network resources, their selfish behaviors affect each other and, as a result, their performance deteriorates. Our research group considers a model of overlay network symbiosis, where overlay networks coexist and cooperate to improve their application-level quality of service (QoS) while sustaining influences from the physical network and other overlay networks. In this paper, we propose a mechanism for pure P2P networks of file-sharing applications to cooperate with each other. In our proposal, cooperative peers establish logical links among two or more P2P networks, and messages and files are exchanged among cooperative P2P networks through these logical links. For efficient and effective cooperation, we also propose an algorithm for selection of these cooperative peers. Simulation results show that our proposed mechanism improves the search efficiency of P2P file-sharing applications and reduces the load in P2P networks.

1 Introduction

To provide application-oriented network services, a variety of overlay networks are deployed over physical IP networks. Each overlay network independently measures network conditions such as the available bandwidth and latency through active or passive measurement schemes. Based on its observations, each overlay network controls traffic, chooses routes, and changes topologies in a selfish manner to satisfy its own application-level QoS. Since overlay networks share and compete for the same physical network resources, their selfish behaviors affect each other and their performance deteriorates [1, 2]. For example, to communicate faster with other nodes, a node measures bandwidth and latency to other nodes and changes its neighborship accordingly. As a result, the load in the physical network dynamically changes and consequently the quality of communication perceived by other overlay networks which compete for the same links and routers in the physical networks deteriorates. Those affected overlay networks then adapt data rate, routes, and topologies to satisfy or improve their application-level QoS. This further affects other overlay networks and it

A.J. Ijspeert et al. (Eds.): BioADIT 2006, LNCS 3853, pp. 33–47, 2006.

causes frequent changes of routing and introduces congestions in the physical network. Finally, the selfish behavior of overlay networks trying to improve their application-level QoS in fact results in the deterioration of application-level QoS.

Recently there are several publications on cooperative overlay networks to enhance their collective performance and efficiently utilize network re sources [3, 4, 5, 6]. In [3], the authors investigate a spectrum of cooperation among competing overlay networks. For example, they propose an architecture where overlay networks cooperate with each other in inter-overlay routing where a message from one overlay network is forwarded to another which provides a shorter path to the destination. In [4], mechanisms are proposed to exchange information among overlay networks without knowing the destination addresses by using an overlay network called i3 (Internet Indirection Infrastructure) network. The i3 network is an network architecture consisted of some servers. In the i3 network, a user sends *trigger* messages with a service identifier and user's address to the i3 network. A service provider sends *packet* messages with a service identifier to the i3 network. The i3 network transfers *packet* messages to users whose *trigger* messages have the same or similar service identifier.

The analysis on coexistence of competitors has been investigated in the field of biology. In an ecosystem, organisms live together in the same environment with direct and/or indirect interactions with each other. In [7], the authors established a mathematical model of the metabolic pathways of bacterial strains to elucidate mechanisms of coexistence of living organisms of closely related species. They revealed that the coexistence emerged not only from interactions among competitors, but also from changes of their internal states.

Taking inspirations from biology, our research group considers the symbiosis among competing overlay networks [8]. We regard an overlay network as an organism. In the model of symbiotic overlay networks, overlay networks in a system evolve, interact with each other, and dynamically change internal structures, but they still behave in a selfish manner, as living organisms in the same environment do. Overlay networks meet and communicate with each other in a probabilistic way. Overlay networks that benefit from each other reinforce their relationship, eventually having many inter-overlay links, and merging one overlay network. Otherwise, they separate from each other. All evolutions, interactions, and internal changes are performed in a self-organizing way. Each node independently decides its behavior based only on locally available information. Symbiosis among overlay networks emerges as a consequence of the independent and autonomous behaviors of nodes and networks.

For this purpose, we need mechanisms for overlay networks to communicate with each other as in biological systems. In this paper, we propose a mechanism for pure P2P networks of file-sharing applications to interact and cooperate with each other in an efficient and effective way. In a P2P network, hosts called peers directly communicate with each other and exchange information without the mediation of servers. According to user's intention, peers consisting in a P2P network behave on its own decision as an individual does in a group or society. One typical example of P2P applications is a file-sharing system. Gnutella and

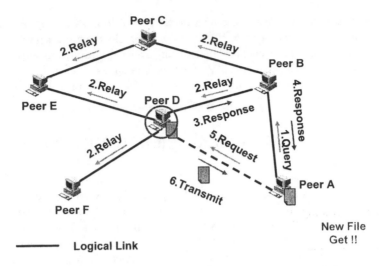

Fig. 1. Flooding in a pure P2P file-sharing network

Winny are categorized as pure P2P networks without a server for searching files. Thus, a peer has to find the desired file by itself by emitting a query message into the network. Other peers in the network reply to the query with a response message and relay the query to their neighbor peers (Fig.1). Flooding, in which a peer relays a query message to every neighbor peer, is a powerful scheme for finding a desired file in a P2P network. However, it has been pointed out that the flooding scheme lacks scalability because the number of query messages that traverses a network significantly increases with the growth in the number of peers [9].

The cooperation among pure P2P networks is accomplished by exchanges of search and reply messages among them through logical connections established among so-called cooperative peers. With such cooperation, we can expect that search messages are disseminated more effectively and a peer finds file more efficiently. Since a peer receives more reply messages for a file, it can choose a more appropriate peer, i.e., faster and more reliable, among many candidate peers, leading to a higher application-level QoS. Furthermore, when a P2P network is disconnected by failures or disappearance of peers, search and reply messages can propagate among separated parts of the P2P networks through cooperative P2P networks. However, to accomplish the efficient and effective cooperation without introducing much load on logical and physical networks, some careful considerations must be made. For example, if a cooperative peer is located at the edge of a P2P network, it has to set a large TTL (Time to Live) value for search messages to spread over the network. As a result, the number of rejected duplicated search messages over P2P networks increases. They waste network bandwidth and causes network congestions. Therefore, we propose an algorithm to choose appropriate cooperative peers. We should note here that a cooperative mechanism should leave peers selfish. Cooperation should emerge from selfish behavior of peers who want to enhance and improve their own QoS. We give some considerations on incentives that a peer begins cooperation.

The rest of this paper is organized as follows. In Section 2, we propose a mechanism for cooperation among pure P2P networks of file-sharing applications. In Section 3, we evaluate our mechanism through several simulation experiments from the viewpoint of the reachability of search messages, the number of found files, and the load on peers. Finally, we conclude the paper and describe future works in Section 4.

2   Cooperative Mechanism for Pure P2P File-Sharing Networks

In this section, we propose a mechanism for pure P2P networks of file-sharing applications to cooperate with each other in an efficient and effective way. In the cooperation of pure P2P networks of file-sharing applications, a logical link is first established between designated peers, called cooperative peers, which are selected among candidate peers in each P2P network. Candidate peers are those which are willing to play the role for cooperation to enhance and improve their own QoS. And then search and reply messages are transmitted through the logical link between cooperative peers (Fig.2).

The mechanism consists of the following steps. First, a peer in a P2P network is promoted to a candidate peer by running a cooperative program. Second, candidate peers construct a candidate network to exchange information for the selection of cooperative peers. Third, a tentative cooperative peer is selected in candidate peers, and then it confirms whether it is appropriate as a cooperative peer or not. Finally, after the confirmation, a tentative cooperative peer is promoted to a cooperative peer. We describe in the following the selection of cooperative peers, the discovery of other P2P networks, the decision of starting

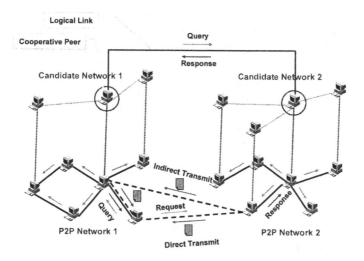

Fig. 2. Cooperation of pure P2P file-sharing networks

a cooperation, the relay of messages and the transfer of files, and the decision of finishing a cooperation in detail.

2.1 Establishing a Candidate Network

When a peer is not satisfied with an application-level QoS received from a P2P network of file-sharing application, it considers to enhance and improve its application-level QoS by its own decision. For example, when a peer cannot find a desired file at all, when a peer cannot find enough number of files against its query, or when a peer cannot tolerate the delay in retrieving a file from a provider peer, a peer, i.e., a user should have some frustrations. A peer will consider that it can receive the higher QoS by connecting to another P2P network which provides it with the higher probability of successful search, the larger number of provider peers, and the smaller delay in file retrieval. In such a case, intending to enhance and improve its application-level QoS, a peer runs the cooperation program independently of others, that is, a peer does not care whether the other peers in the same P2P network will benefit from the cooperation or not. Then, it becomes a candidate peer, i.e., a candidate for cooperative peers. As illustrated in Fig.2, candidate peers in a P2P network construct a candidate network to communicate with each other to select cooperative peers.

A new candidate peer first finds another candidate peer in the same P2P network by flooding a special message over the P2P network or using the i3 network. In the latter case, a new candidate peer registers itself to an i3 service repository by sending a *trigger* message containing a service identifier and its address to the i3 network. On the other hand, candidate peers in a candidate network send *packet* messages containing a service identifier and its address to the i3 network periodically. A new candidate peer receives one of their *packet* messages and establishes a logical link to the candidate peer. After that, the new candidate peer deletes its *trigger* message from the i3 service repository.

For this purpose, candidate peers must have a similar service identifier in the same P2P network but different from those of other P2P networks. In our proposal, a service identifier consists of $l + m + n = 256$ bits. The first l bits are for the cooperation service and common among all cooperation programs. The following m bits correspond to the P2P network. To have the same m bits among candidate peers in the P2P network, we use the IP address of a bootstrapping node. To join a P2P network, a new peer first contacts a bootstrapping node, which should always be available online, to obtain one or more IP addresses of other peers. Since peers in a P2P network know the same bootstrapping node, by applying a hash function to the IP address of the boot strapping node, all candidate peers can have the same network identifier of m bits. We should note here that there is a small possibility that two or more P2P networks have the same m bits identifier. However, we consider that we can avoid the problem without introducing any mediation mechanism. Peers in a P2P network tend to exist close to each other due to a service discovery mechanism of pure P2P applications. Since the i3 network forwards a *packet* message to a node which registers a matching *trigger* message and is close to the sender of the *packet* message, we can expect that a *packet* message is forwarded to another candidate peer of the same P2P network. The last n bits are generated at random. In the i3 network, *inexact matching* is used where the *packet* message has a service identifier matching the longest pattern of bits with the *trigger* message. Therefore, a new candidate peer finds a randomly chosen candidate peer in the same P2P network.

2.2   Selecting Cooperative Peers

Cooperative peers are selected among the candidate peers on receiving a cooperation request. A new cooperation request is generated by a newly joined candidate peer, generated by a candidate peer on its own decision, or sent from other P2P network.

Cooperative peers must be carefully selected to effectively disseminate search messages in P2P networks and distribute the load among peers and networks. It is shown in recent studies [10] that the Internet and many overlay networks have a power-law topology whose degree distribution follows $p(k) \propto k^{-\alpha}$. In [11], it is shown that peers can find files effectively through high-degree peers. It means that by choosing peers with a large number of neighbor peers as cooperative peers, we can expect effective query dissemination. However, high-degree peers are closely connected with each other and thus such selection leads to the concentration of load and causes congestions.

For the efficient and effective message dissemination, we propose a selection method of cooperative peers as follows. First, every candidate peer advertises its degree, i.e., the number of neighbor peers, by flooding a message over a candidate network. Second, each peer ranks candidate peers in descending order of degree. A candidate peer which ranks itself highest advertises a candidacy message to all other candidate peers over a candidate network to become a tentative cooperative peer. On receiving a candidacy message, a candidate peer checks the rank of the tentative cooperative peer in its ranking list. If it is not on the first in the list, a candidate peer sends a conflict message to the tentative cooperative peer. A tentative cooperative peer gives up its candidacy and removes itself from the list on receiving more conflict messages than a predetermined threshold T. The threshold T is introduced to consider the case that a candidate peer, who accidentally missed an advertisement of a tentative cooperative peer, will send a conflict message. Otherwise, a tentative cooperative peer floods a confirmation message with a TTL n in a P2P network. If any cooperative peer already exists within the range, it sends a reject message to the tentative cooperative peer. On receiving a reject message, a tentative cooperative peer gives up its candidacy and advertises its cancellation to the other candidate peers. The tentative cooperative peer is removed from the list and another selection is conducted again. By this mechanism, cooperative peers are kept apart from each other by more than $n + 1$ hops. When a tentative cooperative peer does not receive any reject message in a given time, it finally becomes a cooperative peer. To select two or more cooperative peers, each candidate peer removes a new cooperative peer from the list and repeats the same procedures.

2.3 Finding Other P2P Networks

A newly chosen cooperative peer first finds a candidate peer in other P2P networks by using the i3 network. A cooperative peer sends a trigger message containing a service identifier and its address to the i3 network. The last $m + n$ bits of the service identifier are generated at random, where m bits must be different from its own network identifier.

When a cooperative peer receives a packet message which matches the trigger message by inexact matching, it sends a cooperation request to the candidate peer, i.e., the sender of the packet message, in another P2P network. Next, the selection of a cooperative peer is initiated by the candidate peer in a newly found P2P network. Then, the cooperation request is forwarded from the candidate peer to a new cooperative peer. Finally, a logical link is established between those cooperative peers.

2.4 Decision of Starting Cooperation

Through a logical link established in the preceding step, cooperative peers exchange information to decide whether they cooperate with each other or not. In a biological system, there are varieties of cooperation, coexistence, or, symbiosis, i.e., mutualism, where both species benefit from each other, commensalism, where one species benefits from the other, but the other is unaffected, and parasitism, where one species benefits from the other, but the other suffers. In the case of P2P file-sharing applications, we consider mutualism. However, the decision is still selfish. A peer begins cooperation to enhance and improve its own QoS. A peer maintains an inter-network logical link as far as it considers it is beneficial to itself. When both sides of a logical link consider it is worth connecting, the link is kept. Cooperation is a consequent of selfish behavior of cooperative peers. The decision to start cooperation is made taking into account some criteria, such as the compatibility between P2P file-sharing protocols, the size of P2P networks such as the number of peers and files, and the type of files shared in P2P networks.

When application protocols are different, cooperative peers must convert one protocol into the other. Therefore, it is desirable that protocols are the same or compatible to reduce the load on cooperative peers. When P2P networks are different in their size, peers in a larger P2P network cannot expect the benefit from the cooperation very much. However, the newly introduced load from a smaller cooperative P2P network is considered not much. On the other hand, peers in a smaller P2P network can share and find more files by the cooperation, but they receive a considerable amount of search messages from a larger P2P network. Therefore, cooperative peers must consider the trade-off between the benefit in the application-level QoS and the cost in the increased load by the cooperation. When the type and category of files shared in P2P networks are different, the effect of cooperation is rather small from the viewpoint of the application-level QoS. Therefore, it is desirable that P2P networks sharing similar files such as movies, music, and documents cooperate with each other. A cooperative peer obtains that information and defines priorities to each of them.

When the weighted sum is beyond a threshold for both cooperative peers, the cooperation is started. We should note that weight values and the threshold are determined by an application and details of its strategy and policy are left as one of future research topics.

2.5   Relaying Messages and Getting Files

A search message sent from a peer is disseminated in a P2P network by a flooding scheme. When a search message reaches a cooperative peer, it is forwarded to a cooperative peer in another P2P network after protocol conversion is applied if needed. A TTL value of a search message is reduced by one in transmission between cooperative peers. We hereafter call a P2P network from which a search message originated as a guest network and the other as a host network. A cooperative peer in a host network disseminates the search message in the host P2P network by flooding. When there are two or more pairs of cooperative peers, the same search message would be relayed to a host network. To eliminate the duplication, search messages have the same identifier independently of cooperative peers they traverse. Peers in a host network silently discard duplicated search messages with the same identifier.

If a file is found in a host P2P network, a reply message is generated by a provider peer and it reaches a cooperative peer in a host network along a reverse path of the corresponding search message. A cooperative peer in a host network transmits the reply message to a cooperative peer in a guest network after protocol conversion if needed. In the case that a different protocol is used for file retrieval, a cooperative peer in a guest network cashes a reply message and replaces the address of a provider peer with its own address in the reply message. A reply message reaches the source peer of the search message along a reverse path of the search message in a guest P2P network. The searching peer establishes a connection to a provider peer to obtain a file. In the case that a protocol for file retrieval is different, the peer regards a cooperative peer as a provider peer. Then, the cooperative peer retrieves the file from the original provider peer on behalf of the searching peer. Finally, the file is sent to the searching peer. Therefore, peers do not need to recognize such cooperation to receive the benefit of the cooperation.

2.6   Decision of Finishing Cooperation

Cooperation of P2P networks is terminated by disconnection of all logical links established between all pairs of cooperative peers. A logical link is maintained by the soft-state principle. When no message is transmitted through a logical link for a predetermined duration of time S, it is disconnected. In addition, a peer intentionally disconnects a logical link when it considers that it pays too much for the cooperation. As a consequent of the cooperation, which was initiated by a peer itself, the peer helps peers in a cooperating network in finding files by relaying query and response messages. Taking into account the trade-off between the benefit and the cost of the cooperation, a peer decides whether it maintains the link or not. For example, a cooperative peer monitors the number of outgoing messages and that of incoming messages, then compare their ratio to the threshold R, which is determined by an application or a user. We should note here that details of criteria are left as one of future research topics.

3   Simulation Evaluation

In this section, we conduct several preliminary simulation experiments to evaluate our proposed mechanism. To see what happens when two P2P networks cooperate with each other, we consider two cooperative and static P2P networks. Metrics of our evaluation are the reachability of search messages, the number of found files, and the load on peers. The reachability of search messages is the average fraction of the number of peers which a search message reaches among all peers. As the number of reachable peer becomes higher by cooperation, the possibility of successful search also increases. In addition, a searching peer can choose the most preferable, i.e., the fastest or the most reliable, provider peer among the increased number of file-holders. Therefore, with a higher reachability we can expect a higher application-level QoS in P2P file-sharing applications. The number of found files is the average number of files found in P2P networks per search message. The number of found files is equivalent to the number of found file-holders in our experiments. The load on peers is the average sum of search and reply messages which a peer sends, relays, and receives. The load corresponds to the cost which is introduced by cooperation.

3.1   Simulation Environments

We generate two power-law networks of 10,000 peers based on BA model [12] by a topology generator, BRITE [13]. We assume that logical links among peers have infinite capacity and zero latency. We consider static and stable networks where there is no change in their topologies due to joins and leaves of peers. There are F kinds of files in both P2P networks. Their popularity is determined by Zipf distribution of $\alpha=1.0$. The number of files also follows Zipf distribution of $\alpha=1.0$, where the number of the least popular file is 1. For example, in a P2P network of 10,000 peers, there are 5,000 kinds of 45,473 files and the number of the most popular file is 5,000. Files are placed on randomly chosen peers.

A search message is generated at a randomly chosen peer for a file determined in accordance with the popularity. It is disseminated by flooding within the range limited by TTL, which ranges from 1 to 10 in our simulation experiments. To keep the distribution of files to follow Zipf, a peer does not retrieve a file in our evaluation.

We change the number of cooperative peers from 1 to 100. Cooperative peers are chosen among all peers, that is, all peers are candidate peers in our simulation experiments. In all cases, 20,000 search messages are generated in P2P networks.

3.2   Evaluation of Reachability of Search Messages

Figures 3 and 4 illustrate the reachability of search messages. In these figures, "Descending Order of Degree" shows the result of the case that cooperative peers

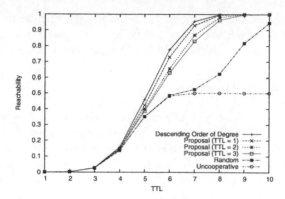

Fig. 3. Relationship between the reachability of search messages and TTL value

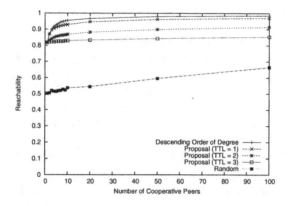

Fig. 4. Relationship between the reachability of search messages and the number of cooperative peers

are selected in descending order of degree of a peer. "Proposal (TTL = n)" shows the result of the case that cooperative peers are selected by our proposed algorithm. In our proposal, a TTL value of a confirmation message is set at n so that the number of hops among cooperative peers are kept more than $n + 1$. "Random" shows the result of the case that cooperative peers are selected at random. "Uncooperative" shows the result of the case that there is no cooperation among P2P networks.

Figure 3 illustrates the relationship between the reachability of search messages and an initial TTL value of a search message where the number of cooperative peers is 10. It is shown that, by the cooperation of P2P networks, search messages reach more peers, and consequently peers can find desired files with a higher probability. In addition, by selecting high-degree peers as cooperative peers preferentially, search messages reach more peers even if a TTL value is small. For example, the reachability of "Uncooperative" and "Random" with TTL of 7 is lower than that of "Descending Order of Degree" and "Proposal" with TTL of 6.

Figure 4 illustrates the relationship between the reachability of search messages and the number of cooperative peers where a TTL value is set at 7. The reachability becomes lower as the number of hops between cooperative peers increases in our proposal. In a power-law network, high-degree peers tend to be located closer, that is, they are connected with each other. Therefore, as n increases, low-degree peers begin to be chosen. Since a low-degree peer cannot disseminate search messages effectively, the number of reachable peers decreases. Furthermore, Fig. 4 shows that in all degree-dependent selection algorithms, the amount of increase in the reachability becomes smaller as the number of cooperative peers increases. Therefore, peers benefit from cooperation with only a few cooperative peers. For example, in the cooperation of two P2P networks of 10,000 peers, about 10 cooperative peers are enough.

3.3 Evaluation of Number of Found Files

Figure 5 illustrates the relationship between the number of found files and the popularity. The number of cooperative peers is 10 and a TTL value is set at 7. It is shown that degree-dependent selection algorithms provide twice the performance of the random selection algorithm and the uncooperative networks. The number of found files of "Random" is almost the same as that of "Uncooperative", that is, the cooperation of P2P networks by randomly chosen cooperative peers does not improve the application-level QoS at all. Since the majority are low-degree peers in a power-law network, a random selection algorithm often chooses low-degree peers as cooperative peers. As a result, the random selection algorithm cannot effectively disseminate search messages in a host network. The reason of step-shaped lines in Fig. 5 is that the number of files, which follows Zipf distribution, takes integer values based on the popularity.

Figure 6 illustrates the cumulative distribution function of the number of found files against the number of hops between a searching peer and file-holders. It is shown that the number of found files within four-hops neighbors is almost

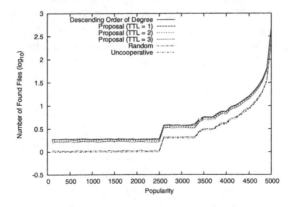

Fig. 5. Relationship between the number of found files and the popularity

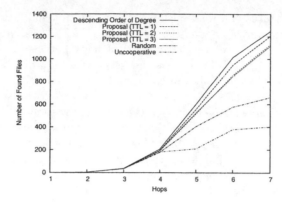

Fig. 6. CDF of the number of found files against the number of hops between a searching peer and file-holders

the same among algorithms. However, degree-dependent selection algorithms can find more file-holders distant from a searching peer. This comes from the fact that degree-dependent selection algorithms disseminate search messages more effectively in a host network as shown in Fig. 3. However, it takes long time for response messages generated at distant file-holders in a host network to reach a searching peer, since they traverse a reversed path of the corresponding query peer in a logical P2P network. Therefore, to have more file-holders for a higher application-level QoS, it is necessary that a searching peer wait for a longer duration of time.

3.4   Evaluation of Load on Peers

Figures 7 and 8 illustrate the load on peers. Figures 3 and 7, and Figs. 4 and 8 show similar tendency respectively, because the number of search and reply messages increases in proportional with the number of peers that search messages reach, i.e., the reachability. However, the load increases slower than the reachability against a TTL value, because the number of duplicated search messages becomes small in low-degree peers. For example, the load of "Proposal (TTL = 3)" with TTL of 6 is almost the same as the load of "Uncooperative" with TTL of 7 (Fig. 7), whereas the reachability of the former is higher than that of the latter (Fig. 3).

Figure 9 illustrates the distribution of the number of duplicated search messages that a peer receives. The number of cooperative peers is 10 and a TTL value is set at 7. The duplicated search messages are redundant and lead to the waste of physical network resources and the processing power of peers. In comparison with "Descending Order of Degree", our proposal can reduce the number of duplicated messages especially at peers with a degree smaller than 100. In "Descending Order of Degree", since high-degree peers are selected as cooperative peers, search messages via cooperative peers can reach to distant peers. It often happens that search messages are redundant at any peer. On the

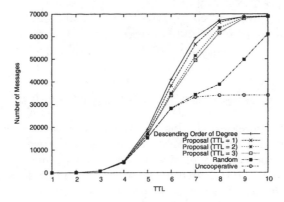

Fig. 7. Relationship between the load on peers and TTL value

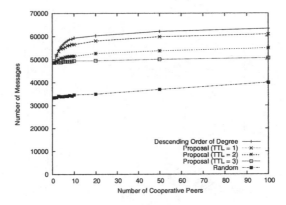

Fig. 8. Relationship between the load on peers and the number of cooperative peers

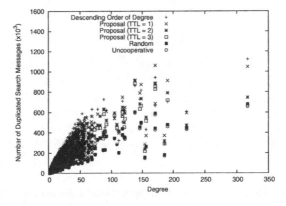

Fig. 9. Distribution of the number of duplicated search messages

other hand, in our proposal, cooperative peers are far from each other and consist of both high-degree peers and low-degree peers. Only search messages with a larger TTL value are redundant, as the number of hops between cooperative peers increases.

On the other hand, as Fig. 10 illustrates, the number of search and reply messages including duplicated messages at the highest-degree peers is considerably high in our proposed methods. In addition, as the number of hops between cooperative peers increases, the load on the highest-degree peers increases. A peer with degree 317 and one with degree 221 have the highest degree in each of P2P networks and they are always chosen as cooperative peers. As the number of hops increases, low-degree peers, who disseminate search messages less effectively, are chosen as cooperative peers. Then, the number of peers that search messages originated from a high-degree peer reach increases. As a result, the number of reply messages becomes higher at a high-degree peer with larger n.

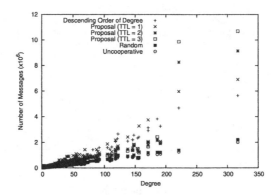

Fig. 10. Distribution of the number of search and reply messages

4   Conclusions

In this paper, in a context of the overlay network symbiosis, we proposed a mechanism for pure P2P networks of file-sharing applications to cooperate with each other. Through simulation experiments, it was shown that application-level QoS was improved by selecting high-degree peers as cooperative peers in the cooperation of power-law P2P networks. Furthermore, it was shown that by keeping cooperative peers apart from each other, the load on the P2P network was reduced, but a few cooperative peers were burden with heavy load.

As future research works, first we consider a mechanism to distribute the load among cooperative peers while keeping the high reachability. We also investigate behaviors of cooperation among dynamic P2P networks, which change their topology as consequences of cooperation. Furthermore, we should evaluate influences of cooperation to a physical network.

Acknowledgements

This research was supported in part by "New Information Technologies for Building a Networked Symbiosis Environment" in The 21st Century Center of Excellence Program of the Ministry of Education, Culture, Sports, Science and Technology of Japan.

References

1. L. Qiu, Y. R. Yang, Y. Zhang, and S. Shenker, "On Selfish Routing in Internet-Like Environments," in *Proceedings of ACM SIGCOMM Conference 2003*, pp. 151–162, Aug. 2003.
2. M. Seshadri and R. H. Katz, "Dynamics of Simultaneous Overlay Network Routing," in *Technical Report of Electrical Engineering and Computer Sciences (EECS), University of California Berkeley (UCB), UCB/CSD-03-1291*, Nov. 2003.
3. M. Kwon and S. Fahmy, "Toward Cooperative Inter-overlay Networking," in *Poster in the 11th IEEE International Conference on Network Protocols (ICNP)*, Nov. 2003.
4. I. Stoica, D. Adkins, S. Zhuang, S. Shenker, and S. Surana, "Internet Indirection Infrastructure," in *Proceedings of ACM SIGCOMM Conference 2002*, pp. 73–88, Aug. 2002.
5. A. Nakao, L. Peterson, and A. Bavier, "A Routing Underlay for Overlay Networks," in *Proceedings of ACM SIGCOMM Conference 2003*, pp. 11–18, Aug. 2003.
6. D. Andersen, H. Balakrishnan, F. Kaashoek, and R. Morris, "Resilient Overlay Networks," in *Proceedings of the 18th ACM Symposium on Operating Systems Principles (SOSP)*, Oct. 2001.
7. T. Yomo, W.-Z. Xu, and I. Urabe, "Mathematical Model Allowing the Coexistence of Closely Related Competitors at the Initial Stage of Evolution," in *Researches on Population Ecology, vol.38, no.2*, pp. 239–247, 1996.
8. N. Wakamiya and M. Murata, "Toward Overlay Network Symbiosis," in *Proceedings of the Fifth IEEE International Conference on Peer-to-Peer Computing (P2P2005)*, Aug. 2005.
9. R. Schollmeier and G. Schollmeier, "Why Peer-to-Peer (P2P) Does Scale: An Analysis of P2P Traffic Patterns," in *Proceedings of the Second IEEE International Conference on Peer-to-Peer Computing (P2P2002)*, Sept. 2002.
10. M. E. J. Newman, "The Structure and Function of Complex Networks," in *SIAM Review, vol.45, no.2*, pp. 167–256, 2003.
11. L. A. Adamic, R. M. Lukose, A. R. Puniyani, and B. A. Huberman, "Search in Power-law Networks," in *Physical Review E, vol.64, 046135*, Sept. 2001.
12. A. L. Barabasi and R. Albert, "Emergence of Scaling in Random Networks," in *Science, vol.286*, pp. 509–512, Oct. 1999.
13. A. Medina, A. Lakhina, I. Matta, and J. Byers, "BRITE: An Approach to Universal Topology Generation," in *Proceedings of the International Workshop on Modeling, Analysis and Simulation of Computer and Telecommunication System (MASCOTS'01). available at http://www.cs.bu.edu/brite/*, 2001.

Resilient Multi-path Routing Based on a Biological Attractor Selection Scheme

Kenji Leibnitz, Naoki Wakamiya, and Masayuki Murata

Graduate School of Information Science and Technology,
Osaka University, 1-5 Yamadaoka, Suita,
Osaka 565-0871, Japan
{leibnitz, wakamiya, murata}@ist.osaka-u.ac.jp

Abstract. In this paper we propose a resilient scheme for multi-path routing using a biologically-inspired attractor selection method. The main advantage of this approach is that it is highly noise-tolerant and capable of operating in a very robust manner under changing environment conditions. We will apply an enhanced attractor selection model to multi-path routing in overlay networks and discuss some general properties of this approach based on numerical simulations. Furthermore, our proposal considers randomization in the path selection which reduces the selfishness and improves the overall network-wide performance.

1 Introduction

It is a well known fact that mechanisms found in biological systems are very robust and can handle changes in the environment very well. Therefore, many methods have been implemented in information science which mimic certain behavior found in nature. Some well known techniques like artificial neural networks, simulated annealing, or genetic algorithms are capable of performing well for certain problem types, especially in the presence of incomplete or fuzzy input data. In artificial neural networks, the concept of *attractors* is often used, which are equilibrium points or curves in the solution space to which the system converges depending on its initial condition. Attractors are a key issue in chaos theory and are often applied in mathematical models found in physics and bioinformatics.

Living organisms in nature continuously face a fluctuating environment and adaptation to these changing conditions is essential for the survival of the species. However, due to the high dimensionality of the habitat, each of the upcoming environmental changes rarely repeats itself during the lifetime of an individual organism. Therefore, the development of adaptation rules is not always feasible since learning and evolutionary processes require multiple occurrences of events to which the organisms adapt. Applying pattern-based learning techniques like in artificial neural networks is only possible, if input patterns and a desired target value exist. When no such input patterns exist, the adaptation to new situations is performed in a more self-organized manner. For example, cells can switch from

A.J. Ijspeert et al. (Eds.): BioADIT 2006, LNCS 3853, pp. 48–63, 2006.

one state to another depending on the availability of a nutrient [1]. These self-adaptive mechanisms are not necessarily optimal from the viewpoint of overall performance, but their main advantages lie in robustness and sustainability. This is a highly important feature for surviving in an unpredictable and fluctuating environment.

In this paper we extend the model of *adaptive response by attractor selection* (ARAS) which was introduced in [1] and apply it to the problem of multi-path routing. ARAS is originally a model for its host E. coli cells to adapt to changes in the availability of a nutrient for which no molecular machinery is available for signal transduction from the environment to the DNA. We will use this mechanism for switching between paths in a multi-path routing environment in communication networks. We consider an underlying IP layer with an overlay network in which an application specific routing is performed. This facilitates the implementation, as no modification to the existing IP layer is necessary. Each source may have several paths to the destination and splits its traffic depending on the current condition of the network over each path. However, one of the paths is chosen as primary path over which the majority of traffic will be routed, while the secondary paths are simply kept alive with a small proportion of the traffic. Attractor selection will be applied here to determine the primary path for a given traffic condition. When the environment, hence link qualities, changes such that the primary path is no longer appropriate, a new primary path is automatically selected. The advantage of our proposal is that there is no explicit routing rule for doing so, but everything is implicitly included in the differential equations describing the dynamics of the system. Furthermore, we use an inherent noise term to drive the system from one attractor to another, making the whole system also very stable to influences from noise.

The reason why we choose a dynamic system for self-adaptive routing instead of simple rule-based mechanisms is because our focus is on adaptiveness and stability of the system. Unlike most other routing papers like [2] which define a target function and perform an offline optimization of the OSPF weights using linear programming, we prefer a highly distributed sub-optimal solution, which is robust in the presence of fluctuations of environment conditions.

The remainder of this paper is organized as follows. In Section 2 we will briefly discuss the problem of multi-path routing in overlay networks and relevant work that is related to this topic. Then, in Section 3 we introduce the biological attractor selection model and extend the original model from $M = 2$ to a higher dimension. In Section 4 we illustrate how to use this proposed model for multi-path routing in overlay networks and we perform some simple simulations and discuss the results in Section 5. Finally, in Section 6 this paper is concluded with a short outlook on future work.

2   Related Work on Overlay Routing

Overlay networks have the appealing feature that their routing can be configured in an application-specific manner without modifying the underlying IP routing scheme. Before we discuss some related work, we would like to clarify the term of multi-path routing as we will use it in the following. The term multi-path routing has been used with different connotations. In all of them multiple paths are used from the source to destination over which traffic is transported. One interpretation of multi-path routing is to increase the resilience of the network, by simultaneously transmitting duplicates of the same packet over each path. This technique is often used in wireless ad-hoc networks [3] and it is sometimes referred to as *redundant multi-path routing*. Another way of using multiple paths is by distributing the traffic volume over these paths. Although by introducing this path diversity the routing is made more robust to failures of individual links, its main purpose is rather on performing load balancing [4]. We will use the latter notion of multi-path routing in our paper. An important issue in this type of multi-path routing which we will not address here is the topic of *packet reordering*, as some packets may overtake each other on different paths. The destination node must buffer the received packets and place them in the right order before delivering them to higher layers.

The issue of routing in overlay networks has been discussed, e.g. for *resilient overlay networks* (RON) [5], as an overlay network architecture which is able to improve the loss rate and throughput over conventional BGP routing due to its faster reaction to path outages. However, end-to-end route selection schemes as employed in overlay routing are of a highly selfish nature, as they greedily choose paths that offer the highest performance, regardless of the implications on the performance and stability of the whole network.

Several publications have investigated selfish routing using a game theoretical approach, e.g. [6, 7]. However, routing optimization is often performed with a global view of the network and its solution is computed by linear programming techniques. In our paper we wish to only consider the limited scope of information that a node can obtain from measurements of its links. In such a case, Seshadri and Katz [8] make suggestions to improve the overall stability of the system by imposing some restraints on the degree of selfishness of each flow. Randomization in path selection is one of such possibilities which we will also adopt in our approach. Another way to improve the overall system stability is to use a hysteresis threshold when updating the path decision.

User-optimal or selfish routing achieves a *Wardrop equilibrium* [9], which states that users do not have the incentives to unilaterally change their routes. Xie et al. [10] present a routing scheme which takes into account the user-optimal routing and network-optimal routing, where the former converges to the Wardrop equilibria and the latter to the minimum latency. In [11] an analytical model is constructed for multi-path routing which leads to an optimal number of links over which dynamic multi-path routing should be conducted. Su and de Veciana [11] propose a policy of routing the traffic to the set of least loaded links and show that this is especially suitable for high speed networks carrying bursty traffic flows.

An adaptive multi-path routing algorithm is proposed by Gojmerac et al. [12] that operates with simple data structures and is independent of the underlying network layer routing protocol. This is achieved by local signaling and load balancing resulting in the reduction of signaling overhead. Another measurement based multi-path routing scheme is given by Güven et al. [13]. This method is similar to the work by Elwalid et al. [14], but does not require the explicit knowledge of the cost derivatives and due to stochastic approximation theory they use noisy estimates from measurements for estimating the cost derivatives. Other papers have dealt with improving the performance by sharing any unused other paths between different users. Approaches to MPLS [15] and WDM networks [16] have been proposed where the backoff capacity is shared, resulting in a better performance especially when supporting quality of service sensitive applications.

3 Biological Attractor-Selection Scheme

In this section we will give an outline of the principle of attractor-selection which is the key component in our method. The original model for adaptive response by attractor-selection is given by Kashiwagi et al. [1] and a first application to multi-path routing is performed in [17]. We will briefly summarize the basic method in an abstract problem formulation in this section, before introducing our extensions and discussing the proposed application to multi-path routing.

Basically, we can outline the attractor selection method as follows. Using a set of differential equations, we describe the dynamics of an M-dimensional system. Each differential equation has a stochastic influence from an inherent Gaussian noise term. Additionally, we introduce an *activity* α which changes the influences from the noise terms. For example, if $\alpha \to 1$ the system behaves rather deterministic and converges to attractor states defined by the structure of the differential equations, see Fig. 1. However, for $\alpha \to 0$ the noise term dominates the behavior of the system and essentially a random walk is performed. When the input values (*nutrients*) require the system to react to the modified environment conditions, activity α changes accordingly causing the system to search for a more suitable state (dotted line in Fig. 1). This can also involve that α causes the previously stable attractor to become unstable.

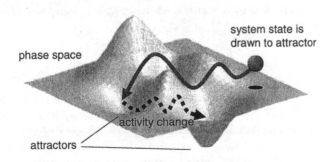

Fig. 1. General concept of attractor selection

The random walk phase can be viewed as a random search for a new solution state and when it is found, α decreases and the system settles in this solution. This behavior is similar to the well known *simulated annealing* [18] optimization method, with the main difference that the temperature is not only cooled down, but also increased again when the environment changes.

3.1 Basic Biological Model

The biological model describes two mutually inhibitory operons where m_1 and m_2 are the concentrations of the mRNA that react to certain changes of nutrient in a cell. The basic functional behavior is described by a system of differential equations, see Eqns. (1).

$$\frac{dm_1}{dt} = \frac{syn(\alpha)}{1 + m_2^2} - deg(\alpha)\, m_1 + \eta_1$$
$$\frac{dm_2}{dt} = \frac{syn(\alpha)}{1 + m_1^2} - deg(\alpha)\, m_2 + \eta_2 \tag{1}$$

The functions $syn(\alpha)$ and $deg(\alpha)$ are the rate coefficients of mRNA synthesis and degradation, respectively. They are both functions of α, which represents cell activity or vigor. The terms η_i are independent white noise inherent in gene expression.

The dynamic behavior of the activity α is given as:

$$\frac{d\alpha}{dt} = \frac{prod}{\prod\limits_{i=1}^{M}\left[\left(\frac{nutr\_thread_i}{m_i + nutrient_i}\right)^{n_i} + 1\right]} - cons\,\alpha, \tag{2}$$

where *prod* and *cons* are the rate coefficients of the production and consumption of α. The term $nutrient_i$ represents the external supplementation of nutrient i and $nutr\_thread_i$ and n_i are the threshold of the nutrient to the production of α and the sensitivity of nutrient i, respectively.

A crucial issue is the definition of the proper $syn(\alpha)$ and $deg(\alpha)$ functions. In our case, the ratio between $syn(\alpha)$ and $deg(\alpha)$ must be greater than 2 to have two different solutions of Eqn. (1) when there is a lack of one of the nutrients. When $\frac{syn(\alpha)}{deg(\alpha)} = 2$, there is only a single solution at $m_1 = m_2 = 1$. The functions $syn(\alpha)$ and $deg(\alpha)$ as given in [1] are shown in Eqn. (3).

$$syn(\alpha) = \frac{6\,\alpha}{2 + \alpha} \qquad\qquad deg(\alpha) = \alpha \tag{3}$$

The system reacts to changes in the environment in such a way that when it lacks a certain nutrient i, it compensates for this loss by increasing the corresponding m_i value. This is done by modifying the influence of the random term η_i through α, see Fig. 2. When α is near 1, the equation system operates in a deterministic fashion. However, when α approaches 0, the system is dominated by the random terms η_i and it performs a random walk.

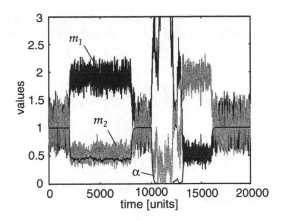

Fig. 2. Biological attractor selection model

In Fig. 2 an example is given over 20000 time steps. We can recognize the following behavior. When both m_i values are equal, the activity is highest and $\alpha = 1$. As soon as there is a lack of the first nutrient ($2000 \leq t < 8000$), m_1 compensates this by increasing its level. When both nutrient terms are fully available again ($8000 < t \leq 10000$), the activity α becomes 1 again. An interesting feature of this method can be observed between $10000 < t < 13000$. Here, the random walk causes the system to search for a new solution, however, it first follows a wrong "direction" causing α to become nearly 0 and the noise influence is highest. As soon as the system approaches the direction toward the correct solution again, α recovers and the system gets stable again. Such phases may always occur in the random search phase.

3.2 Multi-dimensional Attractor Selection Model

In its original form, the attractor selection model only takes a dimension of $M = 2$ into account. Let us now consider a system of $M > 2$ equations as shown in Eqn. (4). The difference to Eqn. (1) is that we now have in the denominator the difference of the m_i value from its maximum $\hat{m} = \max_j m_j$. This does not fully have the direct mutual inhibitory effect anymore like in the original biological model, but makes it easier to extend.

$$\frac{dm_i}{dt} = \frac{syn(\alpha)}{1 + \hat{m}^2 - m_i^2} - deg(\alpha)\, m_i + \eta_i \qquad\qquad i = 1, \ldots, M \qquad (4)$$

Furthermore, for the sake of simplicity we define in the following:

$$\varphi(\alpha) = \frac{syn(\alpha)}{deg(\alpha)}. \qquad (5)$$

Equilibrium Points. The equilibrium points have the condition

$$\frac{dm_i}{dt} = 0 \qquad\qquad \forall i = 1, \ldots, M$$

and can be easily computed from (4) when we assume without restriction of generality that m_i is maximal for an index $i = k$. Inserting this into Eqn. (4) we obtain M resulting vectors of the type

$$\mathbf{x}^{(k)} = \left[x_1^{(k)}, \ldots, x_M^{(k)}\right]^T \qquad k = 1, \ldots, M$$

with components

$$x_i^{(k)} = \begin{cases} \varphi(\alpha) & i = k \\ \frac{1}{2}\left[\sqrt{4 + \varphi(\alpha)^2} - \varphi(\alpha)\right] & i \neq k \end{cases} \qquad (6)$$

These results are all of the type

$$\mathbf{x}^{(k)} = [L, \ldots, L, H, L, \ldots, L]$$

with a single high value H at the k-th entry and all others are a low value L. Note that at

$$\varphi^* = \frac{1}{\sqrt{2}} \qquad (7)$$

we have a special point, as the solutions $\mathbf{x}^{(k)}$ are only defined when $\varphi(\alpha) \geq \varphi^*$. For $\varphi(\alpha) = \varphi^*$ we obtain a single solution $\mathbf{x}$ with the same entries.

$$\mathbf{x} = [x_1, \ldots, x_M] \qquad \text{with} \quad x_i = \varphi(\alpha) \quad \forall i = 1, \ldots, M.$$

This structure of solution vectors is extremely useful to indicate that from all possible M paths, the k-th path is chosen as primary path or there is no specific primary path and the traffic is equally split among all paths.

Determination of the Activity Dynamics. To fully specify the model, we need to define the basic dynamic behavior of the activity α and the functions $syn(\alpha)$ and $deg(\alpha)$. The eigenvalues of the Jacobian matrix at the solutions $\mathbf{x}^{(k)}$ always reveal negative values, leading to stable attractors [19].

Recalling the original biological model, we could identify three distinct stages during the convergence process: there was case (*i*) when all m_i were nearly equal due to a balanced condition at $\alpha = 1$. Then, there was case (*ii*) with one m_i taking a high value and the other m_j with $j \neq i$ a low value. In this case we had different attractor locations and the activity α was fixed at some level between 0 and 1. Finally, in case (*iii*) with activity $\alpha = 0$, we only had random influence.

In the following, we will slightly modify this general behavior. Our goal is to almost always perform a selection of a primary path out of the M possible paths. We will therefore definitely need case (*ii*) stated above. However, we merge cases (*i*) and (*iii*) to consider the scenario when all paths are nearly equal and we don't have a preference; we still choose one of them rather randomly as a primary path. Therefore, this modified method will always yield a primary path except for the time when a new solution is searched. Additionally, we shift the domain for α to the interval $[1, 2]$, since at $\alpha = 1$, we have the lowest absolute value of α and the highest influence from noise. On the other hand, all m_i are at the same value $\varphi(\alpha)$ which helps to recover from this state of equality among the paths and quickly drives one path to become the primary path.

Based on the above mentioned constraints, the quotient $\varphi(\alpha)$ should be a increasing function in $[1, 2]$ with $\varphi(1) = \varphi^*$. We use the following function given in (8).

$$ syn(\alpha) = \alpha \left[(\alpha - 1)^2 + \varphi^* \right] \qquad deg(\alpha) = \alpha \qquad (8) $$

Let us now discuss the desired behavior of α. In order to specify its behavior, we must define what activity should indicate. In this paper, we consider the transmission delay on path i as performance metric l_i, so a "better" path is characterized by a smaller value of l_i. The output values m_i should reflect them by considering the minimum values of l_i. Hence, when an $\check{l} = l_k$ is the minimum of all input values, we wish that the system obtains m_k maximally. The dynamics of the activity behavior is shown in Eqn. (9). We introduce with Δ a hysteresis threshold in order to limit unnecessary oscillations between paths. The use of such a hysteresis was reported in [8] to reduce the selfishness and help improve the overall system performance.

$$ \frac{d\alpha}{dt} = \delta \left(\left[\prod_{i=1}^{M} \left(\left(\frac{m_i}{\hat{m}} \, \frac{\check{l}}{l_i + \Delta} \right)^n + 1 \right) \right]^{\beta} - \alpha \right) \qquad (9) $$

Like in the original model, the rate δ corresponds to the growth (*prod*) and decay (*cons*) rate of α, which we choose to be equal at $\delta = 0.01$. The parameter n given here, is an exponent which must be selected very large, e.g. $n = 100$ in order to "filter out" any unwanted intermediate values. Furthermore, we scale the output levels for H and L with the exponent β. A value of $\beta = 1.75$ has proven to be most effective. Within the product in (9) we could also add further input parameters for evaluating the current system condition in greater detail.

4   Application to Multi-path Routing

The main problem that we focus on here is that for a certain source-destination pair, exactly one path is chosen as primary path based on the current environment condition. When the situation changes and the current primary path is no longer the best choice, the scheme adapts to selecting a different primary path which is better suited. The desired behavior is shown in Fig. 3. There are M paths from source s to destination d and one of these is the primary path over which the main traffic volume is transported. If a link or node fails on this path, the primary path is automatically switched to the best secondary path. The switching of paths should not only occur in such drastic conditions as link failures, but also of course when due to changed load conditions one of the secondary paths seems more appropriate as primary path.

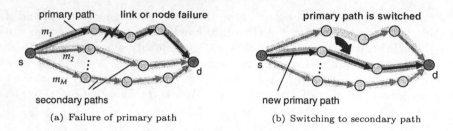

(a) Failure of primary path   (b) Switching to secondary path

Fig. 3. Desired behavior of routing method

The basic sequence of the routing algorithm consists of two steps: (i) route setup phase and (ii) the route maintenance phase. In the following sections we will discuss the operation of both of these phases.

4.1   Route Setup Phase

In the route setup phase we use a decentralized method similarly like in AODV routing. When a request for a new route to a destination arrives at the source node, it broadcasts *route request* (RREQ) packets to the overlay network. When a neighboring node receives an RREQ message and it has no route to the destination, it continues broadcasting the packet to its neighbors. However, if it receives an RREQ message that it has already processed, the request is discarded. In case the RREQ packet arrives at the destination node or another node which already has a route to the destination stored in its table, it replies with a *route reply* (RREP) packet to the source node requesting the route. As soon as the first RREP message arrives at the source it will have knowledge of a route to the destination node and will start using this route in its transmission. In such a way up to M routes are collected gradually and the route maintenance phase with the attractor selection algorithm will proceed with these M paths.

The route setup phase is initiated when the transmission request to an unknown node arrives at the source. After that the route maintenance phase is entered, in which the scheme will operate most of the time. However, in the case that paths are lost in the course of that phase and a minimum threshold of M_{min} is reached, route setup for additional paths is again invoked to add new paths.

4.2   Route Maintenance Phase

Once the first path from source to destination has been established, the route maintenance phase is performed. In this phase, the attractor selection model introduced in Section 3 is used to select the primary path for transmitting packets. This selection is done according to the metric values of each path. We assume that the transmission delay obtained from measurements of the round trip time (RTT) of each packet can be captured by inline measurements to reduce any overhead from active delay measurements.

The main problem in overlay network routing is that the best path is often chosen in an entirely selfish manner and the overall system performance is

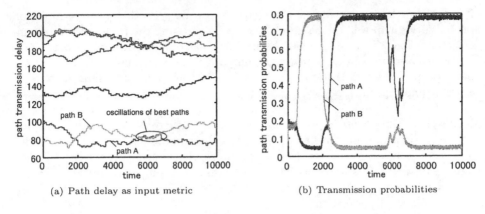

(a) Path delay as input metric   (b) Transmission probabilities

Fig. 4. Input metric and transmission probabilities with P-ARAS

neglected. This may lead to undesired instability and oscillation in the network load. Seshadri and Katz [8] have studied this issue and suggest three restraints on this greedy behavior to improve the overall system-wide performance: (i) randomization in the route selections, (ii) route changes performed with a hysteresis threshold, and (iii) increase of the time interval between route changes. They present three extensions of simple greedy routing where the route selection for each packet is performed with randomization: ARAND, GRAND, and SRAND. The basic operation of these three methods is sketched below. Further details can be found in [8].

ARAND: The path is randomly selected from the set of potential path with probabilities proportional to their metric.

GRAND: The path is randomly selected from the best K potential paths.

SRAND: A subset of K paths is chosen from the potential paths among which the path with the highest metric is selected.

We can integrate randomization of path selections easily in our model, by using path transmission probabilities p_i which are obtained as normalized values of m_i.

$$p_i = \frac{m_i}{\sum\limits_{j=1}^{M} m_j} \qquad\qquad i = 1, \ldots, M \qquad\qquad (10)$$

For this reason we will consider two variants of ARAS distinguishing between a probabilistic version and a deterministic version.

P-ARAS: The path is chosen with probabilities p_i.

D-ARAS: The path with the highest m_i level is selected.

An example of the input metric generated by a Wiener process is shown in Fig. 4(a) for each path and the resulting transmission probabilities for the

P-ARAS method are given in Fig. 4(b). It can be seen that the transmission probabilities map well to the input metrics by choosing the path with minimum delay. At about time step 2000 the primary path is switched from path B to A. It can also be seen that although the path with best input metric oscillates between paths A and B around time step 6000, our method maintains path A as its primary path.

Using only a single metric value like in this case, makes the problem easy to tackle if we simply use a greedy approach, since there is an obvious mapping between input and output values. It should be emphasized, however, that our objective is not only to attempt to optimize the transmission delay of each individual user (as is done in the greedy case). By using randomization in the path selection we accept a slightly worse subjective performance in favor of an improved overall performance.

5   Numerical Results

In this section we will some discuss numerical results of our proposed method. The main performance metric we consider is the *average rate of path changes*. The *average transmission delay* would account only for the subjective performance, but we are more interested in observing the overall objective behavior. However, we will later also consider this metric.

Packets are generated in each slot with a certain probability p_{arr} which corresponds to a geometric time between arrival instants. For each packet arrival occurring at time t, the path over which it is transmitted is chosen by ARAS. If a path is selected that differs from the path used for the previous packet, we consider this a path change. Its total number is divided by the duration of each simulation run to obtain the path selection rate. A high value is, however, not necessarily an indicator for bad performance, since we assume that the paths have already been set up and there is no additional overhead for switching a path. It can be rather regarded as an indicator for the degree of path diversity. Clearly, a too high diversity results in a bad subjective performance since many "bad" paths are used and packet reordering may become necessary. On the other hand, a too small value indicates that the system operates rather deterministically. The whole problem narrows down to finding a good tradeoff between the user's subjective quality and the objective overall network performance.

Each simulation run has a duration of 10000 time steps and is repeated 1000 times. Since the confidence intervals are very small, we omit plotting them. We will focus our study on some of the parameter settings for the randomized version P-ARAS. The simulation scenario which we consider consists of a single source destination pair having $M = 6$ paths with metrics varying over time, see Fig. 5. The background traffic is modeled by initially uniformy distributed random path latencies and the evolution is performed by a Wiener process characterized by its standard deviation σ. Note that we will sometimes refer to this value simply as variation of background traffic. We restrict the possible values of the path latency to be between a lower limit of 10 and an upper limit of 500.

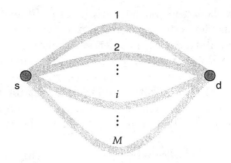

Fig. 5. Simple multi-path layout used in simulations

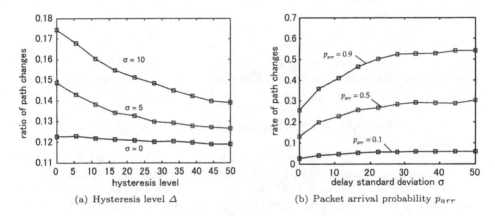

(a) Hysteresis level Δ (b) Packet arrival probability p_{arr}

Fig. 6. Influence of parameters on rate of path changes

5.1 Influence of Parameter Settings

Let us consider at first the hysteresis threshold for switching paths. This parameter influences the reaction to sudden changes of the best path. However, when Δ is too large, the system becomes too slow in response to the metric changes and the performance degrades. The ratio of path changes is shown in Fig. 6(a) as a function of Δ.

The purpose of introducing the hysteresis threshold is to reduce the greediness by keeping the current primary path in spite of another one being slightly better. Using hysteresis shows a great advantage, especially when high oscillations among paths are observed . This is illustrated in Fig. 6(a) where the rate of path changes per packet is shown as a decreasing function over Δ. The slope of decrease becomes larger when σ is large.

In general, the hysteresis threshold should be selected depending on the variation of traffic, but the influence of an improper setting is not very crucial in the operation of our method. An algorithm for automatically selecting the hysteresis is proposed by the authors of [8] which could also be applied to our approach.

Next, we examine how the packet arrival rate influences the rate of path changes. Since we consider a discrete time system, we use a packet arrival probability p_{arr} in the simulation with geometrically distributed interarrival times. This corresponds to a Poisson arrival process with exponential interarrival time in the continuous time domain. We assume that the time steps are larger than the transmission time of the packets, leaving no direct interaction between the packets in this simulation scenario. Therefore, there is no influence of p_{arr} on the simulated average delay. The influence of p_{arr} on the rate of path changes is shown in Fig. 6(b).

The highest packet arrival probability causes also the highest path switching rate, as the arrival instants are more frequent and the sensitivity to traffic variations becomes larger. However, the curves flatten for large values of σ. This means that after the traffic variation reaches a certain level, it hardly influences the frequency of path switches. Although, the packet arrival probability does not influence the delay in our scenario, it does have an effect on the rate of path changes.

In this study we only consider a single flow from a source node to a destination node. When we extend our evaluation to a whole network with interacting flows in the future, we expect that the packet arrival rate will show some greater effect on the performance of our method.

5.2   Comparison of ARAS with Randomized Routing Methods

In the following we will compare the performance of D-ARAS and P-ARAS to the other methods introduced in Section 4. In general, there are two types of path selection methods, those with randomization and those without. While Greedy and D-ARAS are deterministic methods, all others use randomization for path selection. The subjective performance of the deterministic methods is naturally expected to be best, but they operate selfishly and thus are not efficient when considering the overall network performance.

Fig. 7(a) shows the average packet delay for each considered method in the presence of variation of the background traffic process. We use a packet arrival probability of $p_{arr} = 0.5$ and a hysteresis value of $\Delta = 5$. Greedy shows the expected best subjective performance with lowest delays. D-ARAS is only slightly higher, since it has a more delayed reaction than Greedy when choosing the paths. Of the randomized methods, P-ARAS is very efficient as it yields only slightly higher average delays than the deterministic algorithms. However, randomization clearly worsens the subjective performance experienced by the user's average end-to-end packet delay.

In Fig. 7(b) the rate of path changes is depicted. Obviously, the purpose of randomization is to balance the traffic among each path, so these methods yield a higher ratio. The Greedy method and D-ARAS have a very small ratio which is caused by paths often staying best paths despite the presence of high variation of the others. Of the randomized methods again P-ARAS has the smallest path switching rate, whereas ARAND, GRAND, and SRAND stay nearly unaffected of the traffic variation. Clearly the highest path diversity is achieved by ARAND due to the proportional splitting of the traffic flow.

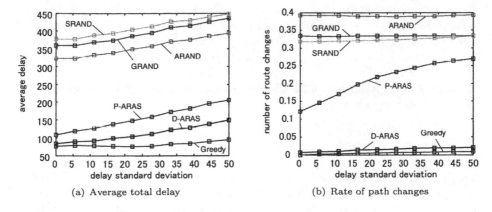

(a) Average total delay   (b) Rate of path changes

Fig. 7. Comparison of ARAS with other methods

In general, we can show that P-ARAS is a good candidate for selecting paths, especially when we compare the results to the other randomized approaches. Its subjective performance reaches nearly that of the deterministic approaches while showing a high degree of path diversity.

6   Conclusion and Outlook

In this paper we presented an application of adaptive response by attractor selection (ARAS) to multi-path routing in overlay networks. ARAS is a biologically-inspired method and is robust to changes in the environment. The method converges to attractor solutions in the phase space and the selection of the appropriate attractor is driven by an activity term α. We have seen that by adequately defining the dynamic behavior of the activity α, we are able to map the input values to the selection of a primary path in an overlay network in a self-adaptive way.

Although the results suggested that the greedy approach appeared to show a good performance, the main drawback of using greedy path selection lies in the instability it introduces to the network. Whenever a new path appears more suitable, traffic flows are shifted and result in *route flapping*. For this reason, we implemented randomization of the path selections to reduce the greediness of each individual source-destination flow, while still achieving a good performance in terms of average packet delay. Furthermore, we investigated the influence of the key parameters of our model, such as the hysteresis threshold for switching paths under different levels of variation of the background traffic. Comparisons to other randomized methods showed the effectiveness of our approach. The main advantage of our proposal is that it operates without explicit rules and is simply implemented by numerical evaluation of the differential equations.

In the future, we wish to focus more on a network-wide view with large scale evaluations of the whole network. When evaluating the network in whole, we expect that our approach will be superior to the greedy method in performance.

So far we considered only a single source-destination pair and the path selection was influenced only by the background traffic without any interaction from other flows operating with our method. As a main goal of further studies, we need to investigate and quantify the benefits of our proposed mechanism in the presence of interacting traffic. In such a way, the activity could be extended by some overall network performance metric resulting in a symbiotic selection of paths for each flow which is best for the whole network.

Acknowledgement

This research was supported by "The 21st Century COE Program: *New Information Technologies for Building a Networked Symbiosis Environment*" and a Grant-in-Aid for Scientific Research (A)(2) 16200003 of the Ministry of Education, Culture, Sports, Science and Technology in Japan.

References

1. Kashiwagi, A., Urabe, I., Kaneko, K., Yomo, T.: Adaptive response of a gene network to environmental changes by attractor selection. submitted for publication (2004)
2. Fortz, B., Thorup, M.: Internet traffic engineering by optimizing OSPF weights. In: IEEE INFOCOM, Tel-Aviv, Israel (2000) 519–528
3. Mueller, S., Tsang, R.P., Ghosal, D.: Multipath routing in mobile ad hoc networks: Issues and challenges. Lecture Notes in Computer Science **2965** (2004) 209–234
4. Andersen, D., Snoeren, A., Balakrishnan, H.: Best-path vs. multi-path overlay routing. In: Internet Measurement Conference (IMC), Miami Beach, FL (2003)
5. Andersen, D., Balakrishnan, H., Kaashoek, M., Morris, R.: Resilient overlay networks. In: 18th ACM Symposium on Operating Systems Principles (SOSP), Banff, Canada (2001)
6. Roughgarden, T., Tardos, E.: How bad is selfish routing? Journal of the ACM **49** (2002) 236–259
7. Qiu, L., Yang, Y., Zhang, Y., Shenker, S.: On selfish routing in internet-like environments. In: ACM SIGCOMM, Karlsruhe, Germany (2003)
8. Seshadri, M., Katz, R.: Dynamics of simultaneous overlay network routing. Technical Report UCB//CSD-03-1291, University of California, Berkeley, CA (2003)
9. Wardrop, J.: Some theoretical aspects of road traffic research, part II. In: Institution of Civil Engineers. Volume 1. (1952) 325–378
10. Xie, H., Qiu, L., Yang, Y.R., Zhang, Y.: On self adaptive routing in dynamic environments – an evaluation and design using a simple, probabilistic scheme. In: International Conference on Network Protocols (ICNP), Berlin, Germany (2004)
11. Su, X., de Veciana, G.: Dynamic multipath routing: asymptotic approximation and simulations. In: ACM SIGMETRICS, Cambridge, MA (2001) 25–36
12. Gojmerac, I., Ziegler, T., Ricciato, F., Reichl, P.: Adaptive multipath routing for dynamic traffic engineering. In: IEEE GLOBECOM, San Francisco, CA (2003)
13. Güven, T., Kommareddy, C., La, R.J., Shayman, M.A., Bhattacharjee, B.: Measurement based optimal multi-path routing. In: IEEE INFOCOM, Hong Kong (2004)

14. Elwalid, A., Jin, C., Low, S.H., Widjaja, I.: MATE: MPLS adaptive traffic engineering. In: IEEE INFOCOM, Anchorage, Alaska (2001) 1300–1309
15. Menth, M., Reifert, A., Milbrandt, J.: Self-Protecting Multipaths - A Simple and Resource-Efficient Protection Switching Mechanism for MPLS Networks. In: 3rd IFIP-TC6 Networking Conference (Networking), Athens, Greece (2004)
16. Gowda, S., Sivalingam, K.M.: Protection mechanisms for optical WDM networks based on wavelength converter multiplexing and backup path relocation techniques. In: IEEE INFOCOM, San Francisco, CA (2003)
17. Leibnitz, K., Wakamiya, N., Murata, M.: Biologically inspired adaptive multipath routing in overlay networks. In: IFIP/IEEE International Workshop on Self-Managed Systems & Services (SELFMAN 2005), Nice, France (2005)
18. Aarts, E., Korst, J.: Simulated Annealing and Boltzmann Machines. Wiley, New York (1989)
19. Murray, J.: Mathematical Biology, I: An introduction. 3 edn. Springer (2002)

Packet Classification with Evolvable Hardware Hash Functions – An Intrinsic Approach

Harald Widiger, Ralf Salomon, and Dirk Timmermann

University of Rostock,
Institute of Applied Microelectronics and Computer Engineering,
Richard-Wagner Str. 31, 18119 Rostock-Warnemuende, Germany
{harald.widiger, ralf.salomon, dirk.timmermann}@uni-rostock.de

Abstract. Bandwidth demands of communication networks are rising permanently. Thus, the requirements to modern routers regarding packet classification are rising accordingly. Conventional algorithms for packet classification use either a huge amount of memory or have high computational demands to perform the task. Using a hash function in order to classify packets is promising regarding both memory and computation time. However, such a hash function needs to be of high performance and cheap in hardware costs. These two design goals are contradictory. To limit the costs of a hardware implementation, known good hash functions, as used for software implementations of encryption algorithms, are applicable to only a limited extend. To achieve the goals mentioned above, an adaptive hash function is needed. In this paper, an approach for a hardware packet classifier using an evolvable hash function is presented. It consists of an evolutionary algorithm which is entirely implemented in hardware.

1   Introduction

In state of the art communication technology, an increasing amount of data has to be transferred. The bandwidth demands of communication networks are rising permanently. Not only the bandwidth demands but also the service demands on state of the art network equipment rise as well. Voice over IP (VoIP) traffic, for example, requires very low latencies. The diversification of data streams in routers driven by the raising quality-of-service (QoS) demands of customers and internet service providers accelerates the packet classification problem in routers rapidly.

1.1   Packet Classification Problem

Network routers must offer a huge variety of services on different flows. These services comprise routing, rate limiting, access control to networks, virtual bandwidth allocation, traffic shaping and policing, and service differentiation. In order to distinguish between different flows, nearly all network components both at the edge and in the core of a network need a packet classifier. Many of the

A.J. Ijspeert et al. (Eds.): BioADIT 2006, LNCS 3853, pp. 64–79, 2006.

aforementioned services are time sensitive. That is why network routers need to classify the packets at wire speed in order to add as less latency as possible before making service decisions.

The classification of packets is based on rules. All rules are stored in a database. The packet classification problem is to determine the rule, that matches for an incoming packet. The database has to be searched in order to find the matching rule. The search must be performed as fast as possible. With higher bandwidths and a large number of rules, a huge database has to be searched in a shorter time. Thus, packet classification is a severe problem in state of the art communication technology for which only limited hardware resources are available. IP lookups in routers for example should be as fast as possible. Conventional algorithms [1] must make a tradeoff between classification speed and memory demands. The algorithms are either implemented in software or in hardware. The software implementations usually lead to comparative low memory requirements but very high search latencies. Many of them use tree structures to classify packets. The HiCuts algorithm [2], for example, partitions the search space guided by heuristics. Each search leads to a leaf, which consists of a small number of rules. The leaves can then be searched linearly to find the best match. The hardware based algorithms on the other hand can perform in wire speed. But therefore either a huge memory amount or specialized and thus expensive hardware or memories like ternary content addressable memories (TCAMs) are required. A TCAM memory array stores all rules (N) in decreasing priority. An input key is compared to all rules in the array in parallel. The N-bit vector indicating all matching rules is read by an N-Bit priority encoder, which indicates the address of the highest priority match. The address is used to index a random access memory (RAM) to find the action associated with the prefix. Besides the potential high costs, another drawback of hardware implementations is the very limited number of rules that can be stored [1].

A solution of the packet classification problem can be the use of hash functions. By the use of a hash function, the two main demands to a packet classifier can be met. Hash functions have a search complexity of ideally $O(1)$. Thus, they are independent of the number of elements searched. With $O(N)$, memory requirements scale only linearly with the number of classification rules. This paper presents a hardware packet classifier that is based on a hash function. Section 2 gives a short overview over the basics of evolutionary algorithms. In section 3, hash functions in general and the evolvable hash functions used for the packet classifier in particular are characterized. Section 4 summarizes the simulation results of the implemented hash functions. Section 5 details the implemented hardware architecture of the packet classifier. Section 6 concludes this paper and presents an outlook to future work.

2 Evolutionary Algorithms

Evolutionary or genetic algorithms are search algorithms based on the mechanics of natural selection and natural genetics [3]. They combine survival of the fittest among string structures with a structured yet randomized information exchange to form a search algorithm with some of the innovative flair of human search. In every generation, a new set of artificial creatures based on the bits and pieces of the old generation is created. Being randomized, genetic algorithms are not simply random walks trough the search space. They efficiently use historical information to speculate on new search points with expected improved performance.

Genetic algorithms work with a coding of a parameter set, instead of the parameter set itself. The search is not done from a single point but a population of points. For determining the quality, a fitness function is used. This fitness function measures the quality of an artificial creature regarding its purpose. In contrary to traditional methods, genetic algorithms use probabilistic transition rules rather than deterministic ones. The mechanism of a simple genetic algorithm involves nothing more than copying strings and swapping partial strings, bit vectors respectively. These transitions are called operators. A simple genetic algorithm is composed of three operators: reproduction, crossover, and mutation.

Reproduction is a process in which individuals are copied depending on the fitness function. A limited number of individuals (the fittest ones) is copied to form the base of the next generation.

Crossover is a process that simulates sexual reproduction (Figure 1). Parts of the bit vectors of two individuals A1 and A2 (the parents) are exchanged producing two offspring (A'1 and A'2) having features of both parents. The individuals created by the reproduction form a mating pool. Members of the pool are mated at random. An integer value k between 1 and the length of the bit vector minus one (1-1) is drawn uniformly. Two new bit vectors are created by swapping all bits between k+1 and l.

Mutation is a process in which bits of the bit vector of the individuals are inverted at random positions. The mutation probability is relatively low. A mean mutation frequency of one mutation per number of bits in the bit vector obtains good results [3]. However, the best mutation rate may be different for each application. If the rate is too high, a random search is performed rather than a genetic algorithm. If it is too low, the speed of the quality improvement of the genetic algorithm is limited needlessly.

If the genetic algorithm is implemented in a hardware structure, it is called an evolvable hardware (EHW). According to [4], EHW can be classified into two categories, extrinsic and intrinsic evolvable hardware. In extrinsic EHW the genetic algorithm is performed externally in software. As a result, only the best configuration obtained is downloaded into hardware. This is done once in each

Fig. 1. Crossover Operator

generation. In the intrinsic approach, the hardware itself simulates the genetic algorithm. This has two main advantages. On the one hand, the genetic algorithm is performed much faster in a specialized hardware than it could be in software on a general purpose processor. On the other hand, such an evolvable hardware can operate autonomously in an Field Programmable Gate Array (FPGA) without an interface to a processor with a software system.

3   Hash Functions

As stated in the introduction, packet classifiers have two main demands, high classification speed with low latency and low hardware (memory) costs. By the use of a hash function the two main demands to a packet classifier can be met. Hash functions have a search complexity of ideally $O(1)$. Thus, they are independent of the number of elements searched in. With $O(N)$ the memory need scales only linearly with the number of classification rules. However, it is problematic to find a sufficient hash function. It has to be both high performance and of low hardware costs. It might be easy to find a good hash function for a specific amount of elements out of a huge search space. But because of changing key sets in packet classifiers, a hash function, that used to be sufficient, might be insufficient for a modified key set. A solution for this problem is a permanently adapting and improving hash function. This goal can be obtained by evolutionary computing completely done in hardware. Such an evolvable hardware hash function is proposed here.

Hash Functions map a value X to its hash value h(X). Usually hash functions do a conversion from a large domain to a much smaller domain. In case of a packet classification, i.e., a 32-bit key (destination IP address) is hashed to a 10-bit wide memory address to store rules for 1024 different keys. Thus, the goal is to map 2^m elements from a search space of 2^n to a much smaller search space of 2^m. The quality of the hash function can be determined by measuring the number of collisions, that occur when hashing all keys into memory. Ideally, every element hashes to a different value. In that case, a hash function is perfect. That would mean for the packet classification that the search for a rule corresponding to a key would be done with just one memory access. Finding such a perfect hash function is very difficult. Depending on the algorithm or the hardware structure of that function, there might be no perfect hash function. Normally a hash function is not perfect. Thus, collisions occur when hashing a number of keys. A collision occurs if two different values are hashed to the same value (equation 1).

$$X \neq Y; h(X) = h(Y) \tag{1}$$

Those collisions must be resolved. This can be done in two different ways [5]. One way is to rehash h(Y) with another hash function that hashes an m-bit value to another m-bit value until no collision occurs and a free entry in the hash memory is found. Another way is to perform a linear collision resolution. For a linear collision resolution a constant value is added to the hash value. This is done until a free memory entry was found. The constant must be a prime number or at least a number which is relatively prime to the number of memory entries. This is required to assure that all existing memory entries are searched before reaching the original entry. In the simplest case the constant is 1. As mentioned above, the quality of a hash function can be measured by counting the number off collisions that occur when all keys are hashed into memory. A perfect hash function would not create any collision. The worst hash function on the other hand would be one that hashes all values to the same hash value. In that case, the maximum number of collisions that would occour is $\frac{n^2-n}{2}$. To limit the number of collisions and to therefore increase the lookup performance, the memory load is usually limited to $\frac{1}{2}$. This means 2^m elements are hashed to (m+1)-bit wide hash values and stored in a memory with 2^{m+1} entries.

Memories accessed by hash functions have the great advantage of fast updates. Both insertions and deletions can be achieved very fast. They have the same complexity as searching. To insert a new entry in a hash memory, the key has to be hashed. Then the memory has to be searched on the bases of $h(key)$ until an empty entry was found. The new entry can be inserted at this position. Deletion is a little more complicated, as the corresponding memory entry cannot simply be freed but must be marked as deleted. Freeing is only possible when rehashing the complete memory. Thus, insertions are not only done when a free memory position is found but also at memory positions that are marked as deleted.

3.1   Evolvable Hardware Hash Functions

To be able to perform many key lookups in a packet classifier with the utilization of a hash function, the hash function should be implemented in hardware. The database of a packet classifier is not static: Permanently rules are added or removed. Thus, a hash function, that used to be sufficient and of good quality for a specific database, gets insufficient with the changes of the database.

A hash function is needed that can be implemented easily and efficiently in hardware. To adapt at any time to an actual set of keys, the hash function shall evolve autonomously. Thus, a complete hardware evolution comes to pass. This is realized by constantly traversing an evolution pipeline comparable with the one in [6]. The system is implemented both as a SystemC software model and a fully synthesizable VHDL description for implementation into an FPGA. A linear collision resolution for the hash functions is used. In the following sections, different hardware architectures of hash functions are explored to determine their potential.

3.2   Hash Architecture 1 and 2

A promising architecture which is high performing and relatively cheap in hardware costs is shown in Figure 2. In the following it is referred to as hash1. It consists of a number of multiplexer elements. The multiplexers are controlled by registers. Those registers form the genome of the hash function. For every output signal, two multiplexer outputs are connected via an xor function. To hash an N-bit value to an M-bit value, $2 \cdot M$ N-to-1 multiplexers are needed. As

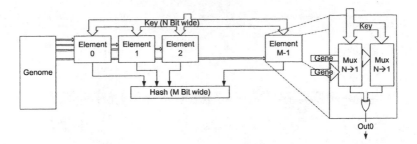

Fig. 2. Architecture of an Evolvable Hash Function (hash1)

every multiplexer can multiplex any of the input bits to its output, controlling a multiplexer demands $\log_2(N)$ bits. These bits controlling the function of the multiplexers form the genome of the hash function. Thus, to hash N bits to M bits, a genome size as stated in expression 2 is needed. To hash 1024 32-bit keys a hash function with a genome size of 100 bit is required.

$$2 \cdot M \cdot \log_2(N) \qquad (2)$$

A variant of the above introduced architecture was developed as well (Figure 3). In the following, it is referred to as hash2. Here the genome is enlarged to increase the possibilities for evolutionary development. It is a two-stage architecture. We use the elements consisting of two multiplexers connected by an xor in the first stage. In the second stage, first stage results are mixed up by multiplexers. To hash N bit to M bit a genome size as stated in expression 3 is needed. To hash 1024 32-bit keys a hash function with a genome size of 370 bit is needed.

$$(2 \cdot N + M) \cdot \log_2(N) \qquad (3)$$

3.3 Hash Architecture 3

In [7], a hardware architecture of a hash function is presented. In the following it is referred to as hash3. The presented architecture was adapted slightly to improve its performance and to limit the hardware costs. The hash function

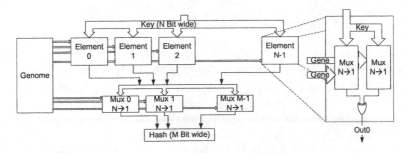

Fig. 3. Architecture of an Evolvable Hash Function (hash2)

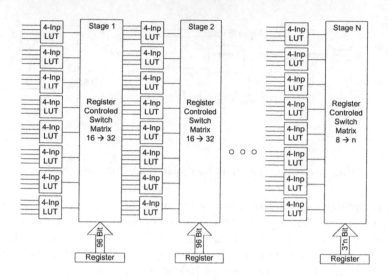

Fig. 4. Architecture of an Evolvable Hash Function (hash3)

matches the structure of FPGAs very well. It mainly consists of four-input-look up tables (LUTs). In those LUTs any logical 4-input function can be performed. To code the function 16 bit are needed. The logical functions are mapped to the FPGAs LUTs. Every slice of i.e. a Virtex2 FPGA comprises of two LUTs. As all LUTs have four inputs, to map an N bit wide key, $\frac{N}{4}$ parallel LUTs are needed for one complete stage. Every stage is followed by a register controlled switch matrix. All but the last switch $\frac{N}{4}$ inputs to N outputs. The last matrix switches $\frac{N}{4}$ inputs to M outputs.

$$\left[\left(N \cdot \log_2\left(\frac{N}{4}\right)\right) + \frac{N}{4} \cdot 16\right] \cdot (S-1) + M \cdot \log_2\left(\frac{N}{4}\right) + \frac{N}{4} \cdot 16 \quad (4)$$

For the whole function with an N-bit key and M-output bits and a depth of S stages a genome as given in expression 4 is needed. To hash 1024 32-bit keys a four staged hash function with a genome size of 830 bit is needed.

4   Simulation Results

The evolvable system comprises the complete evolutionary algorithm. It works autonomously and without any control of a software system. Thus, it is an intrinsic EHW. It was implemented as a SystemC model. The model is functional identical to the VHDL implementation, which is described in chapter 5. All three hash functions were implemented and evaluated with different key sets of up to hundred thousand 32-bit keys. The keys were generated randomly. The memory load of the hash memory was set to different levels ranging from 37% to 87%. All hash functions evolved over thousand generations.

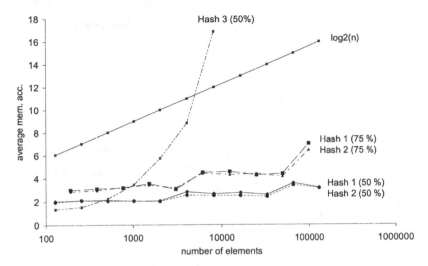

Fig. 5. Lookup Performance of Different Hash Architectures. Average memory accesses needed for finding an entry in the hash memory.

In Figure 5, the graphs reveal, that the architectures of the hash functions performed differently. The hash functions build of multiplexers (hash1 and hash2) showed great performance. The average of required memory accesses over all keys scales only very slightly. For a memory load of 50%, both architectures hash1 and hash2 show a comparable performance. The average number of memory accesses over all keys stored in the memory remains below four even with 2^{17} keys. Finding an entry in a sorted list of 2^{17} keys, sixteen accesses are needed on average. Four accesses outperform the sixteen memory accesses of a sorted list remarkably. The architecture consisting of LUT rows (hash3) showed poorer performance. It scales almost linearly with the size of the key sets. Even with just 8192 keys, an average of 17 memory accesses is needed. Even at this relatively small number of keys, the sorted list outperforms the hash function with just twelve memory accesses. Thus, the architecture is not applicable for implementation in a packet classifier.

When using a memory with a load of 75%, hash1 and hash2 perform well, too. Searching for one of 2^{17} keys requiress six memory accesses on average. Nevertheless the performance has decreased by about 50%. Here we make a tradeoff between search time and memory demands. However, it has to be mentioned that the theoretical upper bound for searching in the memory with the help of a hash function is still $O(N)$. Even if the average memory accesses needed are very low, the worst keys require far more than $log_2(N)$ memory accesses. This is the case at least for the memories with a load of 75%, as emanating from Figure 6.

It shows that the number of needed memory accesses for particular keys are extremely high. Especially when the memory load is at 75%, the maximum needed memory accesses are at 80 for hash1 and at 166 for hash2 respectively. When the memory load was as high as 87%, the worst case memory accesses

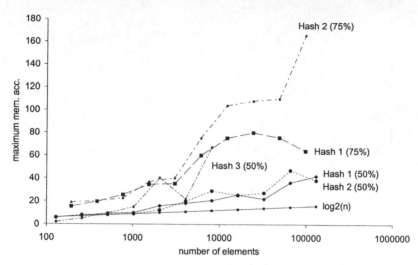

Fig. 6. Lookup Performance of Different Hash Architectures. Maximum memory accesses needed for finding an entry in the hash memory.

needed where at 262 (hash1) and 283 (hash2). Whereas the hash functions with a memory load of 50% show a better performance. Here the maximum needed memory accesses are at 42 (hash1) and 47 (hash2). That is why a memory load of 50% should not be exceeded in a system implementation, as the penalty for the worst case is rising quickly. The memory demand of such architecture has a complexity of $O(N)$. As the hash function evolves constantly, repetitive rehashing of the keys in the memory is required. To do so, there have to be two memory blocks of which one is used in the data path while the other one is rehashed. That means if the memory load is limited to 50%, exactly $4 \cdot N$ memory locations are required to store keys and classification rules.

5   Hardware Architecture of the Packet Classifier

The System was implemented in VHDL. Functionally it equals the SystemC model used for the simulations exactly. The packet classifier consists of two main elements. The data path and the evolution pipeline. The classifier is completely described in VHDL and was implemented into a Xilinx Virtex2 FPGA. The packet classification is done at wire speed. So no external memory is designated to buffer the data packets. Only a FIFO build of internal block RAMs of the FPGA stores the packets until the classification rule is extracted from the memory.

5.1   Data Path

In the data path, incoming packets are parsed and the key is extracted. The packet is stored in a buffer until the corresponding classification rule has been extracted from the memory. Based on the key the packet is classified. The key

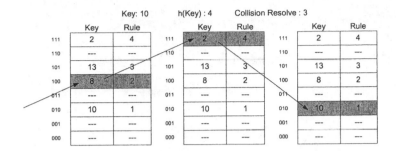

Fig. 7. The hash value for the key 10 is 4. Searching for key 10 leads to memory address 4 in the first run. As the stored key is not equal to 10, the next address is h(key)+3 = 7. As the stored key is not equal to 10 either, the next address is h(key)+3+3=2. At memory entry 2 the right correct is found and the corresponding rule is returned. Three memory accesses were needed.

is hashed by the evolvable hash function. Using the hash value $h(key)$ as start address, the memory is searched. If the stored key does not comply with the search key, a collision occurred. Using linear collision resolution, the next read address in the memory is set to: $h(key) + prime$. The prime number is configurable. Adding the prime number to the read address is repeated until the correct entry or an empty memory entry is found. In Figure 7, an example of such memory access is given. When the correct entry is validated by comparing the search key with the one stored in the memory, the classification rule together with the packet is sent to the output of the classifier. To solve the problem of numerous memory accesses, a small cache can be implemented to the memory module. The eight worst keys, which produce many memory accesses can be held in that cache and therefore be read out in just one memory access. This would improve the overall quality of the packet classifier. However, this feature has yet to be implemented to the packet classifier. The classifiers key parser module extracts the search keys from the incoming packets. The module can extract any combination of bits from a data packet. The bits, the key consists of, can be configured at any time. The bit mask for the key is stored in a memory block which is accessed through a configuration port. The generic architecture of the key parser allows the configuration of the width of the search key at implementation time while the actual bits of the key can be changed while the classifier is in use. In that way, the code guarantees high flexibility.

As the hash function changes during operation of the packet classifier permanently, it needs a repeating reconfiguration. In addition a permanent rehashing of the memory is required. This would interrupt the packet classification process very often for a quite substantial time. This is the reason why the data path consists of two independent hash functions and hash memories. While one path is used for the normal operation of the packet classifier, the other one can adapt to a new evolved and better performing hash function. The reconfiguration of the unused hash function is done without affecting the one used in the data path. Furthermore, the time intensive rehashing of the memory can be done as

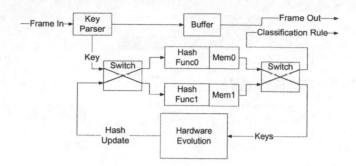

Fig. 8. Architecture of the Data Path

well without interference. The time for the rehashing process depends on the one hand on the number of memory elements to be rehashed and on the other hand on the traffic the classifier is exposed to. To be able to rehash the unused memory, the one utilized in the data path is needed to provide the information that is to be rehashed. In order to not interfere with the functionality, data reads for rehashing can only be gathered when the utilized memory is in an idle state. Memory accesses from the key parser always have the highest priority. Therefore the duration of the rehash process is not determined. When the inactive memory is rehashed and the hash function is reconfigured, the data path is switched to the new configured path. If the maximum memory load is limited to 50% as it is mentioned above, the memory demand of the classifier is 4 times the number of keys. The memory can be implemented either with the internal block RAMs of the FPGA or by using an external memory. A V4FX40 FPGA, i.e., has a total of over 2.5 million bits of block RAM. Assuming a key size of 32 bit and a rule size of 16 bit for classification, 13500 different rules can be stored internally. Therefore, classifiers with small and medium rule sets can be implemented without using external memories.

5.2 Evolution Module

The evolution module performs the whole evolutionary process completely in hardware. It consists of six functional elements. The evolution is performed permanently, stopping only if a perfect hash function was found. Perfect means that all key are hashed to a different value. The evolutionary algorithm used in the hardware is the following: On reset of the system, four individuals, representing four different genomes of the hash function, are generated (pseudo)randomly by a linear feedback shift register (LFSR). The number of bits k, the genome consists of, arises from expressions three, four, or five depending on the chosen hash function. From these four parents an offspring of twelve is generated by random as well. The best of the parents does not have a bias to be chosen with a higher probability. The offspring is then mutated. Due to a simple and efficient hardware implementation the mutation probability p is always as stated in equation 5.

$$p = \frac{1}{2^k}; \quad 2^k \leq l < 2^{k+1} \tag{5}$$

On average, between one and two bits of a genome are mutated. After mutation, the fitness of the offspring f(x) is evaluated. The fitness of an individual is measured by counting all collisions that occur. It is the difference between the theoretically maximal number of collisions and the actual number of collisions c that occur when hashing n keys (equation 6).

$$f(x) = \frac{n^2 - n}{2} - c \tag{6}$$

The four fittest individuals out of the offspring and the fittest parent form the new parent generation. To prevent the fitness form decreasing from one generation to another, the fittest parent is always included in the survivor selection. The new four parents are the starting point for the new run through the evolution module. The used evolutionary operators in the evolutionary algorithm are reproduction and mutation. The crossover operator was set aside. As mentioned above, the evolution module consists of six functional blocks (Figure 9). An evolution cycle starts at the genome update module. This module holds the four individuals of the parent generation in a block RAM. It has an interface to the data path, to update the genome of the hash functions in the data path. A LFSR in the child select module selects twelve times one of the parents for the new offspring. This is done by random and without taking into account the differences in fitness of the parents. The selected genome is read out of the genome update module and transferred in double word portions to the mutate module. The mutate module consists in principle of 32 LFSRs. Every LFSR is responsible for mutating one bit of the genome part at the input of the module. The probability of the mutation of one bit is according to equation 6 between $\frac{1}{l}$ and $\frac{2}{l}$. After being mutated, the genome is used for configuring the hash function used for fitness evaluation. The fitness evaluation module computes the fitness of the actual genome. This is done by holding a memory that has a bit position for every entry of the hash memory. All existent keys are read out of the one memory in the data path that is not in use. Incoming keys are hashed and the

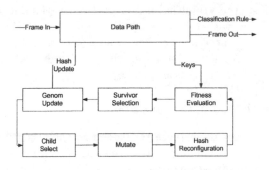

Fig. 9. Structure of the Evolution Module

memory is checked at the position of the hash value. If the memory indicates a free position, it is marked as used. Otherwise a collision counter is incremented and a new memory position is computed by the linear collision resolution. By counting all the collisions that occur when inserting all key to the memory the fitness is measured. After being evaluated the genomes of the offspring are transferred to the survivor selection module, where the four fittest ones are selected and transferred to the genome update module as the new parent generation.

5.3   Performance

The evolutionary algorithm especially the computation of the fitness of a hash function is extremely demanding regarding the computation time. During simulation four individuals, which produced an offspring of twelve, were evolved. To evolve 1000 generations with 100.000 keys with the SystemC model, a computation time of more than a day was needed on a 3.2 GHz machine. A software implementation of the evolutionary algorithm would probably have a computation time consumption comparable to the model. That is why the whole system was implemented in hardware, consisting of the data path and the evolution module. The most time consuming and thus performance critical module is the functional element evaluating the fitness. The fitness evaluation has a complexity of $O(N^2)$. If the initial hash function hashes all keys to the same value, $\frac{N^2-N}{2}$ collisions can occur when storing N keys to the memory. This is the worst case. But as the initial genome of the hash function is always chosen randomly, its quality is always better. The simulations showed that the initial hash functions produce at worst 20 million collisions for 2^{17} keys. The fitness evaluation module can compute one collision per clock cycle. Thus, for the above example of 2^{17} keys and an offspring of twelve, approximately 240 million clock cycles are needed. On a 125 MHz FPGA, the first generation would evolve in less than two seconds. The evolution rate increases rapidly with the hash function getting fitter. This is without any optimizations in the fitness evaluation. In Figure 10, the results of a simulation run with the ModelSim simulator are drawn. Here an evolution of 2048 32-bit wide keys has been performed. The keys were produced by a random generator. Running with 125 MHz, it took the system 1.84 seconds to evolve 1000 generations. As the fitness of the evolving system reached a very high value very fast, the graph is limited to twenty generations. The number of collisions occurring with the fittest individual was 187311 in the first generation (92.46 memory accesses per key) and after twenty generations limited to 923 (1,45 accesses per key). After the whole 1000 generations the number of collisions reached 845 (1,41 accesses per key).

5.4   Increasing the Computation Speed

There are different ways to increase the speed of the evolutionary process. As the time for fitness evaluation dominates the system computation time, the main attention regarding optimizations must refer to that hardware module. There are different ways for speeding up the fitness evaluation.

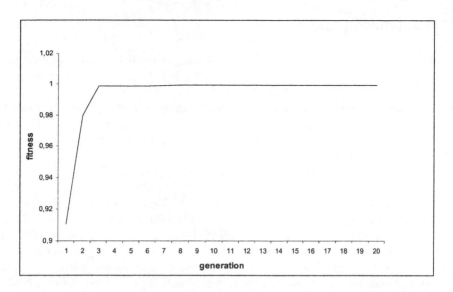

Fig. 10. Fitness of the ModelSim simulation of the packet classifier. The fitness is scaled to 1. Meaning a perfect hashing results in a fitness value of one.

One is the parallel implementation of one fitness evaluation element per off-spring. This would increase the evaluation performance by a factor of twelve, as the fitness of all offspring would be computed at the same time. The computation time is bound to the offspring with the worst fitness. When looking for collisions while evaluating the fitness, a memory interleaving can be used. A linear collision resolve strategy is used. Thus, when the hash value of a key is known, all possible memory positions are known as well. The n-th possible position is at memory address $h(key) + n \cdot prime$. With that knowledge, many potential memory positions can be checked in parallel which speeds up the fitness evaluation process. A third way of speeding up the fitness evaluation is to stop evaluating when the number of collisions an offspring produces exceeds the number of collisions of the four best elements of the offspring. As only the four best elements of the offspring are selected for survival, the computation of an offspring element can be stopped, when it is clear, that the element is not among this group. This way the mean computation time for the fitness evaluation can be reduced.

In order to optimize the evolutionary algorithm, it might be useful to adapt the mutation rate according to the variance of the finesses of all the offspring. This method has been proposed in [7]. When the variance is high, the mutation rate should be decreased. When it is low, the mutation rate can be increased.

5.5 Implementation

The packet classifier was implemented into a Xilinx Virtex2 FPGA (XC2V4000-6-BF957). 2800 slices and 34 block RAMs are needed for the implementation of a packet classifier which can store 2048 classification rules with 32-bit keys and 16-bit rules. The implemented hash function is hash1.

6   Conclusion and Outlook

Both the simulations of the model and the implemented hardware showed that a packet classifier consisting of an evolvable hash function can be very efficient. The time complexity is roughly $O(1)$ and the memory demand is $O(N)$, even for very large rule sets. The actual used hash function is always designed for the momentary rule set by the hardware evolution. Evolving constantly, the hash function improves over time and adapts to changes in the rule set. These are excellent characteristics.

However, a drawback of the actual implementation is the limited range of application. At the moment the size of the key on which a rule search bases is configurable but still after implementation constant. That means, that for standard router applications, where longest prefix searches basing on keys with different lengths are the main application, the packet classifier is not very well suited. The mapping could only be done by setting the prefixes to the standard length. That would lead of course to huge redundancy. To map, i.e., a 28-bit prefix to a 32-bit key, 16 different keys with the same rule would have to be stored in memory. This problem can be solved by the use of multiple hash functions as presented in [8]. Here hash functions of different widths are used to do the prefix search. However, prefixes not matching any of the widths would still produce redundant entries.

The speed of evolutionary process has still to be increased in order to make faster adaptation to changing key sets possible. The four different possibilities that have been presented in this paper must be implemented in hardware. It has to be determined how the improvement of the fitness evaluation module can speed up the evolutionary process. Furthermore, the behavior of the packet classifier with real databases must be researched. At this moment only fabricated data basing on random functions has been used to demonstrate the behavior. Thirdly, the influence of the use of a small cache in the data path to solve the problem of numerous memory accesses for some keys must be tested.

A final evolving system could be implemented in a dynamically reconfigurable environment as mentioned in [9]. In such a system the hash functions would not need to consist of register controlled multiplexers. Instead there are just wires from input to output and some combinatorial logic. The wires are simply rerouted to evolve to a new generation. This is achieved by the FPGAs partial reconfigurability. The whole area of the FPGA, where the hash function is implemented, is reconfigured.

References

1. Gupta, P., McKweon, N.: Algorithms for packet classification. In: IEEE Network. (2001) 24–32
2. Gupta, P., McKweon, N.: Packet classification using hierarchical intelligent cuttings. In: IEEE Micro. (2000) 34–41
3. Goldberg, D.E.: Genetic algorthms in search, optimization, and machine learning. In: Addison-Weseley, 20th printing. (1999)

4. Yao, X., Higuchi, T.: Promises and challenges of evolvable hardware. In: IEEE Transactions on Systems, Man, and Cybernetics - Part C. (1999)
5. Knuth, D.E.: The art of computer programming, vol. 3 sorting and searching. In: Addison-Weseley, 3rd edition. (1998)
6. Tufte, G., Haddow, P.C.: Prototyping a ga pipeline for complete hardware evolution. In: Evolvable Hardware. (1999) 143–150
7. Damiani, E., Tettamanzi, A.G.B.: On-line evolution of fpga-based circuits: A case study on hash functions. In: Evolvable Hardware. (1999) 33–36
8. Broder, A., Mitzenmacher, M.: Using multiple hash functions to improve ip lookups. In: IEEE Infocom. (2001) 1454–1463
9. Kubisch, S., Hecht, R., Timmermann, D.: Design flow on a chip - an evolvable hw/sw platform. In: 2nd IEEE ICAC. (2005) 393–394

Emergence of Two Power-Laws in Evolution of Biochemical Network; Embedding Abundance Distribution into Topology

Chikara Furusawa[1,3] and Kunihiko Kaneko[2,3]

[1] Department of Bioinformatics Engineering,
Graduate School of Information Science and Technology,
Osaka University, 2-1 Yamadaoka, Suita, Osaka 565-0871, Japan
furusawa@ist.osaka-u.ac.jp
[2] Department of Pure and Applied Sciences,
Univ. of Tokyo, Komaba, Meguro-ku, Tokyo 153-8902, Japan
kaneko@complex.c.u-tokyo.ac.jp
[3] ERATO Complex Systems Biology Project, JST,
3-8-1 Komaba, Meguro-ku, Tokyo 153-8902, Japan

Abstract. The evolutionary origin of universal statistics in biochemical reaction networks is studied, to explain the power-law distribution of reaction links and the power-law distributions of chemical abundances. Using cell models with catalytic reaction networks, we confirmed that the power-law distribution in abundances of chemicals emerges by the selection of cells with higher growth speeds, as suggested in our previous study. Through the further evolution, this inhomogeneity in chemical abundances is shown to be embedded in the distribution of links, leading to the power-law distribution. These findings provide novel insights into the nature of network evolution in living cells.

1 Introduction

Recent advances in molecular biology have provided detailed knowledge about individual cellular components and their functions. Despite its enormous success, it is increasingly clear that the nature of intra-cellular dynamics maintaining the living state is difficult to be understood only by building up such detailed knowledge of molecules, since a complex network of reactions among these molecules, such as proteins, DNA, RNA and small molecules, are essential for it. Here, one possible strategy to extract the nature of intra-cellular dynamics is to search for universal laws with regard to the networks of intra-cellular reactions common to all living systems, and then to unravel the dynamics of evolution leading to such universal features.

Indeed, recent large-scale studies revealed two universal features in cellular dynamics. First, the power-law distribution of links in reaction networks was discovered in metabolic and other biochemical reaction networks, as is termed as a scale-free network, where the connectivity distribution $P(k)$ obeys the law

A.J. Ijspeert et al. (Eds.): BioADIT 2006, LNCS 3853, pp. 80–92, 2006.

$k^{-\gamma}$ with $\gamma \approx (2 \sim 3)$[2, 3, 4, 5, 6]. Second, the abundances of chemicals in intra-cellular reaction were found to also exhibit the power-law distributions, as confirmed at the levels of gene expression [1, 7, 8] and metabolic flux [9]. Here, the chemical abundances plotted in the order of their magnitude are inversely proportional to their rank.

However, despite the potential importance of these universal statistical laws, it is still unclear how they developed through evolution, how they are mutually related, and what their biological meaning is. As the efficiency of biochemical reaction process to achieve cellular growth can depend on the statistical distribution of chemical abundances and the network structure, it is then natural to pursue the possibility that both the two statistical laws appear as a result of evolution of cellular reaction dynamics. In the present paper, we demonstrate that this possibility is indeed true, through extensive simulations of evolution of cells with catalytic reaction networks to achieve higher cellular growth, and by proposing a theory for the evolutionary link from the abundance distribution to the network structure.

Employing a simple cell model with catalytic reaction dynamics consisting of a huge number of chemicals, we first found that a power-law distribution in abundances of chemical species emerges by selecting cells with higher growth speeds. Then, this inhomogeneity in the chemical abundances is embedded into the distribution of links in the reaction networks by further evolutionary process. This embedding of abundances into the network is shown to be due to the fact that the probability with which a new reaction path is connected to the chemicals is not uniform *after selection*, but it is higher for a path to be linked to a chemical that has a larger abundance. This abundance-connectivity correlation leads to a power-law distribution in reaction networks, as is consistent with the previous reports in the metabolic networks. On one hand, these findings provide a novel insight into the evolution of intra-cellular reaction dynamics and networks. On the other hand, generality of a proposed theoretical mechanism for the evolutionary embedding of abundance distribution into network connectivity distribution suggests its possible relevance to understand the structure of biological networks in general.

2   Model

Consider a cell consisting of a variety of chemicals. The internal state of the cell can be represented by a set of concentrations $(x_1, x_2, \cdots, x_K)$, where x_i is the intra-cellular concentration of the chemical species i with i ranging from $i = 1$ to K. Depending on whether there is an enzymatic reaction from i to j catalysed by some other chemical ℓ, the reaction path is connected as $(i + \ell \to j + \ell)$. The rate of increase of x_j (and decrease of x_i) through this reaction is given by $x_i x_\ell$, where for simplicity all of the reaction coefficients were chosen to be equivalent $(= 1)$ [10].

Next, some nutrients were supplied from the environment by transportation through the cell membrane with the aid of some other chemicals, i.e., "transporters". Here, we assumed that the transport activity of a chemical is proportional to its concentration, and the rate of increase of x_i by the transportation is given by $Dx_{m(i)}(X_i - x_i)$, where $m(i)$-th chemical acts as the transporter for the nutrient i and $x_{m(i)}$ is concentration of m_i-th chemical. The parameter D is a transport constant, and the constant X_i is the concentration of the i-th chemical in the environment. In addition, we took into account the changes in cell volume, which varies as a result of transportation of chemicals into the cell from the environment. For simplicity, we assumed that the volume is proportional to the sum of chemicals in the cell, which can increase by the intake of nutrients. The concentrations of chemicals are diluted due to increases in volume of the cell, Based on the above assumption, this dilution effect is equivalent to imposing the which imposes the restriction $\sum_i x_i = 1$. When the volume of a cell is doubled due to nutrient intake, the cell is assumed to divide into two identical daughter cells.

To summarize these processes, the dynamics of chemical concentrations in each cell are represented as

$$dx_i/dt = R_i - x_i \sum_j R_j \tag{1}$$

with

$$R_i = \sum_{j,\ell} Con(j,i,\ell)\, x_j\, x_\ell - \sum_{j',\ell'} Con(i,j',\ell')\, x_i\, x_{\ell'}$$
$$(+Dx_{m(i)}(X_i - x_i)), \tag{2}$$

where $Con(i,j,\ell)$ is 1 if there is a reaction $i+\ell \to j+\ell$, and 0 otherwise, while the last term in R_i is added only for the nutrients, and represents its transportation into a cell from the environment. The last term in dx_i/dt with the sum of R_j gives the constraint of $\sum_i x_i = 1$, due to the growth of the volume.

Of course, how these reactions progress depends on the intra-cellular reaction network. Here, we study the evolution of the network in a GA-like rule, by generating slightly modified networks and selecting those that grow faster. First, n mother cells are generated, where the connection paths of catalytic network were chosen randomly such that the number of incoming, outgoing, and catalyzing paths of each chemical is set to the initial path number k_{init}. From each of n mother cells, m mutant cells were generated by random addition of one reaction path to the reaction network of the parent cell. Then, reaction dynamics were simulated for each of the $n \times m$ cells to determine the growth speed of each cell, i.e., the inverse of the time required for division. Within the cell population, n cells with faster growth speeds were selected as the mother cells of the next generation, from which m mutant cells were again generated in the same manner.

3   Result: Power Laws in Abundances and Network Structure Achieved Through Evolution

A number of network evolution simulations were performed using several different initial networks, different parameters and various settings. We found that all

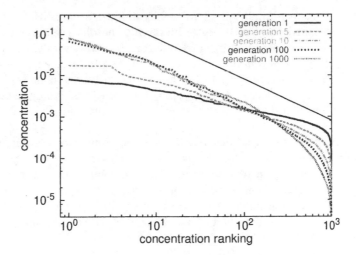

Fig. 1. Rank-ordered concentration distributions of chemical species. Distributions with several different generations are superimposed using different colors. The solid line indicates the power-law $x \propto n^{-1}$ for the reference. This power-law of chemical abundance is established around the 10th generation, and is sustained for further evolutions in the network. In the simulation, the growth speeds of 10×2000 networks were measured, and the top 10 networks with regards to the growth speed were chosen for the next generation. The parameters were set as $K = 1000$, $D = 4.0$, and $k_{init} = 4$. Chemicals x_m for $m < 5$ are considered as nutrient chemicals, and the concentration of them in the environment are set as $X_m = 0.2$. For each nutrient chemical, one transporter chemical is randomly chosen from all other chemicals.

of the simulations indicated common statistical properties with regard to both reaction dynamics and topology of networks. Here, we present an example of simulation results to show the common properties of our simulations.

The rank-ordered concentration distributions of chemical species in several generations are plotted in Fig.1, in which the ordinate indicates the concentration of chemical species x_i and the abscissa shows the rank determined by x_i. The slope of the rank-ordered concentration distribution increased with generation, and within a few generations converged to a power-law distribution with an exponent -1, which was maintained over further generations. Or equivalently, the distribution $p(x)$ of the species with abundance x is proportional to x^{-2} [13].

Indeed, the emergence of such power-law by selecting cells with higher growth speeds is a natural consequence of our previous study [1]. In our previous study, we found that there is a critical amount of nutrient uptakes beyond which the cell cannot grow continuously. When the nutrient uptake is larger than the critical amount, the flow of nutrients from the environment is so fast that the internal reactions transforming them into chemicals sustaining 'metabolism' and transporters cannot keep up. At this critical amount of nutrient uptake, the growth speed of a cell becomes maximal, and the power-law distribution of chemical abundance appears in the intra-cellular dynamics. This power-law distribution at the critical state is maintained by a hierarchical organization of catalytic reactions, and based on this catalytic hierarchy, the observed exponent -1 can be explained using a mean field approximation. Experimentally, the power-law distributions of chemical abundances were confirmed in large-scale gene expression data of various organisms and tissues, including yeast, nematodes, human normal and cancer tissues, and embryonic stem cells, which suggests that the intra-cellular reaction dynamics in real cell systems universally lie close to the critical state (see [1] for the details).

In the evolutionary dynamics of the present simulations, to increase the growth speed of cells, change in the network which enhances the uptake of nutrients from the environment is favored. This nutrient uptake is facilitated by increasing the concentrations of transporters, while if the uptake of nutrient is too large, the cell can no longer grow continuously due to the excess of the critical amount of them, as mentioned above. Now, with the evolutionary process as

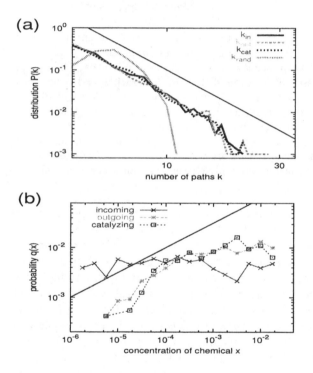

Fig. 2. Evolution of the network topology. **(a)**, Connectivity distribution $P(k)$ of chemical species obtained from the network of the 1000th generation. The solid line indicates the power-law $P(k) \propto k^{-3}$. For comparison, the distribution of k_{rand}, obtained by a randomly generated reaction network with the same number of paths with the network of 1000th generation, is shown. **(b)**, Probability $q(x)$ that a path to a chemical with abundance x is selected in evolution. The probabilities for incoming $(q_{in}(x))$, outgoing $(q_{out}(x))$, and catalyzing paths $(q_{cat}(x))$ are plotted. The data were obtained by 1.5×10^5 trials of randomly adding a reaction path to the network of the 200th generation, and the paths giving the top 0.05% growth speeds were selected.

shown in Fig.1, the nutrient uptakes increase to accelerate the growth speed of cells, until further mutations of the network may result to exceed the above critical value of the nutrient uptake. Here, successive increase in the growth speed by the 'mutation' to the reaction network is possible only when the enhancement of nutrient uptakes by it is in step with the increase in the other catalytic activities. As a natural consequence, selected are such networks that the nutrient uptake is kept near this critical point, where successive catalytic reaction process maximizes the use of nutrients, and form a power-law distribution of abundances.

Next, we investigated the topological properties of the reaction networks. The connectivity distributions $P(k)$ of chemical species obtained from the network of the 1000th generation are plotted in Fig.2a, where k_{in}, k_{out} and k_{cat} indicate the numbers of incoming, outgoing and catalyzing paths of chemicals, respectively. These distributions were fitted by power-laws with an exponent close to -3. Thus, a scale-free network was approached through evolution, while this power-law behavior was maintained for further evolutionary processes.

As shown in Fig.3, in this simple model, the evolved reaction network formed a cascade structure in which each chemical species was mainly synthesized from more abundant species. That is, almost no chemical species disrupted the flow

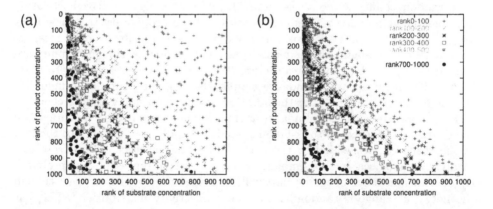

Fig. 3. Changes in the network structure. The abscissa shows the rank determined by the abundance of substrate i, and the ordinate shows the rank for the product j: the top left is the most abundant and the bottom right is the least abundant. A point is plotted when there is a reaction path $i \rightarrow j$, while the abundance of catalyst for the reactions is given by different colors determined by rank. As each product is dominantly synthesized from one of the possible paths, we plotted only the path with the highest flow, since the use of reaction paths from a chemical is quite uneven, and such a path with the highest flow can characterize the flow through the chemicals. (a), The network at the 10th generation, where the network structure is rather random, even though the power-law in abundance has already been established. (b), The network at the 1000th generation. Only a small number of paths are located in the upper-right triangular portion of the figure, indicating that almost all chemical species were synthesized from more abundant species.

of chemical reaction from the nutrients, as the network approached that with optimal cell growth. It should also be noted that the reaction dynamics for each chemical were also inhomogeneous in that synthesis of each chemical species had a dominant reaction path. Such uneven use of local reaction paths was also reported previously in real metabolic networks [9].

4   Mechanism: Embedding the Power Law in Abundances into Network Structure

The reason why the scale-free-type connectivity distribution emerges in this evolution is explained by selection of preferential attachment of paths to the chemicals with larger abundances. Note that the power-law distribution of chemical abundance has already been established through evolution. Here, we found that when a new reaction path is attached to an abundant chemical species, it gives a larger influence on the whole cellular state, as is expected from reaction kinetics. As a natural consequence, change in the growth speed after the mutation of the network is also larger when a path is attached to an abundant chemical species, as shown in Fig.4. Thus, when a certain number of cells with higher growth speeds are selected from the mutant pool, the probability that those selected cells have new links to such abundant chemicals is statistically higher than those expected from random change without selection. Therefore, there is a positive correlation between the abundance of chemical species and the probability that new links are added to such species in evolutionary dynamics, that is, the preferential attachment to such abundant chemicals appears. To represent this probability, we use variable $q(x)$ which indicates the probability that a new reaction path is attached to a chemical with abundance x after selection. For example, assume that change of the growth speed by the addition of a path outgoing from a chemical increases linearly with its abundance x. This assumption is rather natural since the degree of influence on the cellular state is generally proportional to the flux of the reaction path added to the network, i.e., the product of substrate and catalyst abundances. In this simple case, $q_{out}(x)$, which represents the probability of attachment for outgoing path will increase linearly with x, even though the network change is random. Here, the connectivity distribution $P(k_{out})$ is obtained by the transformation of variable as follows. Suppose that the probability of selection of a path attached to a chemical with abundance x is given by $q(x)$, then the path number $k \propto q(x)$. By the transformation $k = q(x)$, the distribution

$$P(k) = \frac{dx}{dk}p(x) = \frac{p(q^{-1}(k))}{q'(q^{-1}(k))} \tag{3}$$

is obtained. By applying the abundance power-law $p(x) \propto x^{-2}$, we obtain $P(k) = k^{-(\alpha+1)/\alpha}$ when $q(x) = x^{\alpha}$. Consequently, a scale-free network with exponent -2 should be evolved if $q_{out}(x) \propto x$.

Numerically, we found that the probabilities $q_{out}(x)$ and $q_{cat}(x)$ were fitted by $q(x) \propto x^{\alpha}$ with $\alpha \approx 1/2$, as shown in Fig.2b. Then, using the above transformation the connectivity distribution was obtained as $P(k) = k^{-3}$. Here,

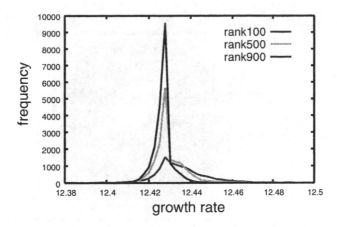

Fig. 4. Changes in growth speed with addition of a reaction path. Reaction paths were added to the network of the 200th generation from the 100th, 500th and 900th most abundant chemical species to investigate the changes in growth speed, while product and catalyst of the path were chosen randomly. Here, the concentrations of 100th, 500th and 900th most abundant chemicals were 1.80×10^{-3}, 2.03×10^{-4} and 2.98×10^{-5}, respectively. The histograms show growth speeds obtained by 20000 trials. In some trials, the growth speeds decreased markedly with the addition of a path, as the amount of nutrient uptake exceeded the limit of cellular dynamics. For the paths from the 100th, 500th and 900th most abundant chemical species, 39%, 23% and 4% of such trials showed growth speeds of less than the given threshold (we choose 12.38), respectively. Such data are not plotted in the figure. As shown in the figure, adding a reaction path from a more abundant chemical was more effective in changing the growth speed of the cell.

it is interesting to note that the connectivity distribution observed from real metabolic and other biochemical networks follows the power-law $P(k) \propto k^{-\gamma}$ with γ between 2 and 3, as often seen in experimental data [2, 3].

The probability $q(x)$ is determined through the evolutionary process. To clarify the reason for $q(x) \sim x^{\alpha}$ with $\alpha < 1$ in outgoing and catalyzing paths, we investigated the relationship between substrate abundance x and catalyst abundance y of a path to be selected. For this, we simulated changes in growth speeds by random addition of a reaction path to the network of 200th generation. For 1.5×10^5 trials, paths giving 0.05% of the highest growth speeds were regarded as being selected, and are plotted in Fig.5 as blue points on the x-y plane, while others are plotted as red points. As shown in the figure, a path with small flux is not selected since adding such path cannot change the cellular state enough, while a path with large flux is not selected also, since such large change destroys hierarchical structure of catalytic reactions, which results the decrease of nutrient intakes or exceeding the critical point so that the "cell" can no longer grow. Then, the fluxes of the selected paths satisfy $\Delta < xy < \Delta + \delta$, with Δ and δ being constants. We also found that the density of paths to be selected is almost constant in the above region. Consequently, for each chemical x, the probability

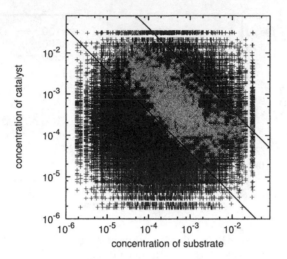

Fig. 5. Relationship between substrate abundance x and catalyst abundance y for the selected paths. A randomly chosen reaction path was added to the network of the 200th generation, and the growth speed of a cell after adding the path was simulated. For 1.5×10^5 trials, paths giving 0.05% of the highest growth speedss were regarded as being selected, and are plotted as blue points on the x-y plane, while others are plotted as red points. As shown, the selected paths satisfy $\Delta < xy < \Delta + \delta$, with $\Delta = 3.8 \times 10^{-8}$ and $\delta = 4.0 \times 10^{-6}$, respectively.

that such a path exists is given by the probability that there is such a partner chemical with abundance y, which satisfies $\Delta/x < y < (\Delta + \delta)/x$.

That is,

$$q(x) = \int_{\Delta/x}^{(\Delta+\delta)/x} p(z)dz \approx p(\Delta/x)(\delta/x) \tag{4}$$

By using the equation (1), we obtain

$$P(k) = \frac{-p(\Delta/y)}{(p(y) + ydp(y)/dy))y^2}, \tag{5}$$

with $yp(y) = k$. Indeed, if $p(x) = x^{-2}$, the above expressions lead to $q(x) \propto x$, as well as $P(k) = k^{-2}$. This expression holds when the evolved network is just at the critical point. The evolved network is near this critical point but there is a slight deviation, as can be seen in the deviation from the power-law in Fig.1, for small abundance of chemicals. Note that the asymptotic behavior for large k is given for small y. Then, the asymptotic behavior for large k is given by $P(k) \approx 1/((p(y) + ydp(y)/dy))$ depends on $p(y)$ for small y. If the asymptotic behavior of $p(y)$ for small y is given by $y^{-\beta}$ with $\beta < 2$, then $P(k) \approx k^{\beta/(1-\beta)}$. As $\beta < 2$, the exponent of the power is smaller than -2. For example, for $\beta = 3/2$ (which corresponds to the relationship between x and rank n as $x \sim n^{-2}$ for large n, as seen in Fig.1), $P(k) \approx k^{-3}$ is obtained. In general, even if the behavior of

$p(y)$ for small y is not fitted by a power-law, its increase with $y \to 0$ is slower than y^{-2}. Then the decrease of $P(k)$ with k is faster than k^{-2}, as often seen in experimental data [2, 3].

On the other hand, the probabilities $q_{in}(x)$ to have incoming path after selection show no dependence on the chemical abundance x, and therefore the above explanation is not directly applicable for the incoming paths. As for incoming paths, we have found 'hot' chemical species which facilitate the synthesis of the transporters for the nutrient uptakes, while others promote the formation of cascade structure of reaction dynamics as shown in Fig.3. These hot species have higher probability to acquire incoming path after selection. Such inhomogeneity of the probability among chemicals results in the inhomogeneity of the number of incoming paths as shown in Fig.2a. Still, further studies are necessary if such inhomogeneity results in the same power law as $q_{out}(x)$ and $q_{cat}(x)$.

5   Universality

Through several simulations, we have found that the emergence of two statistical features here is quite general and we expect that does not rely on the details of our model. To be specific, we have first checked the results by changing the initial conditions of the simulation, i.e., the initial concentrations of chemicals and the reaction network in the first cell, and confirmed that the results are independent of the initial conditions. Next, we have studied a model by changing parameters. Still, by restricting parameter values at which a cell reproduces efficiently, Zipf's law for abundances is generally observed. Furthermore, we have found the Zipf's law for the following class of models, for a cell that reproduces efficiently:

1. universality against network structure: we have studied the models with homogeneous as well as highly inhomogeneous path distribution. The distribution includes Gaussian and the power laws (i.e., the scale-free network).
2. universality against parameter distribution: instead of homogeneous parameter values for for reaction and diffusion coefficients, studied is the case with distributed parameters depending on each chemical species. The distribution includes Gaussian and log-normal.
3. universality against reaction kinetics: studied is the case with higher order catalytic reaction (for example to include the reaction kinetics $x_j x_\ell^2$ instead of $x_j x_\ell$ in eq.(2) for all chemicals)
4. universality against the form of transport of nutrient chemicals: studied is the cases with active transport mediated by some chemical, as well as passive diffusion term for the transport of nutrient.
5. universality against the condition for the cell division: Instead of setting a threshold for cell division by the sum of all chemicals, the condition is set for the amount of a specific chemical accumulated.

For all the cases, the power law distribution is obtained when the cell volume increase is optimal. Hence we believe that the result is general when a reaction network system that synthesizes chemicals in a cell shows recursive growth.

Now it is expected that the Zipf's law generally emerges through evolution, for a "cell" system consisting of the following processes:

(i) intra-cellular reaction dynamics within cells
(ii) intake of nutrients (that may depend on the internal chemical concentration)
(iii) synthesis of chemicals through the above process lead to the cell growth so that the cell is divided when a certain condition is satisfied
(iv) evolutionary process together with this cell division, i.e., random mutations to reaction networks and selection of cells with higher growth speed,

since the higher growth in cell is selected through (iv) and the Zipf's law in abundances is generally reached for a cell with optimal growth. Furthermore, as the embedding mechanism is also general, the evolution to power law in network paths is also expected to be rather universal.

Indeed, we have performed simulations with several different evolutionary criteria, and the results are essentially same, as long as the degree of mutation is not large. For example, when we assume that the probability to be selected as parent cells of the next generation is proportional to cellular growth speed, the evolutionary dynamics is qualitatively same as those presented here. As another example, we have performed simulations in which a fixed (large) number of cells is put in a given environment and when a cell divides into two cells, a randomly chosen cell is removed to keep a total cell number constant, instead of introducing discrete generations as in Genetic algorithm rule adopted in the present paper. In such rules of simulation also, cells having higher growth speeds are selected, and the power-law distribution of chemical abundances emerges as a result of evolutionary dynamics[14].

6   Summary and Discussion

In the present paper, we have shown that the power law in abundances of chemicals and network paths naturally emerges through evolution, by taking a class of cell models consisting of catalytic reaction networks. It is shown that the power law in abundances is later embedded into that of network path distribution, while the relation between the two powers is analyzed.

With regard to evolution of reaction networks, preferential attachment to a more connected node has often been discussed [2, 15]. In the previous models, preference of path attachment is simply defined as a function of number of existing paths, and the origin of such preference in evolutionary dynamics remains obscure. On the other hand, our study is different from them in two important respects. First, the dynamics of chemical abundance in the networks were introduced explicitly (described as node 'strength' in [16]), while previous models generally considered only the topological structure of the network. Second, selection only by cellular growth speed results in such a preference, even though attachment itself is random. Here, we found that more abundant chemical species acquired more reaction links as attachments of new links to such chemicals have both a greater influence on the cellular state and a higher probability of being selected. With these mechanisms, the power-law in abundance is naturally embedded in the intracellular reaction network structure through evolution, which is simply a process of selecting cells with faster growth speeds.

As discussed, the emergence of the power-law distribution of chemical abundance is expected to be a universal feature of growing cells, since this feature seems to necessarily appear in any systems having both intra-cellular reaction dynamics and intake of nutrients from an environment, when the cellular growth speed is maximized. Similarly, our simulations support that the evolutionary dynamics toward the power-law distribution of reaction path numbers emerges when cells having higher growth speeds are selected and mutations are randomly added to reaction networks. An important point here is that the emergence of universal features is independent of details of the system, as long as the conditions required for such features are satisfied. The power-laws of both abundance and connectivity, which are often observed in intracellular reactions, can be simply consequences of our mechanism by Darwinian selection.

Acknowledgements. We would like to thank T. Yomo and K. Sato for stimulating discussions. The work is partially supported by Grant-in-Aids for Scientific Research from the Ministry of Education, Science and Culture of Japan.

References

1. Furusawa, C., and Kaneko, K. Zipf's Law in Gene Expression. (2003) *Phys. Rev. Lett.* **90** (2003) 088102
2. Jeong, H. et al. , Tombor, B., Albert, R., Oltvai, Z. N., and Barabási, A.-L., The large-scale organization of metabolic networks. (2000) *Nature* **407** (2000), 651
3. Jeong, H., et al. Mason, S. P., and Barabási, A.-L., Lethality and centrality in protein networks. (2001) *Nature* **411** (2001), 41
4. Li, S. et al. A map of the interactome network of the metazoan C. elegans. (2004) *Science* **303** (2004), 540
5. Featherstone, D. E. et al. , Broadie, K. Wrestling with pleiotropy: genomic and topological analysis of the yeast gene expression network. (2002) *Bioessays* **24** (2002) 267
6. Guelzim, N. et al. , Bottani, S., Bourgine, P. and Kepes, F. Topological and causal structure of the yeast transcriptional regulatory network. (2002) *Nature Genet.* **31** (2002), 60
7. Ueda, H. R. et al. Universality and flexibility in gene expression from bacteria to human. (2004) *Proc. Natl Acad. Sci. USA* **101** (2003), 3765
8. Kuznctsov, V. A. ot al. *Genetics* **161** (2002) 1321
9. Almaas, E. et al. *Nature* **427** (2004) 839
10. We confirmed that our results are qualitatively same when we use distributed reaction coefficients for the simulations.
11. Kaneko, K., and Yomo, T. *Jour. Theor. Biol.* **199** (1999) 243
12. Furusawa, C., and Kaneko, K. *Phys. Rev. Lett.* **84** (2000), 6130

13. The rank distribution, i.e., the abundances x plotted by rank n can be transformed to the density distribution $p(x)$, the probability that the abundance is between x and $x + dx$. Since $dx = dx/dn \times dn$, there are $|dx/dn|^{-1}$ chemical species between x and $x + dx$. Thus, if the abundance-rank relation is given by a power-law with exponent -1, $p(x) = |dx/dn|^{-1} \propto n^2 \propto x^{-2}$.

14. As for the number distribution of reaction links, the simulation has not yet reached the stage to show the scale-free statistics in a network clearly, (since the simulation requires much longer time than the present method), but still we found that the number distribution of such network show heterogeneity in number of reaction links, with significant deviation from those of random networks.

15. Barabási, A.-L., and Albert, R. *Science* **286** (1999) 509

16. Barrat, A., Barthélemy, M., and Vespignani, A. *Phys. Rev. Lett.* **92** (2004), 228701

Microbial Interaction in a Symbiotic Bioprocess of Lactic Acid Bacterium and Diary Yeast

Hiroshi Shimizu[1], Sunao Egawa[2], Agustin K. Wardani[2],
Keisuke Nagahisa[1], and Suteaki Shioya[2]

[1] Dept. of Bioinformatic Engineering,
Graduate School of Information Science and Technology,
Osaka University, 2-1 Yamadaoka, Suita, Osaka 565-0871, Japan
{shimizu, nagahisa}@ist.osaka-u.ac.jp
http://www-shimizu.ist.osaka-u.ac.jp/mej.html
[2] Dept. of Biotechnology, Graduate School of Engineering,
Osaka University, 2-1 Yamadaoka, Suita, Osaka, 565-0871, Japan
{agustin, shioya}@bio.eng.osaka-u.ac.jp

Abstract. In symbiotic processes, different organisms coexist stably and interact by sharing with same metabolites and environmental conditions. A symbiotic process of a lactic acid bacterium, *Lactococcus lactis* sub species *lactis* (ATCC11454) and diary yeast *Kluyveromyces marxianus* is studied in this paper. A mathematical model of the symbiotic process composed of two microorganisms is developed by integrating two pure cultivation models. A cascade pH controller coupled with the dissolved oxygen (DO) control is newly developed and lactate consumption activity of *K. marxianus* is controlled by changing the DO concentration. The pH and lactate are kept stably at constant levels and both microorganisms grow well. Stability of this symbiotic process with disturbance of inoculums sizes of both microorganisms is investigated. The dynamic behavior of fusion process of independent two bionetworks is also discussed.

1   Symbiotic Process and Microbial Interaction

Microbial ecosystem, which consists of abundant genus of microbial populations, takes an important role for maintaining a microcosm as well as carbon and nitrogen circulation in global environment. From ancient age, people utilize complex microbial functions to produce many substances, such as foods, brewing drinks, pharmaceuticals and so on. Most fermented foods are produced by mixed cultures acting on various substrates. Cheese, yogurt, pickles, whiskey and Japanese rice wine sake are some examples of fermented foods. Numerous interactions, such as competition, predation, commensalism, mutualism, happen between microbial communities. Especially, combination of lactic acid bacteria (LAB) and diary yeasts (DY) is the most popular for making diary and brewing products in the world. And their interaction, which is usually mutualism, affects taste

A.J. Ijspeert et al. (Eds.): BioADIT 2006, LNCS 3853, pp. 93–106, 2006.

and flavors of the product, stability and productivity in their processes. One of typical examples of microbial interaction of LAB and DY is studied in this paper.

Living organisms are complex systems with multidimensional hierarchical networks, composed of gene, protein, and metabolic networks, respectively. Living cells have ability to flexibly change the topology of complex bionetworks in order to survive under many unexpected environmental conditions. In symbiotic systems, bionetworks composed of two different microorganisms fuse together by sharing with same nutrients in the environments. In the case that nutrients are competitively taken by two organisms, competition phenomenon happens among two microorganisms. When metabolic wastes from one microorganism become nutrients for the other microorganism, commensalism phenomenon happens. When the metabolic wastes show inhibitory effect for the producing microorganisms, the cleaning up of the wastes by the different microorganism makes favorable condition and mutualism phenomenon happens [1]. In this paper, we study behavior of a symbiotic process with a lactic acid bacterium, *Lactococcus lactis*, and diary yeast, *Kluyveromyces marxianus*.

Certain strains of *L. lactis* produces a food preservative nisin[2]. In the LAB fermentation process, the growth inhibition happens due to the accumulation of lactate and the decrease in pH [3]. In this study, a new pH control strategy with microbial interaction was developed. The concept of this strategy is shown in Fig.1. The *L. lactis* assimilates maltose as a carbon source and produces lactate. *K. marxianus*, which was isolated from kefir grains, does not have ability to assimilate maltose, while it has ability to assimilate lactate. Since the consumption rate of lactate is affected by dissolved oxygen (DO) concentration, lactate concentration and pH are controlled by manipulation of DO concentration. One measure of symbiotic process is how good growth of both microorganisms is. Since nisin is produced as growth associated, nisin production is a good indicator of how good symbiotic process is working.

The activity of the microorganisms can be represented as specific reaction rates, that is, reaction rates per unit cell concentration. Specific reaction rates of both microorganisms, including specific growth rate and the specific production rate of lactate by *L. lactis*, and the specific consumption rate of lactate by *K. marxianus* are examined in pure cultures. Based on the information of

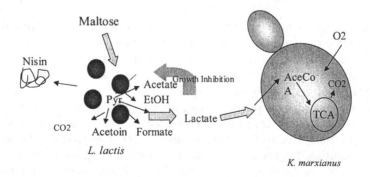

Fig. 1. Microbial interaction and removal of lactate

specific reaction rates of both microorganisms, a symbiotic process with microbial interaction of both microorganisms is developed. Nisin production is used as an indicator of the bioprocess and it is compared with that of pure cultivation process of *L. lactis*.

2   Materials and Methods

2.1   Microrganisms and Methods

L. lactis subsp. *lactis* ATCC 11454 was used as a nisin producing lactic acid bacterium. *K. marxianus* MS1 was isolated from kefir grains by ourselves. Concentrations of maltose, yeast extract, and peptone in main culture were 40, 10, and 10 g/L respectively, and for fermentation with high cell concentration they are set 60, 40, and 40 g/L, respectively.

2.2   Analysis

Cell concentrations of the pure cultivation processes were measured as dry cell mass and optical density (OD). The viable cell concentrations of *L. lactis* and *K. marxianus* in the symbiotic process were determined as colony forming units (CFU) on selection media. Concentrations of L-lactate, acetate, and formate in the medium were analyzed enzymatically. Ethanol concentration was measured by gas chromatography. Glucose concentration was measured using a glucose analyzer (Model 2700, YSI Inc., OH). Maltose concentration was measured after hydrolysis to glucose. Nisin concentration was measured by a bioassay method based on the method of Matsuzaki et al. [4].

2.3   Cultivation Method

Before main cultivation was performed, culture size was scaled up by two steps in order to increase the amount of cells with high growth activity. Main cultures were performed in a 5 L jar fermentor (EPC Control Box, Eyla, Japan) equipped with temperature, pH, dissolved oxygen (DO) concentration and gas flow control systems, respectively. The working volume was 2 L. Air or nitrogen was supplied to the fermentor for aerobic or anaerobic cultivation conditions, respectively. In this study, the cascade control strategy was applied in order to control pH level via DO control by manipulating the agitation speed. Other detailed methods were described previously [5].

3   Pure Cultivation Porcess of *L. lactis*

The time course of pure cultivation process of *L. lactis* under anaerobic conditions without pH control is as shown in Fig. 2. The pH decreased below 5.0 within 3 h due to increase in the produced lactate. The cell growth was completely terminated after 6 h and the concentration of nisin was 7.4 mg/L. The specific growth rate (μ_L) of *L. lactis* and specific production rate of nisin (ρ_N) without pH control were 0.30 h^{-1} and 4.0 mg-nisin/g-cell/h, respectively.

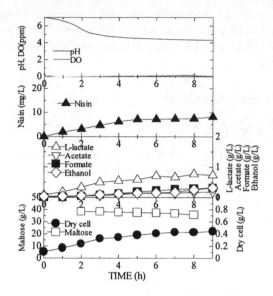

Fig. 2. Nisin production without pH control

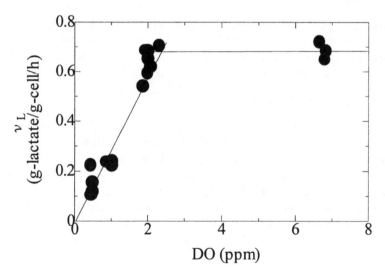

Fig. 3. Effect of DO concentration on the specific rate of consumption of lactate by *K. marxianus*

4   Pure Cultivation Process of *K. marxianus*

The specific lactate consumption rate of *K. marxianus* was determined under aerobic conditions. The effect of dissolved oxygen (DO) concentration on lactate consumption rate by *K. marxianus* is shown in Fig. 3. The maximum specific rate of lactate consumption of $K.$ $marxianus$ (ν_L), was about 0.7 g/g-cell/h, which was greater than the maximum specific rate of lactate production of $L.$ $lactis$ under aerobic conditions. Thus, it was expected that lactate produced by $L.$ $lactis$ would be completely consumed by $K.$ $marxianus$. The ν_L decreased linearly as DO concentration decreased in the range below 2 mg/L as shown in Fig. 3. When the lactate concentration was expected to be decreased, the DO concentration level should be increased and the specific rate of lactate consumption of $K.$ $marxianus$ is enhanced. On the other hand, lactate concentration was expected to be increased; the DO level should be decreased and the specific rate of lactate consumption of $K.$ $marxianus$ is attenuated.

5 Development of Symbiotic Bioprocess of $L.$ $lactis$ and $K.$ $marxianus$

As shown in Fig.1, a symbiotic bioprocess of $L.$ $lactis$ and $K.$ $marxianus$ was developed. In order to keep lactate and pH at constant, a novel cascade control system was designed, taking into account of microbial interaction. Figure 4 shows a flow diagram of the automatic cascade controller of coupling of pH with DO control in the symbiotic process. The PI and PID control strategies were employed for the automatic control of DO and pH controllers.

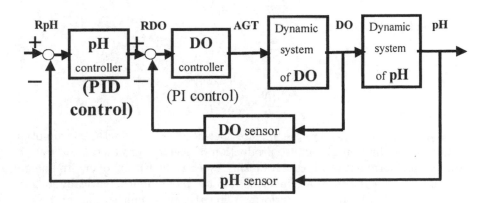

Fig. 4. A cascade pH controller incorporated with DO control

6 Development of Mathematical Model of Symbiotic Process of $L.$ $lactis$ and $K.$ $marxianus$

A mathematical model of a symbiotic process was developed to optimize a pH cascade controller in the symbiotic process consisting $L.$ $lactis$ and $K.$ $marxianus$. The symbiotic process model was developed by integrating individual models of $L.$ $lactis$ and $K.$ $marxianus$ in pure cultivation processes.

6.1   Mathematical Model of L. *lactis*

The Lactic acid bacterium *L. lactis* produce many metabolites hetero-fermenta tively such as lactate, acetate, acetoin, formate, nisin and so on. The concentrations of cell of *L.lactis* (X_L), maltose (S_M), lactate (L), acetate (A), acetoin (AT), formate (F), and nisin (N) are represented, respectively, as follows

Cell growth

$$\frac{dX_L}{dt} = \mu X_L \tag{1}$$

Maltose consumption

$$\frac{dS_M}{dt} = \nu_M X_L \tag{2}$$

Lactate production

$$\frac{dL}{dt} = \rho_L X_L \tag{3}$$

Acetate production

$$\frac{dA}{dt} = \rho_A X_L \tag{4}$$

Acetoin production

$$\frac{dAT}{dt} = \rho_{AT} X_L \tag{5}$$

Formate production

$$\frac{dF}{dt} = \rho_F X_L \tag{6}$$

Nisin production

$$\frac{dN}{dt} = \rho_N X_L \tag{7}$$

where μ_L, ν_M, ρ_L, ρ_A, ρ_{AT}, ρ_F, ρ_N are specific rates of growth, consumption of maltose, production of lactate, production of acetate, production of acetoin, production of formate, production of nisin, respectively. Effects of environmental conditions on specific rates are involved into the model mathematically [6].

Computer simulation was performed for the pure cultivation process of *L. lactis*, using the mathematical model. A satisfactory approximation to the experimental data was given by the mathematical model as shown in Fig. 5. Additionally, oxygen consumption was observed under aerobic condition. Oxygen consumption rate ($q_{O2}X_L$) of *L. lactis* is calculated based on NADH/NAD$^+$ balance from the stoichiometric equations in the metabolic pathway as:

$$q_{O2XL} = \frac{\frac{4\nu_M}{MW_M} + \frac{\rho_A}{MW_A} + \frac{\rho_F}{MW_F}}{2} \tag{8}$$

where MW_M, MW_A, MW_F are molecular weights of maltose, acetate and formate, respectively.

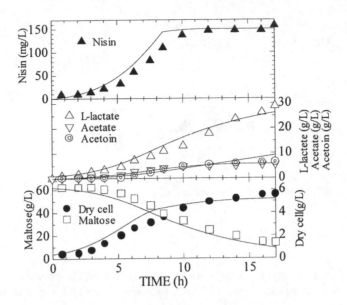

Fig. 5. Simulation and experimental result of pure cultivation process of *L. lactis*

6.2 Mathematical Model of *K. marxianus*

The cell growth and lactate consumption of *K. marxianus* are represented in Eqs. (9) and (10), respectively. Concentrations of cell of *K. marxianus* (X_K) and lactate (L) are represented as follows:

Cell growth

$$\frac{dX_K}{dt} = \mu_K X_K \tag{9}$$

Lactate

$$\frac{dL}{dt} = -\nu_L X_K \tag{10}$$

where μ_K and ν_L are specific rate of cell growth and lactate consumption of *K.marxinaus*, respectively. Effects of DO concentration on specific consumption rate of lactate is shown as in Fig. 3. Computer simulation for the pure cultivation process of *K. marxianus* was performed. It was found that the model gave a satisfactory approximation to the experimental data as shown in Fig. 6.

6.3 Mathematical Model of Symbiotic Process of *L.lactis* and
  K. marxianus

In the symbiotic process, both models of pure cultivation processes of *L. lactis* and *K. marxianus* were integrated into one model. Mass balance of lactate is represented as

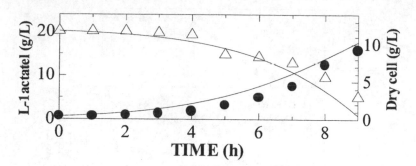

Fig. 6. Simulation and experimental result of pure cultivation process of *K. marxianus*

$$\frac{dL}{dt} = \rho_L X_L - \nu_L X_K \tag{11}$$

Since the dissolved oxygen (DO) concentration affected the specific consumption rate of *K. marxianus* as shown in Fig.3, balance of the DO concentration in the symbiotic process was involved in the model as:

$$\frac{dC}{dt} = k_L a(C^* - C) - M_{O2}(q_{O2} X_L + q_{O2} X_K) \tag{12}$$

where $k_L a$, C, C^*, are the mass transfer coefficient of oxygen, dissolved oxygen concentration and its saturated value, respectively. M_{O2}, q_{O2XL}, q_{O2XK} are the molecular weight of oxygen (defined as 32000 mg-O_2/mol), oxygen consumption of *L. lactis* and oxygen consumption of *K. marxianus*, respectively. The DO concentration was monitored by a DO sensor with delay shown as:

$$\frac{dC_{MES}}{dt} = k_{late}(C - C_{MES}) \tag{13}$$

where C_{MES} is the measured value of oxygen and k_{late} is a time constant, determined experimentally as 1/8 (1/sec). The dynamics of the pH change in the medium with time is described as shown in Eq. (14) as :

$$\frac{dpH}{dt} = \frac{-\left(\frac{\rho_L X_L - \nu_L X_L}{MW_L(1+10^{-pH+pK_L})} + \frac{\rho_A X_L}{MW_L(1+10^{-pH+pK_A})} + \frac{\rho_F X_L}{MW_F(1+10^{-pH+pK_F})}\right)}{K + ln10(10^{-pH} + 10^{pH-14} + term_L + term_A + term_F)} \tag{14}$$

where $term_L$, $term_A$, and $term_F$ are represented, respectively as

$$term_L = \frac{L}{MW_L} \frac{10^{-pH+pK_L}}{(1 + 10^{-pH+pK_L})^2} \tag{15}$$

$$term_A = \frac{A}{MW_A} \frac{10^{-pH+pK_A}}{(1 + 10^{-pH+pK_A})^2} \tag{16}$$

$$term_F = \frac{F}{MW_F} \frac{10^{-pH+pK_F}}{(1+10^{-pH+pK_F})^2} \tag{17}$$

MW_L, pK_L, pK_A, pK_F, and K are the molecular weight of lactate, dissociation constants for lactic acid, acetate and formate, and a consatnt parameter, respectively.

7 Optimization of Symbiotic Control Process of *L. lactis* and *K. marxianus* by Simulation Study

To keep the lactate in low level by microbial interaction of *L. lactis* and *K. marxianus*, the cascade pH control system as shown in Fig. 4 was developed. Because the pH in the medium was controlled by the lactate consumption of *K. marxianus* and the specific lactate consumption rate was controlled by manipulating the DO concentration, a cascade controller coupled with the DO control was developed. The consumption rate of lactate by *K. marxianus* was decreased linearly as the DO concentration decreased in the range below 2 ppm

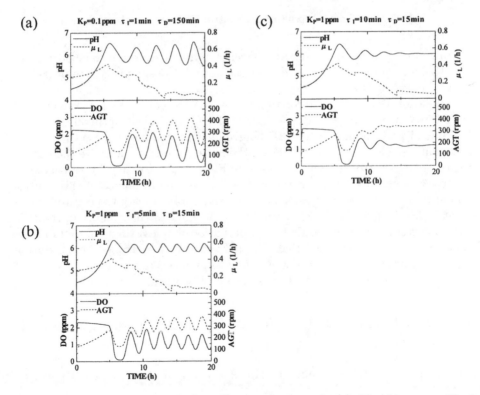

Fig. 7. Simulation results of the pH cascade control. (a) Kp=0.1 ppm, Ti=1 min,Td=150 min; (b) Kp=1 ppm, Ti=5 min, Td=15 min; (c) Kp=1 ppm, Ti=10 min, Td=15 min.

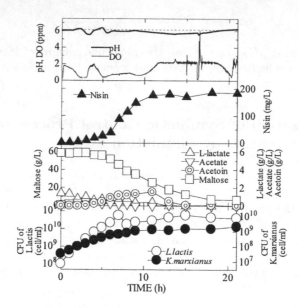

Fig. 8. Experimental result of pH control with microbial interaction

as shown in Fig.3. When the lactate concentration was expected to be decreased, the DO level should be increased, and the specific consumption rate of lactate by *K. marxianus* is enhanced.

Simulation was performed for tuning the control parameters. Parameters of the PID controller to give the set point of DO are tuned optimally, because the control performance of the PID controller was significant for entire control performance. The application of the mathematical model to optimize the performance of this control system, are shown in Figs. 7 (a), (b), and (c), respectively. A pH set point was set 6.0 in this case. The best performance of this control system to stabilize the pH was found when the parameters of the controller was set at Kp = 1 ppm, Ti = 10 min and Td = 15 min. In this condition, the PID control system was tuned so that the fluctuation was less than 0.5 units in the simulation. It was confirmed that The pH value was controlled at 6.0 during the fermentation as shown in Fig. 8. The nisin concentration finally reached at 200 mg/L, indicating the symbiotic process well worked.

8   Robustness and Stability of the Symbiotic Control Process

8.1   Experimental Evidence of the Stability of the Control Process

When inoculum size of *L. lactis* is greater than the expected value, or inoculum size of *K. marxianus* is less than the expected value, lactate is not completely assimilated by *K. marxianus* and pH decreases. In such a case, growth of

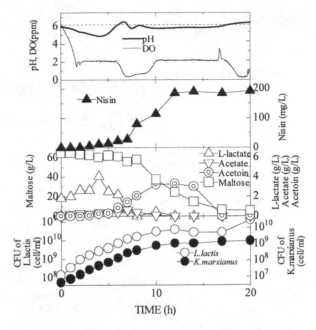

Fig. 9. Stability test for uncertainty of inoculum size

L. lactis is expected to be inhibited. Figure 9 shows the result of the stability test for uncertainty of inoculum sizes of both microorganisms. In this case, imbalance of cell of *K. marxianus* was inoculated, which is 1/10 less than that of optimal inoculum size. Due to imbalance of the cell concentrations of both microorganisms, lactate was accumulated and pH was decreased to 4.9. As a result, growth of *L. lactis* was stopped at 4.5 h. However, lactate was assimilated gradually by *K. marxianus* and both microorganisms well grew after 8h. Nisin concentration reached to 190 mg/L in this case. It was experimentally proved that this control system was robust for such uncertainty of inoculum size of microorganisms.

8.2 Symbiotic Network Analysis

It is found that a symbiotic process of a lactic acid bacterium *L.lactis* and diary yeast, *K. marxianus* shows stable behavior. The environmental conditions such as pH and DO concentration are kept constant levels. Even though the initial cell concentrations of the both cells are imbalanced, the process goes to the stable states. Interaction of both microorganisms in the symbiotic process by sharing the common metabolites and environmental condition are illustrated in Fig.10 (a). Arrows indicate enhancement of microorganisms' activities or increase in the metabolites concentrations in the environment, while stop bars indicate inhibition of microorganisms' activities or decrease in metabolites concentrations in the environmental condition. Solid and dotted lines indicate active and inactive interactions and nodes, respectively.

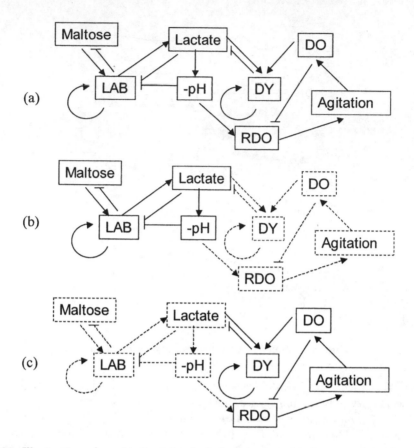

Fig. 10. Illustration of symbiotic network: behavior of symbiotic network in the cases that both microorganisms grow well (a), the *K. marxianus* concentration is much lower than that of *L. lactis* (b), and *L. lactis* concentration is much lower than that of *K. marxianus* (c), respectively. The both cases of (b) and (c) autonomously recovers to the orignial status of (a). Arrows indicate enhancement of microorganisms' activities or increase in the metabolites concentrations in the environment, while stop bars indicate inhibition of microorganisms' activities or decrease in metabolites concentrations in environmental condition. Solid and dotted lines indicate active and inactive interactions (and nodes), respectively. LAB: *L.lactis*, DY: *K. marxianus*.

When *K. marxianus* concentration is much lower than that of *L. lactis*, the action from *K. marxianus* is negligible compared with activity of *L. lactis*. The active network in this situation is illustrated in Fig.10 (b). In this case, lactate is accumulated and pH is decreased, which causes the stop of cell growth of *L. lactis* and dynamic behavior of entire network are slow down for a while. After *K. marxianus* grows as much as *L. lactis* and lactate concentration is decreased gradually, the original activity of network as shown in Fig. 10 (a) recovers autonomously. In the pure cultivation process of *L. lactis*, this autonomous recover is not possible as shown in Fig.2.

On the other hand, when *L. lactis* concentration is much lower than that of *K. marxianus*, lactate concentration goes down for sufficient growth of it K. marxianus. In this case, *K. marxianus* growth is also inactivated due to depletion of lactate, and dynamic behavior of entire network is slow down for a while as shown in shown Fig.10 (c). After *L. lactis* grows as much as *K. marxianus*, and lactate concentration is gradually increased, the original activity of network as shown in Fig. 10 (a) recovers autonomously in this case as well.

In the symbiotic processes, more than one microorganism highly interact each other as shown in the case of this study. In the case that the activity of one microorganism slows down, this issue affects on the activity of other microorganisms and activity of the entire bionetwork slows down. As a result, the entire system waits for the recovery of the activity of the microorganisms, and avoid the stuation that the only one microorganism becomes a winner. When the activity of the microorganism recovers, the entire bionetwork also recovers autonomously. This concept would be useful for creation of a autonomous recovery system in information technology.

9   Conclusions

The symbiotic process of *L. lactis* and *K. marxianus* stably worked well. The pH was well controlled by the cascade controller with the microbial interaction. This controller was robust for uncertainty of inoculum sizes of microorganisms. The indicator of the symbiotic process, nisin concentration reached 200mg/L and this value was 20 times greater than that in pure cultivation process without control of pH. The dynamic behavior and autonomous recovering process are discussed when the cell amounts of the both microorganism are imbalanced.

Acknowledgements

This research was supported in part by The 21st Century Center of Excellence (COE) Program of the Ministry of Education, Culture, Sports, Science and Technology, Japan.

References

1. Shioya, S.: Mixed culture: In Encyclopedia of Bioprocess Technology (Eds. Flickinger M. and Drew S.) John Wiley and Sons, Inc. (1999) 1798-1810.
2. Broughton, J.B.: Nisin and its uses as a food preservative. Food Technol. 44, (1990) 100-117.
3. Taniguchi, M., K. Hoshino, H. Urasaki, and M. Fujii.: (1994) Continuous production of an antibiotic polypeptide (nisin) by *Lactococcus lactis* using a bioreactor coupled to a microfilteration module. J. Ferment. Bioeng. 77, (1994) 704-708.
4. Matsusaki, H., N. Endo, K. Sonomoto, and A. Ishizaki: Lantibiotic nisin Z fermentative production by *Lactococcus lactis* IO-1: relationship between production of the lantibiotic and lactate and cell growth. Appl. Microbiol. Biotechnol. 45, (1996) 36-45.

5. Shimizu, H., Mizuguchi, T., Tanaka, E., and S. Shioya: Nisin production by a mixed culture system consisting of *Lactococcus lactis* and *Kluyveromyces marxianus*. Appl. Environ. Microbiol. 65, (1999) 3134-3141.
6. Wardani, A.K., Egawa, S., Nagahisa, K., Shimizu, H., and Shioya, S.: Inhibitory effect of by-products on cell growth and nisin production in *Lactococcus lactis*, Bio chemical Engineering Journal, submitted (2005).

Responses of Fluctuating Biological Systems

Tetsuya Yomo[1,2,3,5], Katsuhiko Sato[4,5], Yoichiro Ito[1,5],
and Kunihiko Kaneko[3,4,5]

[1] Department of Bioinformatic Engineering, Graduate School of Information Science
and Technology, Osaka University, 2-1, Yamadaoka, Suita, Osaka 565-0871, Japan
yomo@ist.osaka-u.ac.jp
http://www-symbio.ist.osaka-u.ac.jp/sbj.html
[2] Department of Biotechnology, Graduate School of Engineering, Osaka University,
2-1, Yamadaoka, Suita, Osaka 565-0871, Japan
[3] Graduate School of Frontier Bioscience, Osaka University, 2-1, Yamadaoka, Suita,
Osaka 565-0871, Japan
[4] Department of Pure and Applied Sciences, University of Tokyo, Komaba,
Meguro-ku, Tokyo 153-8902, Japan
[5] ERATO, JST, 2-1, Yamadaoka, Suita, Osaka 565-0871, Japan

Abstract. A linear relationship between responses of biological systems and their fluctuations is presented. The fluctuation is given by the variance of a given quantity, whereas the response is given as the average change in the quantity for a given parameter change. By studying experimental evolution where fluorescence per *E.coli* cell increased, we confirmed our relationship with a positive correlation between the evolutionary rate of fluorescence and its fluctuation observed over genetically identical cells. The generality of the relationship and its possible application to other fluctuating systems are discussed.

1 Introduction

Many biological systems fluctuate to some extent because their elements work at a finite temperature and because their surroundings also fluctuate. For example, in the case of genetic networks in living organisms, because the bio-molecules are synthesized and decomposed by chemical processes occurring at finite temperatures, the molecules are inevitably affected by thermal fluctuations, as a consequence of the laws of physics and chemistry. Recently, fluctuations in gene expression have been investigated extensively [1,2,3]. Even with such inevitable fluctuations or noise in their elements, living organisms have responded adaptively to unpredictably fluctuating environments by mutation of some parameters of their genetic networks to change their states or phenotypes in response to environmental changes.

This raises the question of whether there is a general relationship between the adaptive response and fluctuation. In general optimization processes of systems to accomplish high responsiveness, fluctuation or noise has been treated as suppressed. On the other hand, it is clear that network with a greater degree of fluctuation respond more flexibly to environmental changes as they are "soft". Here,

A.J. Ijspeert et al. (Eds.): BioADIT 2006, LNCS 3853, pp. 107–112, 2006.

we propose a linear relationship between fluctuation and response that should hold true in a broad class of systems, and discuss an experimental demonstration of the relationship in a process of optimization of protein fluorescence in a cell. We compared our proposed theoretical relationship with the experimental results and found good agreement. We also discuss the relevance of fluctuations to system optimization in the framework of our fluctuation-response relationship.

2 Linear Fluctuation-Response Relationship

Our linear fluctuation-response relationship is as follows: When we change the value of a parameter, a, slightly to, $a + \Delta a$, the change in the average value of a variable, x, will be proportional to its variance at the initial parameter, a, i.e.:

$$\langle x \rangle_{a+\Delta a} - \langle x \rangle_a = b\Delta a \langle (x - \langle x \rangle_a)^2 \rangle_a$$

where the coefficient, b, is a constant independent of the parameter, a, and $\langle x \rangle_a$ and $\langle (x - \langle x \rangle_a)^2 \rangle_a$ are the average and variance at the initial parameter value, a, respectively. They are defined explicitly as $\langle x \rangle_a = \int x P(x,a) dx$ and $\langle (x - \langle x \rangle_a)^2 \rangle_a = \int (x - \langle x \rangle_a)^2 P(x,a) dx$, where $P(x,a)$ is the normalized distribution function of x at the parameter, a. In this paper, the symbol $\langle \ \rangle_a$ denotes the average of a given function of x in the brackets with respect to the distribution function $P(x,a)$. We assume that the parameter, a, and the variable, x, are both scalar. This equation indicates that the response is proportional not only to the parameter change, Δa, but also to the fluctuation or the variance. The relationship is essentially the same as the fluctuation-dissipation theory in statistical physics.

To derive the above linear relationship, we assume a "Gaussian-like" distribution. The distribution with $a + \Delta a$ is written as follows:

$$P(x, a + \Delta a) = P(x,a)e^{Log(P(x,a+\Delta a)) - Log(P(x,a))} = P(x,a)e^{\varepsilon(x,a,\Delta a)}$$

Here, "Gaussian-like" means that $\varepsilon(x, a, \Delta a)$ can be written with the expansion around $\langle x \rangle_a$ by not more than the second-order as follows:

$$\varepsilon(x, a, \Delta a) = \varepsilon_0(a, \Delta a) + \varepsilon_1(a, \Delta a)(x - \langle x \rangle_a) + \frac{\varepsilon_2(a, \Delta a)}{2}(x - \langle x \rangle_a)^2$$

With the constant, N, for normalization, the distribution is rewritten as:

$$P(x, a + \Delta a) = P(x,a)Ne^{\varepsilon_1(a,\Delta a)(x - \langle x \rangle_a) + \frac{\varepsilon_2(a,\Delta a)}{2}(x - \langle x \rangle_a)^2}$$

The change in the average can be calculated using the above equation valid to the first-order of Δa:

$$\langle x \rangle_{a+\Delta a} - \langle x \rangle_a = \int (x - \langle x \rangle_a) P(x, a + \Delta a) dx = b(a)\Delta a \langle (x - \langle x \rangle_a)^2 \rangle_a$$

where $b(a)$ is the first-order derivative of $\varepsilon_1(a, \Delta a)$ with respect to Δa. This equation shows that larger variance leads to a larger response to the parameter change, Δa. If the dependency of $b(a)$ on a is negligible for a certain range of a, we obtain our linear relationship. The a-independence should be examined experimentally as follows. A more formal derivation of our proposition has been presented elsewhere [4].

3   Experimental Demonstration

To determine whether the optimization process of biological systems follows the above relationship, we conducted experimental evolution in a cellular system. Fig. 1 outlines the experimental procedure (details in [5]).

The initial material for the evolution was a mutant green fluorescent protein (GFP), which was composed of GFP with a random polypeptide (RP3-34) attached to its N terminus of GFP. RP3-34 is composed of 149 amino acid residues, and has no homology with any known natural proteins in the SwissProt database as analyzed by BLAST 2.2.2. The fused protein was subjected to random mutagenesis to prepare a mutant pool of about 2000 *E. coli* clones, each of which possessed a different mutant GFP gene with a few substitutions in its RP3-34 fragment only. Among the clones, we selected several by eye that showed high fluorescence and inoculated them into liquid media to choose the clone with the highest level of fluorescence by spectrofluorometry. Then, we subjected a DNA fragment encoding the RP3-34 portion of the selected clone to random mutagenesis and reattached the mutated fragments to the N terminus of GFP to prepare a mutant pool for the next generation. The fluorescence of the selected clones at each generation was measured using a fluorescence-activated cell sorter (FACS).

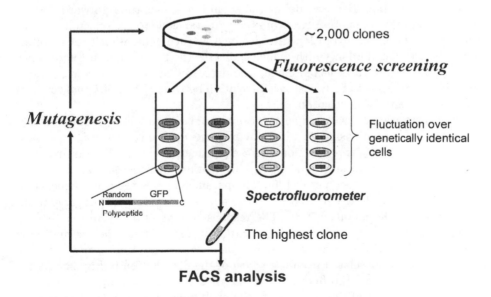

Fig. 1. Schematic drawing of the selection process

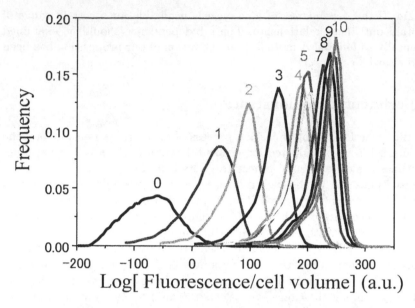

Fig. 2. Distribution in fluorescence per cell modified from Fig. 1 in Ref. [4]

Fig. 2 shows the distribution in fluorescence per cell of the selected clones at each generation. Note that there was always some diversity or fluctuation in fluorescence among the cells of the selected clones grown in the same environment, even though they possessed identical genetic information. It is clear that the peak fluorescence of each progressive generation, indicated by numbers, increased as a result of selection. Here, we define the evolution rate as the rightward-shift in the peak position of fluorescence from the parental clone to the selected clone at each generation. The evolution rate declined as each generation passed. Interestingly, the distribution width, which indicates the fluctuation in fluorescence among the cells of the selected clone, also decreased as each generation passed. Briefly, there seems to be a positive correlation between the evolutionary rate of fluorescence and its fluctuation.

The correlation observed experimentally was shown to follow the fluctuation-response linear relationship, in which the response or change in average of a variable, $\langle x \rangle_{a+\Delta a} - \langle x \rangle_a$, is proportional to the parameter change, Δa, multiplied by the variance of the variable, $\langle (x - \langle x \rangle_a)^2 \rangle_a$. In the experimental evolution, x is logarithm of fluorescence per cell [6]. The parameter, a, is the gene sequence of the fused GFP, and Δa corresponds to the number of mutations per generation, which we call the mutation rate. The response or evolutionary rate is defined as the change in peak position per generation in Fig. 2, while the fluctuation is defined as the variance of the fluorescence on a logarithmic scale over genetically identical clones, calculated from the width of the distribution in Fig. 2. The expected linearity from the fluctuation-response linear relationship was observed (Fig. 3) in the plot of the response or the evolutionary rate on the x-axis with

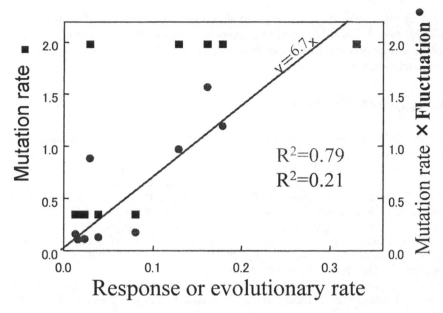

Fig. 3. Linear relationship expected from response-fluctuation theory

the mutation rate, Δa, multiplied by the variance at each generation, $\langle (x - \langle x \rangle_a)^2 \rangle_a (R^2 = 0.79)$, but not with only $\Delta a (R^2 = 0.21)$.

The linear relationship indicates that the response was larger when the same parameter change was applied to the network with larger fluctuation. This corresponds to a larger rightward-shift in peak position at an earlier generation when the cellular distribution was wider.

4   Discussion

The fluctuation-response linear relationship that was proposed and confirmed experimentally can be interpreted in connection with optimization as follows. In the course of evolution or optimization processes, the primordial biological networks may have had a large number of elements acting independently or with a high degree of freedom. The self-organization or optimization of systems occurred with fixation of relationships among their elements or in "soft-wiring" their elements. With a decrease in the number of freely acting elements or the degree of freedom, there must have been a decline in the evolutionary rate or optimization rate due to the decrease in number of parameters that could otherwise be used to optimize the systems even further. At the same time, the decrease in number of freely acting elements may have caused a decrease in the network fluctuation, as networks with a lower degree of freedom have a tendency to show less fluctuation. Briefly, the optimization, which leads to a decrease in the freely acting parts of systems, results in a simultaneous decrease in both the evolutionary rate and the fluctuation. That is, the correlation obtained in the present study may be a general consequence of functional optimization of systems with large degrees of freedom. It would be interesting to apply the linear relationship to optimization processes of other fluctuating networks, such as the WWW or human societies, etc.

References

1. Elowitz, M.B., Levine, A.J., Siggia, E.D., Swain, P.S.: Stochastic Gene Expression in a Single Cell. Science **297** (2002) 1183-1186
2. Swain, P.S., Elowitz, M.B., Siggia, E.D.: Intrinsic and Extrinsic Contributions to Stochasticity in Gene Expression. Proc. Natl. Acad. Sci. USA **99** (2002) 12795-12800
3. Hasty, J., Pradines, J., Dolnik, M., Collins, J.J.: Noise-Based Switches and Amplifiers for Gene Expression. Proc. Natl. Acad. Sci. USA **97** (2000) 2075-2080
4. Sato, K., Ito, Y., Yomo, T., Kaneko, K.: On the Relation Between Fluctuation and Response in Biological Systems. Proc. Natl. Acad. Sci. USA **100** (2003) 14086-14090
5. Ito, Y., Kawama, T., Urabe, I., Yomo, T.: Evolution of an Arbitrary Sequence in Solubility. J. Mol. Evol. **58** (2004) 196-202
6. Furusawa, C., Suzuki, T., Kashiwagi, A., Yomo, T., Kaneko, K.: Ubiquity of Log-Normal Distributions in Intra-Cellular Reaction Dynamics. Biophysics **1** (2005) 25-31

Analysis of Fluctuation in Gene Expression Based on Continuous Culture System

Tadashi Yamada, Makoto Sadamitsu, Keisuke Nagahisa,
Akiko Kashiwagi, Chikara Furusawa, Tetsuya Yomo,
and Hiroshi Shimizu

Department of Bioinformatic Engineering,
Graduate School of Information Science and Technology,
Osaka University, 2-1 Yamadaoka, Suita, Osaka 565-0871, Japan
{nukumori, sadamitsu, nagahisa, akikok, furusawa, yomo,
shimizu}@ist.osaka-u.ac.jp

Abstract. The emergence of heterogeneous cellular state in uniform environment was studied. Using a continuous culture system which provides homogeneous culture environment, we investigated the fluctuation in expression level of *glnA* gene in a cell population. As results, we found that the expression level of *glnA* gene in the cells exhibit a large fluctuation (with two orders of magnitude of protein number), even though expression of the gene is essential for cellular growth and the environment is homogeneous. Furthermore, among several steady states, the transient processes of such heterogeneous cell population were investigated, by changing environmental conditions. The results showed that cells can respond to environmental changes even when their intra-cellular state is accompanied by fluctuations. These results may provide a clue to understand why biological systems can maintain and reproduce themselves robustly.

1 Introduction

In studies of biological systems, it is generally assumed that intra-cellular state of isogenic cells in a fixed environment are homogeneous, and analysis of the systems are based on this assumption. For example, cell concentration is usually measured at the macroscopic level, such as measurement of turbidity of culture medium, which relies on the homogeneity of cells. However, recent developments of experimental technique enable us to measure the intra-cellular state at the single-cell level, and such measurements suggest that heterogeneity of cellular state is ubiquitous in cellular system [1][2]. Thus, to clarify the nature of such cellular heterogeneity is important for further development of biological studies. For this purpose, in this study we investigate the heterogeneity of cellular state in a uniform environment, and adaptation process of such heterogeneous cellular state to environmental changes, using bacteria cells in continuous culture system.

In this study, to characterize intra-cellular state of cells, we adopt expression level of *glnA* gene, since the expression of this gene is essential for nitrogen assimilation in our culture medium, and then it can represent cell viability under

A.J. Ijspeert et al. (Eds.): BioADIT 2006, LNCS 3853, pp. 113–127, 2006.

nitrogen-limited growth condition. In our system, a glutamine synthetase gene
glnA deficient mutant of *Escherichia coli* YMC21 [3] was used as a host bacterium. The plasmid pKGN-EGFP, carrying the *egfp-glnA* [4] fusion gene was
introduced into the *glnA*-deficient mutant. This cells were cultured in a minimal
medium, containing glucose and glutamate as sole carbon and nitrogen sources,
respectively. Glutamine synthetase only catalyze the conversion reaction from
glutamate to glutamine. This pathway is essential for cell growth under the
medium condition using in this study, so that cells must express the *glnA* gene
to grow in the system. Using this recombinant strain, we can monitor the expression level of *glnA* gene at a single cell level, by measuring fluorescence of
EGFP-GlnA fusion protein. This *egfp-glnA* gene is not regulated by wild-type
promoter of *glnA* gene[5][6], instead the expression of this gene is controlled by
tac promoter[7], which is artificially constructed and is not regulated directly by
other factors in the *E. coli* YMC21 cells. And this strain and plasmid used in this
system do not have repressor gene (*lacI*) of *tac* promoter. Use of this promoter
allows us to the nature of heterogeneity in gene expression levels regardless of
regulations in the wild-type strain.

To maintain the environmental conditions constant, we used a continuous
culture system. In this culture system, growth rate, cell concentration, and substrate concentration are kept constant at a steady state by a continuous input
flow of medium and output flow of culture (medium and cells), where the growth
rate of cells is identical to the dilution rate of the medium. At such steady state
of continuous culture, intra-cellular state is also expected to be constant, and
the heterogeneity of cellular state was studied at such steady state conditions.

Furthermore, after reaching such steady state of cell population, we changed
the environmental conditions to study the transitions of intra-cellular state between these steady states. Here, we added two types of environmental changes.
In one experiment, we changed glutamate concentration in the feeding medium,
to change the importance of *glnA* gene under the condition. For example, when
the concentration of glutamate in the medium decrease, it is expected that more
expression of *glnA* is required for cell growth. On the other hand, when the concentration of glutamate in the medium becomes enough high, the importance
of *glnA* expression decreases. In another experiment, we used the glutamate
medium as basis and switched to the mixed nitrogen medium containing glutamate and glutamine. Here, by this environmental change, the importance of
glnA is expected to decrease, since glutamine is the product of the enzymatic
reaction which is catalyzed by *glnA* protein.

Using this system, we investigated the heterogeneity of cellular state at a
steady state of the continuous culture, and the transient process of cellular state
between such steady states. As a result, first we found that even at the steady
state of continuous culture, the expression level of *glnA* gene in the cells showed
a broad distribution (with two orders of magnitude of protein number), even
though the reaction catalyzed by *glnA* protein is essential for cell viability under
our medium condition. Second, it was shown that such heterogeneous cellular
state responded to environmental changes. Since the heterogeneity of cellular

state was maintained in uniform environments, these observations indicate that the fluctuations in cellular states inevitably emerges, and biological systems can be sustained even under such fluctuations in intra-cellular dynamics. To clarify the mechanism that biological systems can work under such fluctuations will allow us to construct the robust artificial systems, such as IT networking.

2 Materials and Methods

2.1 Strain and Plasmid

A glutamine synthetase gene (*glnA*) deficient mutant of *Escherichia coli* YMC21 [3] (genotype is shown in Table 1) was used as a host. The plasmid pKGN-EGFP (shown in Figure 1), carrying the *egfp-glnA* fusion gene downstream of *tac* promoter was introduced into the determined *glnA*-deficient mutant. The plasmid has β-lactamase gene.

2.2 Cultivation Methods

-80°C stock of experimental strain is streaked on M9 like glutamate medium agar (KH$_2$PO$_4$ 4.5g/L, K$_2$HPO$_4$ 10.5g/L, Glutamate 1mM, Glucose 0.4%,

Table 1. The strains used in this study

strain	genotype
Escherichia coli YMC21	Δ(*glnA-glnG*), Δ*lacU169*, *endA1*, *hsdR17*, *thi-1*, *supE44*

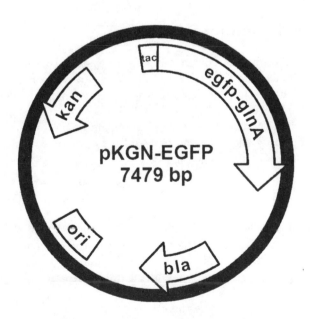

Fig. 1. Vector map of pKGN-EGFP

Thiamine·HCl 5mg/L, MgSO$_4$·7H$_2$O 50mg/L, Ampicilin 50mg/L, agar 1.5%) plate and stored at 37°C for 2 days. Prewormed fresh M9 like glutamate medium (KH$_2$PO$_4$ 4.5g/L, K$_2$HPO$_4$ 10.5g/L, Glutamate 1mM, Glucose 0.4%, Thiamine·HCl 5mg/L, MgSO$_4$·7H$_2$O 50mg/L, Ampicilin 50mg/L) is added to the plate. The colonies are suspended by glass stick. In preculture, the suspended cells are inoculated into 100mL M9 like glutamate medium in Sakaguchi flask and cultured at 37°C, 120rpm for a day(MM-10, Titec Japan). The precultured cells are collected into two 50ml tubes and centrifuged at 6000rpm for 10min twice. The pellet is resuspended by the fresh 10mL fresh M9 like glutamate medium. The 10mL suspended cells are added into the 125mL M9 like glutamate medium in the 200mL fermenter (Titec Japan) which aeration and temperature are controlled by fermentation controller (BMJ-01, ABLE Japan). In main culture system, cultivation is performed at the scale of 125mL. Cultivation conditions of aeration, temperature and dilution rate are 1vvm, 37°C and 0.075(1/h), respectively. The fermenter is prewormed at 37°C before inoculation and stored for 30 minutes after inoculation. After storing for 30 minutes, feeding pumps of input and output flows of medium start to operate and this time is set as a start time (0h) of the culture. The sample from output medium is taken for analysis the cell concentration, glucose concentration, glutamate concentration and population dynamics by flow cytometer (EPICS ELITE, Beckman Coulter), periodically. Cell concentration is analyzed by the particle characterization analyzer (SD-2000, Sysmex) and spectrophotometer (UV mini 1240, Shimazu). The glucose concentration is measured by glucose analyzer (MODEL2700, Y.S.I Co. Ltd.). The glutamate concentration is measured by the Glutamate F Kit (Roche Diagnostics Swiss).

3   Continuous Culture System

In this study, we adopt the continuous culture system to maintain a uniform environment in space and time. Figure 2 illustrates a reactor tank. The configurations of this cultivation method are also called chemostat. The principle of continuous culture is described below in detail[8][9].

At a steady state, concentrations of components in the reactor are kept constant, so we can apply the following material balance equations to any components of the system:

$$\frac{dXV}{dt} = \mu XV - F_{out}X = 0 \qquad (1)$$

$$\frac{dSV}{dt} = F_{in}S_f - F_{out}S - \nu XV = 0 \qquad (2)$$

where X = cell concentration in the reactor and in the effluent stream

F_{in} = volumetric flow rate of feed liquid stream

F_{out} = volumetric flow rate of effluent liquid stream

V = total volume of culture

μ = specific growth rate of the cells

S_f = substrate concentration in the feed stream

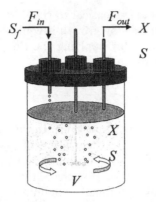

Fig. 2. Schematic diagram of reactor tank

S = substrate concentration in the reactor and in the effluent stream
ν = specific substrate consumption rate.

In the continuous culture system, culture volume V is a constant.

$$\frac{dV}{dt} = 0 \tag{3}$$

$$F_{in} = F_{out} \tag{4}$$

By applying Eq. 3 and Eq. 4 to Eq. 1 and Eq. 2, we obtain the following equations:

$$\frac{dX}{dt} = \mu X - DX = 0 \tag{5}$$

$$\frac{dS}{dt} = D(S_f - S) - \nu X = 0. \tag{6}$$

Here, as noted in Eq. 5 and Eq. 6, the parameter D, called the dilution rate and defined by

$$D = \frac{F_{in}}{V} = \frac{F_{out}}{V} \tag{7}$$

characterizes the holding time or processing rate of the continuous culture system. In Eq. 5, We have equality if

$$X = 0 \tag{8}$$

or

$$\mu = D \tag{9}$$

is approved. In the case of Eq. 8, no cell exists in the reactor. This case is called "wash-out", where all cells are flowed out because their maximum specific growth rate is lower than the dilution rate. In this case, the substrate concentration S becomes S_f. In the case of Eq. 9, the cells can survive in the reactor. The specific growth rate of the cells becomes identical to the dilution rate. This means that the number of the increased cells by growth is equivalent to the number of cells flowed-out. At the steady-state, by applying the Eq. 8 to Eq. 9 the equation of substrate concentration is written as

$$\frac{S_f - S}{X} = \frac{\nu}{\mu}. \tag{10}$$

In Eq. 10, the righthand side is constant value. In this case, the cell concentration is proportional to the substrate concentration of feeding medium if the cells consume the substrate completely (S is almost zero). Then, we can control the cell concentration at the steady-state by changing the substrate concentration. In this study, we use M9 like glutamate medium including glutamate as sole nitrogen source. We kept the glutamate concentration in the feeding medium lower than 1mM, since in this range the culture environment is maintained as the glutamate limited condition. We can cultivate cells under uniform environment and change the environment in the reactor by changing the feeding medium.

4   Results

We performed two kinds of experiments with environmental changes. First, we performed the continuous culture with change in glutamate concentration. After the environmental conditions reached at the steady state, the condition was kept constant until 20 or more generations of cells passed, to obtain the steady state of intra-cellular reaction dynamics. Then, the concentration of glutamate in the feeding medium was changed, in the order of 1mM → 0.1mM → 1mM. Figure 3 shows time courses of cell concentration, glutamate concentration and glucose concentration in the reactor, respectively. Cell concentration was estimated by optical density at 600nm (OD_{600}) and particle number measured by the particle characterization analyzer. At each steady state, we confirmed that glutamate concentration was almost zero and cell concentration was proportional to the glutamate concentration in the feeding medium. Soon after switching high glutamate concentration to lower one (at 270h in Fig. 3), cell concentration started to decrease, and after about 48 hours it reached to the new steady state. In a similar way, soon after switching low concentration to higher one (at 510h in Fig. 3), cell concentration increased and after about 48 hours it reached to the original steady state.

Figures 4 and 5 show the distributions of cellular states at each sampling time, measured by flow cytometer. The axis from front to right back indicates Forward Scattering intensity (FS) of each cell, and the axis from front to left back indicates GFP fluorescent intensity of each cell. The vertical axis indicates the fruquency (%) of each FS-GFP region. Upper layer of each figure shows the 3D histogram of FS-GFP and lower layer shows the density plot. Here, GFP fluorescence intensity indicates the expression level of *glnA* gene, and FS represents the cell size, respectively. In Fig. 4, distributions at the same steady state are compared with each other. The shapes of distributions at the same steady state

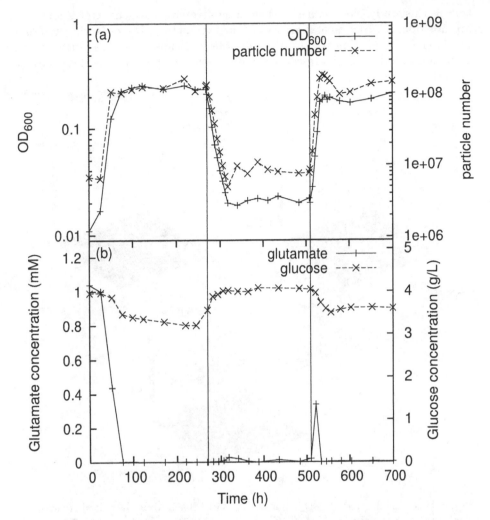

Fig. 3. Time courses of glutamate concentration change experiment. (a) the time courses of cell concentration, and (b) the time courses of substrate concentration. In the graph (a), (+) mark indicates the cell concentration measured by turbidity method (corresponding left vertical axis) and (×) mark indicates cell concentration measured by particle characterization analyzer (corresponding right vertical axis), respectively. In the graph (b), (+) mark indicates the glutamate concentration (corresponding left vertical axis) and (×) mark indicates the glucose concentration (corresponding right vertical axis), respectively. Two vertical lines at 270h and 510h indicate the time of changing the glutamate concentration in the feeding medium.

are similar. An important point here is that the distribution of *glnA* expression level exhibits a large standard deviation (with two orders of magnitude of protein number), even though the environment is homogeneous and the reaction catalyzed by *glnA* protein is essential for cell viability under the medium condi-

tion in this study. We confirmed that these diversities of gene expression levels
are not due to experimental errors of flow cytometry, by measuring standard
beads (BD Living Colors™EGFP Calibration Beads, BD Biosciences) which
have known sizes and fluorescences, and comparing these standard data to the
data of the cells.

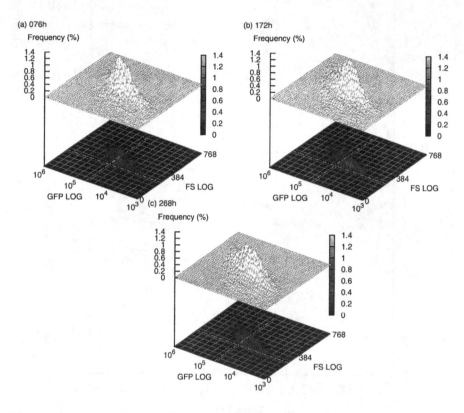

Fig. 4. The distribution of GFP fluorescence and FS signal at the initial steady-state
of glutamate concentration 1mM. The figures show the distribution at (a) 76h, (b)
172h, and (c) 268h, respectively. The shapes of distribution at the same steady state
are similar each other.

When the glutamate concentration in the feeding medium was changed, dynamic changes of cellular states were observed. When the glutamate concentration in the feeding medium decreased, the cell population with a high GFP
fluorescence intensity (*glnA* expression level) became the major group in the
system, and the number of cells with a low GFP fluorescence intensity (*glnA*
expression level) decreased (Figure 5 (a-b)). On the other hand, when the glutamate concentration in the feeding medium increased, the cell population which
had a low GFP fluorescence intensity (*glnA* expression level) became the major
group in the system, and the number of cells which had a high GFP fluorescence
intensity (*glnA* expression level) decreased (Figure 5 (c-d)). Interestingly, the

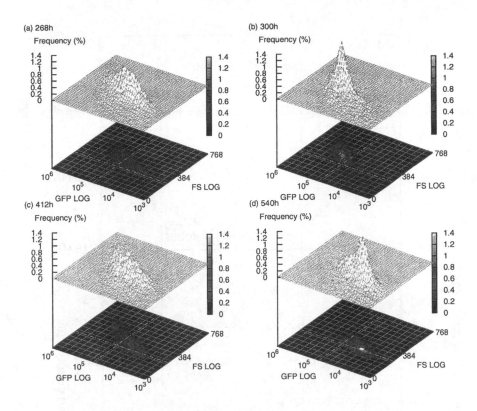

Fig. 5. The distributions of GFP and FS signal at the transient state of glutamate concentration change. Figures (a) and (b) show the distributions at the transient when the glutamate concentration in feeding medium was changed from 1mM to 0.1mM. Figure (a) shows the distribution at the initial steady state (268h) at 1mM glutamate, and figure (b) shows the distributions at 30h after change of the glutamate concentration (300h) during this transient process, subpopulation with low GFP intensity (low expression level of *glnA*) disappeared. This change was not maintained and the distribution was recovered to the original one around 48h after change of the glutamate concentration. Figures (c) and (d) show the distributions at the transient when the glutamate concentration in feeding medium was changed from 0.1mM to 1mM. Figure (c) shows the distribution at the initial steady state (508h) at 0.1mM, and figure (d) shows the distributions at 30h after change of the glutamate concentration (540h). In this case, subpopulation with high GFP intensity (high expression level of *glnA*) disappeared. Also, this change was not maintained and the distribution was recovered to the original one around 48h after change of the glutamate concentration.

cell population with the high or low *glnA* expression level was not maintained, and the original distribution with a large standard deviation reappeared, after reaching the steady state.

Next, we performed the continuous culture in which the feeding medium was changed from the medium containing glutamate as a sole nitrogen source to one containing both glutamate and glutamine. In a similar way to the previous ex-

122   T. Yamada et al.

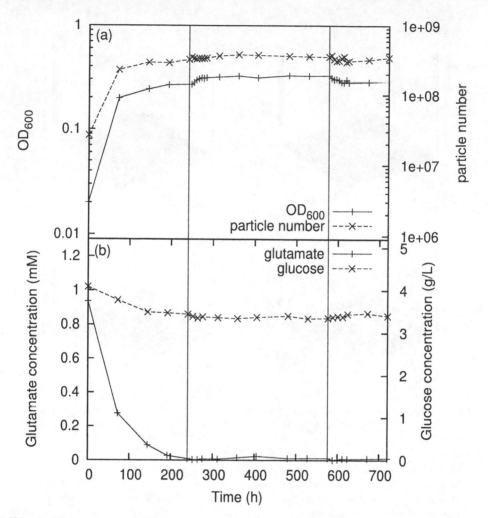

Fig. 6. Time courses of glutamate concentration change experiment. Figure (a) shows the time course of cell concentration, and figure (b) shows the time courses of substrate concentration, respectively. In the figure (a), (+) mark indicates the cell concentration measured by turbidity method (corresponding left vertical axis) and (×) mark indicates cell concentration measured by particle characterization analyzer (corresponding right vertical axis), respectively. In the figure (b), (+) mark indicates the glutamate concentration (corresponding left vertical axis) and (×) mark indicates the glucose concentration (corresponding right vertical axis), respectively. Two vertical lines at 240h and 576h indicate the time of changing the glutamine concentration in the feeding medium.

periment, to obtain the steady intra-cellular state, we kept the system for 20 or more generations passed after the environmental condition settled down. After that, the feeding medium was changed in the order of (1mM glutamate) → (1mM glutamate and 0.1mM glutamine) → (1mM glutamate). Figure 6 shows

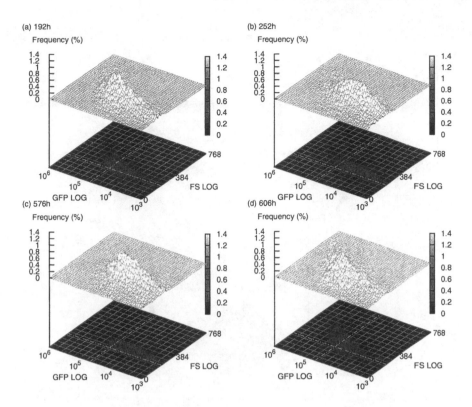

Fig. 7. The distributions of GFP and FS signal at the transient when glutamine is added to or removed from the feeding medium. Figures (a) and (b) show the distributions at the transient when glutamine concentration in feeding medium was changed from 0mM to 0.1mM. Figure (a) shows the distribution at the initial steady state (192h) at 1mM glutamate only medium, and figure (b) shows the distributions at 30h after change to the glutamine added medium (252h). After addition of glutamine, subpopulation with high GFP intensity (high expression level of *glnA*) disappears. Figures (c) and (d) show the distributions at the transient when glutamine concentration in feeding medium was changed from 0.1mM to 0mM. Figure (c) shows the distribution at the initial steady state (576h) at 0.1mM glutamine, and figure (d) shows the distributions at 30h after removal of glutamine (606h). In this case, Also, this change was not maintained and the distribution was recovered to the original one around 48h after change of the glutamate concentration. In this case, subpopulation with low GFP intensity (low expression level of *glnA*) disappears. These distributions were maintained as long as the culture conditions were kept constant.

the time courses of the glutamine addition culture. At all the steady states, that cell concentration and glucose concentration were constant, and glutamate concentration was almost zero. The addition of glutamine to the feeding medium made the cell concentration increasing about 20%. In the microscopic viewpoint, when the feeding medium was switched from glutamate only medium to glutamine added glutamate medium, dynamic change of intra-cellular states was

124   T. Yamada et al.

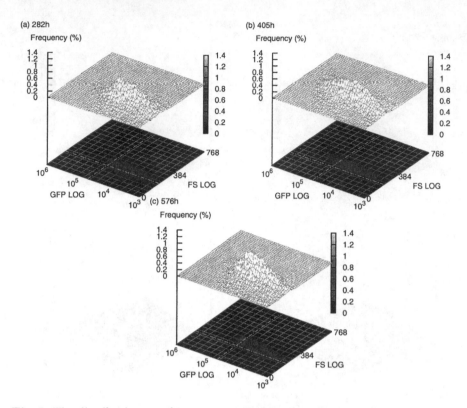

Fig. 8. The distributions at the steady state of glutamine added medium. The figures show the distribution at (a) 252h, (b) 405h, and (c) 576h, respectively. The shapes of distribution with low GFP intensity are maintained at the same steady state.

observed as shown in Figure 7 (a-b). In the steady state of glutamate medium, the distributions of *glnA* expression exhibited a large standard deviation as the previous experiments. On the other hand, when feeding medium was changed to the glutamine added medium, the number of the cells which had a high expression level of *glnA* decreased. This population change continued to the next steady state and this distribution was maintained during the steady state in this condition(Figure 8). When the addition of glutamine was cut, the original distribution was recovered as shown in Fig. 7 (c-d).

5   Discussions

Continuous cultures of the isogenic cells in an uniform environment were carried out, to investigate the nature of heterogeneity in intra-cellular state which is characterized by the analysis using the flow cytometer. As results, first we found that even in uniform environments in space and time, the cells generally show heterogeneity of intra-cellular states. Even though the expression level of *glnA* gene is essential for cell viability under the medium condition in this study, the distribution of the expression level exhibited a broad distribution (with two orders of magnitude of protein number) in the uniform environment. This result clearly showed that such heterogeneity is inevitable in cell population, presumably due to the stochastic nature of intra-cellular dynamics[10].

Second, we found that the distribution of *glnA* gene expression dynamically changed when the substrate concentrations in the feeding medium were changed. When the glutamate concentration in the feeding medium decreased, cells with low *glnA* expression disappeared, and only cells having high *glnA* expression levels remained. Conversely, when glutamate concentration increased, cells with high *glnA* expression disappeared, and only cells with low *glnA* expression remained. Furthermore, we found that at the steady state of cells in the medium containing both glutamate and glutamine, the subpopulation with a high *glnA* expression level decreased. This change of distribution was maintained as long as glutamine was added to the feeding medium.

One may cast a question whether this dynamical change of cell population is given by flow out of subpopulation with lower growth speed, or it is due to the change of intra-cellular state in response to the environmental change. To answer it, we analyzed the change in the distribution of *glnA* expression in detail. In the continuous culture with the addition of glutamine to the feeding medium (Figure 7 (a-b)), the histograms of *glnA* expression level at the steady state in glutamate only medium and at the transient state (12h after switching to glutamine added medium) were plotted in Fig. 9. As shown in the figure, the

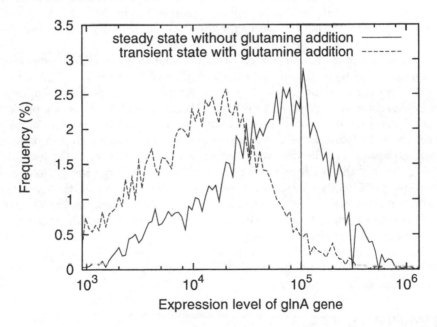

Fig. 9. The histogram of GFP intensities (expression level of *glnA* gene) at the steady state (dotted line) and transient state (solid line) of glutamine addition. The distribution of GFP intensity (expression level of *glnA* gene) moved to lower side for 12h.

expression level decrease in the transient state, and the question here is whether this change of the distribution can be explained by the difference in the growth speeds of cell populations or not. Since the flow out of the medium and cells is kept constant in the continuous culture system, we can determine the maximal change of cell population in a certain period, when the intra-cellular state of cells do not change and there are only differences in the growth speed of cells. Assume that there is a subpopulation of cells which cannot grow in the new environmental condition, their specific growth rate is zero ($\mu = 0$). The change in the population of such cells is represented as follows.

$$\frac{dX_{sub}}{dt} = -DX \tag{11}$$

Here, a survival ratio of subpopulation is defined as

$$\frac{X_{sub}(t)}{X_{sub}(0)} = \exp(-D \cdot t). \tag{12}$$

Since the dilution rate D was set at $0.075(1/h)$ in our experiments, when a subpopulation of cells stop to grow due to the environmental change, we can estimate that about 40% of these cells remains in the reactor 12h after the environmental change. This indicates the maximal change of cell population in the reactor without changing their intra-cellular state. In the transient process shown in Fig. 9, the fraction of cells which have more than 10^5 GFP intensity (a.u.) remains only 15% at 12h after the environmental change. This means that, the decrease of such subpopulation cannot explained by the difference of growth speed among cells, instead, the *glnA* expression level of cells changes in response to the environmental change.

It should be noted that in our experiments, the change of *glnA* expression level seems to be regulated in accordance with its requirement. For example, when the concentration of glutamate in the feeding medium is decreased, more *glnA* expression may be required to cell growth, and then the expression of *glnA* actually increases. On the other hand, when glutamine, which is product of reaction catalyzed by GlnA protein, is added to the feeding medium, the importance of *glnA* expression may be decrease, and in fact the expression of the gene decreases. The fact that such regulation is possible even though the promoter of this gene is not directly controlled by other factors suggests that the existence of another mechanism for the adaptation of cellular state. Such mechanism may provide a clue to understand why biological systems can maintain and reproduce themselves robustly, even though their intra-cellular reaction network are inevitably accompanied by large fluctuations. Also, we believe that to understand such nature of this mechanism will be available to make a robust artificial systems, such as IT networking.

Acknowledgements

This work was partially supported by the grant of the 21st century center of excellent (COE) program from the Japan Society for Promotion of Science (JSPS).

References

1. Natarajan A and Srienc F: Glucose uptake rates of single *E. coli* cells grown in glucose-limited chemostat cultures. J Microbiol Methods, 42(1). Sep, 2000, 87-96
2. Natarajan A and Srienc F: Dynamics of glucose uptake by single *Escherichia coli* cells. Metab Eng, 1(4). Oct, 1999, 320-333
3. Xu,W-Z and A.Kashiwagi and T. Yomo and I. Urabe: Fate of a mutant emerging at the initial stage of evolution. Researches on Population Ecology, Vol.38. (1996) 231-237
4. Zhang G and Gurtu V and Kain SR: An enhanced green fluorescent protein allows sensitive detection of gene transfer in mammalian cells. Biochem Biophys Res Commun, 227(3). Oct, 1996 707-711
5. Mariette R. Atkinson and Timothy A. Blauwkamp and Vladamir Bondarenko and Vasily Studitsky and Alexander J. Ninfa: Activation of *glnA*, *glnK*, and *nac* Promoters as *Escherihia coli* Nitrogen Starvation. Journal of Bacteriology, 184(19). Oct, 2002, 5358-5363
6. Shizue Ueno-Nishio and Keith C. Backman and Boris Magasanik: Regulation at the *glnL*-Operator-Promoter of the Complex *glnALG* Operon of *Escherichi coli*. Journal of Bacterioloty, Mar, 1983 1247-1251
7. Herman A. De Boar and Lisa L. Comstock and Mark Vaser: The *tac* promoter: A functional hybrid derived from the *trp* and *lac* promoters. PNAS, Vol.80. Jan, 1983 (1)21-25
8. Butler, G.J. and G.S.K. Wolkowicz: A mathematical model of the chemostat with a general class of functions describing nutrient uptake. SIAM Journal of Applied Mathematics, Vol.45. (1985) 138-151
9. James Edwin Bailey and David F. Ollis: Biochemical Engineering Fundamentals. McGrow-Hill, 1986
10. Nitzan Rosenfeld and Jonathan W. Young and Uri Alon and Reter S. Swain and Michael B. Elowitz: Gene Regulation at the Single-Cell Level. SCIENCE, Vol. 307. Mar, 2005 1962-1965

Bio-inspired Computing Machines with Self-repair Mechanisms

André Stauffer, Daniel Mange, and Gianluca Tempesti

Ecole polytechnique fédérale de Lausanne (EPFL),
Logic Systems Laboratory, CH-1015 Lausanne, Switzerland
andre.stauffer@epfl.ch

Abstract. Developmental biology requires three principles of organization characteristic of living organisms: multicellular architecture, cellular division, and cellular differentiation. Implemented in silicon according to these principles, new computing machines become able to grow, to self-replicate, and to self-repair. The introduction of a new algorithm for cellular division, the so-called Tom Thumb algorithm, necessitates new self-repair mechanisms of structural configuration, functional configuration, microscopic cicatrization, and macroscopic regeneration. The details of these mechanisms constitutes the core of this paper.

1   Introduction

The *Embryonics* project (for *embryonic electronics*) [2] aims at creating radically new computing machines inspired by Nature and able to grow, to self-repair, and to self-replicate [4] [8] [1]. The embryonic development of living creatures fascinates engineers who dream of designing computing machines mimicking living organisms in a completely different environment, the two-dimensional world of silicon. Our Embryonics project aims at creating such machines which, starting from a one-dimensional blueprint, an "artificial genome", will be able to grow and give birth to computers endowed, as their living models, with original properties such as self-repair and self-replication. These properties are highly desirable for "extreme" applications of computer engineering (space exploration, radioactive environments, avionics, etc.) and, more importantly, are indispensable for the design of the future nanoscale electronic components whose characteristics will be very close to those of living organisms [3]. In conclusion, the challenge to be met is to make perfect systems out of imperfect components.

Borrowing three principles of organization (multicellular architecture, cellular division, and cellular differentiation) from living organisms, we have already shown [5] how it is possible to grow an artificial organism in silicon thanks to two algorithms: an algorithm for cellular differentiation, based on coordinate calculation, and an algorithm for cellular division, the Tom Thumb algorithm [6].

The goal of this paper is to perform the Tom Thumb algorithm many times so that self-repair could be introduced and make it possible the cicatrization (microscopic self-repair) and the regeneration (macroscopic self-repair) of the

A.J. Ijspeert et al. (Eds.): BioADIT 2006, LNCS 3853, pp. 128–140, 2006.
© Springer-Verlag Berlin Heidelberg 2006

original organism. Starting with a very simple artificial organism with only three cells, the "SOS" acronym (for Save Our Souls), Section 2 will recall the definitions of cicatrization and regeneration. We will then introduce the growth processes, based on the Tom Thumb algorithm, leading to the structural configuration (Section 3) and functional configuration (Section 4), as well as to the cicatrization mechanism (Section 5) and regeneration mechanism (Section 6) of the artificial cell. A brief conclusion (Section 7) summarizes the whole procedure.

2   Cloning, Cicatrization and Regeneration

Even if our final goal is the development of complex machines, in order to illustrate the basic mechanisms of self-repair we shall use an extremely simplified example, the display of the acronym "SOS". The machine that displays the acronym can be considered as a one-dimensional artificial organism, *Acronymus elegans*, composed of four cells (Fig. 1a). Each cell is identified by a X coordinate, ranging from 1 to 4. For coordinate values $X = 1$ and $X = 3$, the cell should implement the S character, for $X = 2$, it should implement the O character, while for $X = 4$ it should implement a *spare* or *totipotent cell*. A totipotent cell (in this example, a cell capable of displaying either the S or the O character) comprises $4 \times 6 = 24$ molecules (Fig. 1b), 21 of which are invariant, one displays the S character, and two display the O character. An incrementer—an adder of one modulo 4—is embedded in the final organism; this incrementer implements the X coordinate calculation according to the following cycle: $X = 1 \rightarrow 2 \rightarrow 3 \rightarrow 4 \rightarrow 1$.

The *self-replication* (or *cloning*) of a multicellular artificial organism (the "SOS" acronym, for example), i.e. the production of one or several copies of the original, rests on two assumptions: (1) There exists a sufficient number of spare totipotent cells in the array (at least four in our "SOS" example) to contain one copy of the additional organism. (2) The calculation of the coordinates produces a cycle $X = 1 \rightarrow 2 \rightarrow 3 \rightarrow 4 \rightarrow 1$ implying $X+ = (X + 1) \bmod 4$. As the same pattern of coordinates produces the same pattern of genes (in our example, the same alphabetical pattern "SOS"), self-replication of an organism can be easily accomplished if the incrementer, embedded in each totipotent cell, counts modulo n, thus producing several occurrences of the basic pattern of coordinates. Given a sufficiently large space, the self-replication of the organism can be repeated for any number of specimens in the X and/or Y axes.

In order to implement the self-repair of the organism, we decided to use one or several spare cells to the right of the original organism (Fig. 1a). The existence of a fault is detected by a KILL signal (Fig. 1c) which is calculated in each cell by a built-in self-test mechanism realized at the molecular level (see below). The state KILL=1 identifies the faulty cell, and the entire column of all cells to which the faulty cell belongs is considered faulty and is deactivated (column $X = 2$ in Fig. 1a; in this simple example, the column of cells is reduced to a single cell). All the functions (X coordinate and gene) of the cells to the right of the column $X = 1$ are shifted by one column to the right. Obviously, this process requires as many spare columns to the right of the array as there are faulty cells or columns

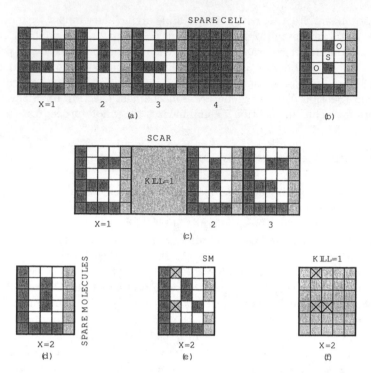

Fig. 1. Self-repair of *Acronymus elegans*, the acronym "SOS" (for Save Our Souls). (a) One-dimensional organism composed of four cells; a spare totipotent cell takes place at the right of the organism, with coordinate $X = 4$. (b) Totipotent cell. (c) The faulty cell ($X = 2$) and all the cells to the right of the faulty cell ($X = 3$) are shifted by one column to the right; the price to pay is an empty space, or a "scar". (d) Initial configuration of the healthy cell displaying O ($X = 2$). (e) Self-repaired cell ($X = 2$) with 2 faulty molecules; the price to pay is a deformation of the original O character; SM=spare molecule. (f) Faulty cell ($X = 2$) with 2 faulty molecules in the same row (KILL=1).

to repair (one spare column tolerating one faulty cell, in the example of Fig. 1a). It also implies that the cell needs to be able to bypass the faulty column and to divert to the right all the required signals (such as the artificial genome and the X coordinates). Given a sufficient number of cells, it is obviously possible to combine self-repair in the X direction and self-replication in both the X and Y directions.

The introduction in each cell of one or several columns of spare molecules (Fig. 1d), defined by a specific structural configuration, and the automatic detection of faulty molecules (by a built-in self-test mechanism which constantly compares two copies of the same molecule) allows cellular self-repair: each faulty molecule is deactivated, isolated from the network, and replaced by the nearest right molecule, which will itself be replaced by the nearest right molecule, and so on until a spare molecule (SM) is reached (Fig. 1e). The number of faulty molecules handled by the cellular self-repair mechanism is necessarily limited:

in the example of Fig. 1d, we tolerate at most one faulty molecule per row. If more than one molecule is faulty in one or more rows (Fig. 1f), cellular self-repair is impossible, in which case a global KILL=1 is generated to activate the organismic self-repair described above (Fig. 1c).

Salamanders, starfish, polyps and zebra fish can regenerate new heads, limbs, internal organs or other body parts if the originals are lost or damaged. The prolific properties of planarian worms make them an ideal starting point for investigating regeneration. A flatworm contains dormant stem cells distributed throughout its body. When damage occurs, stem cells near the injury rely on signals from neighboring damaged tissues to work out their location, and hence what repairs are needed [7]. According to Wolpert [10], regeneration is closely related to embryonic development; many aspects of regeneration seem related to embryonic regulation and can be considered in terms of replacing the positional values of cells that have been lost. Coming back to the Embryonics project, one may consider that the first step of repair, i.e. cellular self-repair where faulty molecules are replaced by spare molecules, can be regarded as a kind of *artificial cicatrization*, while the second step of repair, i.e. organismic self-repair where faulty cells are replaced by spare totipotent cells, is the equivalent of *artificial regeneration*.

3 Structural Configuration

For a better understanding of the *structural growth process*, performing the *structural configuration* by applying the Tom Thumb algorithm, we will give up the "SOS" acronym example, yet too complex, and we will start with a minimal self-repair cell. This cell is made up of six molecules organized as an array of two rows by three columns, one column (two molecules) being dedicated to self-repair (SM=spare molecule) (Fig. 2a). Each molecule is now able to store in its five memory positions five characters of the artificial genome, and the whole cell embeds 30 such characters. The structural genome G1 for the minimal self-repair cell is organized as a string of twelve characters, i.e. two characters for each molecule in the cell, moving anticlockwise by one character at each time step ($t = 0, 1, 2, ...$). The characters composing the alphabet of our structural genome are detailed in Fig. 3a. They are either *empty data, flag data* (from "north connect flag" to "north connect and branch activate flag") or *structural data*; structural data combine two pieces of information: a position information or *type* (from "top type" to "top-left type") and a state information or *mode* (from "living mode" to "dead mode"). Flag data will be used for constructing the various paths between the molecules, while structural data are indispensable, in a first step, for locating the *living* (normal) and *spare* molecules. Furthermore, each character is given a status and will eventually be *mobile data*, indefinitely moving around the cell, or *fixed data*, definitely trapped in a memory position of a molecule (Fig. 3b).

At each time step, a character of the structural genome is shifted from right to left and simultaneously stored in the lower leftmost molecule (Fig. 2a). The

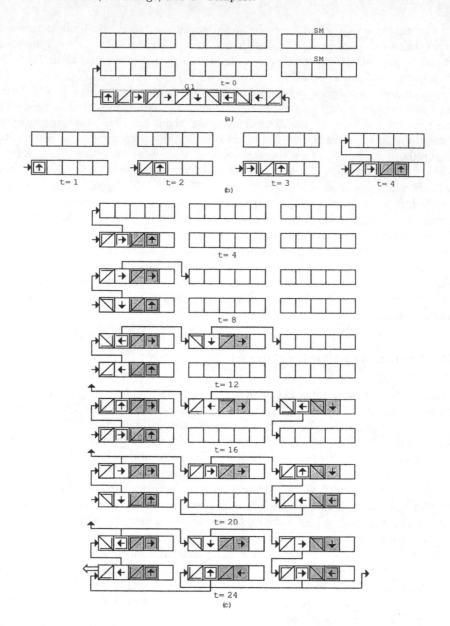

Fig. 2. The minimal self-repair cell made up of six molecules. (a) At time $t = 0$, the cell is empty; the structural genome G1 is ready to enter the first molecule. (b) Four steps of the Tom Thumb algorithm; $t = 1...3$: shift of the genome by one position to the right; $t = 4$: the genome is shifted by one position to the right, while the two right-most characters are trapped in the molecule (fixed data in gray) and a connection is established to the north. (c) State of the connections between the molecules after every four steps of the structural growth process; at time $t = 24$, when the path is closed, the lowermost molecule of the first column delivers a close signal to the nearest left neighbor cell.

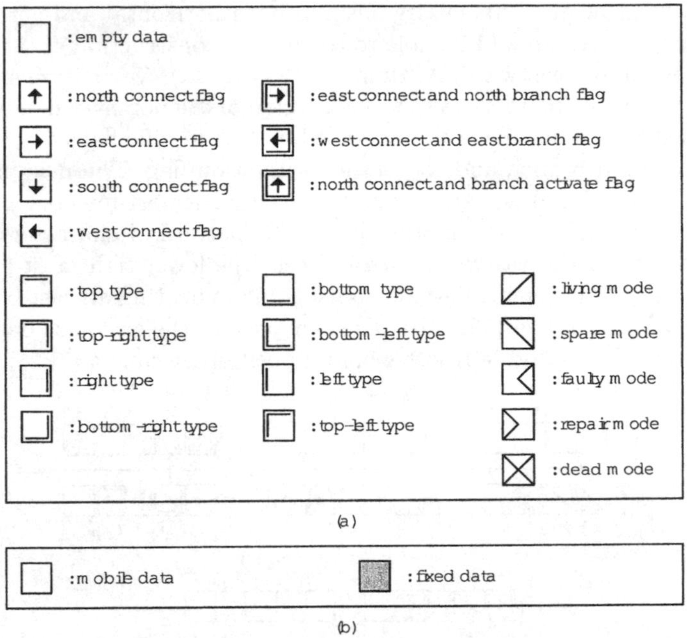

: empty data

↑ : north connect flag   ➡ : east connect and north branch flag

➡ : east connect flag   ⬅ : west connect and east branch flag

⬇ : south connect flag   ⬆ : north connect and branch activate flag

⬅ : west connect flag

: top type   : bottom type   : living mode

: top-right type   : bottom-left type   : spare mode

: right type   : left type   : faulty mode

: bottom-right type   : top-left type   : repair mode

: dead mode

(a)

: mobile data   : fixed data

(b)

Fig. 3. The characters forming the alphabet of an artificial genome. (a) Graphical representations of the characters which are divided in 3 major classes: empty data, flag data describing the paths between the molecules of the cell, and structural data describing both the position (type) and the state (mode) of each molecule. (b) Graphical representation of the status of each character defining mobile or fixed data.

construction of the cell, i.e. storing the fixed data and defining the paths for mobile data, depends on two major patterns (Fig. 2b): (1) If the five, four or three rightmost memory positions of a molecule are empty (blank squares), the characters are shifted by one position to the right ($t = 0, 1, 2$). (2) If the two rightmost memory positions are empty ($t = 3$), the characters are shifted by one position to the right; in this situation, the two rightmost characters are trapped in the molecule (fixed data), and a new connection is established from the second leftmost position toward the northern, eastern, southern or western molecule, depending on the fixed flag information (for $t = 3$: "north connect and branch activate flag", and the connection is toward the northern molecule). At time $t = 24$, the connection path between the molecules is closed and 24 characters, i.e. twice the contents of the structural genome, have been stored in 24 memory positions of the cell (Fig. 2c). The lowermost molecule of the first column delivers a *close signal* to the nearest left neighbor cell, while twelve characters are fixed data, defining the structure of the final cell, and the twelve remaining ones are mobile data, composing a copy of the structural genome. Mobile data are ready for starting the growth of other cells, in both northern and eastern directions.

In order to grow an artificial organism in both horizontal and vertical directions, the mother cell should be able to trigger the construction of two daughter cells, northward and eastward. At time $t = 15$ (Fig. 4a), we observe a pattern of characters which is able to start the construction of the northward daughter cell; the upper leftmost molecule is characterized by two specific flags, i.e. a fixed flag indicating a north branch and the branch activation flag. The new path to the northward daughter cell will start from the second leftmost memory position, at time $t = 16$. At time $t = 21$, another particular pattern of characters will start the construction of the eastward daughter cell; the lower rightmost molecule is characterized by two specific flags, i.e. a fixed flag indicating an east branch, and the branch activation flag (Fig. 4b). The new path to the eastward daughter cell will start from the second leftmost memory position at time $t = 22$.

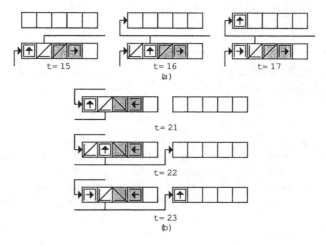

Fig. 4. Artificial cell division. (a) North directed branch starting the growth of a northward neighboring cell. (b) East directed branch starting the growth of an eastward neighboring cell.

The final cell shown in Fig. 2c will now start a *load process*, triggered by the close signal delivered by its nearest right neighbor cell ($t = i$), when this has finished its own structural growth process. A *load signal* will then propagate east-west and bottom-up according to Fig. 5 ($t = i+1$ to $i+3$). At each step, this signal will transform the corresponding molecule in two ways: (1) The structural data in the third position are shifted in the fifth, i.e. rightmost position, of the molecule memory. (2) The four leftmost memory positions are cleared (i.e. empty data). At the end of this process ($t = i + 4$), we finally obtain an homogeneous tissue of molecules, with four memory positions empty, and the fifth filled with the structural data, defining both the boundaries of the cell and the position of its living and spare molecules. This tissue is ready for being configured by a second artificial genome, the functional genome.

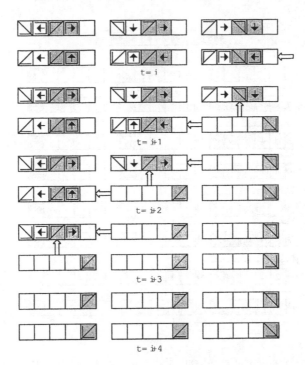

Fig. 5. Triggered by the the close signal of the nearest right neighbor cell ($t = i$), the load process stores the molecular types and modes of the artificial cell in the rightmost memory position of the molecules while the four leftmost ones are cleared ($t = i + 1$ to $i + 4$)

4   Functional Configuration

The goal of *functional configuration* is to store in the homogeneous tissue which already contains structural data (Fig. 5, $t = i + 4$) the functional data needed by the specifications of the current application. This configuration is a *functional growth process*, performed by applying the Tom Thumb algorithm with the following conditions: only the molecules in the "living mode" participate to the growth process, while the molecules in the "spare mode" are simply bypassed. The final cell is made up of four "living mode" molecules organized as an array of two rows by two columns (Fig. 6b, $t = 16$), while one row of two "spare mode" molecules are bypassed. Each molecule is now able to store in its four empty memory positions four characters of the functional genome G2 (Fig. 6a), which is implemented as a string of eight characters. These characters are either *empty data*, *flag data* (Fig. 3a) or *functional data*; functional data are indispensable for defining the final specifications of the cell under construction.

The Tom Thumb algorithm is executed according to the rules of structural configuration (Section 3) if we consider that the fifth position of each molecule is empty. At time $t = 16$ (Fig. 6b), 16 characters, i.e. twice the contents of the

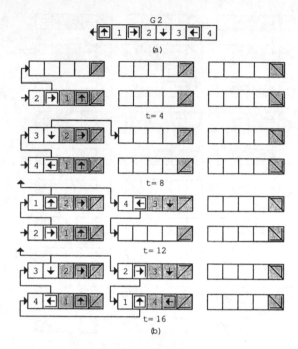

Fig. 6. Functional configuration of the "living mode" molecules. (a) Artificial genome G2. (b) State of the functional growth process after every four steps.

functional genome G2, have been stored in the 16 memory positions of the "living mode" molecules of the cell. Eight characters are fixed data, forming the phenotype of the final cell, and the eight remaining ones are mobile data, composing a copy of the original genome G2, i.e. the genotype. Both *translation* (i.e. construction of the cell) and *transcription* (i.e. copy of the genetic information) have been therefore achieved.

5   Cicatrization Mechanism

Fig. 6b, at time $t = 16$, shows the normal behavior of a healthy minimal cell, i.e. a cell without any faulty molecule.

A molecule is considered as *faulty*, or in the "faulty mode" (Fig. 3a), if some built-in self-test, not described in this paper, detects a lethal malfunction. Starting with the normal behavior of Fig. 6b ($t = 16$), we suppose that two molecules are suddenly in the "faulty mode" (Fig. 7, $t = i$): (1) The lowermost molecule in the first column, which was in previously in the "living mode". (2) The uppermost molecule in the third column, which was before in the "spare mode". While there is no change for the uppermost molecule, which is just no more able to play the role of a "living mode" molecule, the lowermost one triggers the following *cicatrization mechanism*, made up of a *repair process* followed by a *reset process* (Fig. 7).

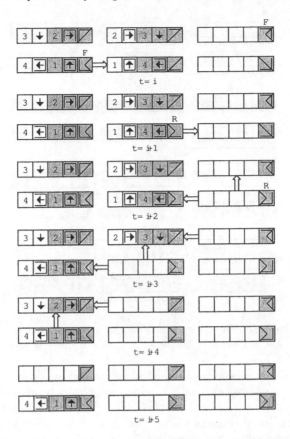

Fig. 7. Cicatrization mechanism performed as a repair process ($t = i + 1$ and $i + 2$) followed by a reset process ($t = i + 3$ to $i + 5$); at the start ($t = i$), two molecules are supposed in the "faulty mode" (F); two molecules are given the "repair mode" (R) at time $t = i + 1$ and $i + 2$

- In a first step, a *repair signal* sent by the lowermost cell transforms the first nearest right "living mode" neighbor in the "repair mode" ($t = i + 1$).
- In a second step, this signal continues to propagate eastward and transforms the next nearest right "spare mode" neighbor in the "repair mode" ($t = i+2$).
- The repair signal having converted a "spare mode" molecule into a "repair mode" one, a *reset signal* comes back in the opposite direction in order to clear the four first memory positions of each "living mode" molecule ($t = i+3$ and $i + 4$).
- In the last step ($t = i+5$), the reset signal erases the contents of the memory positions of the last molecule, the uppermost molecule in the first column.

In this mechanism, the contents of the four memory positions of any "faulty mode" molecule is not erased, as these molecules are obviously not able to perform any function.

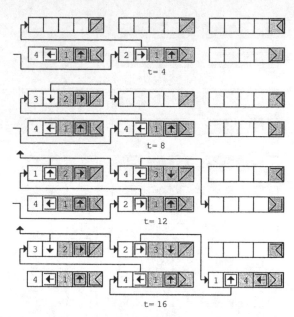

Fig. 8. Functional reconfiguration, based on the artificial genome G2, following the cicatrization mechanism; state of the functional growth process after every four steps

We finally obtain a new topological array containing four healthy molecules ("living mode" and "repair mode"), which is able to be reconfigured in order to emulate the original minimal cell, in its rectangular implementation (Fig. 6b, $t = 16$). A functional reconfiguration, exactly similar to that of Section 4, is launched. The preceding functional genome G2 (Fig. 6a) is introduced into the trapezoidal array of Fig. 7 ($t = i + 5$) and produces a new version of the original minimal cell (Fig. 8, $t = 16$).

6   Regeneration Mechanism

In the general discussion about cicatrization (Section 2), we have already pointed out that only one faulty molecule was tolerated between two spare molecules. A second faulty molecule in the same row will trigger the death of the whole cell, and the start of a regeneration mechanism with recalculation of the X coordinate. Fig. 9 ($t = i$) illustrates such a case: the cicatrized cell of Fig. 8 ($t = 16$) is given a new faulty molecule ("faulty mode") in its uppermost molecule of the second column. The *regeneration mechanism*, made up of a *repair process* and a *kill process*, takes place as follows (Fig. 9):

– In a first step, the new faulty cell sends a *repair signal* eastward, in order to look for a "spare mode" molecule, able to replace it ($t = i$).
– In a second step, the supposed "spare mode" molecule, which is in fact a "faulty mode" one, enters the lethal "dead mode" and triggers *kill signals* westward and southward ($t = i + 1$).

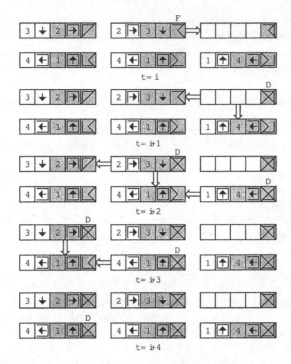

Fig. 9. Regeneration mechanism performed as a repair process ($t = i + 1$) followed by a kill process ($t = i + 2$ to $i + 4$); at the start ($t = i$), a new molecule is supposed in the "faulty mode" (F); all the molecules are then successively given the "dead mode" (D) from time $t = i + 1$ to $i + 4$

- In the three next steps, the other molecules of the array are given the "dead mode" ($t = i + 5$); the original minimal cell is dead, and a general KILL=1 signal is emitted so that the recalculation of the coordinates might take place.

7   Conclusion

While the Tom Thumb algorithm is a rather straightforward tool for designing self-repairing patterns of any complexity, its implementation in systems which are able to self-repair, involves a succession of four possible mechanisms:

- First, a structural configuration, defined by an artificial genome G1, is injected in a homogeneous array of Tom Thumb cellular automata in order to fix the boundaries of the cell ("top type", "bottom type", etc.) and the state of each molecule ("living mode" or "spare mode").
- Second, a functional configuration, described by an artificial genome G2, is injected in the sole "living mode" molecules of the previously defined array; the artificial organism under construction is then obtained.

- Third, a minor fault, one molecule in the "faulty mode", is detected between two "spare mode" molecules; the cicatrization mechanism modifies the original array in order to replace the "faulty mode" molecule by a "repair mode" one; a reconfiguration process with the functional genome G2 concludes this mechanism.
- Fourth, a major fault may happen, with two molecules in the "faulty mode" between two "spare mode" molecules; the cell is no more able to self-repair, and the regeneration mechanism kills all the molecules in the cell, before generating a global KILL=1 signal triggering the recalculation of the X coordinate.

The detailed architecture for the data and signals cellular automaton (DSCA) which constitutes the basic molecule of the Tom Thumb algorithm has been described in [6], while the modifications of this DSCA for performing the self-repair mechanisms are presented in [9].

References

1. R. Canham and A. M. Tyrrell. An embryonic array with improved efficiency and fault tolerance. In J. Lohn et al., editor, *Proceedings of the NASA/DoD Conference on Evolvable Hardware (EH'03)*, pages 265–272. IEEE Computer Society, Los Alamitos, CA, 2003.
2. H. de Garis. Evolvable hardware: Genetic programming of a Darwin machine. In R. F. Albrecht, C. R. Reeves, and N. C. Steele, editors, *Artificial Neural Nets and Genetic Algorithms*, pages 441–449. Springer-Verlag, Heidelberg, 1993.
3. J. R. Heath, P. J. Kuekes, G. S. Snider, and R. S. Williams. A defect-tolerant computer architecture: opportunities for nanotechnology. *Science*, 280(5370):1716–1721, June 1998.
4. D. Mange, M. Sipper, A. Stauffer, and G. Tempesti. Toward robust integrated circuits: The Embryonics approach. *Proceedings of the IEEE*, 88(4):516–541, April 2000.
5. D. Mange, A. Stauffer, E. Petraglio, and G. Tempesti. Embryonics machines that divide and differentiate. In A.J. Ijspert, D. Mange, M. Murata, and S. Nishio, editors, *Biologically Inspired Approaches to Advanced Information Technology*. Proceedings of The First International Workshop Bio-ADIT 2004, Lecture Notes in Computer Science. Springer-Verlag, Heidelberg, 2004.
6. D. Mange, A. Stauffer, E. Petraglio, and G. Tempesti. Self-replicating loop with universal construction. *Physica D*, 191(1-2):178–192, April 2004.
7. H. Pearson. The regeneration gap. Nature, 414(6):388–390, 2001.
8. L. Prodan, M. Udrescu, and M. Vladutin. Survivability of embryonic memories: Analysis and design principles. In R. S. Zebulum et al, editor, Proceedings of the NASA/DoD Conference on Evolvable Hardware (EH'04), pages 130–137. IEEE Computer Society, Los Alamitos, CA, 2004.
9. A. Stauffer, D. Mange, and G. Tempesti. Embryonic machines that grow, self- replicate and self-repair. In J. Lohn et al, editor, Proceedings of the 2005 NASA/DoD Conference on Evolvable Hardware (EH'05), pages 290–293. IEEE Computer Society, Los Alamitos, CA, 2005.
10. L. Wolpert. The Triumph of the Embryo. Oxford University Press, Oxford, 1993.

Perspectives of Self-adapted Self-organizing Clustering in Organic Computing

Thomas Villmann[1,*], Barbara Hammer[2], and Udo Seiffert[3]

[1] University of Leipzig, Clinic for Psychotherapy
thomas.villmann@medizin.uni-leipzig.de
[2] University of Technology, Institute of Computer Science
[3] IPK Gatersleben, Pattern Recognition Group, Division Cytogenetics

Abstract. Clustering tasks occur for various different application domains including very large data streams e.g. for robotics and life science, different data formats such as graphs and profiles, and a multitude of different objectives ranging from statistical motivations to data driven quantization errors. Thus, there is a need for efficient any-time self-adaptive models and implementations. The focus of this contribution is on clustering algorithms inspired by biological paradigms which allow to transfer ideas of organic computing to the important task of efficient clustering. We discuss existing methods of adaptivity and point out a taxonomy according to which adaptivity can take place. Afterwards, we develop general perspectives for an efficient self-adaptivity of self-organizing clustering.

1 Introduction

Efficiency ... *the capacity to produce desired results with a minimum expenditure of energy, time, or resource (Merriam-Webster Online Thesaurus)*

Organic Computing (OC) offers efficient biologically inspired self-adaptive approachess to achieve desired results. Thereby, the desired results are usually not specified in an exact mathematical or formal way. Rather, the task is to keep a system which is interacting with the environment or a human user in a state comfortable for the environment or the human user. Since the system, the environment, and the demands of the users are changing, solutions need to be adaptive – machine learning solutions are a popular technique to achieve this goal. The lack of exact mathematical objectives has the consequence that unsupervised machine learning methods are most suitable for these tasks. Clustering constitutes a key issue of unsupervised learning and it is related to a broad variety of problems concerning data mining, information extraction, information presentation, visualization, etc. It plays an essential role in OC tasks, e.g. to cluster the states or sensor data of a system, to allow a human understandable inspection of the state of the system, or to allow a state dependent adaptation of the system. Clustering can be considered as a prerequisite for self-regulation and self-adaptation mechanisms, and it can efficiently be achieved by OC-methods imitating clustering behavior as observed in biological matter.

---

* Correponding author.

A.J. Ijspeert et al. (Eds.): BioADIT 2006, LNCS 3853, pp. 141–159, 2006.
© Springer-Verlag Berlin Heidelberg 2006

We will focus on efficient biologically inspired self-organizing clustering algorithms. The term efficiency implies three different requirements and three partially overlapping forms of adaptivity of the models. Efficiency with respect to energy, time, or resource of the *hardware system* aims at using the given hardware in an optimum way. The implementation of the basic algorithms should be optimally adapted to the given amount of memory, computation power, communication channels, its respective ratio and its current reliability. Efficiency with respect to energy, time, or resource of the *user* refers to an optimum adaptivity to the expectation of the user with respect to the presentation of the result, the type of the extracted information, its level of detail and focus. Based on possibly weak and possibly interactive signals of the user or the environment, the implicit goal and explicit representation of the clustering model need to adapt itself to the possibly changing desired results. Finally, efficiency with respect to energy, time, or resource of the *data* and *data presentation* covers the adaptivity of the clustering model with respect to the given information involved in the data. The method should use the given, usually heterogeneous information in an optimum way and extract all relevant information in a form which suits the given data. In particular, it should use this information to guide learning systems in an optimum way anticipating the hardware setting and user demands. Thereby, these three axes are closely interrelated and optimum self-adaptive algorithmic design can only be achieved if all three aspects are taken into account. We discuss existing approaches and perspectives for efficient adaptive self-organizing clustering methods which adapt itself continuously to the given hardware configuration, user demands, and prerequisites of the given data.

2   Self-organizing Clustering

The need for clustering occurs frequently in biological as well as technical systems: animals need to separate other living beings into predators, preys, and other (neutral) animals. A human web user has to classify documents into web sites about interesting topics and those which are not relevant. An authentication server must cluster potential users into legal ones and illegal hackers. Thereby, the desired taxonomies and categories and their exact form are not a-priori known and the circumstances of the setting change frequently. However, efficient, fast, and reliable clustering is of vital importance. Thus, efficient anytime and anywhere clustering constitutes an important part of OC systems.

There exists a broad variety of clustering methods including graph clustering [9, 19], statistical solutions [118, 128], joining and splitting methods [70], and many other [50]. Here the focus will lie on intuitive prototype-based clustering methods [12, 65, 75, 83, 84]. These models integrate organic behavior such as neighborhood competition and cooperation, local and distributed operations, local simplicity and scalability, the possibility of incremental learning and control of the stability and plasticity of the models. Due to their flexibility and statistical integration of signals and events they show very robust behavior which can be adapted to the specific requirements. The atomic prototypes and similarity based operations provide a human-understandable and controllable base of the models and offer a natural way for adaptivity driven by the environment or system invariants. In addition, the local and scalable design of the models allows an efficient parallel implementation and any-time adaptivity of the model and its specific mode. Thereby, only few models have so far been implemented as hardware realizations such as [63, 79, 92, 94] and only first, although promising, attempts for anytime adaptivity with respect to different continuous axes such as hardware load, data type and user demands have been considered, e.g. [22, 100].

A variety of different, often biologically inspired prototype-based clustering algorithms exist. The algorithms differ with respect to their objective – modeling of biological phenomena such as direction selectivity in the visual cortex [13, 23, 120], statistical modeling of given data [6, 54, 104], learning prototypical representations [31, 32], extraction of relevant (possibly nonlinear) dimensions [58, 78], minimizing the distortion error or variants [5, 75], developing topologically faithful representations [75, 109], or visualization [63, 71, 72], to name just a few.

The basic ingredients of prototype based clustering algorithms are: (1) A number of prototypes which represent the classes; thereby, the number might be fixed a priori or it might be adapted during learning in an optimum way [18, 24, 86]. Depending on the application and current hardware, flat or hierarchical topologies might be appropriate [52, 125]. (2) An assignment method of data points to the classes; the assignment might be fuzzy or crisp, and possibilistic versions, outlier detection, or vigilance can be introduced to measure the novelty of data points [31, 51, 56]. (3) A similarity measure to determine the similarity of data points and prototypes, or the similarity of two prototypes or two data points, depending on the model. The similarity measure is often provided by the Euclidean distance; however, fast alternatives, versions better adapted to parallel hardware solutions, or general measures for non-Euclidean data are also relevant [22, 29, 30, 34, 64, 79, 93, 100]. The similarity measure constitutes a basic local computation which widely influences the efficiency of the algorithms. Metric operations are independent for each basic constituent and can be performed in parallel. (4) A communication strategy or neighborhood structure of the basic constituents which allows to integrate the local computations in an appropriate way [75, 83, 104]. The communication load constitutes another important factor which influences the efficiency. Within parallel implementations, efficient implementation of the communication method is widely influenced by the current hardware system. (5) Postprocessing methods to interpret the results. This might include visualization and highlighting of important information, component planes, supervised postprocessing, extraction of clusters and information about the metric, or description by symbolic rules [8, 62, 102, 105, 121]. Unlike many other neural methods such as feed-forward neural networks, prototype-based clustering allows direct insight into its behavior and does not constitute a black-box mechanism, thus directly initiating a couple of different interesting postprocessing possibilities.

Applications of prototype-based clustering algorithms range from data mining for large text or multimedia databases [55, 69], robotics and control [2, 28, 84], finance [62], computational biology [49, 61, 74, 125], medicine [89, 110, 126], up to large scale satellite image processing [100, 113]. For simple applications, standard algorithmic solutions are readily available. However, large scale applications require efficient and self-adaptive parallel implementations optimized for the specific requirements to offer an attractive anytime and anywhere information processing tool [63]. Thereby, different requirements have to be taken into account, depending on the number of prototypes, dimensionality of the data, the used metric, the user expectation, time scale of learning, and, most important, current hardware system. So far, only static solutions mostly for the standard self-organizing map as proposed by Kohonen and k-means as proposed by Bezdek have been realized on parallel hardware [5, 22, 33, 36, 37, 63, 66, 77, 79, 85, 92, 127]. Several approaches explicitly consider the interaction of key ingredients of the algorithm and the hardware implementation and provide promising results [22, 85, 92]. However, an anytime adaptive integration of the algorithmic design, data requirements, hardware configuration, and user expectation has not yet been investigated.

3   Dimensions of Adaptivity

3.1   Adaptivity with Respect to Statically Diverse or Dynamically Changing Computer Hardware

Since a certain algorithm has always to be considered against the background of the underlying computer hardware it is run on, these hardware issues are of essential interest. Particularly when attempting to deal with efficient adaptive implementations the utilized or generally available computer hardware moves into the focus of interest.

In general there are two *structural* levels where an adaptation of an algorithm on particular computer hardware can be achieved: 1.) *verbal algorithmic formulation* and 2.) *compilation*.

While the latter is mandatory to get the algorithm run at all and is usually done more or less automatically and without many options for the user, the first one offers much more potential to achieve improved performance. On account of this it is rather astonishing that even this opportunity is utilized that scarcely.

Early attempts date back to the 1980ies/1990ies [60, 67]. The probably best known example of an adapted verbal algorithmic formulation is the FFT (Fast Fourier Transformation) software library within the ATLAS (Automatically Tuned Linear Algebra Software) [124] framework. However, many of these approaches often assume a rather fixed hardware. Dynamically adaptive components dealing with computer hardware changing at run-time are reported in more recent work [20].

In addition to the structural domain there exist three kinds of *temporal* layers where hardware adaptability can be implemented (Fig. 1): 1.) *install-time*, 2.) *before-execute-time*, and 3.) during *run-time*.

Both the inherent complexity and challenge on the one side and the possible benefit on the other increase from top to bottom of this list. Thus the most promising but also most challenging level is undoubtedly at run-time. Finally this is the only one where the above mentioned dynamic adaptation is efficiently feasible.

Parallel implementations of neural methods, in particular prototype-based models, which are dedicated to efficient implementations on different computer hardwar can be found e.g. in [15, 88, 92, 116]. The architectures range from dedicated neural hardware, such as the CNAPS parallel processor architecture by Adaptive Solutions either as PCI acceleration board (64 processors) or development system with up to 512 parallel processors (in [92]) up to very powerful general purpose parallel clusters (32 Dual Pentium III/IV with Myrinet interconnect) and shared memory systems (e.g. 64 parallel

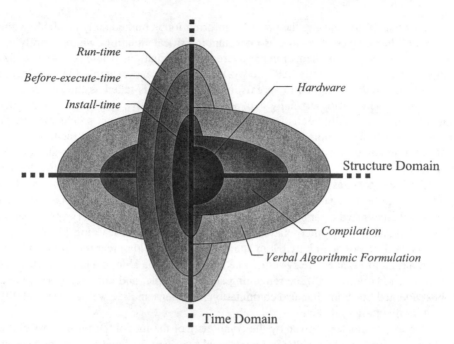

Fig. 1. Two different domains to implement a computer hardware adaptive algorithm. While the structural domain is divided into *compilation* and *verbal algorithmic formulation* the time domain consists of *install-time*, *before-execute-time*, and *run-time*.

HP N-class processors, 32 Alpha EV7 processors) [15, 88]. An exemplary demonstration of the differences of several computer hardware for of a showcase Self-Organizing Map has been pesented in [87]. Thereby, the impact of limited communication bandwidth and latency is demonstrated which gives a shared memory machine (fastest interprocessor communication) a significant lead over the inherently faster processors of the Beowulfs. These implementations still assume fixed resources availability during run-time, although trends and starting points for the hardware adaptivity at run-time, as developed beforehand, have already been identified. Within this line, OC technologies have already been successfully realized to guide a biologically inspired automatic parallelization process [57, 117].

3.2 Adaptivity with Respect to User Specific Models

For an efficient implementation of prototype-based clustering at run-time according to the current hardware configuration and requirements, one has to identify basic algorithmic design concepts which can be adapted according to the current situation. The adaptivity of self-organized clustering algorithms can be seen in the light of its relations to the underlying model, user specific requirements, or post-processing tasks.

A first focus in this direction is the general *time characteristics* of the adaptation scheme. One can distinguish several modes: 1.) *instantaneous learning*, 2.) *rapid learning*, and 3.) *life-long learning*.

In *instantaneous learning* the provided information is immediately available within the model. Instantaneous learning is important in critical situations where entirely new or only few data are provided, or in hardware critical situations where prototype update and communication is costly. ART-networks constitute one example [31]: an incoming pattern is either assigned to an existing cluster or it is taken as the generator for a new one. The decision crucially depends on the respective control parameter (vigilance) which is usually heuristically determined. *Rapid learning* is characterized by methods which allow short learning with only few available data and medium update and communication load, although, unlike instantaneous learning, faults and outliers can be corrected due to (limited) integration. Rapid models generate a rough description which can serve as a base for fine tuning work or hypothesis testing later on. Batch versions of the self organizing map (SOM) constitute a basic example [63]. More advanced schemes are the parameterized SOM (PSOM), which uses a very sparse neuron lattice with subsequent interpolation [82], or attention based learning [7, 16], which controls the force of adaptivity by an attention level. *Life-long* learning frequently occurs in autonomous adaptive systems. The system must be able to adapt in a changing environment, however, all-time remaining stable, reliable, and consistent. This yields robust adapted behavior, but also computational burdens and the well-known stability-plasticity dilemma [38].

A second parameter is given by the *complexity* of the model. Different possibilities include: 1.) fixed or adapted, flat or hierarchical *topology*, 2.) fixed or growing / shrinking number of *prototypes*.

Sparse models allow fast learning with only weak communication load, however, the data domain might only insufficiently be covered. Thus, adaptive and hierarchical variants constitute interesting alternatives since they allow a control of the complexity and easy parallelization. Models with adaptive topology and model complexity cover ART networks [31] and variants of neural gas (NG), SOM, or the generative topographic map (GTM) [4, 25, 101]. These models include an incremental and, hence, hierarchical growing, but no subsequent model reduction techniques. Several approaches have been proposed in the context of growing and shrinking dynamics [26, 27, 38]; however, a satisfying approach is still open.

A third important parameter of the models is the *evaluation measure and user perception*. This topic is related to the fundamental issue that the usually only imprecise and varying question 'what is adequate' must be expressed in a formal way to implement the algorithm on computer hardware. One can distinguish several different evaluation criteria which can drive the algorithmic design: 1.) *topology preservation*, 2.) representation of the underlying *statistical* distribution, 3.) *geometric* aspects, and 4.) subsequent *supervised* tasks.

Various different measures for topology preservation in SOMs have been proposed [3, 109], some of which are complex to compute. Further approaches try to capture topology preservation by internal forces such as in multi-dimensional scaling [68]. Alternative evaluation measures include different types of partition entropy, intra-inter cluster correlations, or information based evaluation criteria [5, 21, 81]. Most of these proposals have not yet been integrated within a hardware implementation, however, they would offer a starting point to continuously guide design choices of models and map the topology to the current hardware topology. A particularly promising step towards any-time adaptivity of the topology is offered by growing models: A special multidimensional topology including an adapted neighborhood relationship to process image sequences was developed in [90]. This basic algorithm has been equipped with a growing feature [86] and was successfully implemented also on parallel hardware [92]. Further proposals for very successful automatically growing technologies have been developed e.g. in [4, 107]. Among other applications, these models have been successfully applied to remote sensing images and biomedical data [112, 113, 114].

Vector quantization can be optimized with respect to information transfer depending on user or system specific requirements. One possibility is offered by a control of the so-called magnification [84] which can be adapted e.g. by attention based learning [108]. There exist further possibilities to estimate and control the magnification factor as discussed in [11, 106, 108, 108, 111]. A further evaluation measure is offered by user controlled posterior labeling of clusters, such as supervised-SOM, counterpropagation, or learning vector quantization [31, 63]. This feature also allows the inclusion of fuzzy assignments [73]. In addition, it offers a natural interface to human interaction. Yet, the anytime adaptivity of models according to these objectives adapted to the given situation and hardware is not explicitly integrated in current algorithms.

3.3   Adaptivity with Respect to Specific Data Structures

Self-organizing clustering can be adapted with respect to the user model in different ways to meet optimum algorithm-hardware interaction, including three (continuous) axes as specified above: an optimum time scale of learning, an optimum model complexity, and an adaptive learning objective. Further adaptation schemes are offered if the data level is taken into account.

The efficiency of prototype-based models is essentially determined by the choice of the metric and the local topological cooperation of neurons. These two ingredients interact and the complexity of the computation can be varied among these two ingredients. Strong neighborhood cooperativity causes a smoothness of the map such that approximate values for the single similarities are sufficient for a valid evaluation of the algorithm. If no topological cooperation is present, the winner determination has to be precise. Naturally, the hardware configuration suggests an optimum choice of the ratio of precision of local similarity versus cooperativity since the former can be done in parallel whereas the latter requires communication processes. A key factor within this process is the data format and the respective *similarity measure*. Important factors are: 1.) the *dimensionality* of the data, 2.) the *availability* of similarity information in case of missing or proximity data, and 3.) the *complexity* of similarity computation in case of real-life structured data.

Naturally, the complexity of the similarity computations directly scales with data *dimensionality*, and it is worth integrating efficient parallel versions, dynamic or hierarchical computation, and neighborhood integration for high dimensionality. Thereby, static metrics are often not appropriate since they require (usually not available) prior knowledge on the data. Recent alternatives are offered by learning metrics which adapt the similarity measure according to the given situation, such as proposed in [10, 47, 48, 62, 76, 115]. Thereby, the metric changes within the system and, consequently, an optimum implementation has to be adapted according to the current basic algorithmic setting. Interestingly, the beneficial effects can also be accompanied by a theoretical counterpart [46]. Naturally, criteria to adapt the metric appropriately have to be identified. Criteria which are solely based on general paradigms of unsupervised processing have been proposed in [8, 47], for example.

Often, in particular for *proximity* data where no explicit metric calculation is available, data are sparse and entries might be lacking. There exists a variety of different proposals to tackle this scenario from an algorithmic point of view, such as [14, 30, 64, 80, 93]. However, efficient parallel realizations have not yet been considered. The situation is even more difficult if real-life *structured data* such as text sequences, biomedical data, graphs, etc. are considered. Recent proposals deal with general data structures and general metrics [34, 35, 44, 119]. Since metric calculation might even include NP-hard problems if complex structures such as graphs are considered, an efficient and parallel implementation is here mandatory. Particularly promising approaches where the recursive data dynamics guides the model design have recently been integrated into a general framework, which allows an adaptation of the model and context representation according to the specific needs inherent in the data [44, 95, 96]. In general, real life data containing additional structure inject a fundamentally new quality towards algorithm design including problems with respect to the efficiency of the models, but also opening new possibilities for efficient high-level human-system interaction based on structure induced high-level information as demonstrated e.g. in [39, 40, 41, 42, 43, 45, 96].

Emphasizing the data layer offers another striking possibility for OC-solutions: one key paradigm of OC is *self*-adaptivity, i.e. the system should optimize itself with respect to the current environment taking the current state of the hardware system into account and anticipating the user expectation as much as possible. Since (signal) data, system and user demands change frequently, adaptivity and self-control need to happen online and in real time. Information to *automatically control* self-adaptivity must be directly extracted from the data and its interaction with the system. Thus, adaptivity with respect to the given data constitutes an essential part of OC systems which allows an automatic supervision of the algorithmic and hardware interaction.

Naturally, a couple of techniques exists to control parameters of adaptive components of self-organizing clustering: several approaches in this direction are based on information theoretic data evaluation such as optimal information transfer (maximum mutual information) in clustering and vector quantization in *conscience learning* [104]. The algorithm developed by DeSieno [17] and the frequency sensitive competitive learning (FSCL) [1] are further realizations of these ideas. A generalization of this framework is offered by *perceptual learning* [53]. These techniques help to automatically tune hyperparameters of the models. Thereby, data *invariances* are of particular interest to guide the system in a systematic and objective way. Self-organizing clustering offers a couple of techniques to automatically extract appropriate data invariances within the given system, such as: 1.) extraction of relevant possibly nonlinear *directions* with principal or independent component analysis and variants [58, 104], 2.) *grouping* and clustering at different hierarchical levels such as exemplarily demonstrated within the semantic map or competitive layer models (CLM) [63, 123], and 3.) explicit *feature* learning and extraction such as in the adaptive subspace SOM (ASSOM) or learning CLM [122].

These methods provide efficient self-organizing models to automatically extract low-dimensional representations of the given information. However, this information has only partially been integrated into a control of the algorithm design so far, and it has not yet been integrated into efficient hardware implementations.

Data adaptivity goes far beyond simple parameter optimization. Efficient models must be adapted to the specific data structures and information contained in the data and its interaction with the hardware. Depending on the situation, fundamental qualitative changes of data presentation, data handling, or the learning paradigm might be necessary. Apart from automatic adaptations, user feedback is desirable or necessary at some points to confirm the optimum settings as extracted from data. Information contained in the data offers a natural way to initiate a user-feedback cycle by means of human-understandable information in critical situations. Due to their intuitive basic principles, prototype-based algorithms offer insight into their behavior. However, in human-computer interaction, explicit representative *symbolic descriptions* can speed up and focus the information transfer. Various different approaches include 1.) description by *decision trees* [45, 103], and 2.) first models for *spatio-temporal* data [95, 96].

These techniques have mainly been implemented for one-shot information extraction from given data. In principle, they offer an interesting data-driven possibility for continuous high-level human-computer interaction.

4   Perspectives

Based on this taxonomy and existing integrative work towards efficient any-time self-adaptive self-organizing clustering, several particularly promising perspectives can be identified.

4.1   Adaptivity with Respect to Hardware

In the light of a dynamic adaptation of algorithms to changing computer hardware as well as the temporal levels mentioned in Sect. 3.1, a number of special properties and requirements of parallel computing arise. While at a sequential run of a particular algorithm, for example on a single PC, a changing hardware at run-time is not very likely, at distributed processing, especially on computer clusters (e.g. Beowulfs) and compute farms, a dynamically changing environment is quite common. Along with increasing spread, popularity, and utilization of computer clusters the demand on the one side but also the reward on the other side are increasingly high.

This concerns to a lesser extend a complete failure or breakdown of an entire computation node, which is often handled by load balancing systems on operating system level, but rather an incremental shift of available resources (e.g. processor time, transmission bandwidth, memory access) caused by concurrent processes which are asynchronously started or stopped. Looking from this angle, this concerns all platforms of potential hardware – from the above mentioned clusters and general purpose shared memory systems up to dedicated neural hardware.

As described above, real hardware adaptivity and self-organization has to take place at run-time level and can not be achieved by conventional load balancing systems, no matter how sophisticated they might be. In fact, a combination of the verbal algorithmic formulation level (from the structure domain) with the run-time level (from the time domain) is desired. That means the formulation, and not just the numerical implementation, of a considered algorithm has to be modified in time, in fact at run-time.

So far this is the definition of a quite general and formal aim. Now the question is, are there algorithms allowing a preferably continuous but at least stepwise adjustment of their demand for different resources. Obviously there are basic algorithms, in the sense of basic software modules, possessing this feature. Undoubtedly the Fast Fourier Transformation is a prominent example, because it can at least incrementally be formulated, for example, more processor time demanding for the sake of less memory consumption and vice versa.

In terms of computer hardware adaptability the research focus has to go far beyond the above described techniques. This perfectly accompanies the data-driven adaptation of the algorithms as described above. Besides the need to parallel implement these mainly novel algorithms to make them applicable to large-scale data sets and to make them available to the scientific community as well as their general suitability to be run in parallel (due to their inherent parallelism), they particularly offer structural set screws to adjust their demands for several resources. Especially in the cases of variable neighborhood integration, high-dimensional metrics, hierarchical parallelization, growing / shrinking techniques, and variable time-scale of learning this seems to be most promising.

This consequently leads to an analysis of the above described neural methodologies to figure out, whether at all, to what extend and how they can be formulated and implemented to reflect changing hardware resources availability at run-time. This marks up a focal point of research in this direction. As reported in section 2, a variety of different prototype-based models exist. These different design choices have to be integrated and implemented in such a way that a full pairwise combination is possible including possible switching or adaptation of the choices, whereby the algorithmic formulation has to be optimally adapted to the current hardware system.

4.2   Adaptivity with Respect to User Specific Models

As pointed out in section 3.2, three continuous axes can be identified which allow an adaptation with respect to model choices: the time scale of learning, the model complexity, and the model objective. Different concrete realizations have been proposed in the literature, however, a full combination of all possibilities within one framework is not available so far. This would be mandatory to allow a continuous adaptation of the parameters and, in particular, state dependent switching between different possibilities. As for the previous context, a unified formulation of the parameter choices has to be investigated with particular focus on its respective optimum implementation on a given hardware configuration.

Depending on the given hardware, in particular the communication channels and capacity and memory of local units, different algorithmic settings can be implemented efficiently. If communication is costly, neighborhood cooperation should be sparse and mostly realized on single processors. This fact indicates that hierarchical or dynamic settings are better suited in this scenario than other topologies. In addition, neighborhood cooperativity and, consequently, the learning objective might change. Thereby, not only the overall communication flow but also the exact local connectivity of hardware components on the one side and local algorithmic units on the other side are of fundamental importance. Methods to adapt the *current neighborhood cooperativity* in an optimum way with respect to the current hardware topology have to be investigated within this context.

The efficiency of different *time scales* of learning widely depends on the capacity of the basic units used to compute the weight updates and its storage capacity. If updates are costly or not possible at all, instantaneous learning has to be implemented. If changes are fast, life-long learning might be better suited in order to achieve optimum robustness and adaptivity of the system.

The *learning objective* constitutes a third parameter which is closely connected to the question of the topology. An explicit focus on the current learning objective can be of particular interest to guarantee stable behavior if the algorithmic implementation changes. An explicit learning objective can describe the current function of the clustering in an objective, algorithm independent way. Thus, it can be used to guarantee robustness if the algorithmic design is changed because of a varying hardware load.

Since the design choices interact – a large neighborhood cooperation can be used together with only small update steps, as an example – their pairwise connection and combination has also to be investigated. Thus, unified possibilities to adapt these design choices of the model according to the given hardware and pairwise compatibility in real-time have to be developed and examined both, from a general algorithmic perspective as well as within large-scale parallel hardware implementations.

4.3   Adaptivity with Respect to Specific Data Structures

Focusing on the data offers a fourth adaptation axes: the *metric* of the model. Of particular interest are thereby adaptive and non-Euclidean metrics which allow an application of the systems to virtually every type of real-life data containing missing values, relational information, etc. A particularly promising direction consists in the integration of the rapidly developing area of adapted non-standard metrics into a unified efficient implementation of the models. Subsequently, an efficient online hardware implementation as well as its compatibility to other design choices can be investigated. Depending on the metric type and its algorithmic integration into the model, parallel implementations also of the basic metric might be interesting. Similarity of very high dimensional data or graphs, as an example, is a computationally demanding problem. On the other side, these distances can benefit from locally similar graphs for which parts of the computation might be shared. Thus, a parallelization on the level of the metric is also promising.

A second, fundamentally different aspect provided by the data is the possibility to automatically guide self-adaptivity of the system on the one side and to provide high level information for human-computer interaction on the other side. This possibility goes beyond an optimum matching of the given hardware and it can also anticipate semantic issues. Both possibilities, self-adaptation and high level human-computer interaction, have to be studied in depth and investigated with respect to its effect on optimum hardware implementations.

For an *adaptive control* of the algorithmic design by means of data information, it is very important to automatically extract relevant information and invariances of the data. Invariances such as the overall density, distinct directions, relevant features, correlations, information content, etc. can be used to determine appropriate parameter choices which optimum fit the data if no further prior information is available. As a simple example, the degree of novelty of a new data point depends on the principled data characteristic. The vigilance parameter which controls the setup of a new cluster in ART should thus depend on this data characteristic. Much more involved control schemes are possible if abstract data characteristics can be extracted: one can think of information-based adaptation of metric parameters, a dependency of the time scale of learning and the time characteristic of data, a data adapted hierarchy level which mirrors invariant features, etc. These possibilities have a direct effect on the efficiency of the models. Since they change the overall algorithmic design, they need to be integrated into hardware adapted elements of the models.

Human-computer interaction has no direct influence on the current hardware configuration and algorithmic setting. Rather, it provides an explicit way to control the system and its objectives by human feedback and it thus has an indirect effect on the design. Nevertheless, this point is of particular interest with respect to the overall control and reliability of the models. For critical situations an explicit user feedback is desirable. High level human understandable information thereby provides the most efficient and most reliable way to initiate a human-system interaction and explicit control steps. Thereby, critical situations can be automatically detected from the data and the model referring to system invariances which are hurt at these time points.

Thus, data information can offer both, additional algorithmic design possibilities which interact with model properties, and implicit any-time as well as explicit control information to adaptively guide the system in an optimum way.

5   Conclusions

Clustering constitutes an ubiquitous problem which occurs in one form or the other for nearly every type of automatic information transfer. Efficient parallel implementations are required if large amounts of data or high dimensional and complicated structures are to be processed. This is a standard setting in different application areas including symbolic domains such as text or web mining and technical applications such as processing sensor data in robotics or spectral data in life-science. Thus, the development of an efficient parallel realization of a fundamental class of OC algorithms, adaptive prototype-based clustering, which have wide application areas also for very large data sets (e.g. image processing, bioinformatics) and in distributed environments (e.g. robotics, internet) is higly desirable. Efficient self-adaptive hardware realizations are of fundamental relevance. Since the load of the hardware system, the user requirements, and data prerequisites change frequently, adaptivity is of vital importance to achieve efficient and reliable behavior. Prototype-based clustering algorithms are based on OC principles such as local distributed basic processing and neighborhood interaction, such that they offer interesting and efficient possibilities of parallelization, and they show robust behavior. Thus, adaptivity of these essential OC-models can be based on robust and effective OC-principles itself to allow an optimum control with respect to the hardware context, user context and model context as discussed in this article.

References

1. S. C. Ahalt, A. K. Krishnamurty, P. Chen, and D. E. Melton. Competitive learning algorithms for vector quantization. *Neural Networks*, 3(3):277–290, 1990.
2. F. Azam and H. F. V. Landingham. Adaptive self organizing feature map neuro-fuzzy technique for dynamic system identification. In *Proceedings of the 1998 IEEE International Symposium on Intelligent Control (ISIC) held jointly with IEEE International Symposium on Computational Intelligence in Robotics and Automation (CIRA) Intelligent Systems and Semiotics (ISAS)*, pages 337–41. IEEE, New York, NY, USA, 1998.
3. H.-U. Bauer and K. R. Pawelzik. Quantifying the neighborhood preservation of Self-Organizing Feature Maps. *IEEE Trans. on Neural Networks*, 3(4):570–579, 1992.
4. H. U. Bauer and T. Villmann. Growing a hypercubical output space in a self-organizing feature map. *IEEE Transactions on Neural Networks*, 8(2):218–26, 1997.
5. J. Bezdek. *Pattern Recognition with Fuzzy Objective Function Algorithms*. Plenum, New York, 1981.
6. C. Bishop, M. Svensen, and C. Williams. Developments of the generative topographic mapping. *Neurocomputing*, 21(1):203–224, 1998.
7. C. M. Bishop, M. Svensen, and C. K. I. Williams. Magnification factors for the SOM and GTM algorithms. In *Proceedings of WSOM'97, Workshop on Self-Organizing Maps, Espoo, Finland, June 4–6*, pages 333–338. Helsinki University of Technology, Neural Networks Research Centre, Espoo, Finland, 1997.
8. T. Bojer, B. Hammer, M. Strickert, and T. Villmann. Determining relevant input dimensions for the self-organizing map. In L. Rutkowski and J. Kacprzyk, editors, *Neural Networks and Soft Computing (Proc. ICNNSC 2002)*, Advances in Soft Computing, pages 388–393. Physica-Verlag, 2003.
9. U. Brandes, M. Gaertler, and D. Wagner. Experiments on graph clustering algorithms. In *ESA 2003*, pages 568–579, 2003.
10. V. Cherkassky, D. Gehring, and F. Mulier. Comparison of adaptive methods for function estimation from samples. *IEEE Transactions on Neural Networks*, 7:969–984, 1996.
11. J. Claussen and T. Villmann. Magnification control in winner relaxing neural gas. *Neurocomputing*, 63(1):125–137, 2005.
12. M. Cottrell, J. Fort, and G. Pages. Theoretical aspects of the SOM algorithm. *Neurocomputing*, 21(1):119–138, 1998.
13. M. Cottrell and J. C. Fort. A stochastic model of retinotopy: a self-organizing process. *Biological Cybernetics*, 53:405–411, 1986.
14. M. Cottrell, P. Letremy, and E. Roy. Analysing a contingency table with kohonen maps: A factorial correspondence analysis. In *IWANN 1993*, pages 305–311, 1993.
15. T. Czauderna and U. Seiffert. Implementation of MLP networks running Backpropagation on various parallel computer hardware using MPI. In *Proceedings of the 5th International Conference on Recent Advances in Soft Computing*, Dec 2004. submitted.
16. R. Der and M. Herrmann. Attention based partitioning. In M. V. der Meer, editor, *Bericht Des Status–Seminar Des BMFT Neuroinformatik*, pages 441–446. DLR (Berlin), 1992.
17. D. DeSieno. Adding a conscience to competitive learning. In *Proc. ICNN'88, Internat. Conf. on Neural Networks*, pages 117–124, Piscataway, NJ, 1988. IEEE Service Center.

18. M. Dittenbach, A. Rauber, and D. Merkl. Recent advances with the growing hierarchical self-organizing map. In *Proc. 3rd Workshop on Self-Organizing Maps*, pages 140–145, Lincoln, England, 2001.
19. H. A. D. do Nascimento and P. Eades. A system for graph clustering based on user hints. In P. Eades and J. Jin, editors, *Selected papers from Pan-Sydney Workshop on Visual Information Processing*, Sydney, Australia, 2001. ACS.
20. J. Dongarra and V. Eijkhout. Self-adapting numerical software for next generation applications. *Int. J. of High Performance Computing and Applications*, 17(2):125–131, 2003.
21. R. Duda and P. Hart. *Pattern Classification and Scene Analysis*. Wiley, New York, 1973.
22. M. Estlick, M. Leeser, J. Theiler, and J. J. Szymanski. Algorithmic transforms in the implementation of k-means clustering on reconfigurable hardware. In *FPGA 2001, Ninth International Symposium on Field Programmable Gate Arrays (Association for Computing Machinery)*, pages 103–110, 2001.
23. I. Farkas and R.Miikkulainen. Modeling the self-organization of directional selectivity in the primary visual cortex. In *Proceedings International Conference on Artificial Neural Networks*, pages 251–256, 1999.
24. B. Fritzke. Growing cell structures – a self-organizing network for unsupervised and supervised learning. *Neural Networks*, 7(9):1441–1460, 1994.
25. B. Fritzke. A growing neural gas network learns topologies. In G. Tesauro, D. S. Touretzky, and T. K. Leen, editors, *Advances in Neuralm Information Processing Systems 7*, pages 625–632, Cambridge MA, 1995. MIT Press.
26. B. Fritzke. The LBG-U method for vector quantization - an improvement over LBG inspired from neural networks. *Neural Processing Letters*, 5(1):35–45, 1997.
27. B. Fritzke. A self-organizing network that can follow non-stationary distributions. In W. Gerstener, A. Germond, M. Hasler, and J.-D. Nicoud, editors, *Artificial Neural Networks – Proceedings of International Conference on Artificial Neural Networks (ICANN'97) Lausanne*, pages 613–618. LNCS 1327, Springer Verlag Berlin Heidelberg, 1997.
28. U. Gerecke and N. Sharkey. Quick and dirty localization for a lost robot. In *Proceedings 1999 IEEE International Symposium on Computational Intelligence in Robotics and Automation. CIRA'99.*, pages 262–7, Piscataway, NJ, 1999. IEEE Service Center.
29. S. Gold, A. Rangarajan, and E. Mjolness. Learning with preknowledge: clustering with point and graph matching distance measures. In *NIPS*, 1995.
30. T. Graepel and K. Obermayer. A stochastic self organizing map for proximity data. *NeuralComputation*, 11:139–155, 1999.
31. S. Grossberg. Adaptive pattern classification and universal recoding: I. parallel development and coding of neural feature detectors. *Biological Cybernetics*, 23:121–134, 1976.
32. S. Grossberg and J. R. Williamson. A self organizing neural system for learning to recognize textured scenes. *Vision Research*, 39:1385–1406, 1999.
33. H. Guan, C. Li, T. Cheung, and S. Yu. Parallel design and implementation of SOM neural computing models in PVM environment of a distributed system. In *Advances in Parallel and Distributed Computing*, pages 26–31. 1997.
34. S. Günter and H. Bunke. Self-organizing map for clustering in the graph domain. *Pattern Recognition Letters*, 23:401–417, 2002.
35. M. Hagenbuchner, A. Sperduti, and A. Tsoi. A self-organizing map for adaptive processing of structured data. *IEEE Transactions on Neural Networks*, 14:191–505, 2003.
36. T. Hämäläinen. Parallel implementations of self-organizing maps. In U. S. et al., editor, *Self-organizing neural networks. Recent advances and applications*, pages 245–278. 2001.
37. T. Hämäläinen, H. Klapuri, J. Saarinen, and K. Kaski. Mapping of SOM and LVQ algorithms on a tree shape parallel computer system. *Parallel Computing*, 23:271–289, 1997.
38. F. Hamker. Life-long learning cell structures - continously learning without catastrophic inference. *Neural Networks*, 14:551–573, 2001.

39. B. Hammer. *Learning with Recurrent Neural Networks*. Lecture Notes in Control Theory and Information Sciences. Springer, 2000.
40. B. Hammer. Compositionality in neural systems. In M. Arbib, editor, *Handbook of Brain Theory and Neural Networks*, pages 244–248. MIT Press, 2nd edition, 2002.
41. B. Hammer. Recurrent neural networks for structured data – a unifying approach and its properties. *Cognitive Systems Research*, 3(2):145–165, 2002.
42. B. Hammer. Perspectives on learning symbolic data with connectionistic systems. In R. Kühn, R. Menzel, W. Menzel, U. Ratsch, M. Richter, and I. Stamatescu, editors, *Adaptivity and Learning*, pages 141–160. Springer, 2003.
43. B. Hammer and B. Jain. Neural methods for non-standard data. In M. Verleysen, editor, *ESANN'2004*, pages 281–292. D-side publications, 2004.
44. B. Hammer, A. Micheli, A. Sperduti, and M. Strickert. A general framework for unsupervised processing of structured data. *Neurocomputing*, 57:3–35, 2004.
45. B. Hammer, A. Rechtien, M. Strickert, and T. Villmann. Rule extraction from self-organizing maps. In J.R.Dorronsoro, editor, *Artificial Neural Networks – ICANN 2002*, pages 877–882. Springer, 2002.
46. B. Hammer, M. Strickert, and T. Villmann. On the generalization ability of GRLVQ networks. *Neural Processing Letters*, 21:109–120, 2005.
47. B. Hammer, M. Strickert, and T. Villmann. Supervised neural gas with general similarity measure. *Neural Processing Letters*, 21:21–44, 2005.
48. B. Hammer and T. Villmann. Generalized relevance learning vector quantization. *Neural Networks*, 15(8-9):1059–1068, 2002.
49. J. Hanke, G. Beckmann, P. Borck, and J. Reich. Self-organizing hierarchic networks for pattern recognition in protein sequence. *Protein Sciences*, 5(1):72–82, 1996.
50. J. A. Hartigan. *Clustering Algorithms*. John Wiley, 1975.
51. C. He and M. Girolami. Novelty detection employing an l2 optimal nonparametric density estimator. *Pattern Recognition Letters*, 25(12):1389–1397, 2004.
52. J. Herrero, A. Valencia, and J. Dopazo. A hierarchical unsupervised growing neural network for clustering gene expression patterns. *Bioinformatics*, 17(2):126–136, 2001.
53. M. Herrmann, H.-U. Bauer, and R. Der. The 'perceptual magnet' effect: A model based on self-organizing feature maps. In L. S. Smith and P. J. B. Hancock, editors, *Neural Computation and Psychology*, pages 107–116, Stirling, 1994. Springer-Verlag.
54. T. Heskes. Self-organizing maps, vector quantization, and mixture modeling. *IEEE Transactions on Neural Networks*, 12:1299–1305, 2001.
55. T. Honkela, S. Kaski, K. Lagus, and T. Kohonen. WEBSOM– self-organizing maps of document collections. In *Proceedings of WSOM'97, Workshop on Self-Organizing Maps, Espoo, Finland, June 4–6*, pages 310–315. Helsinki University of Technology, Neural Networks Research Centre, Espoo, Finland, 1997.
56. F. Höppner, F. Klawonn, R. Kruse, and T. Runkler. *Fuzzy Cluster Analysis*. Wiley, 1999.
57. J. Huhse, T. Villmann, P. Merz, and A. Zell. Evolution strategy with neighborhood attraction using a neural gas approach. In J. Merelo, A. Panagiotis, and H.-G. Beyer, editors, *Parallel Problem Solving from Nature VII*, LNCS 2439, p. 391–400. Springer, 2002.
58. A. Hyvärinen, J. Karhunen, and E. Oja. *Independent Component Analysis*. Wiley, 2001.
59. T. Imamura and K. Naono. An evaluation towards an automatic tuning eigensolver with performance stability. In *Proceedings of Symposium on Advanced Computing Systems and Infrastructures (SACSIS)*, pages 145–152, 2003.
60. H. Karner and C. W. Ueberhuber. Portable high performance fft algorithms. Tech. Report AURORA TR1997-14, Vienna University of Technology, 1997.
61. S. Kaski, J. Nikkilä, M. Oja, J. Venna, P. Törönen, and E. Castren. Trustworthiness and metrics in visualizing similarity of gene expression. *BMC Bioinformatics*, 4:48, 2003.

62. S. Kaski, J. Sinkkonen, and J. Peltonen. Bankruptcy analysis with self-organizing maps in learning metrics. *IEEE Transactions on Neural Networks*, 12:936–947, 2001.

63. T. Kohonen. *Self-Organizing Maps*. Springer, 1995.

64. T. Kohonen and P. Somervuo. How to make large self-organizing maps for nonvectorial data. *Neural Networks*, 15(8-9):945–952, 2002.

65. P. Koikkalainen. Tree structured self-organizing maps. In *Kohonen Maps*, pages 121–130. Elsevier, 1999.

66. P. Kotilainen, J. Saarinen, and K. Kaski. Mapping of som neural network algortihms to a general purpose parallel neurocomputer. In *ICANN'1993*, pages 1082–1087. 1993.

67. A. R. Krommer and C. W. Ueberhuber. Architecture adaptive algorithms. *Parallel Computing*, 19(4):409–435, 1993.

68. J. B. Kruskal and W. M. *Multidimensional Scaling*. Sage Publications, 1977.

69. J. Laaksonen, J. Koskela, S. Laakso, and E. Oja. PicSOM - content-based image retrieval with self-organizing maps. *Pattern Recognition Letters*, 21(13-14):1199–1207, 2000.

70. G. N. Lanc and W. T. Williams. A general theory of classificatory sorting strategies. *Computer Journal*, 9:373–380, 1967.

71. J. Lee, A. Lendasse, and M. Verleysen. Nonlinear projection with curvilinear distances: Isomap versus curvilinear distance analysis. *Neurocomputing*, 57:49–76, 2004.

72. J. Lee and M. Verleysen. Nonlinear projection with the isotop method. In J. R. Dorronsoro, editor, *ICANN 2002*, pages 933–938. Springer-Verlag, 2002.

73. S. Livens, P. Scheunders, G. van de Wouver, and D. V. Dyck. Wavelets for texture analysis, an overview. In *Proceedings of 6th International Conference on Image Processing and its Applications*, pages 581–585, 1997.

74. F. Luo, L. Khan, F. Bastani, I.-L. Yen, and J. Zhou. A dynamically growing self-organizing tree for hierarchical clustering gene expression profiles. *Bioinformatics*, to appear, 2004.

75. T. Martinetz, S. Berkovich, and K. Schulten. 'Neural gas' network for vector quantization and its application to time series prediction. *IEEE Transactions on Neural Networks*, 4(4):558–569, 1993.

76. F. Mulier. *Statistical Analysis of Self-Organization*. PhD thesis, Univ. of Minnesota, 1994.

77. G. Myklebust and J. G. Solheim. Parallel self-organizing maps for actual applications. In *Proceedings ICNN'95*, volume 2, pages 1054–1059, 1995.

78. E. Oja and J. Lampinen. Unsupervised learning for feature extraction. In *Computational Intelligence Imitating Life*, pages 13–22, 1994.

79. M. Porrmann, M. Franzmeier, H. Kalte, U. Witkowski, and U. R"uckert. A reconfigurable SOM hardware architecture. In M. Verleysen, editor, *ESANN'2002 proceedings*, pages 337–342. D-side publications, 2002.

80. J. Puzicha, T. Hofmann, and J. Buhmann. A theory of proximity based clustering: Structure detection by optimization. *Pattern Recognition*, 33(4):617–634, 1999.

81. A. Renyi. On measures of entropy and information. In *Proceedings of the Fourth Berkeley Symposium on Mathematical Statistics and Probability*. Univ. of California Press, 1961.

82. H. Ritter. Parametrized Self-Organizing Maps for vision learning tasks. In M. Marinaro and P. G. Morasso, editors, *Proc. ICANN'94, International Conference on Artificial Neural Networks*, volume II, pages 803–810, London, UK, 1994. Springer.

83. H. Ritter. Self-organizing maps in non-euclidean spaces. In E. Oja and S. Kaski, editors, *Kohonen Maps*, pages 97–108. 1999.

84. H. Ritter, T. Martinetz, and K. Schulten. *Neural Computation and Self-Organizing Maps: An Introduction*. Addison-Wesley, Reading, MA, 1992.

85. S. Rueping, M. Porrmann, and U. Rueckert. SOM accelerator system. *Neurocomputing*, 21:31–50, 1998.

86. U. Seiffert. Growing multi-dimensional Self-Organizing Maps for motion detection. In U. Seiffert and L. C. Jain, editors, *Self-Organizing Neural Networks: Recent Advances and Applications*, volume 78 of *Studies in Fuzziness and Soft Computing*, pages 95–120. Springer-Verlag, Heidelberg, Germany, 2001.
87. U. Seiffert. Artificial neural networks on massively parallel computer hardware. In M. Verleysen, editor, *Proc. of the 10. European Symposium on Artificial Neural Networks ESANN 2002*, pages 319–330, Evere, Belgium, 2002. D-Side Publications.
88. U. Seiffert. Artificial neural networks on massively parallel computer hardware. *Neurocomputing*, 57:135–150, March 2004.
89. U. Seiffert. Biologically inspired image compression in biomedical High-Throughput Screening. In A. J. Ijspeert, D. Mange, M. Murata, and S. Nishio, editors, *Bio-ADIT 2004 On-Conference Proc.*, pages 185–196, Lausanne, Switzerland, Jan 2004. Swiss Federal Institute of Technology (EPFL), EPFL.
90. U. Seiffert and B. Michaelis. Estimating motion parameters with three-dimensional Self-Organizing Maps. *Information Sciences*, 101:187–201, 1997.
91. U. Seiffert and B. Michaelis. Quasi-Four-Dimensional-Neuroncube and its application to motion estimation. In A. B. Bulsari, J. F. de Canete, and S. Kallio, eds., *Engineering Benefits from Neural Networks: Proc. of the Int. Conf. on Engineering Applications of Neural Networks EANN '98*, pages 78–81, Turku, Finland, 1998. Åbo Akademis Tryckeri.
92. U. Seiffert and B. Michaelis. Multi-dimensional Self-Organizing Maps on massively parallel hardware. In N. Allinson, H. Yin, L. Allinson, and J. Slack, editors, *Advances in Self-Organizing Maps: Proc. of the 3. Workshop on Self-Organizing Maps WSOM 2001*, pages 160–166, London, U.K., 2001. Springer-Verlag.
93. S. Seo and K. Obermayer. Self-organizing maps and clustering methods for matrix data. *Neural Networks*, to appear, 2004.
94. H. P. Siemon and A. Ultsch. Kohonen networks on transputers: implementation and animation. In *Proc. INNC-90 Int. Neural Network Conf.*, pages 643–646, Dordrecht, Netherlands, 1990. Kluwer.
95. M. Strickert and B. Hammer. Neural gas for sequences. In *WSOM'03*, pages 53–57, 2003.
96. M. Strickert and B. Hammer. Self-organizing context learning. In M. Verleysen, editor, *ESANN'04*, pages 39–44. D-side publications, 2004.
97. M. Strickert and B. Hammer. Merge SOM for temporal data. *Neurocomputing*, submitted.
98. M. Strickert, B. Hammer, and S. Blohm. Unsupervised recursive sequence processing. *Neurocomputing*, to appear.
99. K. Takahiro, K. Kise, H. Honda, and T. Yuba. Fiber: A general framework for auto-tuning software. In A. Veidenbaum, K. Joe, H. Amano, and H. Aiso, editors, *Proceedings of The Fifth International Symposium on High Performance Computing*, volume 2858, pages 146–159, Heidelberg, 2003. Springer Verlag.
100. J. Theiler, J. Frigo, M. Gokhale, and J. J. Szymanski. Co-design of software and hardware to implement remote sensing algorithms. In *Proc. SPIE*, vol. 4480, pages 86–99, 2001.
101. P. Tino and I. Nabney. Hierarchical GTM: constructing localized non-linear projection manifolds in a principled way. *IEEE Transactions on Pattern Analysis and Machine Intelligence*, 24(5):639–656, 2002.
102. A. Ultsch. The neuro-data-mine. In H. Bothe and R. Rojas, editors, *Proceeding of the ICSC Symposia on Neural Computation (NC'2000) May 23-26, 2000 in Berlin, Germany*. Philipps-University of Marburg, Dep. of Computer Science, ICSC Academic Press, 2000.
103. A. Ultsch and H. Siemon. Kohonen's self organizing feature maps for exploratory data analysis. In *Proc. INNC'90*, pages 305–308. Kluwer, 1990.
104. M. M. van Hulle. *Faithful Representations and Topographic Maps From Distortion- to Information-based Self-organization*. J. Wiley & Sons, Inc., 2000.

105. J. Vesanto and E. Alhoniemi. Clustering of the self-organizing map. *IEEE Transactions on Neural Networks*, 11(3):586–600, May 2000.
106. T. Villmann. Controlling strategies for the magnification factor in the neural gas network. *Neural Network World*, 10(4):739–750, 2000.
107. T. Villmann and H.-U. Bauer. Applications of the growing self-organizing map. *Neurocomputing*, 21(1-3):91–100, 1998.
108. T. Villmann and J. Claussen. Magnification control in self-organizing maps and neural gas. *Neural Computation*, 18(2): in press, 2006.
109. T. Villmann, R. Der, M. Herrmann, and T. M. Martinetz. Topology preservation in self-organizing feature maps: exact definition and measurement. *IEEE Transactions on Neural Networks*, 8(2):256–266, 1997.
110. T. Villmann, W. Hermann, and M. Geyer. Variants of self-organizing maps for data mining and data visualization in medicine. *Neural Network World*, 10(4):751–762, 2000.
111. T. Villmann and M. Herrmann. Magnification control in neural maps. In *Proc. of European Symposium on Artificial Neural Networks (ESANN'98)*, pages 191–196, Brussels, Belgium, 1998. D facto publications.
112. T. Villmann and A. Hessel. Analyzing psychotherapy process time series using neural maps. In *ICANN99. Ninth International Conference on Artificial Neural Networks (IEE Conf. Publ. No.470)*, volume 2, pages 767–72, London, UK, 1999. IEE.
113. T. Villmann and E. Merényi. Extensions and modifications of the Kohonen-SOM and applications in remote sensing image analysis. In U. Seiffert and L. Jain, eds., *Self-Organizing Maps. Recent Advances and Applications*, p. 121–145. Springer-Verlag, Heidelberg, 2001.
114. T. Villmann, E. Merényi, and B. Hammer. Neural maps in remote sensing image analysis. *Neural Networks*, 16(3-4):389–403, 2003.
115. T. Villmann, F. M. Schleif, and B. Hammer. Supervised neural gas and relevance learning in learning vector quantization. In *Proc. International Workshop on Self-Organizing Maps (WSOM'2003)*, pages 47–52, Kitakyushu, 2003.
116. T. Villmann, U. Seiffert, and A. Wismüller. Theory and applications of neural maps. In M. Verleysen, editor, *Proceedings of the 12. European Symposium on Artificial Neural Networks ESANN 2004*, pages 25–38, Evere, Belgium, 2004. D-Side Publications.
117. T. Villmann, B. Villmann, and V. Slowik. Evolutionary algorithms with neighborhood cooperativness according neural maps. *Neurocomputing*, 57:151–169, 2004.
118. A. Vinokourov and M. Girolami. A probabilistic framework for the hierarchic organisation and classification of document collections. *Information Processing and Management*, 2002.
119. T. Voegtlin. Recursive self-organizing maps. *Neural Networks*, 15(8-9):979–992, 2002.
120. C. von der Malsburg. Self-organization of orientation sensitive cells in the striate cortex. *Kybernetik*, 14:85–100, 1973.
121. J. Walter, H. Ritter, and K. Schulten. Non-linear prediction with self-organizing maps. In *Proc. IJCNN-90, International Joint Conference on Neural Networks, San Diego*, volume 1, pages 589–594. IEEE Service Center, Piscataway, NJ, 1990.
122. S. Weng and J. Steil. Learning compatibitlity functions for feature binding and perceptual grouping. In *Proc. of ICANN/ICONIP 2003*, pages 60–67. Springer Verlag, 2003.
123. H. Wersing, J. J. Steil, and H. Ritter. A competitive-layer model for feature binding and sensory segmentation. *Neural Computation*, 13:357–387, 2001.
124. C. Whaley, A. Petitet, and J. Dongarra. Automated empirical optimizations of software and the atlas project. *Parallel Computing*, 27(3):3–35, 2001.
125. H. Whang, J. Dopazo, and J. Carazo. Self-organizing tree growing network for classifying amino acids. *Bioinformatics*, 14:376–277, 1998.

126. A. Wismuller, F. Vietze, D. R. Dersch, K. Hahn, and H. Ritter. The deformable feature map—adaptive plasticity for function approximation. In L. Niklasson, M. Bodén, and T. Ziemke, editors, *Proceedings of ICANN98, the 8th International Conference on Artificial Neural Networks*, volume 1, pages 123–128. Springer, London, 1998.

127. M. Yasunaga, K. Tominaga, and J. H. Kim. Parallel self-organization map using multiple stimuli. In *Proceedings IJCNN'99*, volume 2, pages 1127–1130, 1999.

128. A. Ypma and T. Heskes. Categorization of web pages and user clustering with mixtures of hidden markov models. In *Proceedings WEBKDD'02*, pages 31–43, 2002.

MOVE Processors That Self-replicate and Differentiate

Joël Rossier, Yann Thoma, Pierre-André Mudry, and Gianluca Tempesti

Ecole Polytechnique Fédérale de Lausanne (EPFL),
Cellular Architectures Research Group (CARG),
CH-1015 Lausanne, Switzerland
j.rossier@epfl.ch

Abstract. This article describes an implementation of a basic multi-processor system that exhibits replication and differentiation abilities on the POEtic tissue, a programmable hardware designed for bio-inspired applications [1, 2] . As for a living organism, whose existence starts with only one cell that first divides, our system begins with only one totipotent processor, able to implement any of the cells required by the final organism, which can also fully replicate itself, using the functionalities of the POEtic substrate. Then, analogously to the cells in a developing organism, our just replicated totipotent processors differentiate in order to execute their specific part of the complete organism functionality. In particular, we will present a working realization using MOVE processors whose instructions define the flow of data rather than the operations to be executed [3]. It starts with one basic MOVE processor that first replicates itself three times; the four resulting processors then differentiate and connect together to implement a multi-processor modulus-60 counter.

1 Introduction

Multi-cellular organization is one of the key concepts for a lot of living creatures. In fact, almost every organism, except viruses and bacteria, is based on this structure that enables an individual to develop an astounding complexity, starting from only one relatively simple cell. Moreover, being a multi-cellular organism offers more possibilities like being able to tolerate some faults, to self-repair or to exhibit self-healing capabilities.

For several reasons, such abilities could obviously be of great interest for multi-processor systems. One of the first reasons is the programmability of a group of processors having to execute collectively a specific task. Today, we can still program individually each processor of the set and give it a specific code. But the size of the electronic components is continuously shrinking and we will soon enter in the era of nano-electronics. In such a case, the processor arrays will have to be realized on an homogeneous substrate consisting in a lot of massively parallel basic nano-components. As a result, it will be very difficult, perhaps even impossible, to initialize one by one each processor of such an array.

A.J. Ijspeert et al. (Eds.): BioADIT 2006, LNCS 3853, pp. 160–175, 2006.

Consequently, the multi-processor systems of tomorrow could take advantage of a self-replication/differentiation mechanism to be more easily configured.

Then, as the scale of electronics will decrease, faults will happen in the circuits with a greater probability than today. Consequently, it could be useful to have a system that could tolerate some faults or, at least, avoid some parts of the circuit where the faults are detected.

In this paper, we propose an implementation of a system showing such capabilities consisting in one totipotent processor, i.e. a processor capable of executing all the sub-tasks required by an application, that first replicates itself. Then, the cloned processors bind themselves and differentiate in order to achieve a full multi-processor system. To illustrate this process, we will use a simple system that implements a watch counter using four processors. The system has been realized in a slightly modified version of the POEtic tissue [1, 2], a reconfigurable logic circuit structure especially designed for bio-inspired applications that will be presented in section 2.2.

In the following sections, we will first describe the background used to realize our system: we will succinctly present the Embryonics project in section 2.1. Then in section 2.2 we will recall the main characteristics of the POEtic tissue. In section 2.3, we will then expose briefly the MOVE paradigm, also known as Transport Triggered Architecture (TTA), on which our processors are based. These bases in mind, we will present the general architecture of our processor in section 3. Then, the self-replication and the differentiation/connection processes will be explained in sections 4 and 5 respectively. The following section will deal with the hardware realization of the system and its implementation on the BioWall [4]. Finally, we will conclude this article with a section discussing the future developments that our system will undergo.

2 Background

Before describing concretely our system, we will now expose the background from which we started the development of our self-replicating processors that differentiate and bind together. We will briefly present the Embryonics project and its major realization, the BioWatch. Then we will describe more thoroughly the POEtic substrate. To close this section, we will present the Transport Triggered Architecture, also known as the MOVE processor paradigm.

2.1 The Embryonics Project

The application of biological ontogenesis to the design of digital hardware has been studied for several years within the Embryonics project [5]. One of its major contribution to the field is the self-contained representation of a possible mapping between the world of multi-cellular organisms in biology and the world of digital hardware systems, based on 4 levels of complexity, ranging from the population of organisms to the molecule (Fig. 1).

Within this mapping, the Embryonics project defines an artificial organism as a parallel array of cells, where each cell is a simple processor that contains the

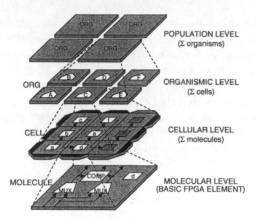

Fig. 1. The four hierarchical levels of complexity of the Embryonics project

description of the operation of every other cell in the organism in the form of a program (the genome). This program, replicated in each cell of the organism as in a living being, is read in parallel in each cell but different parts of it are executed depending on the spatial coordinates of the cell within the organism. The redundancy inherent in this approach is compensated by the added capabilities of the system, such as growth [6] and self-repair [7]. The molecules are defined as the basic elements of the programmable logic circuits; in the Embryonics project, they correspond to simple programmable multiplexers.

A configuration bitstream (the genome of the artificial organisms) is injected into the circuit, causing the molecules to self-assemble into cells. The cells themselves, after a replication phase analogous to cellular division and growth, self-organize to form the final organism.

Using this approach, the Embryonics project demonstrated two basic properties of its substrate with the implementation of the BioWatch [8], an electronic modulus-60 counter made of four cells exhibiting differentiation and fault-tolerance abilities. We have decided to use this same application to demonstrate the capabilities of our system.

2.2   The POEtic Tissue

Bio-inspiration in the design of digital hardware finds its source in essentially three biological models [9, 10]: Phylogenesis (P), the history of the evolution of the species through time, Ontogenesis (O), the development of an individual as directed by his genetic code, from its first cell to the full organism, and Epigenesis (E), the development of an individual through learning processes. All of these models, to a greater or lesser extent have been used as a source of inspiration for the development of computing machines (such as the ontogenesis in the Embryonics project or epigenesis for artificial neural networks) but before the POEtic project [1, 2], no hardware substrate had been developed that could combine the three axes of bio-inspiration into one single circuit.

Indeed, the POEtic tissue draws inspiration from these three axes and from the multi-cellular structure of complex biological organisms. This reconfigurable circuit has been designed to develop and adapt its functionality through the processes of evolution, growth and learning. The organizational architecture of a POEtic system is the same as the one of an Embryonics design: it also follows the four levels of complexity defined in figure 1, once again from the population of organisms to the molecular level.

Physically, the tissue is composed of two layers shown in the left of figure 2: a grid of molecules and a cellular routing layer. As in Embryonics, the smallest units of the POEtic programmable hardware are also called molecules and are also arranged as a two-dimensional array. The cellular routing layer is also a two-dimensional array but contains special routing units that are responsible for the inter-cellular communication. This routing layer implements a distributed routing algorithm based on identifiers allowing the creation of data paths between cells at runtime. Each molecule, as well as each routing unit, are connected to their respective four neighbours in a regular structure, also shown in the left of figure 2. Moreover, the molecules have the capability of accessing the routing units to set up connections among cells.

As shown in the right of figure 2, a molecule mainly contains a 16-bit look-up table (LUT) and a D flip-flop (DFF); its inputs are selected by multiplexers and its outputs are routed to any direction through a switchbox. Moreover, a molecule possesses different configurable operational modes that let it act of different manners. The content of the LUT and of the DFF, as well as the selection of the multiplexers for the inputs and the outputs of a molecule and the mode in which the molecule has to work, are defined by 76 bits of configuration.

In the first four operational modes, that are quite standard in the reconfigurable hardware area, a molecule can be configured as a simple 16-bit LUT, as two 8-bit LUT, as a 8-bit LUT plus a 8-bit shift register, or as a 16-bit

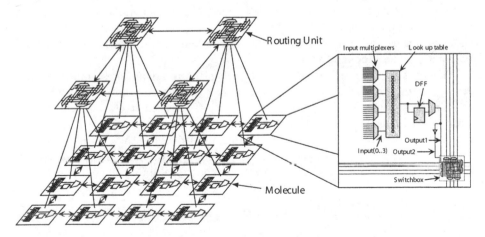

Fig. 2. Left: POEtic two-layer physical structure with the molecules and their routing units. Right: Basic structure of a POEtic molecule.

shift-register. Then there are four additional operational modes that are specific to the POEtic tissue: the first two are the Output and Input modes in which the molecule is connected to its routing unit and contains the 16-bit long routing identifier of the molecule itself, respectively of the molecule from where the information has to arrive. The third special mode is the Trigger mode, in which the task of the molecule is to supply a trigger signal needed by the routing algorithm for synchronization purposes. The last mode is the Configure mode, in which a molecule has the capability of partially reconfiguring its neighbours, i.e. the molecule can modify a fixed subset of the configuration bits of its neighbours (68 bits out of 76).

Inter-molecular communication, i.e. short-range communication between the programmable logic elements in the POEtic circuit, is implemented by a switch box (identical in all molecules) that prevents the possibility of short circuits in the network by using multiplexers and directional lines. There are two of these lines from and to each cardinal direction.

Inter-cellular routing, i.e. long-range communication between the processors implemented using the programmable logic, is implemented using a distributed routing algorithm inspired by Moreno [11], that automatically connects the cells inputs and outputs. A non-connected input (target) or output (source) can initiate the creation of a path by broadcasting its identifier, in case of an output, or the identifier of its source, in case of an input. The path linking them is then created using a parallel implementation of the breadth-first search algorithm, similar to Lee's algorithm [12] that configures multiplexers in the routing units. When all the paths have been created, the organism can start operation, and executes its task, until a new routing is launched.

Note that in the standard POEtic design, in the IO modes, the molecules only have one control signal that forces or not a connection to be established. In addition to this, to implement self-replication we had to slightly modify the standard POEtic design in order to improve the IO molecules with another control signal that makes the molecule to accept or not a connection. As a result, our version of the POEtic IO molecules has two control signals: one to force a molecule to establish a connection, i.e. `ForceConnect`, the other to accept the connections, i.e. `AcceptConnect`.

The routing approach used in POEtic has many advantages compared to a static routing process. First of all, it requires a very small number of clock cycles to finalize a path. Secondly, when a new cell is created it can start a routing process without the need of recalculating all paths already created. Thirdly, a cell has the possibility of restarting the routing process of the entire organism if needed. Finally, this approach is totally distributed, without any global control over the routing process, a clear advantage where scalability is concerned.

2.3   MOVE Processors

We will now present the basic processor structure that has been used for the realisation of our system: the MOVE architecture, also known as the Transport-Triggered Architecture (TTA) [3, 13, 14]. This paradigm was originally developed

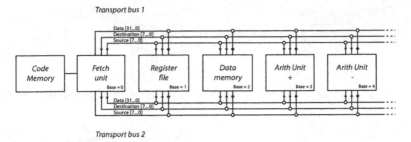

Fig. 3. Internal structure of a TTA processor

for the design of application-specific dataflow processors (processors where the instructions define the flow of data, rather than the operations to be executed).

In many respects, the overall structure of a TTA-based system is fairly conventional: data and instructions can be fetched to the processor from the main memory using standard mechanisms (caches, memory management units, etc.) and are decoded as in conventional processors. The basic differences lay in the architecture of the processor itself, and hence in the instruction set.

Rather than being structured, as is usual, around a more or less serial pipeline, a MOVE processor (Fig. 3) relies on a set of Functional Units (FUs) connected together by one or more transport busses. All the computation is carried out by the functional units (examples of such units can be adders, multipliers, register files, etc.) and the role of the instructions is simply to move data from and to the FUs in the order required to implement the desired operations. Since all the functional units are uniformly accessed through input and output registers, instruction decoding is reduced to its simplest expression, as only one instruction is needed: `move`.

TTA `move` instructions trigger operations which, in the simplest case, correspond to normal RISC instructions. For example, in order to add two numbers a RISC `add` instruction has to specify two operands and, most of the time, a destination register to store the result. The MOVE paradigm requires a slightly different approach to obtain the same result: instead of using a specific `add` instruction, the program moves the two operands to the input registers of a functional unit that implements the add operation. The result can then be retrieved in the output register of this functional unit and moved wherever it is needed.

3 Processor Architecture

After the presentation of the background used for our realization, we will now describe it more precisely. As mentioned, our test system is composed of four processors, the cells, that form a 4-digit modulus-60 counter, the organism, counting seconds and minutes. Each of the processors must then handle one digit. Consequently, two of them count from 0 to 9 while the two others count from 0 to 5. In their final configuration, they are logically organized so as to

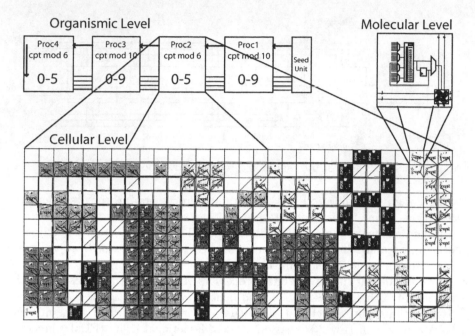

Fig. 4. The three hierarchical levels of our system: organism/counter final configuration, cell/processor mapping on POEtic, molecule/POEtic element

form a chain that is represented in the organismic level of figure 4 (note also the presence of the Seed Unit, whose function will be explained in section 5).

The normal operation of the system is the following: the processor that handles the rightmost digit, i.e. the units of seconds in the clock parallel, permanently counts from 0 to 9. When this processor arrives at 9, it generates a signal (`EnableCount`) telling the next processor, which handles the tens of seconds, to increment its own digit. When the tens of seconds processor arrives at 5, it generates in its turn a signal enabling the next processor on the chain, i.e. the units of minutes, to count. And so on until the tens of minutes.

As exposed in the precedent section, we realized our processors using the MOVE paradigm. Its actual implementation in POEtic molecules is shown in the cellular level of figure 4, while its logical architecture can be seen in figure 5. It resulted in a TTA processor possessing the following Functional Units (FU):

- **FU Cmp** used to compare two values. The result is directly given to the Execution Stack (see below for a short explanation).
- **FU Inc** used to increment one value.
- **FU Position** used to get the position of the processor inside the chain.
- **FU EnableIn** used to get the value of the `EnableCount` signal coming from the precedent processor on the chain.
- **FU EnableOut** used to set the value of the signal enabling the counting of the next processor on the chain.

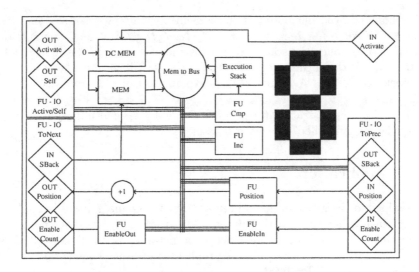

Fig. 5. Detailled architecture of the processor

- **FU IO Active/Self** used to connect one not yet differentiated processor, or used by the processor to connect itself in order to enable the whole system when the differentiation/connection process is finished (see section 5 for more details).
- **FU IO ToPrec** used to set up and configure the connections to the precedent processor on the chain. It is used to receive the processor position inside the chain and the `EnableCount` signal. It is also used to transmit the `Sback` signal whose purpose is explained in section 5.
- **FU IO ToNext** used to set up and configure the connections to the next processor on the chain.

The three FU IOs permit the processor to control the behaviour of the Inputs and Outputs: the processor can access and set up the `ForceConnect` (to force a molecule to establish a connection) and the `AcceptConnect` (to allow a molecule to accept the connections) control signals by setting the appropriate values in the FU IO registers.

Our MOVE processor, as is usual, contains a data bus spanning all the FUs and two memory busses: one for the source addresses and the other for the destination addresses of each `move` instruction. The processor has two memories: one memory (MEM) for the normal operation of the processor (i.e. the counting and the generation of signals) and another memory (DC MEM) that contains the code for the differentiation and connection mechanisms.

Then, as the processor has been realized on the POEtic substrate, which provides a specific molecule mode to implement shift memories (see section 2.2), we decided that, instead of an addressable memory that could support jumps in the code, we would use cyclic memories, where each instruction is read successively, and executed or not, depending on a special unit called Execution Stack.

To summarize the behaviour of the Execution Stack, we can say that, when facing an *"if condition then (x1; x2; ...) else (y1; y2; ...) end"* instruction, if the condition is valid, the stack will permit the execution of the X instructions and then block the Y instructions. Otherwise, it will permit the Y execution and block the X one. A more detailed explanation of this unit can be found in [15, 16].

Finally, for demonstration purposes, we added a special unit that is used to display the digit handled by each processor.

4   Self-replication

As explained in the introduction and in analogy to the majority of living beings, our implementation starts with only one cell/processor containing the information for the entire system to be realized. As a metaphor of the living cell division and multiplication, this first processor replicates in order to generate copies of itself that will then differentiate.

The self-replication process that we have implemented is based on the self-inspection concept [17], where, in order to replicate itself, a system has to generate its description by examining its own structure. This description is then used to create an identical copy of the original system [18].

More precisely, such a self-replication process in our reconfigurable circuit should proceed as follows: first, the cell that wants to replicate itself has to emit the configuration bits of every one of its molecules. Then, in some way, these bits are routed to their destination, i.e. the place where the copy will be constructed. These configuration bits are then injected into molecules that are not yet configured. These molecules receive their new configuration and become copies of the initial molecules. When all the configuration bits of each molecule of the initial system have been emitted, routed and injected in their new place, the cell has replicated itself.

We have to mention one of the requirements for a system to possess the self-replication ability: the order in which the system emits the configuration bits of its molecules, as well as the spatial position of each molecule with respect to the others, have to be the same as the order and position the empty molecules load their new configuration. One of the easiest way to obtain such a behaviour is to have a "path" that goes through each molecule of the system to be replicated. Then the configuration bits are expressed sequentially by shifting them along this path. In parallel, the injection of the configuration into the empty molecules has to construct and follow the same "path". With such an idea, self-replication becomes possible because every molecule is replicated in correct order and in the right place.

For that purpose, we had to separate our self-replicating processor in two parts: a functional part (FP) that contains the object we want to replicate, i.e. the MOVE processor itself, together with its corresponding replication path, and a self-replication part (SRP) that is of course in charge of the self-replication (Fig. 6).

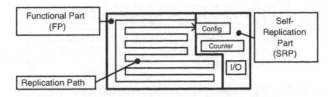

Fig. 6. Mandatory parts for a POEtic self-replication

The SRP contains a counter that knows the total number of configuration bits that have to be emitted by the molecules that want to replicate. It also contains an Input or an Output molecule that is used to connect an emitting SRP to a receiving SRP. Finally, we find in the SRP a molecule in the Configure mode that is used to force the molecules of the FP to shift their configuration bits along the replication path.

We will now detail the self-replication process that uses the self-configuration ability of the POEtic molecules as well as their distributed routing. At the beginning, as shown in figure 6, the system contains the following elements:

- **Functional Part FP** the processor that has to be replicated (Fig. 5).
- **Emitting SRP** that contains an Output molecule and is used to connect to one or more receiving molecules.
- **One or more Receiving SRP** that contain an Input molecule and are used to receive the connection from the Emitting SRP.
- **Replication Paths** that are already configured. The first path span all the molecules of the FP. The others draw the same trajectory as the first path and are placed next to the Receiving SRP.

  The presence of these paths at system startup is a shortcoming due to the impossibility, in the current implementation of the POEtic circuit, to completely configure all the bits of a molecule using the Configure mode. Removing these configuration paths is the next logical step in the development of our system.

The process starts with the Emitting SRP trying to connect to one Receiving SRP. This is done using the distributed routing algorithm of POEtic to link the Output molecule of the Emitting SRP to the Input molecule of the Receiving SRP. As a result, the SRPs can be placed anywhere on the substrate and the routing process will eventually connect the Emitting SRP to the nearest Receiving SRP.

When the two SRPs are connected, their respective Configure molecules start to shift the configuration of their replication paths. The Emitting SRP shifts the configuration of the FP and gets one configuration bit per clock cycle. This bit is duplicated and one copy is transmitted through the connection to the Receiving SRP while the second one is injected again in the FP replication path. Indeed, in order to obtain a replication, it is necessary that after this process, the starting FP finds itself in its initial state. Consequently, during all the process

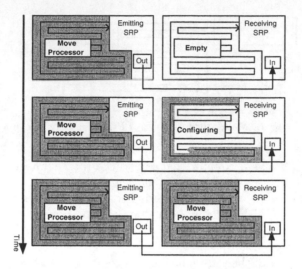

Fig. 7. Three steps of the self-replication process

of transmission of the configuration bits, the Emitting SRP and its replication path emulate a shift register buckling on itself, so that the FP finds again its initial state.

On the other side, the Receiving SRP gets the configuration bit from its Input molecule and injects it in its own replication path. This process repeats itself during a number of clock cycles determined by the SRPs and that is equal to the total number of configuration bits that have to be expressed, i.e. 68 bits that are configurable per molecule times the number of molecules to be replicated.

When the configuration is finished, the system contains two (or more) replicated FP that can start their normal functionality.

Note that this process is not limited to only one processor copy: as the Emitting SRP can connect to more than one Receiving SRP at a time, then the configuration bits can be injected in more than one replication path and consequently the number of copies of the initial processor is not limited. In our case, the processor makes three copies of itself: at the end of the self-replication process, the system contains four processors that are in a quiescent state, simply waiting for an activation signal.

5   Differentiation and Connections

In living organisms, when the first cell has divided, resulting in many totipotent identical cells, these latter have to specialize to handle a specific task that depends on their neighbouring cells and on the place they have inside the entire organism. As a result, the cells differentiate and connect themselves together to form the working organism.

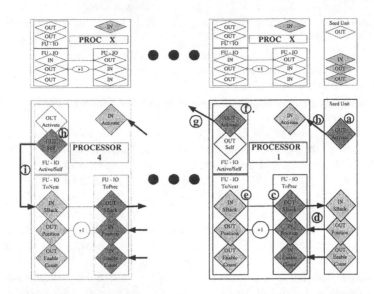

Fig. 8. Processor differentiation and connections. Top: quiescent state of the processors just after the self-replication. Bottom: connection process and differentiated processors.

Similarly, after the self-replication phase, the POEtic substrate contains four identical quiescent totipotent processors that still need to differentiate and connect in order to achieve the whole system functionality. This situation is shown at the top of figure 8 (note that only the IO elements of the processors are represented and that on the top of the figure the labels are not detailled).

In fact, the processor are waiting for an activation signal that will launch the differentiation/connections process. In order to generate this first activation signal, we implemented a special unit: the Seed Unit (SU). It possesses a counter that makes it wait for the end of the processor self-replication. At that time, the SU activates the `ForceConnect` control signal that forces the connection of its Output **OUT Activate**, *(a)* in figure 8. This Output will then initiate a distributed routing process to connect the nearest **IN Activate** molecule that is configured in order to accept the connections *(b)*. Note that all the quiescent processors have their **IN Activate** molecule waiting for a connection, i.e. with their `AcceptConnect` control activated.

As a result, the nearest replicated processor accepts the connection, becomes linked to the SU and receives an activation signal through the newly established connection. This activation signal makes the processor to activate its differentiation and connection memory (DC MEM in figure 5) and start the shifting and the execution of its instructions.

The first instruction makes the `ForceConnect` control of the FU_ IO_ ToPrec be activated *(c)*: the IO molecules of this FU will immediately try to initiate new connections. The only available corresponding molecules that have their `AcceptConnect` control activated are the ones of the SU, consequently these molecules become linked *(d)*. As a result, the processor gets from these new inputs its position inside the chain (zero in this case) as well as its `EnableCount` signal.

Then the DC MEM makes the processor activate the `AcceptConnect` controls of its FU_ IO_ ToNext *(e)*; this is done in order for the next processor on the chain to be able to connect back.

Finally, as the processor now knows it is not the last one of the chain, having already received its position from the FU_ IO_ ToPrec, it will activate the `ForceConnect` control of its **OUT Activate** molecule *(f)*. This molecule will then establish a connection to the next available **In Activate** molecule *(g)*, and launch the differentiation-connection process of the second processor.

The second processor will then execute this process again, connect its FU_ IO_ ToPrec to the first processor (whose FU_ IO_ ToNext now accept the connections). The same process happens for the third processor on the chain.

For the last processor, the points *(f)* and *(g)* are not executed: as the processor knows it is the last one of the chain, it does not need to connect to another processor but must inform the whole chain that the differentiation-connection process is finished and that the system now has to begin its normal multi-processor activity. Consequently, instead of its **OUT Activate** molecule, the fourth processor will activate the `ForceConnect` control of its **OUT Self** molecule *(h)*. This latter will then connect to the **IN SBack** molecule of its FU_ IO_ ToNext *(i)*.

This last connection provides an activation signal that is transmitted through the whole processor chain using the **In SBack** and the **OUT SBack** IOs. This signal activates the processors MEM memories (figure 5), whose instructions contain the code required to execute each of the functionalities needed by the application. The spatial position of the processor inside the chain, defined through the differentiation process, is used to select the appropriate functionality.

6   Hardware Implementation

To have access to a sufficient number of molecules and to be able to integrate our modifications to the design, we decided to emulate the POEtic substrate on the BioWall [4], a two-dimensional electronic wall designed for bio-inspired applications and composed of an array of reconfigurable circuits.

We made two major modifications to the standard POEtic specifications: the first one is the improvement in the control signals of the IO molecules explained in section 2.2. The second one is the following: unlike the standard POEtic connection schema shown in the left of figure 2 where each routing unit is simultaneously connected to four molecules, we realized our POEtic implementation with one routing unit per molecule, permitting a denser connection pattern.

The realization of one of our processor, with its self-replicating part, needs 30x12 POEtic molecules to be implemented. Using the BioWall for the implementation, we have 25x80 POEtic molecules available, which is sufficient to demonstrate the self-replication, the differentiation/connection process and finally the normal operation of our multi-processor system.

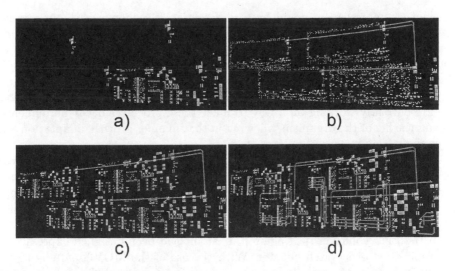

Fig. 9. a) Initialization state. b) Self-replication phase. c) The four totipotent processors before the differentiation/connection phase. d) Operational system.

Moreover, the display capabilities of the BioWall allows us to visually check and demonstrate the correct behaviour of the entire system: some pictures of it are shown in figure 9 and a video of the whole process can be found at http://carg2.epfl.ch/Staff/JR/Videos/PoeMoveSR.avi.

7   Conclusion and Future Developments

We have realized a multi-processor system that exhibits self-replication, differentiation and distributed connection abilities. Moreover, we have implemented the whole system in hardware on the BioWall, demonstrating the feasibility of the concepts. Nevertheless, a number of things can certainly be improved.

With its distributed connection ability, our system can bind together processors that have no fixed predetermined place on the substrate. If the system had a cellular fault-detector, it could detect and disable faulty processors. As a result the differentiation/connections process would automatically avoid the faulty processor and connect to the next correctly working one.

From another point of view, our system can not tolerate individual errors. As a result, one of the improvements that could be added to the POEtic molecules, as in the Embryonics project [7], is a molecular fault-tolerance capability.

Moreover, as already mentioned in section 4, the POEtic substrate has only partial self-configuration abilities (the configuration bits that define the replication path can not be changed by the system). As a result, the replication paths must be pre-configured in order to cross all the molecules that have to be replicated. One major planned improvement consists of changing the POEtic specification by allowing the system to set or reset each configuration bit and consequently enabling a complete self-replication.

174   J. Rossier et al.

Another improvement could be to differentiate the memory: in our system, each processor possesses the same memory and executes the instructions or not, depending on its position in the processor chain. To limit this redundancy we could modify the memories and the differentiation process in order to copy only the instructions needed by a specific processor in its specific memory.

Then, our system replicates and differentiates only once at the beginning. We are currently working on a way to make these processes occur permanently during the life of the organism, allowing in that manner growth, adaptation and re-configuration in case of failures.

Despite all the things that we plan to integrate to future designs, we can already say that in its current state, our realization is a real improvement compared to the existing ones for several reasons. Firstly, contrary to the Embryonics project, where the genome had to be injected in parallel in each cell, in our design we only need to provide the genome one time to the circuit.

In the Embryonics project again, the circuit had been designed expressly for the realization of a watch counter. With the use of the MOVE paradigm, our design is much more versatile and can be modified very quickly to adapt to any logical task, just by adding some Functional Units.

Moreover, as mentioned in the precedent section, compared to the standard POEtic design, we made some improvements on the IO molecules and on the routing layer in our hardware implementation.

Finally we can say that, even if some consequent work remains to be done, our design is one good step ahead in the realization of a really efficient self-replicating electronic system.

References

1. Tyrrell A., Sanchez E., Floreano D., Tempesti G., Mange D., Moreno J.-M., Rosenberg J., Villa A., POEtic Tissue: An Integrated Architecture for Bio-Inspired Hardware, Proceedings of the 5th International Conference on Evolvable Systems: From Biology to Hardware (ICES'2003), pp. 129-140, 2003
2. Thoma Y., Tempesti G., Sanchez E., Moreno J.-M., POEtic: an electronic tissue for bio-inspired cellular applications, BioSystems 76, pp. 191-200, 2004
3. Tabak D., Lipovski G.J., MOVE architecture in digital controllers, IEEE Transactions on Computers C-29, pp. 180-190, 1980
4. Tempesti G., Mange D., Stauffer A., Teuscher C., The BioWall: An Electronic Tissue for Prototyping Bio-Inspired Systems. Proceedings of the 2002 NASA/DOD Conference on Evolvable Hardware, pp. 221-230, 2002
5. Mange D., Sipper M., Stauffer A., Tempesti G., Towards Robust Integrated Circuits: The Embryonics Approach, Proceedings of the IEEE 88(4): pp. 516-541, 2000
6. Mange D., Stauffer A., Petraglio E., Tempesti G., Embryonic Machines that Divide and Differentiate, Proc. 1st Int. Workshop on Biologically Inspired Approaches to Advanced Information Technology (BioADIT04), pp. 328-343, 2004
7. Tempesti G., Mange D., Stauffer A., A robust multiplexer-based FPGA inspired by biological systems, Journal of Systems Architecture 43(10): pp. 719-733, 1997

8. Stauffer A., Mange D., Tempesti G., Teuscher C., A Self-Repairing and Self-Healing Electronic Watch: The BioWatch, Proceedings of the 4th International Conference on Evolvable Systems: From Biology to Hardware (ICES'2001), pp. 112-127, 2001
9. Sanchez E., Mange D., Sipper M., Tomassini M., Perez-Uribe A., Stauffer A., Phylogeny, Ontogeny, and Epigenesis: Three Sources of Biological Inspiration for Softening Hardware, Proceedings of the 1st International Conference on Evolvable Systems: From Biology to Hardware (ICES96), pp. 34-54, 1997
10. Sipper M., Sanchez E., Mange D., Tomassini M., Perez-Uribe A., A phylogenetic, ontogenetic, and epigenetic view of bio-inspired hardware systems, IEEE Transaction on Evolutionary Computation 1(1): pp. 83-97, 1997
11. Moreno J.-M., Sanchez E.,Cabestany J., An in-system routing strategy for evolvable hardware programmable platforms, Proceedings of the 3rd NASA/DoD Workshop on Evolvable Hardware, IEEE Computer Society, 2001
12. Lee C.Y., An Algorithm for Path Connections and Its Applications, IRE Transactions on Electronic Computers EC-10(3): pp. 346-365, 1961
13. Corporaal H., Microprocessor Architectures from VLIW to TTA, John Wiley & Sons, 1998
14. Corporaal H., Mulder H., MOVE: A framework for high-performance processor design, Proceedings of the International Conference on Supercomputing, pp. 692-701, 1991
15. Restrepo H.F., Tempesti G., Mange D., Implementation of a Self-replicating Universal Turing Machine, In Alan Turing: Life and Legacy of a Great Thinker, pp. 241-269, 2004
16. Restrepo H.F., Implementation of a Self-repairing Universal Turing Machine, Swiss Federal Institute of Technology (EPFL), PhD thesis 2457, 2001
17. Ibàñez J., Anabitarte D., Azpeitia I., Barrera O., Barrutieta A., Blanco H., Echarte F., Self-inspection based reproduction in cellular automata, Proceedings of the 3rd European Conference on Artificial Life (ECAL95), pp. 564-576, 1995
18. Laing R., Automaton models of reproduction by self-inspection, Journal of Theoretical Biology 66, pp. 437-456, 1977

The Evolutionary Emergence of Intrinsic Regeneration in Artificial Developing Organisms

Diego Federici

Complex Adaptive Organically-inspired Systems group (CAOS),
Norwegian University of Science and Technology,
N-7491 Trondheim, Norway
federici@idi.ntnu.no

Abstract. Inspired upon the development of living systems, many models of artificial embryogeny are being proposed. These are usually aimed at the solution of some know limitations of evolutionary computation; among these scalability, flexibility and, more recently, fault-tolerance.

This paper focuses on the latter, proposing an explanation of the intrinsic regenerative capabilities displayed by some models of multi-cellular development.

Supported by the evidence collected from simulations, regeneration is shown to emerge as evolution converges to more regular regions of the genotype space.

The conclusion is that intrinsic fault-tolerance emerges as evolution increases the evolvability of the development process.

Keywords: Genetic algorithms, development, fault tolerance.

1 Introduction

Robustness to 'hardware' failures is a fundamental feature for living systems. Having to endure various sources of damage, such as injuries, aging, predators and parasites, organisms that display an endogenous resistance to external tampering and degradation have clearly an advantage when facing natural selection.

It is therefore not surprising that, in order to support life, biological organisms naturally display a strong fault-tolerance.

A possible path towards a good fault resistance is to design devices with some sort of functional redundancy, so that the negative effects of the loss of some components is mitigated by those which are still active.

Multi-cellular living systems display an additional source of robustness derived by their regenerative capabilities. An example is provided by Hydras (Hydra Oligactis). Hidras can regenerate any damaged or dead cell, and severed body parts can even reconstruct the complete organism [1].

Cell regeneration is common also among more complex living organisms. For example the tail of the lizard and the limbs of the salamander regrow after

A.J. Ijspeert et al. (Eds.): BioADIT 2006, LNCS 3853, pp. 176–191, 2006.

being severed. In these cases, regeneration involves the production of highly differentiated tissues.

Notably, it has been shown that transplanted cells can assume specific roles based on the place where they are injected. For example, this technique allows mice to recover from spine injuries with the injection of staminal cells [2].

In these cases, fault-tolerance is based on the same ontogenetic processes which are the conrerstone of the organism's development.

For engineering purposes, devices that could automatically recover from faults are very appealing. Using a re-configurable substrate, we can envision systems that can heal themselves, effectively increasing their life-time without requiring any external support.

Previous work conducted on artificial models of multi-cellular development has highlighted how this class of systems tends to display intrinsic regenerating properties. The term intrinsic refers to the fact that, albeit robustness can be boosted including it in the fitness function [3, 4, 5], recovery of phenotypic faults is also emergent, appearing as well when not selected for during evolution [3, 6, 7].

The fact that these systems are intrinsically fault-tolerant is very important: Even if is it possible to select individuals both on performance and robustness, testing all possible sources of faults can be computationally expensive (if not impossible). Since evolution tends to be very exploitative, faults that are not explicitly tested will most probably not be tolerated by the evolved designs.

On the other hand, if a system presents some degree of intrinsic fault-tolerance, we may expect that a necessarily partial robustness test will better generalize to unforeseen situations.

Still, the fundamental reason that makes this class of embryogeny systems intrinsically fault-tolerant remains unclear.

One may argue that, since the growth program and the variables it acts upon (i.e. cell types, chemicals, etc.) are distributed, development must necessarily provide a low sensitivity to phenotypic perturbations. Still, being based on rewrite rules, phenotype perturbations would be expected to induce a marked morphological divergence as faults get built upon.

An explanation is offered by the canalization concept [8, 9, 10], i.e. that a canalized phenotype evolves to resist perturbations to its developmental process or its genotype: Robustness emerges because of the effects of a stabilizing selection.

Simulations have shown that canalization emerges when developmental noise is present [11, 12]. These results are homologous to those presented in [3, 4, 5] where artificial developing organisms were selected for their phenotypic robustness.

Canalization has also been shown to emerge with the evolution of genotypes with point-stable regulatory networks (independent of their function, [13]). This result is interesting because, as in [3, 6, 7], robustness is achieved in the absence of developmental noise, therefore without an explicit evolutionary advantage.

In this paper we show that canalization and robustness can also emerge simply as a population of developing individuals evolves towards specific targets without developmental noise or the need of point-stable regulatory networks.

Evidence collected from simulations suggests how robustness is connected to a general evolutionary tendency to converge on stable genotype spaces (i.e. presenting a high degree of neutrality[1]).

Altering the mutation rate, we prove how a more aggressive search produces individuals both with more robust phenotypes and converging towards wider neutral spaces.

These results point out a subtle relationship between phylogeny and ontogeny, which does not appear to be explicitly dependant upon the user-defined selection criterion: The intrinsic fault-tolerance emerging in multi-cellular systems appears as a side-effect of the evolutionary preference for more regular regions of the genotype space.

2   Related Work

Typically proposed to increase the scalability and flexibility of evolutionary computation, several indirected encoding schemes have been proposed. These 'Artificial Embryogeny' (AE, [14]) methods recursively construct the mature phenotype following the growth program defined in the genotype.

Since selection operates at the level of the phenotype, the relationship between the evolving genotype and its inclusive fitness is mediated by the development process. This indirect path may trigger complex gene-to-gene interactions, which are captured by the concept of the Gene Regulatory Network (GRN).

Since phenotypic maturation in AE is de facto a rewriting process, early models were based on grammar-based approaches in which the genotype defines the substitution rules which are repeatedly applied to the phenotype. Examples include the Matrix Rewriting scheme [15] and the Cellular Encoding [16].

Some models introduced additional contextual information in each rule definition [17, 18], so that phenotypic trait variations could be generated. Also, it is possible to implicitly define the grammar by means of an artificial GRN [19] and use the accumulated concentrations of simulated chemicals to modulate the characteristics of morphological constituents.

In this direction, and inspired by Cellular Automata, a second approach is to evolve the rules by which cells alter their metabolism and duplicate. Cells are usually capable of sensing the presence of neighboring cells [20], releasing chemicals which diffuse in simulated 2D or 3D environments [21, 22], and moving and growing selective connections to neighboring cells [23].

Closely related to the one presented in this paper, the model proposed in [24] is based upon a fixed cartesian 2D lattice, a checkerboard, in which each cell occupies a given square. Artificial organisms are generated starting from a single

---

[1] Whose changes to the genotype produce none or little change to the phenotype/fitness.

cell. Every cell can replicate in the four cardinal directions taking the organism to maturation in a fixed number of development steps.

All cells share the same genotype encoding the cell growth program (its regulatory network). In [24] the growth program is structured as a sequence of rules. Rules are activated by matching the local neighborhood of a given cell and trigger specific cell responses: duplication, death and cell-state change. Individuals were evolved to produce tesselleting patterns.

In [22], the growth program is represented by a boolean network. Cells belong to 1 of 4 different types and can release chemicals which undergo a simulated diffusion process. Specific evolutionary targets (2D patterns) were evolved and emergent self-healing dynamics were reported for the first time [6].

In [3] the previous model is extended with internal chemicals, which do not diffuse in the environment but are private to each cell. The growth program is encoded by a recursive neural network, and the organism's genotype can contain several chromosomes, each one specifying a complete growth program. Individuals are initialized with a single chromosome which controls the entire development process. During evolution, additional chromosomes can be introduced by duplication (i.e. gene duplication [25]), each one being associated to a specific stage of development. By allowing several independent Embryonal Stages, this method proved capable of increasing overall evolvability in the evolution of specific 2D patterns, also showing a higher scalability then direct encoding. Also in this case, emergent fault-tolerance was reported.

In [24, 22, 3], fitness was concerned only by the topological properties of mature individuals. In [5] the AE model in [22] was used to produce a 2-bit multiplier capable of recovering transient phenotype faults. In [4] the AE model in [3] was used to evolve a regenerating spiking neuro-controller for simulated Kephera robots.

These last results prove the great potential that the evolution of complex fault-tolerant ontogenies can provide to the engineering community.

3   Methods: The Development Model

The AE model used in this paper is introduced in [3]. For clarity the model is explained in detail in this section.

Phenotypes develop starting from a single cell placed in the center of a fixed size 2D checkerboard. Multi-cellular organisms reach maturation in a precise number of developmental steps (N_{ds}). Cells replicate and can release simulated chemicals in intra-cellular space (cell metabolism).

Cell behaviour is governed by a growth program based on local variables, and represented by a simple recursive neural network (Morpher).

3.1   Cell State

Each position in the checkerboard can contain a cell, which is characterized by a state. The following table summarizes the information contained in each checkerboard position:

if a cell is present:
  the cell state: {active, passive}
  the cell type: an integer in $[0, N_t - 1]$
  the cell metabolism: a vector $\in [-1, 1]^{N_m}$
if no cell is present:
  observable cell type 0

In the simulations presented in this paper there is one metabolic chemical ($N_m = 1$) and the number of cell type (N_t) is either 3 or 4.

3.2   The Regulatory System: The Morpher

Cell behavior is governed by an artificial neural network (Morpher) defined by the genotype. The Morpher's inputs define the state of the regulatory system and its outputs encode the cell morphogenic actions.

The Morpher input vector encodes the state of a particular cell (type and metabolism) and of the types of the 4 neighboring cells in the North, West, South and East directions (NWSE).

At each developmental step, under the control of the Morpher outputs, existing active cells can change their own type, alter their metabolism and produce new cells. An active cell can also die or become passive. Each step, up to four new cells can be produced in any of the NWSE directions. In case, the mother cell specifies the daughter cells internal variables (type and metabolism) and whether they are active or passive. If necessary, existing cells are pushed sideways to create space for the new cells. When a cell is pushed outside the boundaries of the grid, it is permanently lost.

The discrete cell type is encoded in a vector $\in [-1, 1]^{N_d}$, in which each vector element is quantized to V values in the $[-1,1]$ range. Therefore the number of cell types N_t equals V^{N_d}. The input and output vectors are exemplified below:

input vector	neuron bias	cell age	cell type	metabolism	neighbors cell types	total
size	1	1	N_d	N_m	$4 \times N_d$	$2 + N_m + 5N_d$

output vector	change state?	new cell type	new metabolism	produce cells?	cell types	metabolisms	total
size	1	N_d	N_m	4	$4N_d$	$4N_m$	$5(N_d + N_m + 1)$

Where: the cell age is set to 1 at cell birth and decays exponentially; 'change state' can take 4 values {no change, go passive, die, change type and metabolism}; 'produce cells' can take three values for each NWES direction {produce an active cell, produce a passive cell, do nothing}.

Passive cells cannot replicate or change their own state.

In the simulations presented herein, $N_d = 1$ and $N_m = 1$. The Morpher has 8 inputs, 15 outputs and contains no hidden layers. The genotype contains a floating point gene for each of the 120 Morpher weights.

3.3   Embryonal Stages

The regulatory system controls gene expression over two orthogonal dimensions: time and space. Development with Embryonal Stages (DES) implements a direct mechanism of Neutral Complexification for the temporal dimension.

As development spans over several consecutive steps, the idea is to start evolution with a single growth program (chromosome/Morpher) which controls all the development steps. As evolution proceeds, a new chromosome can be added by gene duplication.

The developmental steps are therefore partitioned into two groups/stages. The first, controlling the initial steps of embryogenesis, is associated with the old chromosome. The latter, completing growth, is associated with the new, identical, duplicated chromosome. Likewise, new chromosomes can be added one by one, each one controlling a partition of the last development steps.

Being exact copies, new chromosomes do not alter development, and are therefore neutral. But eventual mutations can independently affect each duplicated gene.

By unlocking the gene expression of different development phases, each chromosome can assume more specialized roles, de facto increasing the genotypic resolution around the area represented by the current mature phenotype. In fact, each new chromosome must take care of the maturation of an already partially developed phenotype. This new starting phenotype, as opposed to the zygote, is the result of the evolution of the previous chromosomes and hypothetically provides a flying start for the additional stage. Overall, the effect is an increase in genotype-phenotype correlation leading to higher evolvability [3].

In the simulations presented herein, only the chromosome associated to the latest stage is subjected to the evolutionary operators, while all other chromosomes remain fixed[2].

3.4   Evolutionary Details

Every population is composed of 400 individuals. The best 50 individuals are copied to the next generation and reproduce (elitism). Evolution comprises 1000 generations.

The genotype contains a floating point number for each Morpher's weight. Mutation takes each weight of the Morpher and adds to it Gaussian noise with 0 mean and V_{mut} variance (see Section 4 for actual values).

With a .05 probability an offspring undergoes an additional symmetric mutation. The Morpher's subnet responsible for the production of new cells in a chosen direction overwrites one or more of the other directions subnets. This operator should favor the evolution of phenotypes with various degrees of symmetry, but, since cells are not activated in parallel but follow a top-down left-to-right activation order, perfect symmetrical phenotypes usually require additional changes to the genotype.

---

[2] In [3] it was shown that this restriction does not seem to affect the overall evolutionary dynamics while it speeds up the simulations.

10% of the offspring are produced by crossover. Crossover exchanges all the weights connected to inherited outputs units.

Organisms grow in a 32x32 checkerboard starting from a single active cell in position (16,16), with type 1 and metabolism 0. Development encompasses 12 development steps.

At the end of a evolutionary run, genotypes comprise 12 embryonal stages (one chromosome for each development step). New stages are introduced every $1000/12 = 83.\bar{3}$ generations.

Fitness Function. Each cell in the mature phenotype is interpreted as a pixel, its color provided by the cell type.

Fitness is proportional to the resemblance of an individual to a target pattern and is computed as shown in equation 1. For fitness computation, dead cells are assigned the default type 0 (black color)

$$\text{Fitness}(P,T) = \left(\sum_{x,y} \text{Equals}\,(\,P,T,x,y\,) \right) / \|T\|$$

$$\text{Equals}\,(\,P,T,x,y\,) = \begin{cases} 0 \; if \; P(x,y) \neq T(x,y) \\ 1 \; if \; P(x,y) = T(x,y) \end{cases} \tag{1}$$

where P is the phenotype, T the target pattern. In case of ties, younger individuals are selected.

Notice that in [3, 4], mechanisms devised to contrast premature convergence were present. In this case, we are less interested in evolvability and investigate the relation between phylogeny and ontogeny in the emergence of phenotypic regeneration. For this reason and clarity these mechanisms are not activated in the following simulations.

Target Patterns. The evolutionary targets are plotted in Figure 1.

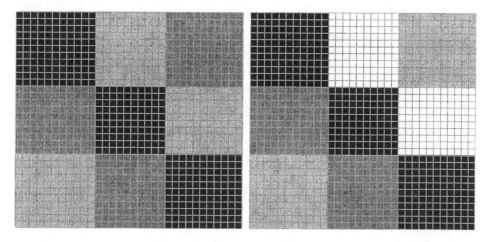

Fig. 1. Evolutionary targets. On the left the 3-color 32x32 pattern ($V = 3$), on the right the 4-color 32x32 pattern ($V = 4$).

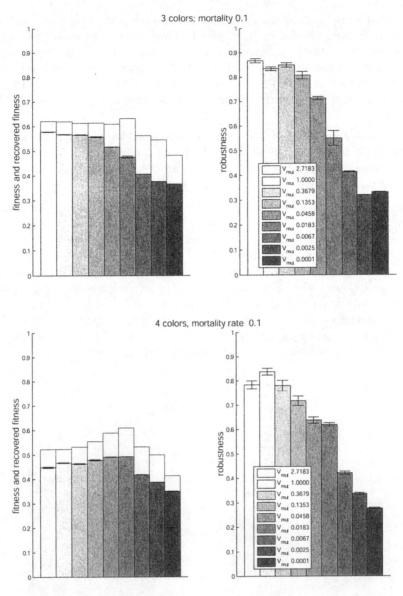

Fig. 2. Emergent fault-tolerance with a 10% mortality rate: fitness and robustness averages over 100 tests. Tested are the fittest individuals of each population and mutation rate. Above individuals with 3 colors, below with 4 colors. Thin boxes display fitness without faults. Individuals were not selected for fault-tolerance.

4   Results

We analyse the results obtained from 36 independent runs with each parameter setting.

We evolve populations whose individuals are selected in base of their resemblance to the targets plotted in Figure 1. After 1000 generations, the intrinsic fault-tolerance of the best individual of each run is tested. While during evolution, development is fault-free, during fault-tolerance tests, each cell at each development step is killed with a given probability (mortality rate). In case of death, cells are simply removed from the checkerboard.

For each tested individual we compute:

fitness recovery: the individual fitness score when subjected to faults.
robustness: the phenotype stability to faults, i.e. a count of the phenotypic differences between the faulty and non-faulty individual averaged over the total number of cells.

The latter is more indicative of the individuals' intrinsic regenerative properties since computing only the recovered fitness score hides phenotypic changes that are neutral towards fitness. For simple combinatorial reasons, these are in fact more probable in less fit individuals.

The averages of both indicators are plotted in Figure 2 for a 0.1 mortality rate. Populations with various levels of mutation variance have been evolved: $V_{mut} = e^i$ with $i = \{1, 0, -1, -2, -3, -4, -5, -6, -7\}$.

It is interesting to notice that, while performance appears maximized for intermediate values of V_{mut}, higher robustness emerges under stronger mutation rates. This intrinsic property of ontogeny appears mediated by the amount

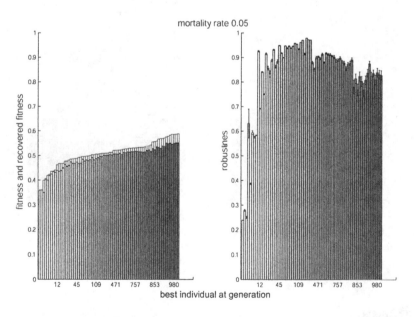

Fig. 3. Intrinsic robustness levels during evolution. Averages over 100 tests for the best individuals of the highest scoring population with $V_{mut} = e^{-2}$ and 4 colors. Robustness emerges during evolution but does not appear to be proportional to fitness. Thin boxes display fitness without faults.

of phylogenetic variation. Since robustness is a feature which is not selected for, this result highlights a relationship between the domains of ontogeny and phylogeny.

4.1   Is Intrinsic Robustness Evolved?

We would like to know whether robustness is an emergent property of development in general, or more specifically it arises during evolution. In [3] it was reported that random individuals appeared less robust than fit ones. In Figure 3 we plot robustness over generations for all the best individuals from the best population evolved with $V_{mut} = e^{-2}$ and 4 colors.

It is observed that, similar to the results obtained in selection experiments [26, 27], robustness emerges after only a few generations. This shows how the most evolvable individuals also present an intrinsic fault-tolerance.

Still robustness does not appear to be strictly proportional to fitness, as it also shown to decrease during evolution. This reflects the fact that robustness is neutral towards selection and its appearance is a byproduct of the evolutionary dynamics.

For example, figure 4 shows how those individuals which are selected for reproduction are not those displaying the highest robustness. Still, the fact that

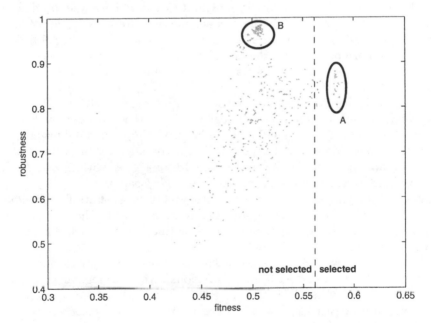

Fig. 4. Scatter plot: intrinsic robustness over fitness. Averages over 100 tests for all the individuals of the last generation of the highest scoring population with $V_{mut} = e^{-2}$ and 4 colors. Individuals laying on the right of the separation line will be selected for reproduction. The fittest individuals are clustered in a group (**A**), while the most robust ones are centered in another (**B**).

the cluster of lower-fitness high-robustness individuals (labeled **B**, in Figure 4) is very dense may explain the reason behind the frequent emergence of fault-tolerant individuals.

4.2   Relation Between Robustness and Neutral Space

The presented results suggest a proportional relation between high mutation rates and phenotypic homeostasis. In this section, we argue that the emergent robustness of ontogeny is connected to the evolutionary preference for genotypes of high mutational robustness.

According to the quasi-species model [28], apart from individuals of high fitness, selection would also prefer genotypes which are robust towards mutation. This is because with full replacement, those individuals which have more probability to produce viable fit offspring have a higher probability to survive as a quasi-species. As a result, populations tend to converge to genotype regions of higher neutrality (i.e. regions of Mutational Robustness, where fewer genotype mutations produce an observable phenotype/fitness change). Being more stable, these regions are in fact attractors of the dynamic evolutionary system, see for example the analysis in [29].

In our case, we use a deterministic method without full replacement (elitism) to select the reproducing/surviving individuals, therefore the quasi-species model should not hold. In fact, individuals of highest fitness will always reproduce and survive no matter how rough is the fitness landscape around their genotype.

Still, the quasi-species analysis is carried at equilibrium (as in [29]). Before reaching equilibrium, we argue, the lack of stochastic fluctuations in the surviving population is replaced by the effects of the randomic exploration of the search space.

For example, let there be two distant genotype regions, R_1 and R_2, so that individuals cannot migrate from one region to the other. R_1 contains few individuals of optimal fitness F_O and many of low fitness F_L (i.e. a promising region but with a rough fitness landscape); while R_2 contains few individuals of low fitness F_L and many of high but sub-optimal fitness F_{SO}, with $F_{SO} < F_O$ (i.e. a less promising region but with regular fitness landscape).

Individuals laying on R_1 have a low probability to generate fit individuals, while those laying on R_2 have a statistically higher yield. The more frequent F_{SO} solutions could take R_1 individuals to extinction if F_O solutions are not discovered in time.

Therefore, even with elitism, the conclusions of the quasi-species model would hold, and evolution would push towards regions with more regular fitness landscapes, i.e. regions of higher mutational robustness. With a more aggressive mutation operator (higher V_{mut}) we also expect populations to converge to regions of more marked neutrality.

We can test the neutrality of the genotype regions occupied by the best individuals of the 5 top scoring populations evolved with each parameter settings. For each tested individual, we alter the genotype and compute the corresponding phenotypic variation. Figure 5 shows the average phenotypic change per unit of genotype change. In the following tables, we report the maximum amplitude of the genotype alteration (G-distance[3]) which causes an average phenotype variation below the given threshold (averages over 48000 random genotype alterations of various amplitudes for each tested individual).

3 colors V_{mut}	G-distance for phenotype distance less then:				average robustness (0.05)
	$< 10^{-4}$	$< 10^{-3}$	$< 10^{-2}$	$< 10^{-1}$	
e^1	0.20	4.50	14.00	≥ 30.00	0.91 ± 0.00
e^0	0.00	0.04	2.50	≥ 30.00	0.89 ± 0.00
e^{-1}	0.00	0.05	1.50	≥ 30.00	0.90 ± 0.01
e^{-2}	0.00	0.01	0.10	18.00	0.86 ± 0.01
e^{-3}	0.00	0.00	0.04	3.00	0.78 ± 0.01
e^{-4}	0.00	0.00	0.04	2.50	0.62 ± 0.03
e^{-5}	0.00	0.00	0.00	0.04	0.48 ± 0.00
e^{-6}	0.00	0.00	0.00	0.01	0.35 ± 0.00
e^{-7}	0.00	0.00	0.00	0.01	0.35 ± 0.00

4 colors V_{mut}	G-distance for phenotype distance less then:				average robustness (0.05)
	$< 10^{-4}$	$< 10^{-3}$	$< 10^{-2}$	$< 10^{-1}$	
e^1	0.07	0.40	9.00	≥ 30.00	0.83 ± 0.01
e^0	0.09	1.00	4.50	≥ 30.00	0.87 ± 0.01
e^{-1}	0.03	0.10	1.00	20.00	0.83 ± 0.01
e^{-2}	0.01	0.06	0.40	6.00	0.76 ± 0.02
e^{-3}	0.00	0.00	0.02	1.50	0.70 ± 0.01
e^{-4}	0.00	0.00	0.01	1.50	0.70 ± 0.00
e^{-5}	0.00	0.00	0.00	0.70	0.49 ± 0.01
e^{-6}	0.00	0.00	0.01	1.00	0.38 ± 0.01
e^{-7}	0.00	0.00	0.00	0.03	0.30 ± 0.01

As expected there is a strong correlation between the mutation rate (V_{mut}) and the average neutrality of the genotype changes. Notably, these results suggest that emergent fault-tolerance is connected to mutational robustness, pointing to a relation between the ontogenetic and phylogenetic domains.

To confirm this hypothesis excluding the effects of fitness scores, we test individuals of equal fitness from the population of Figure 4. We take the most robust individual of the population and compare its neutral space size with the one of the least robust individual with the same fitness score. The most fault-tolerant individual is shown to lay on a larger neutral space:

4 colors fitness	G-distance for phenotype distance less then:				average robustness (0.05)
	$< 10^{-4}$	$< 10^{-3}$	$< 10^{-2}$	$< 10^{-1}$	
0.5088	0.04	0.10	0.40	≥ 30.00	$.9829 \pm .0004$
0.5088	0.01	0.07	0.30	≥ 30.00	$.7073 \pm .0081$

---

[3] Measured as the euclidean distance in the 120-dimensional genotype space.

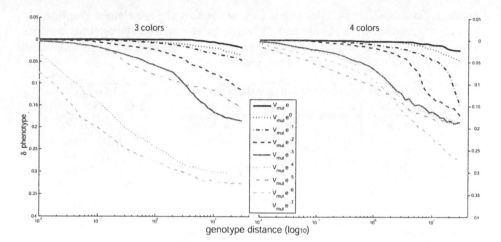

Fig. 5. Individual's neutrality to genotype changes: phenotype variation per unit of genotype change. Averages over 48000 random genotype changes of the 5 best individuals of the 5 top-scoring populations with each parameter settings. Individuals evolved under stronger mutation rates (V_{mut}) usually converge to wider neutral spaces.

5   Conclusions

Related work [22, 6, 3, 7] has show that some Artificial Embriogeny (AE) systems display emergent regenerative properties. With the aim to eventually produce as robust designs as those seen in nature, this tendency can be exploited to produce functional devices with remarkable fault-tolerance [4, 5].

Currently though, there is not a clear understanding of the reasons behind the emergence of the intrinsic robustness displayed by these development systems. It is often assumed that the distributed nature of ontogeny must play a fundamental role in the organism ability to recover from phenotypic faults. Still, logic also suggests that faults should propagate catastrophically as they are built upon during ontogeny.

In this paper we address this issue linking the robustness to phenotypic faults occurring during development to the evolutionary tendency to converge on genotype spaces with a high degree of neutrality.

Simulations conducted on the presented multi-cellular AE model have demonstrated that:

R1: when the mutation rate is increased, evolution converges to more regular genotype regions, i.e. with a high degree of robustness to mutations.

R2: a high robustness to mutations is related to a high degree of tolerance to phenotypic faults during development.

These results are in good agreement with the canalization theory [8, 9], where the emergence of stabilizing selection originates by the evolutionary preference for regular genotype space regions.

Additionally, if R1 fits well with the predictions derived by the quasi-species model [28], we will now argue that R2 is the logic extension of R1 in the case of ontogeny.

In fact, the reason behind the evolutionary emergence of mutational robustness is that individuals converging to more regular fitness landscapes have a higher probability to flood a population with a single strain of related genotypes (i.e. a quasi-species).

This implies that members of such successful quasi-species display a good neutrality to mutations: that when mutated phenotype/fitness changes are negligible.

Without development, this can be achieved by reducing the negative effects of epistasis, see for example [30]. This is because, when mutations alter the genotype, a high level epistasis means that gene to gene interactions will amplify the phenotypic consequences of the change.

With development, the rewriting process allows another path towards the achievement of a good neutrality to mutations: the possibility that a mutation causes a change to the growing phenotype which is cancelled (corrected) later on in development.

Therefore a stable growth program is one that can also neutralize phenotypic variations. When evaluating the intrinsic fault-tolerance of an artificial embryogeny, we are in fact testing a facet of the genotype's mutational robustness, its ability to suppress phenotypic variations caused by mutations.

The conclusion is that fault-tolerance emerges during evolution because, as organisms compete to reach higher levels of evolvability, they converge to more regular (robust) genotype regions.

Future Work. The fact that regeneration of multi-cellular systems emerges as a side effect of the optimization of the development process, allows us to draw two hypotheses: the first, that fault-tolerant developing organisms should be relatively easy to evolve; the second, that it should be possible to use fault-tolerance to measure the evolvability of a development system.

The former is already being validated by recent empirical results [4, 5]. The latter is being investigated, with the hope of producing a theory that would help the design of more evolvable artificial embryogenies.

Acknowledgements. I wish to thank Per Kristian Lehre for the many valuable discussions, and the anonymous reviewers for the quality of their feedback.

References

1. Bode, P., Bode, H.: Formation of pattern in regenerating tissue pieces of hydra attenuata. i. head-body proportion regulation. Dev Biol **78** (1990) 484–496
2. Ramon-Cueto, A., Cordero, M., Santos-Benito, F., Avila, J.: Functional recovery of paraplegic rats and motor axon regeneration in their spinal cords by olfactory ensheathing glia. Neuron **25** (2000) 425–435

3. Federici, D., K.Downing: Evolution and development of a multi-cellular organism: Scalability, resilience and neutral complexification. Artificial Life Journal (in press) **12:3** (2006)
4. Federici, D.: A regenerating spiking neural network. Neural Networks **18(5-6)** (2005) 746–754
5. Liu, H., Miller, J., Tyrrel, A.: Intrinsic evolvable hardware implementation of a robust biological development model for digital systems. In: Proc. of the 6th NASA Conference on Evolvable Hardware. (2005) 87–92
6. Miller, J.: Evolving a self-repairing, self-regulating, french flag organism. In Deb, K., al., eds.: Proc. of Genetic and Evolutionary Compuation, GECCO 2004. (2004) 129–139
7. Roggen, D., Federici, D.: Multi-cellular development: is there scalability and robustness to gain? In Yao, X., al., eds.: Proc. of Parallel Problem Solving from Nature 8, PPSN 2004. (2004) 391–400
8. Waddington, C.: Canalization of development and the inheritance of acquired characters. Nature **150** (1942) 563–565
9. Schmalhausen, I.: Factors of Evolution: The Theory of Stabilizing Selection. Univ. of Chicago Press; reprinted in 1986 (1949)
10. Stearns, S.: Progress on canalization. Proc Natl Acad Sci USA (2002) 10229–30
11. Gavrilets, S., Hastings, A.: A quantitative-genetic model for selection on developmental noise. Evolution **48(5)** (1994) 1478–1486
12. Rice, S.H.: The evolution of canalization and the breaking of von baer's laws: Modeling the evolution of development with epistasis. Evolution **52(3)** (1998) 647–656
13. Siegal, M., Bergman, A.: Waddington's canalization revisited: developmental stability and evolution. Proc Natl Acad Sci USA **99(16)** (2002) 10528–32
14. Stanley, K., Miikulainen, R.: A taxonomy for artificial embryogeny. Artificial Life **9(2)** (2003) 93–130
15. Kitano, H.: Designing neural networks using genetic algorithms with graph generation system. Complex Systems **4:4** (1990) 461–476
16. Gruau, F.: Neural Network Synthesis using Cellular Encoding and the Genetic Algorithm. PhD thesis, Ecole Normale Superieure de Lyon (1994)
17. Hornby, G., Pollack, J.: Body-brain co-evolution using L-systems as a generative encoding. In Spector, L., al., eds.: Proc. of the Genetic and Evolutionary Computation Conference, GECCO-2001, Morgan Kaufmann (2001) 868–875
18. Hornby, G., Pollack, J.: The advantages of generative grammatical encodings for physical design. In: Proc. of the 2001 Congress on Evolutionary Computation, CEC 2001, IEEE Press (2001) 600–607
19. Bongard, J.: Evolving modular genetic regulatory networks. In: Proc. of the 2002 Congress on Evolutionary Computation (CEC2002), IEEE Press, Piscataway, NJ, 2002 (2002) 1872–1877
20. Dellaert, F., Beer, R.: Toward an evolvable model of development for autonomous agent synthesis. In R.Brooks, Maes, P., eds.: Proc. of Artificial Life IV, MIT Press Cambridge (1994) 246–257
21. Eggenbergen-Hotz, P.: Evolving morphologies of simulated 3d organisms based on differential gene expression. In Husbands, P., Harvey, I., eds.: Proc. of the 4th European Conference on Artificial Life (ECAL97). (1997) 205–213
22. Miller, J.: Evolving developmental programs for adaptation, morphogenesys, and self-repair. In Banzhaf, W., Ziegler, J., Christaller, T., eds.: Proc. of the European Congress of Artificial Life, ECAL 2003. (2003) 256–265

23. Cangelosi, A., Nolfi, S., Parisi, D.: Cell division and migration in a 'genotype' for neural networks. Network: Computation in Neural Systems **5** (1994) 497–515
24. Bentley, P., Kumar, S.: Three ways to grow designs: A comparison of embryogenies for an evolutionary design problem. In Banzhaf, W., al., eds.: Proc. of GECCO '99. (1999) 35–43
25. Ohno, S.: Evolution by Gene Duplication. Springer (1970)
26. Kindred, B.: Selection for an invariant character, vibrissa number in the house mouse. v. selection on non-tabby segregants from tabby selection lines. Genetics **55(2)** (1966) 365–373
27. Maynard-Smith, J., Sondhi, K.: The genetics of a pattern. Genetics **45(8)** (1960) 1039–1050
28. Nowak, M.: What is a quasi-species? Trends Ecol. Evol. **7** (1992) 118–121
29. van Nimwegen, E., Crutchfield, J.P., Huynen, M.: Neutral evolution of mutational robustness. Proc. Natl. Acad. Sci. USA **96** (1999) 97169720
30. Edlund, J.A., Adami, C.: Evolution of robustness in digital organisms. Artificial Life **10** (2004) 167–179

Evaluation of Fundamental Characteristics of Information Systems Based on Photonic DNA Computing

Yusuke Ogura[1,2], Rui Shogenji[2], Seiji Saito[1], and Jun Tanida[1,2]

[1] Graduate School of Information Science and Technology, Osaka University,
2-1 Yamadaoka, Suita, Osaka 565-0871, Japan
[2] Japan Science and Technology Corporation (JST-CREST)
{ogura, rui, saito, tanida}@ist.osaka-u.ac.jp

Abstract. In this paper, the characteristics of information systems based on photonic DNA computing are evaluated by simply modeling. Fundamental features of photonic DNA computing clarified with calculations of its performance suggest that selecting applications suitable for photonic DNA computing systems is important. We also considered a simple algorithm for solving the maximum clique problem and found that photonic DNA computing is effective to reduce the amount of DNA strands used and processing time compared to the conventional DNA computing.

1 Introduction

Nature makes a lot of suggestions that are helpful for developing new sophisticated methods relating to information technology. For example, DNA computing is a computational paradigm based on effective utilization of the fundamental structure of processing of DNA in living cells. DNA is the carrier of genetic information, and promotes the evolution of living beings. These facts attest that DNA has potential usability as an information carrier, and much research effort on DNA computing is being made[1, 2].

In DNA computing, to use the characteristics of DNA including massive parallelism of reactions, small size, and capability to react autonomously, information is encoded into the base sequences or the structures of DNA molecules and processed with various bio-chemical reactions. DNA is a powerful tool particularly for parallel information processing at nano-scale. However, information processing based on only the nature of DNA requires hard and complicated tasks: for example, the sequence design and accurate reaction control of the DNA.

In contrast, optical computing is a computational technique for parallel information processing that uses inherent properties of light such as fast propagation, spatial parallelism, and a large bandwidth. The applications include optical interconnection, image processing, and photonic network[3]. The embodiment of a valuable optical computing system requires varieties of optical devices, and some remarkable devices have been developed. These devices are useful for controlling

A.J. Ijspeert et al. (Eds.): BioADIT 2006, LNCS 3853, pp. 192–205, 2006.

optical fields. However, the resolution of the light is restricted in micro-scale due to the diffraction limit; The diffraction limit often determines the density and capacity of information that is dealt with in optical systems. Although near-field optics is a possible idea to overcome the diffraction limit, it is difficult to utilize spatial parallelism of light, which is a large advantage for information processing. Further progress of optical computing systems require a new strategy for manipulating information at nano-scale effectively.

We proposed photonic DNA computing, which uses light and DNA cooperatively[4, 5]. From a viewpoint of applications of optical techniques to DNA computing, an efficient processing or a new operation structure can be introduced. This leads relaxation of constraints in design of DNA sequences, improvement of flexibility in computation, and so on. An electronic technology can be combined to DNA computing because an optical technology bridges the both technologies. In addition, from a standpoint of optical computing, the capacity and density of information increase because the information can be manipulated in molecular scale which is considerably smaller than the diffraction limit. Capability of DNA to react autonomously provides a large tolerance in controlling light and reduces requirements for system packaging.

To realize the concept of photonic DNA computing, we have been developing some optical techniques[6, 7]. An important example is the parallel optical manipulation technique using vertical-cavity surface-emitting laser (VCSEL) array sources. This is applicable to translating ensembles of DNA molecules in parallel. We also demonstrated a method for controlling reactions of DNA in local space by irradiating with a laser beam. These techniques are useful in constructing computing systems.

On the other hand, the characteristics of systems based on the photonic DNA computing have not been clarified. To develop high-performance systems, theoretical consideration is important as well as experiment. The purpose of this study is evaluation of the fundamental characteristics of systems based on photonic DNA computing. The achievement of this study is expected to show a valuable guidance for future research on the field. In analyses, we use a simple model because it is considered to be useful to find the essential features.

In section 2 the concept of photonic DNA computing is described. In section 3 the characteristics of photonic DNA computing are evaluated with a general and simple model. In section 4 we introduce an algorithm for solving maximum clique problems. The performances of conventional DNA computing and photonic DNA computing are compared with respect to the number of DNA molecules of solution candidates and processing time. In section 5 we discuss a few fundamental characteristics of photonic DNA computing.

2   Concept of Photonic DNA Computing

The concept of the information system based on photonic DNA computing is shown in Fig. 1. Information is encoded to the sequences or the structures of DNA molecules as well as conventional DNA computing. A major difference of

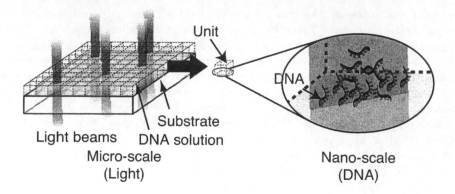

Fig. 1. The concept of photonic DNA computing

photonic DNA computing from the conventional DNA computing is that the volume of a DNA solution is divided to many small units. The units are defined by light spots and the size of the units is comparable to that of the light spot. In the individual units, a lot of DNA molecules react simultaneously, and the reactions in the units are controlled independently. DNA and light are information carrier for computation at nano-scale and micro-scale, respectively. DNA is utilized for autonomous processing, acquiring information in nano-world, controlling nano materials, storing information with high density, and other nano-scale computations. The roles of the light or optical techniques include spatial parallel processing, introducing information from outside, controlling ensembles of information or DNA, communication between units. Information carried with DNA and that with light are interchanged during computation: as a typical example, DNA molecules are manipulated with light and they report their states as fluorescence signals.

3   Evaluation of General Characteristics

A substrate is used in a photonic DNA computing system as shown in Fig. 1. The substrate provides space for DNA reactions, communications between light and DNA, and other operations. We suppose that the volume of a DNA solution on the substrate is divided into $N \times N$ units whose bases are squares with a side length of L.

3.1   Information Density

Let us consider the double helix structure of a double-stranded DNA. The width and the length of one turn, which consists of 10 bases, of the helix are approximately 2 nm and 3.4 nm, respectively. Taking into account that a single base can encode 2-bit data, the information density is estimated to be 2 bit/nm^3. However, with the information density, it is difficult to access and operate data for computing, and the value 2 bit/nm^3 should be considered as local density at the scale smaller than submicrometer.

Another consideration is required for estimating the density of information at micrometer scale or larger. A typical concentration of a DNA solution stored for biological experiments is 100 μM. With this concentration, the density of DNA molecules is 6×10^{-5} nm^{-3}. Figure 2 shows the amount of data in a unit with the volume of $L \times L \times 10$ μm^3 under this condition.

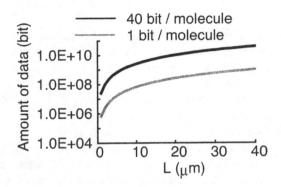

Fig. 2. Dependence of amount of data in each unit on L when the concentration of the DNA solution is 100 μM

The black and gray curves show the amount of data under the assumption that the individual DNA molecules have 40-bit or 1-bit data, respectively. If the data are encoded into the sequences of 20-bases DNA strands, the strands have 40-bit data. In contrast, if the structure of DNA molecules express the data, each of the DNA molecules can be considered to have 1-bit data.

As seen from the figure, more than 1 gigabit data can be dealt with in each unit when $L = 10$ μm and DNA molecules each has 40-bit data. This is equivalent to 1 bit per the volume of a cubic with a side length of 10 nm. In contrast, the spatial resolution of a diffraction-limited optical system using visible light is approximately 1 μm, and the information density of the system is measured as 1 bit/μm^3. This consideration shows that the information density of photonic DNA computing systems can be 10^6 times greater than that of pure-optical systems.

3.2 Processing Time

A basic procedure used in photonic DNA computing is a sequence of distributed processing, data transferring, and global processing, as shown in Fig. 3. The dependence of processing time on the number of units is evaluated by using a simple model of this procedure.

Let us assume that W tasks are necessary for a computation, and the tasks are divided to W_d tasks that are executed by distributed processing and W_g tasks by global processing ($W = W_d + W_g$). In distributed processing, the same number of tasks, namely W_d/N^2 tasks, are executed in the individual units.

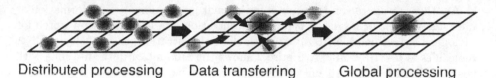

Distributed processing   Data transferring   Global processing

Fig. 3. A basic procedure of photonic DNA computing

Distributed processing is implemented by controlling reactions of DNA in the units independently and in parallel. In contrast, global processing is accomplished with the reaction of the entire solution. We suppose that all reactions take the same amount of time: T_{react}.

Data transfer is required for collecting DNA into a unit for global processing. The procedure for data transfer consists of a pre-process, translation, and a post-process. The amount of time of pre- and post-processes can be expressed as kT_{react}; when DNA reactions are used in these processes, k is integer, and in other cases, k can be decimal number. If the DNA located in a corner's unit is translated to the center unit, the amount of time taken for translation is represented by NT_{trans}, where T_{trans} is amount of time required for translating to an adjacent unit.

The amount of time, T, required for the procedure in Fig. 3 is obtained as

$$T = \frac{W_d T_{\text{react}}}{N^2} + W_g T_{\text{react}} + (NT_{\text{trans}} + kT_{\text{react}}).\tag{1}$$

Introducing parameters α $(0 < \alpha < 1)$ and β $(\beta > 0)$ by defining $W_d : W_g = \alpha : (1 - \alpha)$ and $T_{\text{react}} : T_{\text{trans}} = 1 : \beta$, Eq. (1) is rewritten as

$$T = WT_{\text{react}}\left\{1 - \alpha\left(1 - \frac{1}{N^2}\right) + \frac{\beta N + k}{W}\right\}.\tag{2}$$

Here we estimate k, T_{trans}, T_{react}, and β. We have developed an optical manipulation method with VCSEL array sources to transfer data DNA. Arbitrary spot array patterns are generated by modulating the individual VCSELs on the array, and flexible manipulation of multiple objects is achieved. Direct manipulation of DNA with the optical manipulation technique is difficult because of the scale gap of light and DNA, so that we fabricate DNA clusters. A DNA cluster is an ensemble of DNA molecules attached to a bead by chemical bond. With the DNA clusters, we can deal with a lot of DNA molecules simultaneously.

Our method for data transfer consists of three steps: (i) fabricating DNA clusters, (ii) translating DNA clusters, and (iii) detaching DNA from DNA clusters. DNA reactions are used for fabricating DNA clusters and detaching DNA, and we can obtain $k = 2$. The maximum translation velocity currently obtained by using VCSEL array optical manipulation is approximately 1 μm/sec. With this velocity, $T_{\text{trans}} = 10$ seconds when $L = 10$ μm. On the other hand, DNA reactions often takes hundreds seconds, thousands seconds, or more time, and in this paper we estimate T_{react} as 100 or 1000 seconds; then $\beta = 0.1$ or 0.01.

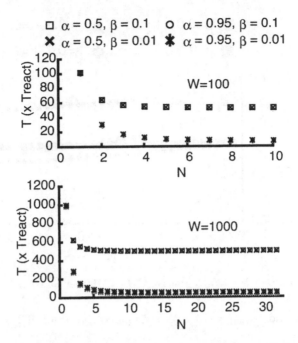

Fig. 4. Relationship between the number of unit N and processing time T. (a) W = 100, (b) W = 1000.

Figure 4 shows plots of T on N when (a) $W = 100$ or (b) $W = 1000$. At $N = (2\alpha W/\beta)^{1/3}$, T takes the minimum value. It can be seen that T strongly depends on N when using small N. In particular, by using distributed processing, processing time can be reduced comparing to the conventional DNA computing ($N = 1$). However, we must emphasize that increase of the number of units causes increase of processing time when data transfer takes much time.

3.3 Data Transfer Rate

In photonic DNA computing, ensembles of DNA molecules are processed and stored in the individual units. This denotes that accessing particular DNA molecules requires to know the position of DNA or the unit in which the target DNA exists. From this point of view, the DNA molecules are considered to have positional addresses to identify them. The positional addresses can be changed by transferring data DNA between units.

The rate, R_{trans}, of data transfer described in section 3.2 is expressed as follows:

$$R_{\text{trans}} = \frac{N_{\text{trans}}}{N T_{\text{trans}} + k T_{\text{react}}} = \frac{N_{\text{trans}}}{(\beta N + k) T_{\text{react}}}, \tag{3}$$

where N_{trans} is the amount of data to be transferred simultaneously. As a reference, Fig. 5 illustrates dependence of R_{trans} on N under the assumption

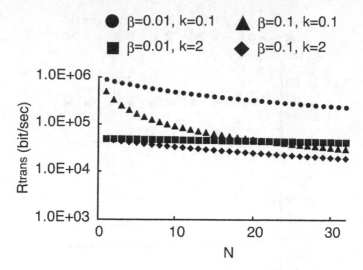

Fig. 5. Dependence of R_{trans} on N. $T_{\text{react}} = 100$ sec and $N_{\text{trans}} = 10^7$

$T_{\text{react}} = 100$ sec and $N_{\text{trans}} = 10^7$. As mentioned in section 3.2, β is estimated to be 0.1 or 0.01.

To meet the demand that the amount of time for translating DNA clusters are much smaller than that for fabricating DNA clusters and detaching DNA, the following requirement must be satisfied:

$$T_{\text{trans}} \ll \frac{k}{N} T_{\text{react}}. \tag{4}$$

For example, we take $k = 2$, $N = 10$, and $T_{\text{react}} = 100$ sec, then $T_{\text{trans}} < 20$ sec. Assuming $T_{\text{trans}} = 2$ sec to achieve this requirement, the velocity faster than 5 μm/sec is necessary when $L = 10$ μm. As mentioned in section 3.2 the present translation velocity of VCSEL array optical manipulation is 1 μm/sec, which fails to meet the above requirement. However, high-power VCSEL arrays are now available, and translation velocity of 5 μm/sec will be achievable by designing special optical systems with high light efficiency.

4   Performance for Solving the Maximum Clique Problem

In this section, we estimate the number of DNA molecules of solution candidates and processing time for solving the maximum clique problem using an algorithm to which photonic DNA computing is applicable. The maximum clique problem is a problem to calculate the largest number of vertices of cliques (complete graphs) among the subgraphs of a given graph $G(V, E)$.

4.1   Algorithm

Ouyang *et al.* proposed a method for solving the maximum clique problem based on DNA computing[8]. Their procedure is as follows:

1. DNA strands that encode each of the vertices are synthesized.
2. DNA strands encoding all subsets of the set of the vertices of the given graph are generated by a method called parallel overlap assembly.
3. DNA strands containing two vertices between which no edge exists are cut by enzyme reactions.
4. The DNA solution is analyzed by electrophoresis. The DNA strand which has the maximum number of vertices is the solution of the given problem.

We modify the algorithm to solve the problem with the procedure shown in Fig. 3. The scheme of the algorithm is illustrated in Fig. 6. This algorithm consists of two steps: obtaining all cliques of each of D subgraphs (distributed processing) and obtaining cliques of the given graph by using the result of the previous step (global processing).

Step. 1

The set, $V(G)$, of vertices of the given graph $G(V, E)$ is divided into D subsets $V(G_i)(i = 1, 2, \ldots D)$ (Fig. 6(a)). The set of edges which link two vertices contained by $V(G_i)$ is referred to as $E(G_i)$, and it is considered as the set of edges of the subgraph G_i (Fig. 6(b)). DNA strands are generated for all subgraphs of $V(G_i)$ as solution candidates. The solution candidates that contain two vertices between which no edge exists are removed. As a result, the solution contains only the DNA strands that encode the sets of vertices $\{V_j(G_i)|j = 1, 2, \ldots, N_{\mathrm{clq}\_i}\}$ of the cliques (Fig. 6(c)). Here N_{clq_i} is the number of cliques contained in G_i.

Step. 2

One element is selected from $V_j(G_i)$ or ϕ (empty set) for individual i (Fig. 6(d)), and the sets of the selected elements are considered as solution candidates in this step (Fig. 6(e)). As same as Step. 1, the solution candidates that contain two vertices between which no edge exists are removed, then the sets of vertices making cliques remain. The largest set of vertices in the remained solution is the maximum clique (Fig. 6(f)).

4.2   Number of Solution Candidates

In Step. 1, the given graph is divided to D subgraphs that contain n/D vertices, where n is the number of the vertices of the given graph, then the necessary number of DNA strands of solution candidates, $N_{\mathrm{cand}}^{(1)}$, is obtained by

$$N_{\mathrm{cand}}^{(1)} = \left(2^{\frac{n}{D}} - 1\right) \times D. \tag{5}$$

This number does not depend on the given graph. In Step. 2, the necessary number of solution candidates, $N_{\mathrm{cand}}^{(2)}$, is expressed by

$$N_{\mathrm{cand}}^{(2)} = \prod_{i=1}^{D}(N_{\mathrm{clq}\_i} + 1) - 1. \tag{6}$$

This number depends on the given graph. The necessary number of solution candidates for the algorithm is larger number between $N_{\text{cand}}^{(1)}$ and $N_{\text{cand}}^{(2)}$.

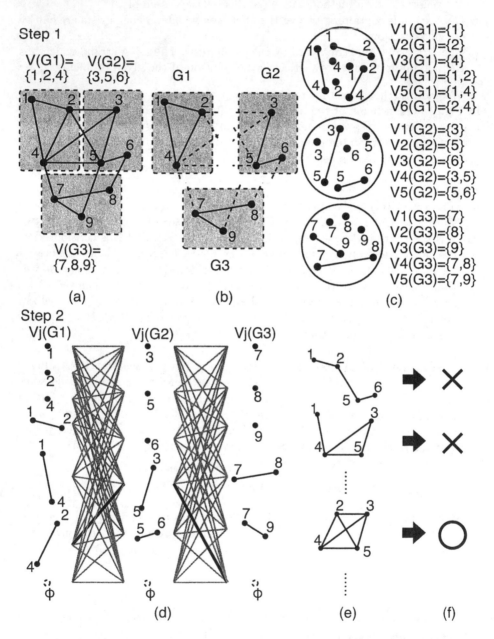

Fig. 6. The algorithm for solving the maximum clique problem. This figure shows an example of a graph consisting of 9 vertices and 14 edges. (a) The given graph is divided, (b) subgraphs G_i, (c) cliques of the individual subgraphs, (d) generation of solution candidates, (e) solution candidates in Step. 2, (f) final solution.

We assume that the edges are distributed uniformly in the given graph $G(V, E)$, then the number, $N_{E(G_i)}$, of the edges of subgraph G_i is estimated as

$$N_{E(G_i)} = \frac{C(\frac{n}{D}, 2)}{C(n, 2)} N_{E(G)}, \tag{7}$$

where $C(u, v)$ is the combination of v elements from a group of u.

Let $N_{clq\_i}^{(\gamma)}$ be the expected number of cliques consisting of γ vertices. When $\gamma = 1, 2$, we obtain $N_{clq\_i}^{(1)} = N_{V(G_i)}$ and $N_{clq\_i}^{(2)} = N_{E(G_i)}$, where $N_{V(G_i)}$ is the number of vertices of G_i. For γ is equal to or more than 3, the following expression can be obtained:

$$N_{clq\_i}^{(\gamma)} = C(N_{V(G_i)}, \gamma) \times \frac{C(C(N_{E(G_i)}, 2) - C(\gamma, 2), N_{E(G_i)} - C(\gamma, 2))}{C(C(N_{V(G_i)}, 2), N_{E(G_i)})}, \tag{8}$$

$$= \frac{N_{V(G_i)} N_{E(G_i)} \left(\frac{n(n-1)}{2} - \frac{\gamma(\gamma-1)}{2} \right)}{\gamma(N_{V(G_i)} - \gamma) \left(\frac{N_{V(G_i)}(N_{V(G_i)}-1)}{2} \right) \left(N_{E(G_i)} - \frac{\gamma(\gamma-1)}{2} \right)}. \tag{9}$$

Because $N_{V(G_i)}$ and $N_{E(G_i)}$ are constant over all i, $N_{clq\_i}^{(\gamma)}$ is also constant and expressed as $N_{clq}^{(\gamma)}$, then Eq. (6) is rewritten as

$$N_{cand}^{(2)} = \left(\sum_{\{\gamma | C(\gamma, 2) \leq N_{E(G_i)}\}} N_{clq}^{(\gamma)} + 1 \right)^D - 1. \tag{10}$$

When $D = 1$, the number of solution candidates is $2^n - 1$: this does not depend on the given graph.

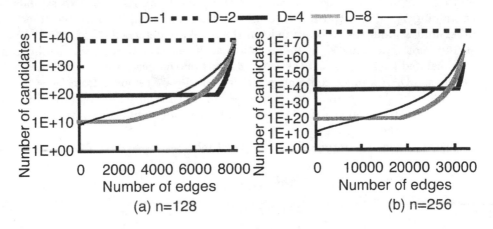

Fig. 7. Dependence of the number of DNA strands of solution candidates on the number of edges. Upper: $n=128$; lower: $n=256$.

Dependence of the number of solution candidates on the number of edges is shown in Fig. 7. The number of vertices is 128 or 256.

We can find that the required number of solution candidates drastically decreases by using distributed processing compared to the conventional DNA computing ($D - 1$). This result shows that distributed processing based on photonic DNA computing is useful to decrease the amount of DNA used. In particular, a significant effect is obtained when the number of edges of the given graph is small because the number of cliques contained in the graph decreases. Comparison of the number on D indicates that increasing D is effective especially for small number of edges. The reason is that the number of solution candidates generated in Step. 1 decreases exponentially with D.

In this calculation, we assume that the edges of the given graph are distributed uniformly. Although the number of solution candidates generated in Step. 2 depends on the distribution of the edges, the result can provide a criterion for determining division number D.

4.3   Processing Time

Generation of DNA strands of solution candidates and removal of DNA of inappropriate candidates (DNA strands that do not encode a clique) are required in each of Steps 1 and 2. DNA strands of solution candidates are generated by repeating reactions of annealing, extension, and denaturing. The amount of the time necessary for generating DNA strands are obtained as $3nT_{react}/2D$ in Step. 1 and $(3\log_2 D)T_{react}$ in Step. 2.

For removing inappropriate candidates, Ouyang et al. use restriction enzyme reactions. However, we consider that this is difficult to apply for scaled-up systems because of limitation of available restriction enzymes and DNA sequences. Here we suppose that the inadequate candidates are removed by using beads. For example, let us consider to remove candidates containing both vertices V_1 and V_2 from unit U_1; namely no edge to link V_1 and V_2 exists. The DNA strands containing V_1 in U_1 are attached to a bead, then this bead is translated to another unit U_2 and the DNA strands on the bead are detached. Next, the DNA strands not containing V_2 in U_2 are attached to another bead, then this bead is translated back to U_1 and the DNA strands on the bead are detached. As a result, the DNA strands containing both V_1 and V_2 are removed from U_1.

Let T_{rm} be the amount of the time necessary for the above removal procedure. The removal procedure should be repeated for the individual edges that are not contained in the given graph.

The total amount of time, T, is expressed by

$$T = \frac{3n}{2D}T_{react} + (3\log_2 D)T_{react}$$
$$+ \left[C(\tfrac{n}{D}, 2) - \min\{N_{E(G_i)}|i = 1, 2, \ldots D\} \right] T_{rm}$$
$$+ \left[C(D, 2) \left(\frac{n}{D} \right)^2 - \left(N_{E(G)} - \sum_i N_{E(G_i)} \right) \right] T_{rm}. \tag{11}$$

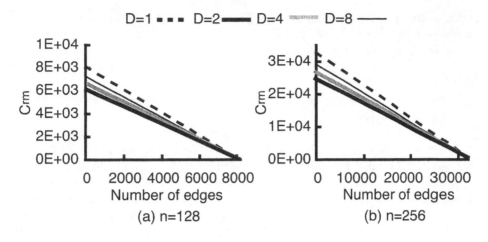

Fig. 8. Dependence of C_{rm} on the number of edges. Upper: $n=128$; lower: $n=256$.

From Eq. (7), the above expression is rewritten as

$$T = 3\left\{\frac{n}{2D} + \log_2 D\right\} T_{\text{react}}$$
$$+ \left[C(\tfrac{n}{D}, 2)\left\{1 - \frac{N_{E(G)}}{C(n,2)}\right\} + C(D,2)\left(\frac{n}{D}\right)^2 - N_{E(G)}\frac{n - \frac{n}{D}}{n-1}\right] T_{\text{rm}}. \quad (12)$$

When $D = 1$, T is represented as follows:

$$T = \frac{3n}{2} T_{\text{react}} + (C(n,2) - N_{E(G)}) T_{\text{rm}}. \quad (13)$$

In Eqs. (12) and (13), the term of T_{react} is much smaller than the term of T_{rm}, and therefore coefficient of T_{rm} was evaluated. The coefficient is expressed as C_{rm}. Dependence of C_{rm} on the number of the edges is shown in Fig. 8. The number of vertices is 128 or 256.

As seen from the figure, C_{rm}, namely processing time, decreases with increasing the number of edges. This is because the number of operations to remove inappropriate candidates decreases. Furthermore, the result shows the effectiveness of distributed processing based on photonic DNA computing. Using this algorithm, processing time is the shortest when $D = 2$. This can be explained as follows: when using larger D, more operations are necessary for Step. 2 although processing time in Step. 1 is reduced. We can find that the ratio of processing time of Steps 1 and 2 is important for efficient computation.

Giving an estimation of T_{rm} for a real system is difficult because the removal procedure includes a complicated combination of DNA reactions and optical operations. However, we expect that T_{rm} is probably between $10^3 - 10^4$ seconds. In this case, from the result of Fig. 8, we can estimate the processing time to be $10^6 - 10^7$ seconds for solving the problem.

Although the algorithm considered here consists of two steps, it is possible to increase the number of steps. By increasing the number of steps, processing

204 Y. Ogura et al.

time is surely reduced because distributed processing is effectively utilized by increasing the size of subgraphs gradually in the algorithm. For applying photonic DNA computing to real problems, the optimal division number should be assessed by considering processing time, the number of solution candidates, and other conditions.

5 Discussion

In photonic DNA computing, multiple units work cooperatively and execute processing of a large amount of data. Referring to Fig. 2, one can estimate the approximate amount of data that can be dealt with in each unit. The individual units contain data of more than 1 megabit when the size of units is defined by a light spot, namely $L > 1$ μm. In addition, the data are encoded into DNA molecules, which interact with each other in a unit. From this consideration, the unit is regarded as a micro-scale processing element capable of manipulating data of more than 1 megabit in parallel.

As seen from Fig. 4, it is possible to reduce processing time drastically by suitable assignment of tasks to the units. A notable point is that the processing time has the minimum value for N owing to the necessity of the operation of data transfer. This result shows that the value of N should be selected adequately for real systems. In addition, the distribution of tasks to the units should be determined with care because necessary time for data transfer between any two units depends on the distance between them.

In section 4 the performance was evaluated using a specific algorithm. The results demonstrate that, comparing to conventional DNA computing, photonic DNA computing has capability of conserving resources and increasing the efficiency of processing. This feature can also be obtained when photonic DNA computing is used in many other applications. On the other hand, the estimated processing time, which was mentioned in the second last paragraph of section 4, suggests that photonic DNA computing is not very suitable for solving simple mathematical problems as most of researchers on DNA computing consider. Note that the algorithm for the maximum clique problem is used for a benchmark analysis in this paper. The systems based on photonic DNA computing can interact with macro-world using light and with nano-world using DNA. The applications of photonic DNA computing should be selected by considering such features that mentioned above.

6 Conclusions

The characteristics of photonic DNA computing are evaluated by simply modeling to clarify the essential features of it. Relationships between performance and the number of units are shown; the results suggest that selecting applications is important to get better performance of the photonic DNA computing. We considered a simple algorithm for solving the maximum clique problem, and demonstrated the effectiveness of distributed processing based on photonic DNA computing in reduction of DNA strands used and processing time. This study is expected to be the basis for applying the photonic DNA computing to various applications.

Acknowledgments

This work was supported by JST CREST and the Ministry of Education, Science, Sports, and Culture, Grant-in-Aid for Scientific Research (A), 15200023, 2003-2005.

References

1. C. Ferretti, G. Mauri, and C. Zandron (eds.), *Lecture Notes in Computer Science* **3384**, Springer-Verlag Berlin Heidelberg (2005).
2. A. Carbone, M. Daley, L. Kari, I. McQuillan, N. Pierce (eds.), *Pre-Proceedings of the 11th international meeting on DNA computing*, London, Ontario (2005).
3. J. Tanida and Y. Ichioka, "Optical computing," The Optics Encyclopedia **3**, Wiley-VCH, Berlin, pp. 1883–1902 (2003).
4. Y. Ogura, T. Kawakami, F. Sumiyama, A. Suyama, and J. Tanida, "Parallel translation of DNA clusters by VCSEL array trapping and temperature control with laser illumination," *Lecture Notes in Computer Science* **2943**, pp. 10–18 (2004).
5. Y. Ogura, F. Sumiyama, T. Kawakami, and J. Tanida, "Manipulation of DNA molecules using optical techniques for optically assisted DNA computing," *Proc. SPIE* **5515**, pp. 100–108 (2004).
6. Y. Ogura, T. Kawakami, F. Sumiyama, S. Irie, A. Suyama, and J. Tanida, "Methods for manipulating DNA molecules in a micrometer scale using optical techniques," *Lecture Notes in Computer Science* **3384**, pp. 258–267 (2005).
7. Y. Ogura, T. Beppu, M. Takinoue, A. Suyama, and J. Tanida, "Control of DNA molecules on a microscopic bead using optical techniques for photonic DNA memory," *Pre-Proceedings of the 11th international meeting on DNA computing*, pp. 78–88 (2005).
8. Q. Ouyang, P. D. Kaplan, S. Liu, and A. Libchaber, "DNA solution of the maximal clique problem," Science **278**, pp. 446–449 (1997).

Hybrid Concentration-Controlled Direct-Proportional Length-Based DNA Computing for Numerical Optimization of the Shortest Path Problem

Zuwairie Ibrahim[1,2], Yusei Tsuboi[2], Osamu Ono[2], and Marzuki Khalid[3]

[1] Department of Mechatronics and Robotics, Faculty of Electrical Engineering,
Universiti Teknologi Malaysia, 81310 UTM Skudai, Johor Darul Takzim, Malaysia
zuwairie@fke.utm.my
[2] Institute of Applied DNA Computing (IADC), Meiji University,
1-1-1 Higashi-mita, Tama-ku, Kawasaki-shi, Kanagawa-ken 214-8571, Japan
{zuwairie, tsuboi, ono}@isc.meiji.ac.jp
http://www.isc.meiji.ac.jp/~i3erabc/IADC.html
[3] Center for Artificial Intelligence and Robotics (CAIRO), Universiti Teknologi Malaysia,
City Campus, Jalan Semarak, Kuala Lumpur, Malaysia
marzuki@utmkl.utm.my

Abstract. DNA computing often makes use of hybridization, whether for vastly generating the initial candidate answers or amplification by using polymerase chain reaction (PCR). The main idea behind DNA computing approaches for solving weighted graph problems is that if the degree of hybridization can be controlled, then it is able to generate more double stranded DNAs (dsDNAs), which represent the answer of the problem during *in vitro* computation. Previously, length, concentration, and melting temperature, have been exploited for encoding of weights of a weighted graph problem. In this paper, we present a hybrid approach, which is called concentration-controlled direct-proportional length-based DNA computing (CCDPLB-DNAC), that combines two characteristics: length and concentration, for encoding and at the same time, effectively control the degree of hybridization of DNA. The encoding by length is realized whereby the cost of each path is encoded by the length of the oligonucleotides (oligos) in a proportional way. On the other hand, the hybridization control by concentration is done by varying the amount of oligos, as the input of computation, before the computation begins. The advantage is such that, after an initial pool generation and amplification, polyacrylamide gel electrophoresis (PAGE) can be performed to separate the survived dsDNAs according to their length, which directly decodes the results. The proposed approach shows significant improvement in term of materials used and scalability. The experimental results show the effectiveness of the proposed CCDPLB-DNAC for solving weighted graph problems, such as the shortest path problem.

1 Introduction

A new computing paradigm based on DNA molecules has appeared in 1994 when Leonard M. Adleman [1] launched a novel *in vitro* approach to solve the so-called

A.J. Ijspeert et al. (Eds.): BioADIT 2006, LNCS 3853, pp. 206–221, 2006.

Hamiltonian Path Problem (HPP) with seven vertices by DNA molecules. Based on Adleman's evolutionary approach, input is encoded by random DNA sequences. Computation is a series of bio-molecular reactions, which involves hybridization, denaturation, ligation, magnetic bead separation, and polymerase chain reaction (PCR). The output of the computation, also in the form of DNA molecules can be read out and visualized by electrophoretical fluorescence operation.

Four years later, in 1998, a length-based DNA computing which is called constant-proportional length-based DNA computing (CPLB-DNAC) for Traveling Salesman Problem (TSP) is proposed by Narayanan and Zorbalas [2]. A constant increase of length of DNA strands is used to encode the actual length of the distances. A draw-back of this method is that, there is a possibility of an occurrence of concatenated DNA strands of two distances which could be longer than the DNA strand of the longest distance that has been encoded. This may lead to errors in computing the shortest path [3]. This scheme, however, has not been realized by any laboratory experiment.

In order to solve the shortcoming of CPLB-DNAC, an alternative approach called direct-proportional length-based DNA computing (DPLB-DNAC) is proposed by Ibrahim *et al.* [4] for solving the shortest path problem. In this approach, the cost of an edge is encoded as a direct-proportional length DNA. After an initial pool generation, numerous solution candidates can be generated. By using PCR, it is possible to amplify the optimal combination which represents the solution to the shortest path problem. The output of the computation can be visualized by applying PAGE, where the DNA duplex representing the solution appears as the shortest band of PAGE.

On the other hand, Yamamoto *et al.* [5] presented concentration-controlled DNA computing (CC-DNAC) for accomplishing a local search for the shortest path problem. Although DNA computing with concentration control method enables local search among all the candidate solutions, it cannot guarantee that the most intensive band is the DNA representing the shortest path in the given graph. In addition, it is technically difficult to extract a single optimal solution from the most intensive band [3]. This difficulty, however, has been solved using denaturating gradient gel electrophoresis (DGGE) and constant denaturant gel electrophoresis (CDGE) [5].

Lee *et al.* [6] proposed a DNA computing approach called temperature gradientbased DNA computing (TG-DNAC) for solving TSP. Denaturation temperature gradient polymerase chain reaction (DTG-PCR) has been introduced where DNA duplex of correct solutions will be denatured and amplified by the PCR operation. As the denaturation temperature increases, other DNA strands will be also subsequently amplified. However, the amount of correct solutions will also be exponentially increased, which does affect the final solution.

In this paper, we propose a combination of both schemes of CC-DNAC and DPLB-DNAC to born a hybrid approach, which is called as concentration-controlled direct-proportional length-based DNA computing (CCDPLB-DNAC). The protocol of CCDPLB-DNAC, in fact, is similar as DPLB-DNAC. But the difference is that the amount of poured DNA representing the edges varies closely to the weight of edges. As a result, the concentration of input during initial pool generation will be different as well, and does influence the degree of hybridization. It is found that the proposed approach offers significant improvements in term of material usage and scalability than that of DPLB-DNAC without concentration-controlled.

In designing and developing the proposed CCDPLB-DNAC, the scopes of the research have been defined. Firstly, the shortest path problem is chosen as a benchmark for this research because the shortest path problem is a kind of problem that involves numerical optimization, even though this problem is not an NP-complete problem. Secondly, a small directed weighted graph, $G = (V, E, \omega)$, which consists of a set of vertices $V = \{ v_1, v_2, v_3, v_4, v_5 \}$, a set of edges $E = \{ [v_1, v_2], [v_1, v_3], [v_3, v_4], [v_4, v_5], [v_2, v_5], [v_2, v_3], [v_2, v_4] \}$, and weight, ω, which is assigned to each edges, will be constructed and used an the input of computation as shown in Figure 1. It is clear that the number vertices $|V|$ and the number of edges $|E|$ are 5 and 7, respectively. Even though this graph is small enough for computation but it is big enough if the computation is to be realized by unconventional DNA computing approach, and thus, is a good example in order to show the feasibility of the proposed direct-proportional length-based DNA computing.

2 A Note on Concentration-Controlled Method

Yamamoto *et al.* carried out CC-DNAC for accomplishing a local search for the shortest path problem [7] by avoiding the generation of hopeless solutions. In this research, the vertices and edges are encoded into DNA sequences. During the encoding process, the vertex sequence is synthesized with the same concentration. The relatively different concentration, D_{ij} of the oligonucleotides encoding an edge $i \rightarrow j$ at cost C_{ij} is calculated by using the following formula:

$$D_{ij} = \left(\frac{Min}{C_{ij}} \right)^{\alpha} \tag{1}$$

where *Min* represent the minimum value among the costs of all edges in the graph, and α is set to 2. After all oligonucleotides for nodes with the same concentration, oligonucleotides for edges with different concentration, and complement oligonucleotides are synthesized, an initial pool generation is done in a test tube. During the initial pool generation, the rate of biochemical reactions depends heavily on the reaction rate constants and reactant concentrations. Thus, as the concentration of DNA strands increase, the paths including them can be generated more frequently and the hopeful DNA paths can be generated with high concentration.

Even though the shortest path problem is belonging to the class P, i.e., it is not hard to solve this problem, it is worth to be solved by DNA computing because numerical evaluations are required during the computation [5]. The input to the shortest path problem is a weighted directed graph $G = (V, E, \omega)$, a start node u and an end node v. The output of the shortest path problem is a (u,v) path with the smallest cost. In the case given in Figure 1, if u is V_1 and v is V_5, the cost for the shortest path will be 100 and the optimal path is clearly shown as $V_1 - V_3 - V_4 - V_5$. If the input graph is shown Figure 1 (a), by using equation (1), all the numerical weights are transformed into relative concentrations as shown in Figure 1 (b).

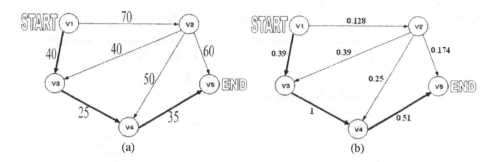

Fig. 1. (a) Example showing a weighted directed graph $G = (V, E)$ with the shortest path shown as V_1 - V_3 - V_4 - V_5 (b) Relative concentration as calculated using equation 1

3 DNA Sequence Design and Synthesis

Let n be the total number of nodes in the graph. The DNA sequences correspond to all nodes and its complements are designed. Let V_i ($i= 1, 2, \ldots , n$) and $\overline{V_i}$ ($i= 1, 2, \ldots , n$) be the 20-mer DNA sequences correspond to the ith node in the graph and its complement respectively. By using the available software for DNA sequence design, DNASequenceGenerator [8], the DNA sequences V_i is designed and listed in Table 1. Melting temperature, T_m is calculated based on Sugimoto nearest neighbor thermodynamic parameter [9]. The GC contents (GC%) and melting temperature (T_m) of each sequence are also shown. Table 2, on the other hand, shows the complement of the node sequences.

We introduce three rules to encode each edge in the graph as follows:

(i)   If there is a connection between V_1 to V_j, where $j \neq n$, design the oligonucleotide (oligo) for that edge as
$$V_1 (20) + W_{1j} (\omega - 30) + V_j (20)$$

(ii) If there is a connection between V_i to V_j, where $i \neq 1, j \neq n$, design the oligo for that edge as
$$V_i (20) + W_{ij} (\omega - 20) + V_j (20)$$

(iii) If there is a connection between V_i to V_n, where $i \neq 1$, design the oligo for that edge as
$$V_i (20) + W_{in} (\omega - 30) + V_n (20)$$

where V, W, and '+' denote the DNA sequences for nodes, DNA sequences for weight, and 'join' respectively. The designed oligos consist of three segments; two node segments and an edge segment. 'ω' denotes the weight value for corresponding DNA sequences for weight W_{ij}, where W_{ij} denotes the DNA sequences representing a cost between node V_i and V_j. The value in parenthesis indicates the number of DNA bases or nucleotides for each segment. Table 3 lists all the oligos based on the proposed rules, where the node segments and edge segments are distinguished by capital and small letters respectively. Again, DNASequenceGenerator [8] is employed. At the end of this stage, the oligos of the complement of nodes and edges are synthesized.

Table 1. DNA sequences for nodes

Node, V_i	20-mer Sequences (5'-3')	GC%	Melting Temperature, T_m (°C)
V_1	AAAGCTCGTCGTTTAGGAGC	50	60.9
V_2	GCACTAGGGATTTGGAGGTT	50	60.3
V_3	GCTATGCCGTAGTAGAGCGA	55	60.5
V_4	CGATACCGAACTGATAAGCG	50	60.6
V_5	CGTGGGTGGCTCTGTAATAG	55	60.5

Table 2. Complement of node

Complement Node, $\overline{V}_i$	20-mer Complement Sequences (3'-5')
$\overline{V}_1$	TTTCGAGCAGCAAATCCTCG
$\overline{V}_2$	CGTGATCCCTAAACCTCCAA
$\overline{V}_3$	CGATACGGCATCATCTCGCT
$\overline{V}_4$	GCTATGGCTTGACTATTCGC
$\overline{V}_5$	GCACCCACCGAGACATTATC

Table 3. DNA sequences for edges

Edge	DNA Sequences
$V_4-W_{45}-V_5$	5'-CGATACCGAACTGATAAGCG ccaagCGTGGGTGGCTCTGTAATAG-3'
$V_3-W_{34}-V_4$	5'-GCTATGCCGTAGTAGAGCGA ccgtcCGATACCGAACTGATAAGCG-3'
$V_1-W_{13}-V_3$	5'-AAAGCTCGTCGTTTAGGAGCacgtcggttc GCTATGCCGTAGTAGAGCGA-3'
$V_2-W_{23}-V_3$	5'-GCACTAGGGATTTGGAGGTT ccgtcttttacccaagtaatGCTATGCCGTAGTAGAGCGA-3'
$V_2-W_{24}-V_4$	5'-GCACTAGGGATTTGGAGGTT acgtgttttaaggaagtacggtaagctgcg CGATACCGAACTGATAAGCG-3'
$V_2-W_{25}-V_5$	5'-GCACTAGGGATTTGGAGGTT gcgtcgcgtaaggcagtaccggactctgcc CGTGGGTGGCTCTGTAATAG-3'
$V_1-W_{12}-V_2$	5'-AAAGCTCGTCGTTTAGGAGC cggtggtttaacgaagtcctgtactatgggttatttgcag GCACTAGGGATTTGGAGGTT-3'

4 Concentration-Controlled Direct-Proportional Length-Based DNA Computing for the Shortest Path Problem

Currently, there are two kinds of initial pool generation methods for solving weighted graph problem: hybridization/ligation and parallel overlap assembly (POA). The hybridization/ligation method has been firstly introduced by Adleman [1] to solve HPP. For hybridization/ligation method, during the operation, the link oligos hybridize through the hydrogen bonds by enzymatic reaction. The hybridization/ligation reaction is well shown in Figure 2 [10].

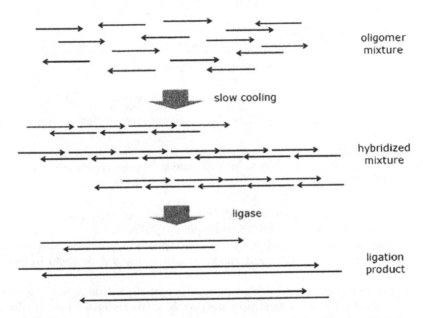

Fig. 2. Hybridization/ligation method for initial pool generation. The arrowhead indicates the 3' end.

POA has been used [11] and broadly applied in gene construction [12-14], gene reconstruction [15], and DNA shuffling [16]. POA involves thermal cycle and during the thermal cycle, the position strings in one oligo anneals to the complementary strings of the next oligo. The 3' end side of the oligo is extended in the presence of polymerase enzyme to form a longer dsDNA. One cycle of parallel overlap assembly is depicted in Figure 3 [10]. After a number of thermal cycles, a data pool with all combinations could be built.

Lee *et al.* [10] did a comparison between hybridization/ligation method and POA for initial pool generation of DNA computing. They came out with a conclusion that for the initial pool generation of weighted graph problems, POA method is more efficient than that of hybridization/ligation method. According to [10], the advantages of POA over hybridization/ligation method for initial pool generation are as follows:

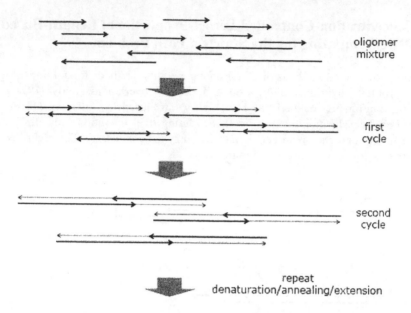

Fig. 3. Parallel overlap assembly for initial pool generation. The thick arrows represent the synthesized oligos which are the input to the computation. The thin arrows represent the elongated part during polymerization. The arrowhead indicates the 3' end.

(i)   The initial pool size generated from the same amount of initial oligos is about twice larger than that of hybridization/ligation method. Though, if a larger problem is considered, the initial pool size is too small to contain the complete pool. POA, however, with more cycle and large experimental scale could include the practical pools.

(ii) Initially, two single-stranded DNA molecules partially hybridize in the annealing step and then they are extended by polymerase. The elongated DNA molecules are denatured to two single-stranded DNA in the next denaturation step, and they are subjected to the annealing reaction at the next cycle. Therefore, POA does maintain the population size and the population size can be decided by varying the initial number of oligos.

(iii) In hybridization/ligation method, the population size decreases as reaction progress. The population size decreased by a factor of the number of components composing it in hybridization/ligation method. As the problem size increases, the required initial pool size increases dramatically. Moreover, initial pool generation by POA requires fewer strands than hybridization/ligation method to obtain similar amount of initial pool DNA molecules because complementary strands are automatically extended by polymerase.

(iv) POA does not require phosphorylation of oligos which is prerequisite for the ligation of oligos.

(v)   POA demands less time than hybridization/ligation method. Hybridization requires one and half hour while ligation required more than 12 hours. Hence, POA for 34 cycles requires only two hours. Therefore, POA is much more efficient and economic method for initial pool generation.

As stated in [3], *"In addition, the fact that larger weights are encoded as longer sequences is contrary to the biological fact that; the longer the sequences are, the more likely they hybridize with other DNA strands, though we have to find the shortest DNA strands"*. From the biological point of view, this argument is definitely true. In order to overcome the limitation of general length-based DNA computing, the authors discovered that by utilizing POA for initial pool generation, a phase where numerous combinations of random routes of the graph are generated in the solution, a shortcoming, which is the biological influence contributed by the length of the oligos could be eliminated.

In order to generate the initial pool of the direct-proportional length-based DNA computing for the example problem by using POA method, the input to the computation are all the synthesized oligos as listed in Table 3 and the complement sequences for each nodes, which are listed in Table 2. These inputs are poured into a test tube and the cycles begin. In fact, the operation of POA is similar as polymerase chain reaction (PCR) but the difference is that POA operates without the use of primers. As PCR, one cycle consists of three steps: denaturation, hybridization, and extension.

At this stage, an initial pool of solution has been produced and it is time to filter out the optimal combinations among the vast alternative combinations of the problem. Unlike conventional filtering, this process is not merely throwing away the unwanted DNA duplex but rather copying the target dsDNA exponentially by using the incredibly sensitive PCR process. This can be done by amplifying the DNA duplex that contain the start node V_1 and end node V_5 using primers. After the PCR operation is accomplished, there should be numerous number of DNA strands representing the start node V_1 and end node V_5 traveling through a possible number of nodes. The output solution of the PCR then undergoes gel electrophoresis operation. During this operation, the dsDNA $V_1 - V_3 - V_4 - V_5$, which representing the shortest path starting from V_1 and ending at V_5 can be visualized by the shortest band of gel electrophoresis with higher intensity than the other dsDNA, if any.

At this moment, based on the shortest length DNA duplex, one only knows that the shortest path begins from V_1 and ends at V_5. However, the information does not contain the nodes that passed through the shortest path. The information regarding all the nodes in the shortest path as well as their sequence can be obtained by applying graduated PCR operation. For the sake of explanation, the DNA molecules representing the answer of the shortest path $V_1 - V_3 - V_4 - V_5$ is taken again for instance. After the shortest band DNA is extracted from the gel, graduated PCR is performed by running four different PCR operations to the solution containing DNA duplex $V_1 - V_3 - V_4 - V_5$ separately. The pair of primers used for every PCR reaction are $V_1 / \overline{V_2}$, $V_1 / \overline{V_3}$, $V_1 / \overline{V_4}$, and $V_1 / \overline{V_5}$. It is expected that for the final solution containing the strand $V_1 - V_3 - V_4 - V_5$, 100 base-pairs (bp), graduated PCR will produce bands of x, 50, 75, and 100 in successive lanes of a gel as depicted in Figure 4. The symbol x denotes the absence of a band corresponding to the omission of nodes V_2 along the DNA duplex. This means that there are intermediate nodes, V_3 and V_4 in between the start node V_1 and the end node V_5. Therefore, the shortest path of the graph can be readout as $V_1 \rightarrow V_3 \rightarrow V_4 \rightarrow V_5$.

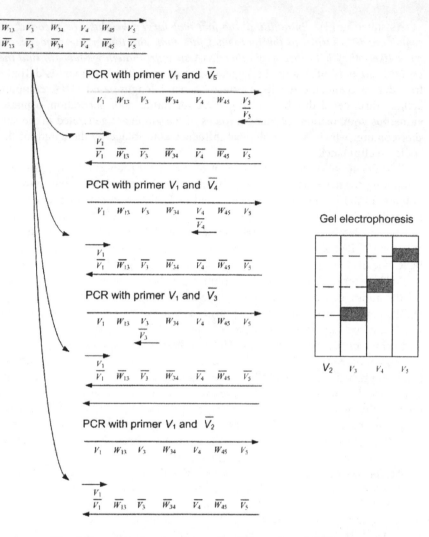

Fig. 4. Examples showing the results of the graduated PCR

6   Experimental Protocols, Results, and Discussions

Firstly, the relative concentration of edges oligos are translated into actually amount of DNA as listed in Table 4. Based on Table 4, the initial pool generation by POA is performed in a 25 μl solution containing 7.842 μl oligos (Proligo Primers & Probes, USA), 2.5 μl dNTP (TOYOBO, Japan), 2.5 μl 10x KOD dash buffer (TOYOBO, Japan), 0.125 μl KOD dash (TOYOBO, Japan), and 12.033 μl double distilled water (ddH$_2$0) (Maxim Biotech). The reaction consists of 25 cycles and for each cycles, the appropriate temperatures and time are as follows:

- 94°C for 30s
- 55°C for 30s
- 74°C for 10s

The product of parallel overlap assembly is shown in Figure 5. In order to select the paths that begin at V_1 and end at V_5, DNA amplification is done by PCR. PCR is performed in a 25 μl solution consists of 2.5 μl for each primers, 1 μl template, 2.5 μl dNTP (TOYOBO, Japan), 2.5 μl 10x KOD dash buffer (TOYOBO, Japan), 0.125 μl KOD dash (TOYOBO, Japan), and 13.875 μl ddH$_2$0 (Maxim Biotech). The reaction consists of 25 cycles as follows:

- 94°C for 30s
- 55°C for 30s
- 74°C for 10s

which is the same as POA. The sequences used as primers are AAAGCTCGTCGTTTAGGAGC (V_1) and GCACCCACCGAGACATTATC ($\overline{V_5}$).

In order to visualize the result of the computation, the product of PCR is subjected to PAGE for 90 minutes at 200V. After that, the gel is stained by SYBR Gold (Molecular Probes) and the gel image is captured. Figure 5 shows the output of the computation of DPLB-DNAC without concentration-controlled. Figure 6 on the other hand, shows the output of CCDPLB-DNAC.

Table 4. Actual amount of each edges oligos

Edge	Without Concentration-Controlled	With Concentration-Controlled
V_4–V_5	1 μl	0.51 μl
V_3–V_4	1 μl	1 μl
V_1–V_3	1 μl	0.39 μl
V_2–V_3	1 μl	0.39 μl
V_2–V_4	1 μl	0.25 μl
V_2–V_5	1 μl	0.174 μl
V_1–V_2	1 μl	0.128 μl
Total	7 μl	2.842 μl

According to the gel image of Figure 5, it is clear that without the concentration-controlled, DPLB-DNAC is able to produce several shortest paths during the computation. In this case, based on the output in lane 2, up to four shortest paths is generated *in vitro* and visualized by gel electrophoresis. In contrast, if concentration-controlled is applied, lane 2 of Figure 6 consists of only one band containing DNA duplex of the shortest path $V_1 - V_3 - V_4 - V_5$ (100bp), which survived after POA and PCR. As expected, it is likely that the concentration of dsDNAs other than dsDNAs representing the answer of the shortest path problem tends to be small. Even though only one band is shown, it is more than enough since the band exactly represent the answer of the shortest path problem.

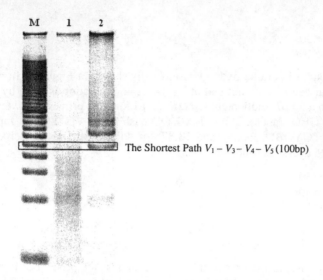

The Shortest Path $V_1 - V_3 - V_4 - V_5$ (100bp)

Fig. 5. Experimental results of gel electrophoresis on 10% PAGE in the case of DPLB-DNAC. Lane M denotes 20-bp ladder, lane 1 is the product of POA, and lane 2 is the product of PCR.

For graduated PCR, 4 identical DNA mixtures, which are the product of PCR of CCDPLB-DNAC are subjected to PAGE for 40 minutes at 200V. After that, the gel is stained by SYBR Gold (Molecular Probes, USA). Quantum Prep^{TM} Freeze 'N Squeeze DNA Gel Extraction Spin Columns (Bio-Rad, Japan) is used during the DNA extraction from the polyacrylamide gel. By using a clean razor blade, the band of interest, which is the shortest band, is carefully excised from the gel. The gel slice is chopped and placed into the filter cup of the Quantum Prep Freeze 'N Squeeze DNA Extraction Spin Column. Then, the filter cup is placed into a dolphin tube. The Quantum Prep Freeze 'N Squeeze DNA Extraction Spin Column is placed in a -20°C freezer for 5 minutes and the sample is spun at 13,000 x g for 3 minutes at room temperature. The purified DNA is collected from the collection tube and ready for PCR.

After the DNA extraction from the polyacrylamide gel, four different PCR, namely PCR1, PCR2, PCR3, and PCR4, is run to the purified solutions. The pair of primers used for every PCR is listed in Table 5.

Each PCR is performed in a 25 μl solution consists of 2.5 μl for each primers, 1 μl template, 2.5 μl dNTP (TOYOBO, Japan), 2.5 μl 10x KOD dash buffer (TOYOBO, Japan), 0.125 μl KOD dash (TOYOBO, Japan), and 13.875 μl double-distilled water (ddH$_2$0) (Maxim Biotech, Inc, Japan). The reaction consists of 25 cycles and for each cycles, the appropriate temperature are as follow:

- 94°C for 30s
- 55°C for 30s
- 74°C for 10s

Again, the product of graduated PCR is subjected to PAGE for 40 minutes at 200V and the gel is stained by SYBR Gold (Molecular Probes, USA). Finally, the gel image is captured. Figure 7 shows the gel image of the product of graduated PCR. Four

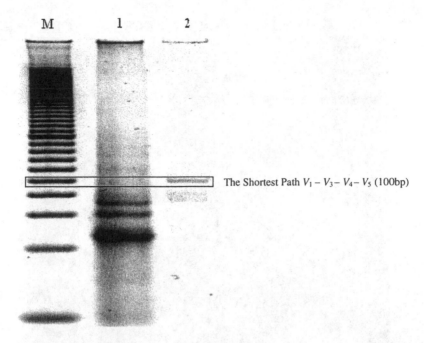

The Shortest Path $V_1 - V_3 - V_4 - V_5$ (100bp)

Fig. 6. Experimental results of gel electrophoresis on 10% PAGE in the case of CCDPLB-DNAC. Lane M denotes 20-bp ladder, lane 1 is the product of POA, and lane 2 is the product of PCR.

Table 5. Four set of primers used for the graduated PCR

Name	Forward Primers	Reverse Primers
PCR1	AAAGCTCGTCGTTTAGGAGC	CGTGATCCCTAAACCTCCAA
PCR2	AAAGCTCGTCGTTTAGGAGC	CGATACGGCATCATCTCGCT
PCR3	AAAGCTCGTCGTTTAGGAGC	GCTATGGCTTGACTATTCGC
PCR4	AAAGCTCGTCGTTTAGGAGC	GCACCCACCGAGACATTATC

bands of x, 50, 75, and 100 base pairs (bp) in successive lanes of the gel are successfully produced and therefore, as expected, the shortest path of the graph can be read-out as $V_1 \rightarrow V_3 \rightarrow V_4 \rightarrow V_5$.

Two significant benefits of graduated PCR for DPLB-DNAC have been identified. The first is due to its capability to show and visualize the detail output of the shortest path computation based on DPLB-DNAC. The other benefit is that at the same time, the correctness of DPLB-DNAC for the computation of the shortest path problem can be proved. Hence, the authors found that graduated PCR should be essentially incorporated in the DPLB-DNAC in order to improve the overall performance of DPLB-DNAC.

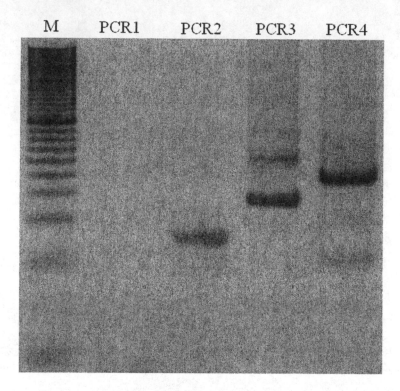

Fig. 7. Experimental results of gel electrophoresis on 10% polyacrylamide gel. Lane M denotes 20-bp ladder.

Scaling is certainly the main problem of DNA computing, especially for generate-and-test DNA computing, as the proposed approach. In order to extend the proposed approach to a larger problem, two issues should be considered: molecular's weight and the capability to select the final solution. As an example, if Adleman's work for solving HPP is further examined, a 70-node problem requires 10^{25} kg of nucleotides, and this is quite a lot for a small test tube [17]. Hence, an advanced high reaction facility, such as microreactor [18], is highly important. In this research, we showed how the scalability of our approach can be improved linearly, in two steps. The first step is during initial pool generation, where POA is employed instead of hybridization/ligation. As previously discussed, POA is able to generate two times bigger initial pool, in term of size, than that of hybridization/ligation. The second step is during the computation, in term of the amount of DNA used for the computation. In our case, we used 2.842 μl edge oligos in the case of concentration-controlled. It is about half of the amount of edge oligos if the computation is done without concentration-controlled, where 7 μl should be used.

In DNA computing for weighted graph problems, after the *in vitro* computation, a subsequent reactions or bio-molecular operations should be employed in order to detect the final solution. As an example, for the CC-DNAC method, separation as DGGE and CDGE should be used, whereas in TG-DNAC method, DTG-PCR separation should be utilized. This operations are relatively complicated than normal gel electrophoresis. In our approach, the adopted protocol for detecting the final solution is simple, where PAGE is more already enough to visualize the result of the computation.

However, one limitation of the proposed approach is that, the minimum weight of edges that can be encoded is limited and the weight falls in a very narrow range. This is mainly because the length of the solution is not only proportional to the length of the path it encodes but also the number of vertices in the path. Hence, the lower bound, in term of minimum weight that can be encoded by the proposed approach is achieved when:

$$\omega - \frac{3}{2}\beta = 0 \tag{2}$$

Hence, the minimum weight, which can be encoded by oligos, ω_{min} is attained as:

$$\omega_{min} = \frac{3}{2}\beta \tag{3}$$

where β is the number of DNA bases used to represent the node sequences [19].

7 Conclusions

Based on massive parallelism inherent in DNA computing, many researchers have tried to solve various NP-complete problems. These are mathematical problems which have exponential complexity and no efficient solution has been found yet. Even though the shortest path problem is not belonging to the class of NP problems, it is important to solve them since this kind of problems occur frequently in many real world problems. Thus, in this paper, we have presented an improve hybrid approach called 'concentration-controlled direct-proportional length-based DNA computing' to solve weighted graph problems using molecular computing. Based on this approach, both length and concentration are used as input and output data is recognized by length only. For the sake of initial pool generation, two kinds of methods are reviewed: hybridization/ligation and POA. Since POA offers several advantages in term of materials usage and reaction time, for a successful demonstration of CCDPLB-DNAC, we found that POA for initial pool generation is critically important. Further, by varying the amount of input DNA, less DNA is used for computation, which further offers the advantage in term of material usage. Since less amount of DNA can be used to generate the combination representing the answer of the problem, indirectly, this will advances the performance of the proposed approach from scalability point of view. Also, in this paper, we have presented graduated PCR, as an extended operation of CCDPLB-DNAC. Based on the proposed approach, the product of PCR of CCDPLB-DNAC is subjected to DNA extraction from polyacrylamide gel, PCR, and PAGE. As supported by the experimental results, graduated PCR is able to visualize detail additional information of the shortest path, such as the intermediate vertices and the order of these vertices in the shortest path. Finally, it is expected that the proposed approach, would extend the applicability of DNA computing for solving intractable weighted graph problems.

Acknowledgements

This research was supported partly by the IEEE Computational Intelligence Society (CIS) Walter J Karplus Student Summer Research Grant 2004 for a research visit in September 2004 at the DNA Computing Laboratory, Graduate School of Information Science and Technology, Hokkaido University, Sapporo, Hokkaido, Japan. The first author would like to thank Masahito Yamamoto for discussions that led to improvements in this work and also the permission to practice various kinds of biochemical experiments in the laboratory. Also, the first author is sincerely grateful to Atsushi Kameda, Satoshi Kashiwamura, and members of DNA Computing Laboratory of Hokkaido University for fruitful explanations and kind assistance during the practice of biochemical experiments. Lastly, the first author is very thankful to Universiti Teknologi Malaysia (UTM) for granting a study leave in Meiji University under SLAB-JPA scholarship.

References

1. Adleman, L.: Molecular Computation of Solutions to Combinatorial Problems," Science, Vol. 266 (1994) 1021-1024
2. Narayanan, A., Zorbalas, S.: DNA Algorithms for Computing Shortest Paths," in Proceedings of Genetic Programming (1998) pp. 718-723
3. Lee, J.Y., Shin, S.Y., Augh, S.J., Park, T.H., Zhang, B.T.: Temperature Gradient-Based DNA Computing for Graph Problems with Weighted Edges, Lecture Notes in Computer Science, Vol. 2568 (2003) 73-84
4. Ibrahim, Z., Tsuboi, Y., Ono, O., Khalid, M.: Direct-Proportional Length-Based DNA Computing for Shortest Path Problem", International Journal of Computer Science and Applications (IJCSA), Technomathematics Research Foundation, Vol. 1 (2004) 46-60
5. Yamamoto, M., Kameda, A., Matsuura, N., Shiba, T., Kawazoe, Y., Ahochi, A.: A Separation Method for DNA Computing Based on Concentration Control, New Generation Computing, Vol. 20 (2002) 251-262
6. Lee, J.Y., Shin, S.Y., Augh, S.J., Park, T.H., Zhang, B.T.: Temperature Gradient-Based DNA Computing for Graph Problems with Weighted Edges," in Preliminary Proceedings of the Eighth International Meeting on DNA Based Computers (2002) 41-50
7. Yamamoto, M., Matsuura, N., Shiba, T., Ohuchi, A.: DNA Solution of the Shortest Path Problem by Concentration Control. Genome Informatics (2000) 466-467
8. Udo, F., Sam, S., Wolfgang, B., Hilmar, R.: DNA Sequence Generator: A Program for the Construction of DNA Sequences," In Proceedings of the Seventh International Workshop on DNA Based Computers (2001) 23-32
9. Sugimoto, N., Nakano, S., Yoneyama, M., Honda, K.: Improved Thermodynamic Parameters and Helix Initiation Factor to Predict Stability of DNA Duplexes, Nucleic Acid Research, Vol. 24 (1996) 4501-4505

10. Lee, J.Y., Lim, H.W., Yoo, S.I., Zhang, B.T., Park, T.H.: Efficient Initial Pool Generation for Weighted Graph Problems using Parallel Overlap Assembly, in Preliminary Proceedings of the Tenth International Meeting on DNA Based Computers (2004) 357-364
11. Kaplan, P.D., Ouyang, Q., Thaler, D.S., Libchaber, A.: Parallel Overlap Assembly for the Construction of Computational DNA Libraries, Journal of Theoretical Biology, Vol. 188, Issue 3 (1997) 333-341
12. Ho, S.N., Hunt, H.D., Horton, R.M., Pullen, J.K., Pease, L.R.: Site-Directed Mutagenesis by Overlap Extension using the Polymerase Chain Reaction, Gene, Vol. 77 (1989) 51-59
13. Jayaraman, K., Fingar, S.A., Fyles, J.: Polymerase Chain Reaction-Mediated Gene Synthesis: Synthesis of a Gene Coding for Isozymec of Horseradish Peroxidase, Proc. Natl. Acad. Sci. U.S.A., Vol. 88 (1991) 4084-4088
14. Stemmer, W.P., Crameri, A., Ha, K.D., Brennan, T.M., Heyneker, H.L.: Single-Step Assembly of a Gene and Entire Plasmid from Large Numbers of Oligodeoxyribonucleotides, Gene, Vol. 164 (1995) 49-53
15. DeSalle, R., Barcia, M., Wray, C.: PCR Jumping in Clones of 30-million-year-old DNA Fragments from Amber Preserved Termites, Experientia, Vol. 49 (1993) 906-909
16. Stemmer, W.P.: DNA Shuffling by Random Fragmentation and Reassembly: In Vitro Recombination for Molecular Evolution," Proc. Natl. Acad. Sci. U.S.A., Vol. 91 (1994) 10747
17. Zucca, M.: DNA Based Computational Models: Ph.D. Thesis, Politecnico di Torino, Italy (2000)
18. Noort, D., Gast, F.U., McCaskill, J.S.: DNA Computing in Microreactors, Lecture Notes in Computer Science, Vol. 2340 (2001) 33-45
19. Ibrahim, Z., Tsuboi, T., Ono, O., and Khalid, M.: A Study on Lower Bound of Direct-Proportional Length-Based DNA Computing for Shortest Path Problem, Lecture Notes in Computer Science, Vol. 3314 (2004) 71-76

Modeling of Trees with Interactive L-System and 3D Gestures

Katsuhiko Onishi, Norishige Murakami, Yoshifumi Kitamura,
and Fumio Kishino

Graduate School of Information Science and Technology,
Osaka University, 2-1 Yamadaoka, Suita, Osaka 565-0871, Japan
{onishi, norishige, kitamura, kishino}@ist.osaka-u.ac.jp
http://www-human.ist.osaka-u.ac.jp/

Abstract. We propose a modeling system that enables users to create
tree models with 3D gesture input and Interactive L-system. It generates
tree models by using growth simulation based on the trunk or silhouette
shapes of trees given by user gestures. The Interactive L-system is one
of the growth simulation algorithm, having spatial information of tree
models, and allows users to generate, manipulate, and edit the shape
of tree models by user's direct input interactively. The system carefully
addresses the fragile balance and tradeoff between the freedom of user
interaction and the autonomy of tree growth. Users intuitively and easily
create tree models that have the exact features of branching structures or
the silhouette shape of trees according to user intentions and imagination.

1 Introduction

Plants or trees is attracting a great deal of attention because of the earth's
environmental problems. Even in a virtual space, people try to cultivate plants
or trees to simulate environmental assessments or education. Here, we have to
take care how the system carefully addresses the fragile balance and tradeoff
between the freedom of user interaction and the autonomy of tree growth, which
are inherent in natural botanical environment in real space.

Much literature has been devoted to generating realistic tree models based on
unique ideas [1, 2, 3, 4, 5]. Almost all of these ideas use procedural algorithms organized by procedural rules and/or numerical parameters; however, for ordinary
users, they are not so intuitive. In addition, their branching structures depend on
given parameters as initial conditions and production rules defined heuristically
beforehand. Therefore, it is difficult for ordinary users to generate the shape of
branches that completely correspond to imagination. Moreover, existing methods tend to rely on conventional 2D GUIs; however, this hampers the generation
or interaction with trees in a 3D environment.

In this paper, we propose a modeling system that enables users to create the
shape of tree models with 3D gesture input and Interactive L-system, as shown
in Figure 1. Here we carefully address the fragile balance and tradeoff between
the freedom of user interaction and the autonomy of tree growth by using an

A.J. Ijspeert et al. (Eds.): BioADIT 2006, LNCS 3853, pp. 222–235, 2006.
© Springer-Verlag Berlin Heidelberg 2006

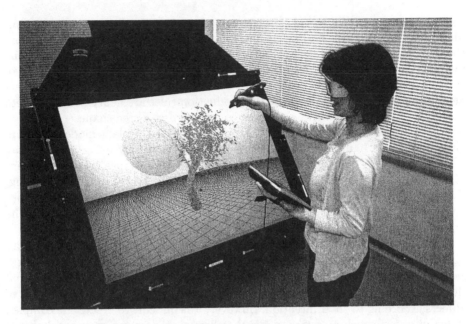

Fig. 1. Interactive modeling system for tree models

Interactive L-system as a tree's growth engine. Interactive L-system has an efficient data structure of tree models and enable to use three-dimensional(3D) spatial information as an attribute of the growth simulation, enabling users to interactively control tree shape [6]. Therefore, users intuitively and easily create tree models that have the exact branching structures or silhouette shape features of trees according to their intentions and imagination.

2   Related Work

Much literature has been devoted to generating realistic tree models based on many unique simulation algorithms.

The L-system [2], a very famous algorithm for growth simulation, is a string rewriting system that operates on a set of rules. This approach is extended to allow tree models to adapt to environmental effects. *L-studio*[3] and *Xfrog*[4] are mentioned as tree generation modelers using L-system's algorithm. In these systems, by using numerical parameters and graphically-defined functions, users can control the angle and length of branch growth, the shape of leaves, etc. *Xfrog* generates tree models based on tree model components assembled hierarchically in a graphical user interface. This component consists of tree elements (leaves and a trunk) and an arrangement type. This allows users to change the geometric shape of tree models by changing the numerical values. *AMAP*[1] simulation software is another such system designed to generate realistic tree models by generating tree models using numerical parameters defined by measuring many tree shapes in the real world. Users input these parameters and run the simulation to produce the desired geometry of the tree model. Tree models from these systems are very realistic. But the silhouette of the entire tree and the imagined branching structure are not always generated, because the shape of the tree model depends on production rules defined beforehand and parameters as initial conditions. Also, because the production rules are heuristically defined, it is difficult to change them according to intentions for tree shape.

Another system, ilsa[7], can directly edit the shapes of plant models that are already created. It manipulates the bending of branches by using inverse kinematics technology. A method that generates new tree shapes by editing parts of existing tree shape might be a solution for intuitive tree shape modeling. However, users have to create models beforehand, and they can only manipulate branches. Therefore, it is difficult for users to reflect their intention in the branching structure.

Techniques that model 3D objects in virtual environments by using 3D gesture inputs have been proposed [8, 9]. Such modeling systems are intuitive and allow easy comprehension of the relation between input information and the created shape of objects. Therefore, they allow users to generate and modify the shape of objects according to their intention. However, it is difficult to create the complex shape of objects such as a tree model that has many component parts, because users must create the local shape of all leaves and branches. A system that models 3D tree models from 2D sketches is also proposed [10], but it is not easy to generate tree models that have characteristic branch structure in 3D.

We propose an Interactive L-system that enables users to directly control growth simulation results. The Interactive L-system enables users to control the generated tree models by introducing 3D spatial information to the L-system. In this paper, we control the Interactive L-system by using 3D gesture input to generate the complex shape of tree models according to user intentions.

3   Interactive L-System

This section describes the Interactive L-system that allows users to interactively generate, manipulate, and edit tree shape models based on a growth simulation. The Interactive L-system is established by expanding the idea of the well-known L-system for enabling users to control the result of growth simulation interactively [6].

3.1   L-System

The L-system makes a string data of symbols, an L-string, by adapting production rules to the initial symbol, the axiom, for generating shapes of tree models. The system runs the modeling process by using this L-string as an instruction group. Examples of symbols are shown in Table 1. Moreover, the L-string is described using turtle geometry[11].

A production rule has a format roughly as shown in equation (1).

$$pred : cond \rightarrow succ \qquad (1)$$

Table 1. Examples of Symbols

Symbol	Order
F	Draw tube & move forward
+	Turn left
−	Turn right
&	Pitch down
^	Pitch up
\	Roll right
/	Roll left
[	Save state, start new branch
]	Restore state, end branch

pred is the strict predecessor symbols, *succ* is the successor symbols, and *cond* is the condition. The Lsystem process replaces the agreed symbols of *pred* within the L-string to the symbols of *succ*.

The numerical parameters of symbols included in the L-string are used to generate such complex shapes of tree models as weeping or branch thickness. In addition, the system controls these shapes by changing the number of times the production rules are adapted.

3.2   Interactive L-System

To control the result of the L-system by using the user's direct input interactively, the Interactive L-system adapts an extended data structure by adding the 3D spatial information as an attribute of the L-string. Here the L-strings are generated by the production rules which are affected by the 3D positional information. Details are described below.

Constructing the Structure of L-String. The Interactive L-system is that constructing the structure of L-string to hierarchical structure to aim at the increase in efficiency of a process of generating tree models. Figure 2 shows the construction process of the L-string structure. The structure of A in Figure 2 is a former structure of L-string. The structure of B in Figure 2 is the hierarchical structure that classified the data of each branch by using symbols "[" and "]". To classify the data of each branch and use the hierarchical data structure, it is enabled to run a process of generating and drawing the tree models at each branch independently. In Figure 2, a suffix of symbol "F" is used in order to explain hierarchy of branches and a trunk.

Table 2. Grouping of symbols

Group	Symbols
Shape	F, f
Transformation	+, −, &, ^, /, \
Structure	[,]

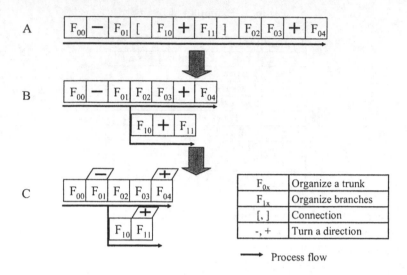

Fig. 2. Reconstruct of L-string

Moreover, the structure of C in Figure 2 is the structure of L-string that is classified symbols by these definition. Table 2 shows major symbols which are classified three groups. Symbols classified "Shape" group are defined modeling some geometric shape. Symbols classified "Transformation" group are defined rotating these geometric shape. Symbols classified "Structure" group are defined the structure of trees.

The Attributes for Indicating Global and Spatial Information. The attributes which indicate the global and spatial information of tree models is used to generate, manipulate and edit tree models interactively. These attributes added as "state" of the symbols which are defined shape of trees. In our method, two of them are used. One of these attributes is positional information of each symbol, $V(x, y, z)$, which defined 3D position of each symbol. And another is the angle of relative rotation (H, L, U) which is an angle of coordination of each symbol based on the global coordination. Moreover, when an angle of a branch is changed by user's manipulation, it is necessary to modify an angle similarly about the branches and leaves which accompany this branch. Therefore, an attribute parameter which defines a variation of an angle "M" that is settled at each branch. The system used these new attributes is enabled users to generate tree models by manipulating based on the global shape of tree models.

Table 3. Configuration of a partial region

Symbol	Order
In	Apply this rule, if "*pred*" is in a region.
Out	Apply this rule, if "*pred*" is out of a region.

Table 4. Configuration of a relative rotation

Symbol	Order
<	Turn left along an user's eye.
>	Turn right along an user's eye.

Configuration of New Parameters. The Interactive L-system needs some configuration of production rules to generate tree models by shown in Table 3 and Table 4. At the format of the production rule, *cond* means the condition. That is, the system used production rules which included "*In*" and "*Out*" shown in Figure 3 is enabled to change the shape of trees in the inside/outside of a certain area. And the system used production rule included these symbols at *succ* allows users to rotate branches based on his/her coordination.

4 Modeling of Trees with Interactive L-System and 3D Gestures

To generate the shape of tree models according to user images, we use hand gesture to determine the shape of tree models. Here, the tree model is generated based on two different concepts, as shown in Figure 3. One is "trunk-based modeling" that generates a tree model by defining the trunk shape with hand gestures. The other is "silhouette-based modeling" that generates a tree model with a silhouette defined by hand gestures. These two concepts are sometimes used individually, however, they can be used in combination according to the situation of modeling.

4.1 Trunk-Based Modeling

The trunk and main branches are components that define the branching structure and the entire shape of the tree model. The shape of such tree model components as trunk and branches is given by gestures. Then, the complex shape of tree models is created by using the Interactive L-system based on the given parts. To achieve this, we propose a method that translates the path of hand gestures to the simulation data (L-string) of the L-system. In the method, hand gesture paths are captured as point sets, and then the symbols that define trunk shape according to the paths are generated from the point sets. Trunk shapes are also corrected to avoid trunk collisions. Details are described below.

Acquisition of Point Sets. The trunk grows in the same direction as the stroke of a user's hand. Therefore, a user has a 3D tracker on his/her hand and move it as if drawing a line. The path of the hand gesture is captured as a set of 3D position information $V(x, y, z)$ at even intervals of time/space, as shown in Figure 4(a).

Analysis of Point Sets. In the Interactive L-system, the L-string symbols have some attributes. As shown in Figure 4(b), the symbol and attribute values of

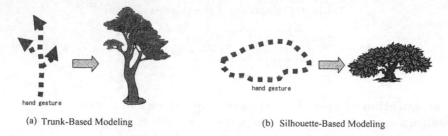

(a) Trunk-Based Modeling   (b) Silhouette-Based Modeling

Fig. 3. Concepts of modeling a tree by hand gestures

the L-string are determined based on the captured 3D position information. In the Interactive L-system, trunk L-strings consist of two groups of symbols, i.e., Transformation and Shape. The symbols of the "Shape" group denote the form of any tree part. The symbols of the "Transformation" group denote the angle of rotation between the growth directions. Symbol "F" is defined as the form of part of the trunk. This symbol has some attributes, including 3D position information $V(x, y, z)$, angle of relative rotation (H, L, U), and a variation of angle M. The values of these attributes are given from the captured 3D position information. Symbol "F" is defined as a part of a trunk/branch. The length of the form given from symbol "F_n" is the distance for two continuous points (V_{n+1}, V_n). The 3D position information of symbol "F_n" is V_n. And H_n is the direction in which the trunk is growing, defined as the vector from V_n to V_{n+1}, as shown in equation (2):

$$H_n = V_{n+1} - V_n \tag{2}$$

L and U are defined as arbitrary vectors that exist on the plane whose normal vector is H. But L is determined by rotating U 90 degree counterclockwise on the plane. M is derived from the "Transformation" symbols group determined by the method described below. Finally, these calculations are made with both continuous points of the captured 3D position information.

Generation of L-String. Here, we explain the determination of the "Transformation" group symbol, which is another L-string component.

The determination of the"Transformation" group symbol is based on the calculated attribute values about the angle of the relative rotation of a trunk. And the L-string of a trunk is generated from the created "Transformation" group symbols and "Shape" group symbols, as shown in Figure 4(c). The "Transformation" group symbols exist among the "Shape" group symbols. The "Transformation" symbol is determined from attribute values of the neighboring symbols of the "Shape" group. The symbol of the "Shape" group calculates the attribute values of the next "Shape" symbol by arbitrary rotation on the axes of its local coordinate system (H, L, U). Also it may rotate two or more times on the same axis. Therefore, the degree of the angle and the order of axes rotation are underspecified by calculating only with vectors that define the angle of the relative rotation of trunk parts. However, generating the L-string in

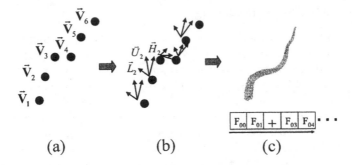

(a)   (b)   (c)

Fig. 4. Translation process from positional information to L-string. (a) Positional information. (b) Angles of relative rotation (H, L, U). (c) L-string.

real-time is required to interactively create tree models. To simplify the derivation of "Shape" symbols, it is assumed that the attribute values about the angle of the relative rotation of the next symbol of the "Shape" group is calculated by rotating the axes in the order of U, L, H in the local coordinate system of the present symbol. Consequently, the relationship between the continuous "Shape" group symbols is defined as three symbols of the "Transformation" group.

Our method translates trunk shape given by gestures to the L-string. When the trunk is generated by gesture inputs, the 3D positional information input later is translated to an L-string as branches of an already generated trunk. Therefore, the method enables users to edit the tree models by the Interactive L-system without considering whether the trunk is given by gestures.

Generation of Growth Points. A trunk that defines branching structure is created by using gesture inputs. Branches and leaves and so on are generated by growth simulation based on the trunk. To achieve this, the growth points of branches are created on the trunk's generated L-string. Symbol "A" as a growth point is generated by L-system simulation with production rules of the growth points, as shown in Figure 5. The attributes (position, angle of shape, and diameter) of symbol "A_1" have the same values as the attributes of symbol "F_{01}" that draw part of a trunk as a root of a generating branch based on symbol "A_1". Branches are generated by the Interactive L-system with the attribute values of the growth points as initial conditions.

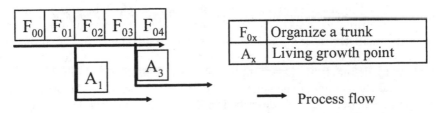

Fig. 5. Placement of growth points

4.2 Silhouette-Based Modeling

Next, a method to generate a tree model based on silhouette shape is described.

First, silhouette shape is determined in two different ways. One simply determines the silhouette shape as a sphere, and the other determines the shape as a supertoroid, which is a special form of superquadrics. Users freely generate the region's shape as superquadrics by 3D gesture inputs. Therefore, the silhouette of the tree model is generated according to user imagination. Superquadrics formulas have some parameters. By adjusting them, a large variety of 3D shape can be generated easily. Two bounding contours of the silhouette are generated by hand gestures captured in the same way as generating trunks and input as the left and right sides of the region's silhouette. The feature points of the contour paths are given from sets of the 3D positions by Vector Tracer. The axes of the generating supertoroids are derived from those continuous feature points. Supertoroids as silhouette shape are generated based on those axes and feature points with a set of equations (3).

$$\begin{cases} x(u,v) = a_x(\alpha_x + \cos^n u) \cos^e v + b_x \\ y(u,v) = a_y \sin^n u + \alpha_y \\ z(u,v) = a_z(\alpha_z + \cos^n u) \sin^e v + b_z \end{cases} \tag{3}$$

$$-\pi \leq u \leq \pi, -\frac{\pi}{2} \leq v \leq \frac{\pi}{2}.$$

Two parameters (b_x, b_z) are introduced into the supertoroid formulas to reflect the slopes of those axes in the supertoroids.

Finally, tree models in this region are generated by using the Interactive L-system [6]. The growth rules of the Interactive L-system are applied only to the part of the symbols at the L-string, which is in the region. If no symbols exist in that region, the axiom at an arbitrary point in the region is applied to the growth rules of the Interactive L-system. Therefore, with the L-system using the generated region of interest, users can directly generate and edit the shape of tree models, whose silhouette reflects user images.

5 The System

5.1 System Summary

Figure 1 shows the interface and a screenshot of our system. The path of the hand gesture is captured as a set of 3D positions obtained in regular time intervals from a stylus in the user's hand. A 3D tracker is attached to the stylus and the Region Of Interest (ROI) is given by the motion of the stylus. There are two ways to define ROI. One simply defines its shape as a sphere, and the position and the radius of the sphere are given by the stylus. The other defines its shape as a supertoroid, as described in 4.2, whose shape is determined from the trajectory of the stylus. After the shape of the ROI is defined, its position and size can be manipulated by the stylus. After the position and size of the ROI are determined, the system adapts the production rule to the parts of the model in the ROI with the Interactive L-system. Users can interactively observe the generated tree models by using stereoscopic LCD shatter glasses. The system is implemented on a personal computer (Xeon 2GHz, Mem 2GB, 3Dlabs WildcatII5110(TM),Windows 2000).

5.2   Interaction with Tree Models Through the L-Strings

Our system allows users to interact with the tree models by using the L-strings that is constructed by Interactive L-system. One of these methods is that it allows users to see the actual L-strings of any part of the tree model and the structure of the actual L-strings. Figure 6 shows an example in which L-strings of branches are superposed on the tree models. Here, the symbols of the parts of the tree model in a ROI are displayed. Black strings show symbols of the "Shape" group defined as geometric shapes of the model, and red strings show symbols of the "Transformation" group that rotate the geometric shapes, as explained in 4.1.

Another is that it allows users to edit the shape of tree models by changing the structure of the L-string. Figure 7 shows an example in which the structure of L-string are displayed at the tree view dialog. As shown in Figure 7(a), the system enables users to select the symbols in the L-string. And the users can change the structure of L-string by using the tree view dialog. The shape of tree

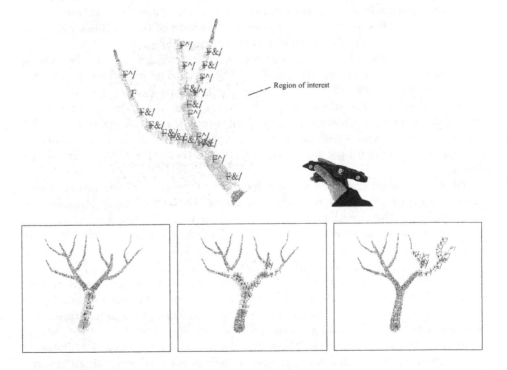

Fig. 6. L-string superposed on tree model

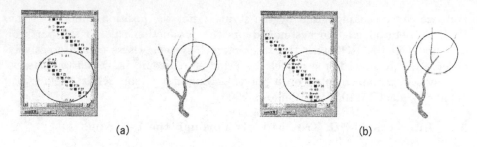

(a)   (b)

Fig. 7. Tree models editted by changing the structure of L-strings

model described by this L-string is modified according to the changing result of it, as shown in Figure 7(b).

5.3   Example of Interactions

In this section, we describe the creation process of tree models. In our system, the hand gesture path is captured as a data set of 3D positions obtained from the stylus in the users' hand. As shown in Figure 8(a), L-string is generated based on the data set and our proposed method, and the system shows the trunk shape drawn based on L-string. As visual feedback, this interaction starts when user gesture input begins to enable users to recognize their gesture inputs. Also, collision detection of trunks to correct the data of the path is carried out immediately when the 3D position is obtained from the stylus.

When the shape of a trunk is generated from gesture inputs, the system requires users to designate the point on the created trunk where trunks are jointed, which is difficult to do correctly because our system uses 3D direct manipulation, and the displaced place of tree models and the gesture input place are separated. Therefore, our system calculates and shows a joint point on the created trunk closest to the pointer controlled by users. Trunk diameter increases in inverse proportion to the velocity of the stroke that generates the trunk.

Branches are generated by the Interactive L-system. Users determine size by controlling the region of interest that they themselves created freely. Branches are generated from the growth points on trunks in the region by adapting production rules for branches, as shown in Figure 8(b). Therefore, our system enables users to easily generate the shape of a tree model that has the silhouette and trunk shapes that reflect their demands.

Users can also directly edit the shape of the generated tree model with the Interactive L-system. The system edits part of the tree model in the region selected by the users, who can obtain various results by selecting the production rules defined beforehand for editing, as shown in Figure 8(c). The system takes about 1.3sec to edit this tree models. Therefore, the user can edit tree models interactively. In the production rules, our system defines generating/erasing blossoms and leaves, bending and pruning branches, and the trunk. As shown in Figure 9,

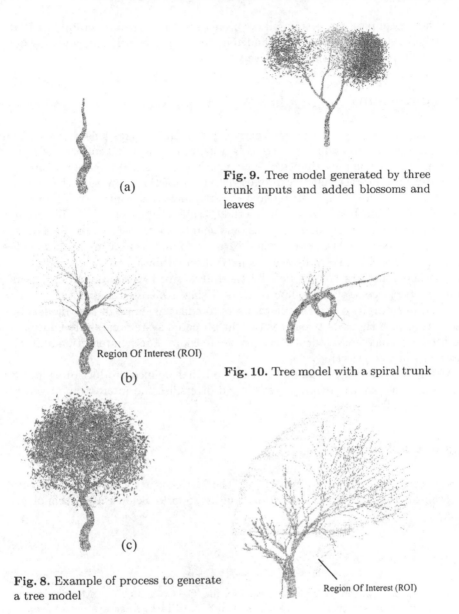

(a)

Fig. 9. Tree model generated by three trunk inputs and added blossoms and leaves

Region Of Interest (ROI)

(b)

Fig. 10. Tree model with a spiral trunk

(c)

Fig. 8. Example of process to generate a tree model

Region Of Interest (ROI)

Fig. 11. Tree model generated by a silhouette input with a supertoroid ROI

tree models are generated by three trunk inputs and added blossoms and leaves. In Figure 10 the trunk is spiral, a shape easily generated by a beginner with this system. As shown in Figure 11, a branching structure is generated from only inputting the region of interest as a silhouette of the entire tree.

In these examples, our system allows users to edit trunks and manipulate ROI by using one stylus. By using two-handed interaction, the users can generate and manipulate tree models more intuitively.

6 Conclusions

In this paper, we proposed an interactive system that makes tree models with 3D gesture input and the Interactive L-system. This system enables users to make intuitively complex shapes of imagined tree models. To create the shapes efficiently and interactively, we proposed the Interactive L-system that has a hierarchal structure of the L-string, and the attributes that control the 3D spatial information of the L-string. In our method, trunk shapes and tree silhouettes are given by the path of hand gestures, and shapes are translated to the data of Interactive L-system. Also, our method corrects "unnatural" trunk shapes made by users to avoid trunk collisions. Using translated data as initial conditions, our method generates tree models by the Interactive L-system, enabling users to interactively control the shape of trees. Using a hierarchal structure of the L-string, our proposed system allows users to edit the shape of tree models by interacting with these L-strings easily. Our proposed system carefully addresses the fragile balance and tradeoff between the freedom of user interaction and the autonomy of tree growth.

As future work, we are planning a method that defines production rules for L-system from shapes given by gesture and diversifies the interaction of generating tree models.

Acknowledgments

This research was supported in part by "The 21st Century Center of Excellence Program" of the Ministry of Education, Culture, Sports, Science and Technology, Japan.

References

1. Gordin, C., Guedon, Y., Costes, E., Gordin, C., Caraglio, Y.: Measuring and analyzing plants with the amapmod software. In: Plants to ecosystems-Advances in computational life sciences. CISRO (1997) 54–84
2. Prusinkiewicz, P., Lindenmayer, A.: The algorithmic beauty of plants. Springer-Verlag New York (1990)
3. Prusinkiewicz, P., Mundermann, L., Karwowski, R., Lane, B.: The use of positional information in the modeling of plants. In: Proc. of SIGGRAPH '01. (2001) 289–300
4. Lintermann, B., Deussenm, O.: Interactive modeling of plants. IEEE Computer Graphics & Application 19(1) (1999) 2–11
5. Boudon, F., Prusinkiewicz, P., Federl, P., Godin, C., Karwowski, R.: Interactive design of bonsai tree models. cgforum 22(3) (2003) 591–599

6. Onishi, K., Hasuike, S., Kitamura, Y., Kishino, F.: Interactive modeling of trees by using growth simulation. In: Proc. of ACM VRST. (2003) 66–72
7. Power, J.L., Brush, A.J.B., Prusinkiewicz, P., Salesin, D.H.: Interactive arrangement of botanical l-system models. In: Proc. of SI3D. (1999) 175–182
8. Schkolne, S., Pruett, M., Schroder, P.: Surface drawing: Creating organic 3d shapes with the hand and tangible tools. In: Proc. of CHI '01. (2001) 261–268
9. Llamas, I., Kim, B., Gargus, J., Rossignac, J., Shaw, C.D.: Twister: A space-warp operator for the two-handed editing of 3d shapes. In: Proc. of SIGGRAPH '03. (2003) 663–668
10. Okabe, M., Igarashi, T.: 3D modeling of trees from freehand sketches. In: SIGGRAPH '03 on Sketches & applications. (2003) 1
11. Abelson, H., diSessa, A.: Turtle geometry. MIT Press, Cambridge (1982)

New Vision Tools from the Comparative Study of an "Old" Psychophysical and a "Modern" Computational Model

Kuntal Ghosh, Sandip Sarkar, and Kamales Bhaumik

Microelectronics Division, Saha Institute of Nuclear Physics,
1/AF Bidhannagar, Kolkata-64, India
kuntal.ghosh@saha.ac.in

Abstract. A comparative study has been made between a one and half century old psychophysical model of vision and a modern computational model. The Mach band illusion has been studied from a new angle, that led to concluding that a Bi-Laplacian of Gaussian operation is a likely possibility in the visual system along with the traditional Laplacian operation. As a follow-up to this, exploring the human visual system through a two-pronged approach, based on the two models mentioned above, has helped in the construction of a new image sharpening kernel, on one hand and possibilities of new algorithms for robust visual capturing and image halftoning and compression on the other.

1 Introduction

Anyone acquainted with the fundamental aspects of image processing and vision, is probably also familiar with the "theory of edge detection" propounded by the late David Marr and his colleagues [1]. Although more efficient edge-detection algorithms have till then been designed, like for example Canny [2], the beauty of Marr's work, was that his algorithm for edge detection was derived as a part of a general investigation on the mechanism of visual perception in nature. Marr and Hildreth [3], claimed that the response function for the Receptive Fields (RF) of the Ganglion cells in the retina or the cells in Lateral Geniculate Nucleus (LGN) behaves as a Laplacian of Gaussian (LOG) filter that convolves the two-dimensional intensity array on the retina and this information is then sent to the visual cortex in the brain, where a "raw primal sketch" of the external world is detected in the form of an edge-map. While Marr and Hildreth [3] speculated a role of the small cells in monkey striate cortex in edge detection, based on the findings of Hubel and Wiesel [4], two later works by Richter and Ullman [5] and Hochstein and Spitzer [6] found further concrete evidences in favour of the existence of such edge detecting Simple cells in primary visual cortex of cats. Moreover, it was shown by Marr-Hildreth [3] that the LOG operator in fact approximates the lateral inhibition based Difference of Gaussian (DOG) model of Ganglion cell RF, as proposed by neurophysiologists [7]. Such RF-s, they claimed, are therefore capable of computing the LOG of any intensity array falling on the retina.

A.J. Ijspeert et al. (Eds.): BioADIT 2006, LNCS 3853, pp. 236–251, 2006.

It may be very interesting to note at this point that, both of these interrelated retinal phenomena, namely lateral inhibition in physiology and Laplacian operation in computation, were predicted almost a century prior to these developments in neurophysiology and artificial intelligence by the eminent physicist Ernst Mach [8]. Mach relied upon psychophysical experiments to arrive at his model. The most important of these observations was what is now popularly known as the Mach band illusion, which inspired Mach to predict a role of lateral inhibition in visual perception. This phenomenon was then explained mathematically by a linear combination of the original intensity distribution on the retina and its second differential coefficient, a model which Mach now proposed as the computational mechanism for visual signal processing [8]. This mid-nineteenth century computational approach to vision based on psychophysics and without any raw physiological data in his time, naturally deviated more towards a holistic (Gestalt) approach to vision rather than a step by step information processing approach from a two-dimensional retinal array to the reconstruction of three-dimensional world view in area 17-19 in the brain, as was David Marr's conjecture another century further on. Yet it was probably the first attempt to mathematically model visual signal processing.

Equipped with the contemporary developments simultaneously in the domain of neurophysiology and computational science in the later part of the twentieth century, David Marr put forward a strong three-level scheme for studying the visual system through an information processing approach [1]. In his approach, convolution of an intensity array by LOG, followed by zero-crossing detection, is a very primary but crucial step. In this paper, we are first of all going to show that an integration of Mach's observation (the Mach bands) and Marr's scheme demands a new operator, namely the Bi-Laplacian of Gaussian (Bi-LOG), prior to zero-crossing detection. Then we are going to adopt two different approaches in modeling this phenomenon. The first of these would resemble the holistic approach of Mach and yield a new image enhancement kernel, that is comparable in simplicity to the Laplacian kernel often used for unsharp masking, but one that performs better. The second approach would resemble Marr's methodology and discuss on how a Bi-LOG operation and subsequent zero-crossing detection is realizable in the visual system, through a simple modification of the existent RF model. Such a modification, it would be shown, leads to an explanation of some of the brightness-contrast illusions hitherto unexplained by LOG or equivalently DOG models. The modified model may therefore, as pointed out in a related work by Yu et al. [9], find application in designing robust visual capturing or display systems and in areas where accurate perception of intensity level is crucial. Another consequence of this later approach, it would be shown, is a new and unconventional process of image compression, that utilizes the inherently present noise in a natural image. Evidences of such utilization of noise (like for example pupil noise in human) in visual perception has already been found in the peripheral nervous system of crayfish [10], and also in some other animals.

2   The Existent Models

2.1   The Approach of Ernst Mach

In order to understand Mach's approach, let us take a look at a commonly used image for understanding the Mach band illusion shown in Fig. 1a. By scanning this image in a direction in which the luminance increases or decreases our visual system perceives an actually non-existent darker bar at the location where the figure just starts getting lighter. Similarly, a brighter bar is perceived at the point where brightness just stops increasing. This observation led Ernst Mach to foresee a mechanism of lateral inhibition in the retina and propose a mathematical model for visual processing based on a linear combination of the intensity function and its second differential coefficient. If we make a finite difference approximation of this second order derivative, i.e. for $\frac{\partial^2}{\partial x^2} + \frac{\partial^2}{\partial y^2}$, then we can easily arrive at an orientation-independent filter mask L [11].

By convolving the image, shown in Fig. 1a with this mask, we get a new image, the horizontal line profile of which has been shown in Fig. 1b. Adding the convolved image to the original, is the same as convolving the original with the filter mask L' [11]:

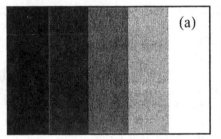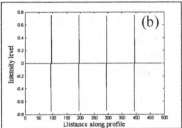

Fig. 1. (a) The Mach band illusion of dark and bright borders around bright and dark regions respectively (b) horizontal profile of this image, convolved with L

$$L = \begin{bmatrix} -1 & -1 & -1 \\ -1 & 8 & -1 \\ -1 & -1 & -1 \end{bmatrix} \qquad L' = \begin{bmatrix} -1 & -1 & -1 \\ -1 & 9 & -1 \\ -1 & -1 & -1 \end{bmatrix}$$

If we convolve Fig.1a with L' and view a horizontal line profile of the resultant image in Fig. 2a., we clearly see a replica of our illusion which is unlike the reality as we can see by comparing with a similar line scan of the original image (Fig. 2b).

The undershoots and overshoots at each step transition bears resemblence to our illusive perception. If we apply this mask to any image it will enhance the image by sharpening the edges. This has been shown in Fig. 3.

Such an operation is sometimes referred to as unsharp masking. The reason behind such enhancement is that the light Mach bands around dark regions

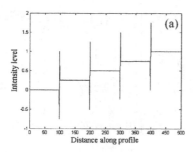
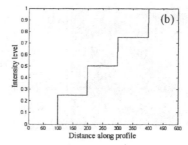

Fig. 2. (a) The horizontal profile of the Mach band image, convolved with L'. A mimetic of the illusory perception is reproduced (b) horizontal profile of the original image shown in Fig. 1a.

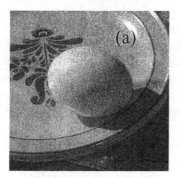

Fig. 3. (a) The bench-mark image of egg on a plate. (b) The image has been enhanced with L'.

and dark ones around lighter, apart from being illusions, also serve a purpose. They actually represent a mechanism of lateral inhibition or in other words the contrast-sensitivity in the eye, that enables one to clearly isolate an object from its background, thus helping in image enhancement. The sharpening operator L', being the discrete version of the rotationally symmetric Laplacian operator, will therefore form such Mach bands in all orientations so that, thus enhancing an object of any arbitrary shape. This is actually the essence of Ernst Mach's model for visual perception, based on the phenomenon of contrast sensitivity alone.

2.2   The Approach of David Marr

David Marr looked upon the Laplacian operator from another angle. He identified three levels at which any machine carrying out information processing task must be understood, namely the computational, algorithmic and implementational levels [1]. Marr's computational view of image processing, consisted of the formation of a "raw primal sketch", which signifies a transition from the

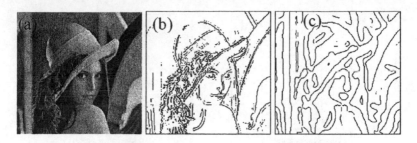

Fig. 4. (a)The famous bench-mark image of Lena. Zero-crossings detected with LOG at (b) a fine scale, the Gaussian $\sigma = 1$ (c) a coarse scale; the Gaussian $\sigma = 4$.

analog, gray scale image to a more-or-less symbolic representation of image based features in terms of spatial primitives like edges, lines, blobs etc. The luminance edges according to Marr, were computed with the help of an LOG filter that resembles the RF structure of retinal Ganglion cells and the LGN cells, at various fine and course scales, i.e. at different variances of the Gaussian. Marr and Hildreth [3] further explained how such an algorithm might be implemented in neural hardware that detects these zero-crossings through an AND gate arrangement of some of the cortical simple cells. Zero-crossings from an image at such fine and a coarse scale has been shown in Fig. 4. Marr then went on to deal with the problem of scale integration, the construction of the "full primal sketch" and so on.

3   Integrating the Two Approaches

If we take a careful look at the Mach band illusion (Fig. 1a) once again, and judge the same from Marr's viewpoint by looking upon this event in terms of the "raw primal sketch", then it amounts to the detection of three edges at each gray level transition. One of these three edges, the central and major one is to represent the real transition in gray level, while the two minor edges are to represent the illusory transitions in gray level on either side of the real one. This is only possible if the operator that convolves this figure, is $\nabla^4 G$ and not Marr's $\nabla^2 G$ operator. This has been shown for a one-dimensional step edge in Fig. 5. The $\frac{\partial^2 G}{\partial x^2}$ operator produces only one zero-crossing (i.e. one edge) at the step transition, but the $\frac{\partial^4 G}{\partial x^4}$ operator produces one major zero-crossing and two minor ones on either side of it, or in other words three edges, one strong and two weak.

Now if these zero-crossings from Bi-LOG operation are detected through a straightforward thresholding approach as in the case of LOG, then it will not be possible to distinguish between the minor and the major zero-crossings, i.e. the strong and the weak edges, though we understand that it might be crucial to include the Bi-LOG operator in the model for visual processing. Accordingly, we adopt two different routes, in order that we might make such incorporation.

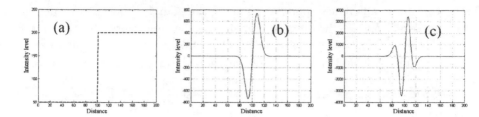

Fig. 5. (a) A one dimensional step image. Convolution with (b) second order derivative of Gaussian produces a single zero-crossing (c) the same with fourth order derivative produces two additional smaller crest and trough on either side of the central zero-crosing, resulting in two additional zero-crossings.

The first of these two, is based upon the holistic approach of Mach. It simply proposes a linear combination of the Laplacian and the Bi-Laplacian opeartor, with varying weights, added to the original intensity distribution, keeping similarity with Mach's model. We shall show how such a combiantion can be made using finite difference approximation. What is interesting is that, we come up with a new and better-performing digital filter for image sharpening. Then we shall take a second route to incorporate the computation of the Bi-Laplacian of Gaussian, into the algorithmic and implementational schemes of Marr and Hildreth and discuss on the advantages thereof.

3.1   The Modified Mach Model

First of all, we discuss on the construction of a computationally handy kernel for the ∇^4 operator following the methodology of construction of the convolution matrix for the ∇^2 operator, using finite difference approximation of second order partial derivative. We may recall [12] that at the outset we represent $\frac{\partial^2}{\partial x^2}$ by the vector $\begin{bmatrix} -1 & 2 & -1 \end{bmatrix}$. Then $\frac{\partial^2}{\partial y^2}$ is represented by the transpose of the above vector. When these two are combined together, we obtain the kernel L_1 for the isotropic ∇^2 operator. Using the property of isotropicity, the diagonal directions are now incorporated by taking the co-ordinates along these applying a 45^0 rotation so that we arrive at a new kernel L_2 :

$$L_1 = \begin{bmatrix} 0 & -1 & 0 \\ -1 & 4 & -1 \\ 0 & -1 & 0 \end{bmatrix} \qquad L_2 = \begin{bmatrix} -1 & 0 & -1 \\ 0 & 4 & 0 \\ -1 & 0 & -1 \end{bmatrix}$$

By combining L_1 and L_2, we get the omnidirectional edge-detector L or the sharpening kernel L' shown in section 2.1.

We now construct the convolution matrix corresponding to the ∇^4 operator following the above example. Clearly,

$$\nabla^4 = \frac{\partial^4}{\partial x^4} + \frac{\partial^4}{\partial y^4} + 2\frac{\partial^2}{\partial x^2}\frac{\partial^2}{\partial y^2}$$

From the finite difference approximation of the fourth order partial derivative, the kernel for $\frac{\partial^4}{\partial x^4}$ in discrete domain can be represented by the vector $\begin{bmatrix} 1 & -4 & 6 & -4 & 1 \end{bmatrix}$. By transposing this kernel we may construct the corresponding vector for $\frac{\partial^4}{\partial y^4}$, add these, so that we get the corresponding matrix for a linear combination of these two terms. The matrix corresponding to the cross-term $\frac{\partial^2}{\partial x^2}\frac{\partial^2}{\partial y^2}$ can be, by using the expressions for $\frac{\partial^2}{\partial x^2}$ and $\frac{\partial^2}{\partial y^2}$ shown above, easily computed also, so that:

$$
\frac{\partial^4}{\partial x^4} + \frac{\partial^4}{\partial y^4} =
\begin{bmatrix}
0 & 0 & 1 & 0 & 0 \\
0 & 0 & -4 & 0 & 0 \\
1 & -4 & 12 & -4 & 1 \\
0 & 0 & -4 & 0 & 0 \\
0 & 0 & 1 & 0 & 0
\end{bmatrix}
\qquad
\frac{\partial^2}{\partial x^2}\frac{\partial^2}{\partial y^2} =
\begin{bmatrix}
0 & 0 & 0 & 0 & 0 \\
0 & 1 & -2 & 1 & 0 \\
0 & -2 & 4 & -2 & 1 \\
0 & 1 & -2 & 1 & 0 \\
0 & 0 & 0 & 0 & 0
\end{bmatrix}
$$

From the above expression for ∇^4 we arrive at the kernel BL_1 for the Bi-Laplacian operator. As in the case of deriving the Laplacian kernel the diagonal directions are now incorporated by taking the co-ordinates along the diagonals through a 45^0 rotation and adding the same to the above kernel so that we get Bi-Laplacian mask BL_2:

$$
BL_1 =
\begin{bmatrix}
0 & 0 & 1 & 0 & 0 \\
0 & 2 & -8 & 2 & 0 \\
1 & -8 & 20 & -8 & 1 \\
0 & 2 & -8 & 2 & 0 \\
0 & 0 & 1 & 0 & 0
\end{bmatrix}
\qquad
BL_2 =
\begin{bmatrix}
1 & 0 & 1 & 0 & 1 \\
0 & -6 & -6 & -6 & 0 \\
1 & -6 & 40 & -6 & 1 \\
0 & -6 & -6 & -6 & 0 \\
1 & 0 & 1 & 0 & 1
\end{bmatrix}
$$

We again apply a $22\frac{1}{2}^0$ rotation so that we may also incorporate the intermediate directions and once again adding the same to the above kernel the final form that the Bi-Laplacian mask assumes is:

$$
BL =
\begin{bmatrix}
1 & 1 & 1 & 1 & 1 \\
1 & -12 & -12 & -12 & 1 \\
1 & -12 & 80 & -12 & 1 \\
1 & -12 & -12 & -12 & 1 \\
1 & 1 & 1 & 1 & 1
\end{bmatrix}
$$

The modified Mach model, proposed in this paper is a weighted sum of L and BL, combined with the original image. These weights may be arbitrarily assigned. But from our discussion on major and minor edges, we understand that the Laplacian deserves a larger weight compared to the Bi-Laplacian. If we give a 90% weight to the Laplacian we arrive at a new 5×5 digital filter comparable in simplicity to the 3×3 L mask. We call this new filter M in memory of Ernst Mach. The corresponding mask for image enhancement as before is represented by M'.

$$M = \begin{bmatrix} -1 & -1 & -1 & -1 & -1 \\ -1 & 3 & 3 & 3 & -1 \\ -1 & 3 & -8 & 3 & -1 \\ -1 & 3 & 3 & 3 & -1 \\ -1 & -1 & -1 & -1 & -1 \end{bmatrix} \qquad M' = \begin{bmatrix} -1 & -1 & -1 & -1 & -1 \\ -1 & 3 & 3 & 3 & -1 \\ -1 & 3 & -7 & 3 & -1 \\ -1 & 3 & 3 & 3 & -1 \\ -1 & -1 & -1 & -1 & -1 \end{bmatrix}$$

M being derived out of a linear combination of two isotropic operators L and BL is naturally isotropic as well. We have made a comparative study of L' and M' in image enhancement in the result section. In fact by modeling the non-linear non-classical receptive fields in human visual system, this same kernel has been derived from another approach and it has already been shown in the same work how it outperforms the standard Laplacian kernel in image enhancement [12].

3.2   The Modified Marr Model

From the perspective of modeling the Extended Classical Receptive Field (ECRF) of retinal Ganglion cells and its implications at the cortical level, some works on the modification of Marr's model have already been initiated in a recently published work [13]. According to this work, the contribution from the amacrine cells in the retina may be incorporated into the physiological DOG model of RF, by effectively adding a wider disinhibitory Gaussian to the DOG. We call it a modified DOG or MDOG model. It has been shown [13], that it is possible to approximate a Bi-LOG operation by such a linear combination of three Gaussians, representing an excitatory, an inhibitory and a disinhibitory neural layer respectively. Taking into consideration the assumption of Marr, that the visual system operates at both fine and coarse scale, this model, it has been shown, reduces to a replacement of Marr's LOG operator with a linear combination of LOG and the Dirac-delta ($\delta(x, y)$) function. We are now going to study the implications of such a modification of Marr's model in some application areas of image processing and vision.

Although, many low-level brightness-contrast illusions can be explained by the LOG or equivalently DOG model, there are happens to be many other brightness-contrast illusions which cannot also be explained by this model. Since, the crux matter of this paper has developed from an attempt to explain the minor edges in Mach band illusion, it is tempting to make an attempt to explain the Mach bands as well such unexplained brightness-contrast illusions mentioned above with the MDOG model. As has already been mentioned, in one dimension this model may be written as:

$$MDOG(\sigma_1, \sigma_2, \sigma_3) = A_1 \frac{1}{\sqrt{2\pi}\sigma_1} \exp(-\frac{x^2}{2\sigma_1^2}) - A_2 \frac{1}{\sqrt{2\pi}\sigma_2} \exp(-\frac{x^2}{2\sigma_2^2})$$
$$+ A_3 \frac{1}{\sqrt{2\pi}\sigma_3} \exp(-\frac{x^2}{2\sigma_3^2})$$

where MDOG represents the response function for the modified RF of retinal Ganglion cells, σ_1, σ_2 and σ_3 represent the scales of the center, the antagonistic surround and the extended disinhibitory surround respectively and A_1, A_2 and

A_3 and represent the corresponding amplitudes. Interestingly, the inverse DoG (IDoG) model of Yu et al. [9] based on a similar disinhibitory property of retinal cells of the arthropod Limulus has also been able to explain the unexplained subtle features of Hermann grid illusion through such simple feedforward networks. We shall see in the result section how the MDOG model not only explains these features, but also explains the hitherto unexplained through low-level modelling the well-known White effect and Todorovic effect phenomena [14].

Next we study the implications of operating the linear combination of LOG and Delta function, as has been mentioned above, in the domain of biological and digital image processing. In the traditional view of image processing, noise in an image is always unwanted. It is the common practice to remove noise by smoothing images with Gaussian filters, before applying image processing algorithms. We will now show that noise can help in retaining the original intensity information in the zero-crossing (ZC) map, when such an operator is employed in image processing. It is quite obvious that any derivative computation (LOG in this case) removes the constant intensity information of the original image and retains only the rate of intensity change. On the other hand, zero-crossings of the LOG-convolved image represents only the peaks and troughs of this rate of intensity change. So any information contained in the monotonic rate of intensity change is not retained in the zero-crossing map. However, we are going to show that with an operator like $h = k_1 \nabla^2 G(x,y) + k_2 \delta(x,y)$, as mentioned above, the computed ZC map is found to retain intensity information of the original image in the sense of a half toning, where the intensity variation is mapped to the density variation of the ZC points. The ZC map therefore is virtually a compressed form of the original image. It is interesting to note here, that though we are dealing with a modified Marr model, the operator h is again virtually same as the Mach model. So the dialectical relationship between these two models, one following inductive logic and the other one deductive, remains prevalent throughout this study. In the present situation we are using it for identifying the ZC map, while previously we have done the same for image enhancement.

4   Results and Discussion

In Fig. 6, we compare the performance of M' with L', in image enhancement or unsharp masking. M' is shown to perform as a more effective sharpening operator.

It may easily be verified for other images as well. The proposed kernel may therefore replace the Laplacian in the opeartion unsharp masking, commonly used in image processing softwares.

Next, we come to the illusions. The Mach band illusion (Fig.7a) has been successfully explained using MDOG model in 7c. For all the illusory figures we have used horizontal line scans to reproduce the results, as is normally the practice [9, 15]. The results are comparable to the solution by DOG model shown in Fig. 7b.

Fig. 6. (a)The bench-mark image of egg on a plate shown in Fig. 3a has been enhanced with L' (b) the image in Fig. 3a has been enhanced with M'. M' clearly performs better as a sharpening operator as per visual inspection. It may be noted that the Mach bands have been further enhanced by M' compared to L'.

The same can easily be verified for other brightness-contrast illusions solvable by DOG, like Simultaneous Brightness Contrast illusion or Grating Induction effect etc. In Hermann Grid illusion, the human vision perceives the crossings in the grid, to be darkest while the streets appear brighter than the peripheral region (Fig. 8a). Convolution with DOG (Fig. 8b), though provide a gross explanation to this effect, cannot reproduce these subtle features, but like the IDOG model [9], the proposed MDOG model is able to reproduce these (Fig. 8c). Most interestingly, the White effect illusion (in a square grating of black and white bars, if identical gray segments are used to replace part of the black bars and also part of the white bars, then former gray segments look brighter than the later), where the Marr model (DOG) fail completely and gives a result exactly opposite to our perceptual experience , has also been faithfully explained with the MDOG model (Fig. 9). Another unexplained illusion called the Todorovic effect (occluding a test patch on a black background by four white squares and

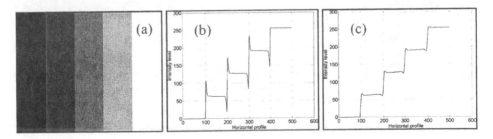

Fig. 7. (a) The Mach band illusion. (b) explanation of the illusion by DOG model (c) explanation by MDOG model.

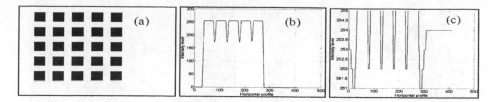

Fig. 8. (a) The Hermann Grid illusion. (b) Partial explanation of the Hermann Grid illusion by convolving the image with conventional DOG filter along a horizontal line profile through one of the streets in the convolved image. (c) Explanation of the Hermann Grid illusion with the MDOG filter.

vice-versa), which like the White effect cannot be explained by DOG, was thought of to be the result of high level perceptual grouping, rather than low-level contrast sensitivity. This illusion has also been sucessfully explained by MDOG as shown in Fig. 10. Potential application of this algorithm may therefore be in the direction of designing novel robust visual capturing or display systems and automatic detection and correction of perceived incoherence in luminance of video display panels, where accurate perception of intensity level is critical.

Finally we come to the application of the operator h mentioned in section 3.2 in image processing. Two kinds of images were considered for these studies. They are synthetic images that are perfectly noise free and natural images that generally contains intrinsic noise. In Fig. 11 - Fig. 13 synthetic images were used to demonstrate the role of noise by adding noise externally and in Fig. 14, we demonstrate the effect of inherent noise in the natural image of a flower in such processing. Fig. 11(a) is the original image I of constant normalized grayscale of 0.5, Fig. 11(b) is the horizontal profile of the image $I \otimes h$, i.e. the image convolved with the operator h and Fig. 11(c) is the zero-crossing map computed from the image of Fig. 11(b). Next, Fig. 11(d) is the original image I of constant normalized grayscale of 0.5 contaminated with Gaussian noise, Fig. 11(e) is the horizontal profile of the image $I \otimes h$ and Fig. 11(f) is the zero-crossing image

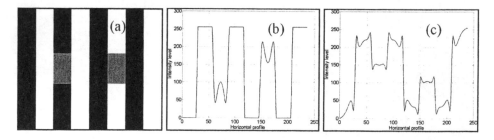

Fig. 9. (a) The White effect illusion. (b) Attempted explanation of the White effect illusion with conventional isotropic DOG filter along a horizontal line profile through the gray segments in convolved image produces results contrary to our perceptual experience. (c) Explanation of the White effect illusion by convolving the image with the MDOG filter.

Fig. 10. (a) The Todorovic effect (b) Explanation of the illusion by convolving the image with MDOG filter along a horizontal line profile through the two test patches in the convolved image

computed from the image of Fig. 11(e). As discussed in section 3.2 Fig. 11(c) does not contain intensity information of the original image but Fig. 11(f) is similar to the half toned map of Fig. 11(d). This is due to the presence of noise that produced zero-crossings as shown in Fig. 11(e). The role of noise depicted in Fig. 11 is also demonstrated in Fig. 12 for the case of ramp image (I_R) where the intensity changes linearly from 0 (black) to 1 (white).Original ramp image and the noise contaminated ramp image is shown in Fig. 12(a) and Fig. 12(d), Fig. 12(b) and Fig. 12(e) are the horizontal profile plots of the convolved ($I_R \otimes h$) ramp image and the convolved noise contaminated ramp image respectively. It is also clear from Fig. 12(f) that intensity information of Fig. 12(a) is mapped to a density variation of zero-crossing points.

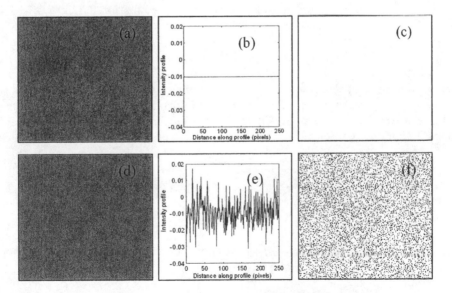

Fig. 11. Influence of noise on ZC image for the case of constant intensity image (a) original constant intensity (gray value=0.5) image (I), (b) $I \otimes h$ image profile, (c) zero-crossing image of $I \otimes h$, (d) image (I_n) contaminated with Gaussian noise, (e) $I_n \otimes h$ image horizontal profile and (f) the resulting zero-crossing image computed from $I_n \otimes h$. No new information is found.

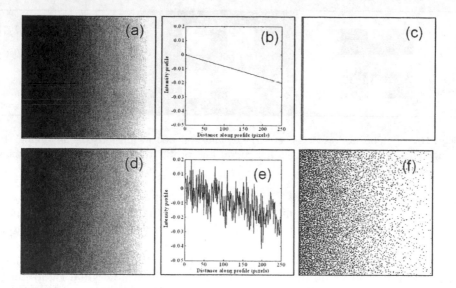

Fig. 12. Influence of noise on ZC image for the case of constant ramp image (a) original (gray value=0-1) image (I_R), (b) $I_R \otimes h$ image profile, (c) zero-crossing image of $I_R \otimes h$, (d) image (I_{Rn}) contaminated with Gaussian noise, (e) $I_{Rn} \otimes h$ image horizontal profile and (f) the resulting zero-crossing image computed from $I_{Rn} \otimes h$. Intensity information can be found.

The picture in Fig. 13(a) is constructed using the function $0.5 \sin(a/x) + 0.5$. Fig. 13(b) is the zero-crossing map for the noise added to this image.

The effect of noise in a natural image is depicted in Fig. 14. Picture in Fig. 14(a) is the original image, picture in Fig. 14(b) is the zero-crossing image of the LOG convolved image of Fig. 14(a). As discussed this ZC image does not retain much of the intensity information of the original image but the image in Fig. 14(c) retains much of the intensity information of the original image. This due to the fact that lily image have some inherent noise that helps in retaining intensity information. Fig. 14(d) is the zero-crossing image of the noise

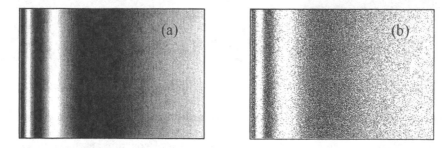

Fig. 13. Influence of noise on ZC image for the case of (a) original image $0.5 \sin(a/x) + 0.5$, (b) zero-crossing image after adding noise added to it. Again we find intensity information in ZC map.

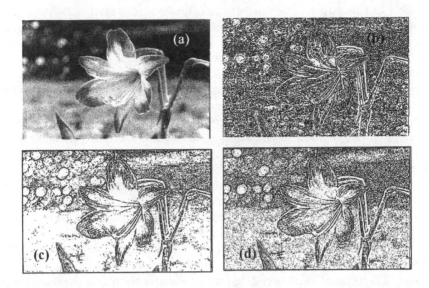

Fig. 14. Influence of noise on ZC image for the case of natural image (a) original lily flower image (I_L), (b) zero-crossing image of $I_L \otimes LOG$ at low threshold, (c) zero-crossing image of $I_L \otimes h$, (d) zero-crossing image computed from Gaussian noise contaminated lily image. Added noise makes halftoning effect more prominent.

contaminated original image in Fig. 14(a). In this case also we observe some improvement in the intensity information, through visual inspection, with respect to the given intensity information. This may be due to the fact that though natural image contains noise the amount of noise become optimum after the addition of some external noise to the original image. So noise (like pupil noise for example) can be made to play a constructive role in preserving intensity information in the zero-crossing images by computing the ZC map from the operator

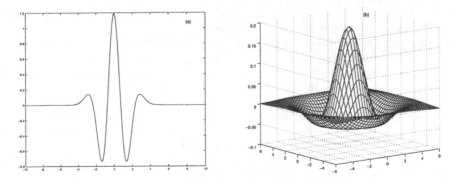

Fig. 15. Graphical representation of the Bi-Laplacian of Gaussian mask in (a) one dimension, (b) two dimension

proposed in this paper. The intensity information may further be improved by adding some appropriate amount of external noise to the original image. Evidences of similar operation has been found in the peripheral nervous system of crayfish [10], and also in some other animals. Such a ZC map which may be detected in the cortical simple cells in fact provides a compressed version of the original image. The compression, we have tested for various images, is about three-fold. We therefore arrive at a new methodology of unconventional image compression. The two different routes that we have chosen to incorporate a Bi-Laplacian operation in the visual system have therefore endowed us with possible new tools for image enhancement, visual capturing and video display as well as in image halftoning and compression.

Finally, we have reproduced a graphical representation of the Bi-Laplacian of Gaussian opeartor in both one and two dimension in Fig. 15. It looks very much like the profile of a Gabor filter. The main difference is that Gabor filters are directional, while the Bi-Laplacian of Gaussian operator is isotropic. The relation between Gabor filters and the Mach band illusion has also been studied [16] and the wavelet transform has been found to contain signatures of the illusory features. The present work serves to further substantiate and develop this idea.

Acknowledgement

The authors are specially thankful to Mr. Subhajit Karmakar for lending a great help in preparing the camera-ready manuscript. The authors also express their thanks to Mr. Ratan kumar Saha and Mr. Manas kumar Roy for similar helps.

References

1. Marr, D.: Vision: A Computational Investigation into the Human Representation and Processing of Visual Information. W. H. Freeman and Company. New York (1982).
2. Canny, J.: A computational approach to edge detection. IEEE Transactions on Pattern Analysis and Machine Intelligence **8** (1986) 679-698.
3. Marr, D., Hildreth, E.: Theory of edge detection. Proceedings of Royal Society of London B **207** (1980) 187-217.
4. Hubel, D. H. and Wiesel, T. N.: Receptive fields and functional architecture of monkey striate cortex. Journal of Physiology **195** (1968) 215-243.
5. Richter, J. and Ullman, S.: Non-linearities in cortical simple cells and the possible detection of zero-crossings. Biological Cybernetics **53** (1986), pp. 195-202.
6. Hochstein, S. and Spitzer, H.: Zero-crossing detectors in primary visual cortex. Biological Cybernetics **51** (1984) 195-199.
7. Rodieck, R.W. and Stone, J.: Analysis of receptive fields of cat retinal ganglion cells. Journal of Neurophysiology **28** (1965) 833-849.
8. Ratliff, F.: Mach Bands: Quantitative Studies On Neural Network In The Retina. San Francisco CA, Holden-Day (1965) 253-332.
9. Yu, Y., Yamauchi, T., Choe, Y.: Explaining low-level brightness-contrast illusions using disinhibition. Biologically Inspired approaches to Advanced Information technology, Springer, LNCS **3141** (2004) 166-175.

10. Douglass, J. K., Wilkens, L., Pantazelou, E., Moss, F.: Noise enhancement of information transfer in crayfish mechanoreceptors by stochastic resonance. Nature (London) **365** (1993) 337-340.
11. Gose, E., Johnsonbaugh R., Jost, S.: Chapter 7: Processing of Waveforms and Images, in: Pattern Recognition and Image Analysis, PHI second Indian reprint, New Delhi (2000) 263-327.
12. Ghosh, K., Sarkar, S., Bhaumik K.: Image Enhancement By High-order Gaussian Derivative Filters Simulating Non-classical Receptive Fields in the Human Visual System. Proceedings of First International Conference on Pattern Recognition and Machine Intelligence, Springer LNCS 3776 (2005) 453-458.
13. Ghosh, K., Sarkar S., Bhaumik, K.: A possible mechanism of zero-crossing detection using the concept of extended classical receptive field of retinal ganglion cells. Biological Cybernetics. **93** (2005) 1-5.
14. Palmer, S.E. Vision Science: Photons to Phenomenology, MIT Press, Cambridge, Massachusetts (1999) 115-118.
15. Blakeslee, B. and McCourt, M. E.: A multiscale spatial filtering account of the White effect, simultaneous brightness contrast and grating induction. Vision Research **39** (1999) 4361-4377.
16. Sierra-Vazquez, V.,Garcia-Perez, M.A.: Psychophysical 1-D Wavelet Analysis and the Appearance of Visual Contrast Illusions. IEEE Transactions on Systems, Man, and Cybernetics **25** (1995) 1424-1433.

Photonic Information Techniques Based on Compound-Eye Imaging

Satoru Irie, Rui Shogenji, Yusuke Ogura, and Jun Tanida

Graduate School of Information Science and Technology,
Osaka University, 2-1 Yamadaoka, Suita, 565-0871 Osaka, Japan
{irie, rui, ogura, tanida}@ist.osaka-u.ac.jp
http://www-lip.ist.osaka-u.ac.jp

Abstract. Insects and arthropods have compound eyes consisting of multiple small eyes as their visual system. Various interesting features can be utilized in the applications of the compound eye to information systems. A compact image capturing system named Thin Observation Module by Bound Optics (TOMBO) is an effective instance of the photonic information systems based on compound-eye imaging. The TOMBO retrieves a high-resolution image from multiple low-resolution images captured by the compound eye. In this paper, wide distance-range imaging, 3-D information acquisition, and 3-D object interface are presented as effective applications of the TOMBO system.

1   Introduction

As is well known, many kinds of insects and arthropods have a different visual system from ours. That is a compound eye consisting of multiple small eyes, which survives as an alternative form of the visual system of creatures for long time. Various interesting features can be obtained by applying the compound eye to information systems. Therefore, many imaging systems based on compound-eye imaging were presented[1][2][3]. Especially, an imitated compound imaging system using a microlens array is a typical form of the implementation due to convenience and compactness of the hardware. However, such an imitated compound imaging system can not capture high-resolution images because each small lens comprising the compound eye is used to detect the signal of a single pixel of the target image. To overcome the problem, the authors presented a compact image capturing system named Thin Observation Module by Bound Optics (TOMBO)[4][5]. In the TOMBO system, each lens is used to form an image of the target, and a set of the images are processed to retrieve a high-resolution image of the target.

In this paper, effective applications of the photonic information systems based on compound eye imaging are presented. As instances of the photonic information techniques, wide distance range imaging, 3-D information acquisition, and 3-D object interface are considered and their implementations are demonstrated.

A.J. Ijspeert et al. (Eds.): BioADIT 2006, LNCS 3853, pp. 252–264, 2006.

2   Compound Eye

A compound eye is an organ composed of a multiple number of small imaging systems consisting of a corneal lens and an optic nerve as shown Fig. 1. The compound eye has interesting features such as wide angle of view, thin hardware structure, and lightweight implementation of the system. Arrangement of the elemental optical systems on a curved basement provides wide angle of view. Short working distance of the elemental lenses contributes to thin and lightweight form of the system.

Figure 2 shows a conceptual diagram of the image capturing process by a compound eye. By the effect of the elemental lens, an inverted image of the object is imaged onto the retina. Although a complete copy of the object is imaged on the retinal plane, a pixel signal at the position of the optic nerve is only sampled in the original form of the compound eye. The positions of the

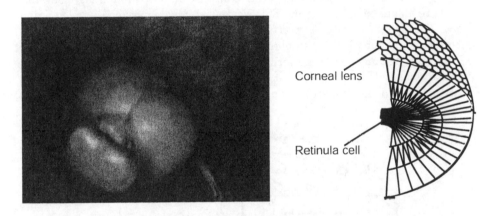

Fig. 1. Compound eyes of a dragonfly and the structure

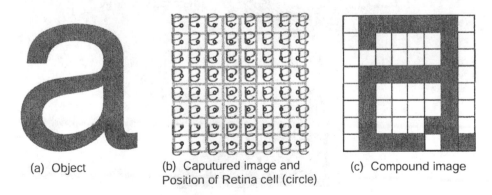

(a) Object   (b) Caputured image and   (c) Compound image
                    Position of Retina cell (circle)

Fig. 2. Image capturing process by a compound eye

optic nerves are indicated by small circles in Fig. 2(b). As shown in the figure, each optic nerve captures a different part of the object due to the geometrical arrangement of the elemental lenses. Therefore, the set of the acquired signals comprise the image of the object as shown in Fig. 2(c). Note that the number of the spatially resolved points of the captured image is equal to the number of the elemental eyes.

3   TOMBO: Thin Observation Module by Bound Optics

3.1   TOMBO System

The TOMBO system is an image capturing system based on compound-eye imaging. The TOMBO system consists of an array of microlenses, a signal separator, and an array of photo detectors as shown in Fig. 3. A set of a microlens and a divided area of the photo detectors comprise an individual imaging system to capture an image of the object. This elemental imaging system is called a unit optics. The signal separator is inserted to prevent crosstalk between the adjacent unit optics. In general, the minimum working distance of an imaging lens, i.e., the required distance for image formation by a lens, is approximately the same as the aperture of the lens. So that, the hardware thickness can be reduced by substitution of a large aperture lens with a set of small aperture lenses. This

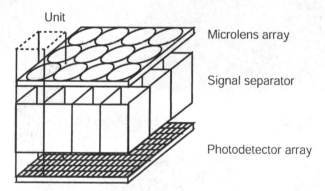

Fig. 3. Hardware composition of the TOMBO system

Fig. 4. Sensor module of the TOMBO system

Table 1. Specifications of TOMBO system

Units per system	8×8
Pixels pr unit	120×120
Pixel size	6.25μm×6.25μm
Device technology	0.35μm CMOS
Microlens property	f=750μm D=750μm

is one of the significant benefits of the compound-eye imaging system. Figure 4 shows a picture of the sensor module of the TOMBO system. The specifications of the TOMBO system are summarized in Table 1.

As a problem of image formation by a compound-eye, the image captured by a unit optics, called a unit image, is a low-resolution one. The TOMBO system employes postprocessing to combine information of the multiple unit images and to retrieve a high-resolution image of the object. As the image retrieval, the pixel rearrange method and other methods have been presented [4][6].

3.2 Image Retrieval

As an example of image retrieval, the procedure of the pixel rearrange method is described[4]. The principle is that the pixel data on the unit images are remapped onto a virtual image plane as shown in Fig. 5. The registration parameter describing the correspondence between the individual unit images and the virtual image plane is determined by the geometrical arrangement of the unit optics, the imaging property of the unit lenses, the distance of the target, etc. Figure 6 shows the optical setup of the TOMBO system. The TOMBO system consists of

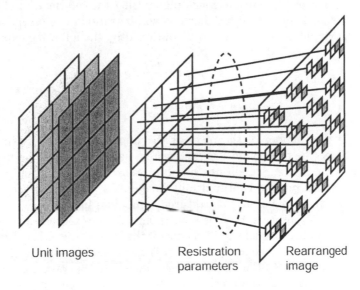

Unit images   Resistration   Rearranged
                     parameters   image

Fig. 5. Schematic diagram of pixel rearrange method

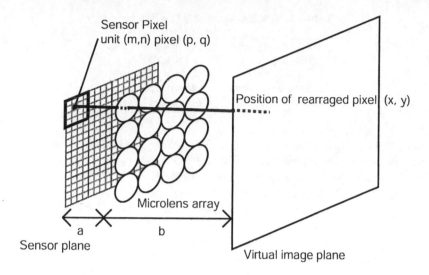

Fig. 6. Schematic diagram of the TOMBO optical setup

an image sensor and a microlens array. The distance between the image sensor and the microlens array is a. We refer to the plane where the image sensor is imaged as a virtual image plane. The distance between the microlens array and the virtual image plane is b. The coordinate system used is shown in Fig. 7. The position of a unit is expressed by (m, n). The position of a pixel of the unit is represented by the local coordinate (p, q). The images obtained by the individual units are mapped on the virtual image plane using the information of the system setup. Let us assume that the lens has no aberration. The pixel coordinate (x, y) on the virtual image plane can be obtained by the following expressions:

$$x = -\nu sm - \frac{bsp}{a},$$

$$y = -\nu sn - \frac{bsq}{a}.$$

Here, ν is the number of the pixel of the unit image and s is the size of the pixels. Since the compound imaging system captures a multiple number of unit images with different conditions simultaneously, the registration parameter can be estimated from the captured unit images. As a result, we can retrieve information of the target from the captured compound image.

In the remapping process, there is a key point of the pixel rearrange method. Ideally, the unit image is a demagnified copy of the target object. However, in the pixel rearrange method, the area of a pixel is not magnified during the remapping from a unit image to the virtual image plane. This operation is considered as a reverse projection of the pixel signal captured as a unit image under the assumption of neglecting image degradation caused by diffraction and aberration of the imaging system.

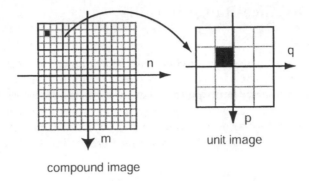

compound image

Fig. 7. Schematic diagram of the coordinate system of a compound image and unit image

After the remapping process, there exist pixels unmapped on the virtual image plane due to inhomogeneous sampling coverage of the unit images. Thus pixel interpolation is employed to retrieve a complete image. This procedure is rather simple, but we confirmed that good results can be obtained conveniently.

3.3 Experimental Result

Figure 8 shows an experimental result of image capture by the experimental TOMBO system[7]. As the target object, an enlarged portrait of 10 cm × 10 cm was set 26 cm distant from the lens array. Figure 8(a) is the captured compound image consisting of 6 × 6 units of 40 × 40 pixels. Shading effect was compensated beforehand. Figure 8(b) shows an enlarged unit image and Fig. 8(c) is the reconstructed image by the pixel rearrange method. Comparing these images, we can verify the effect of the image reconstruction processing.

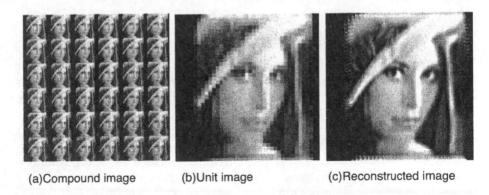

(a)Compound image   (b)Unit image   (c)Reconstructed image

Fig. 8. Experimental result of image retrieval: (a) captured compound image, (b) enlarged unit image, (c) reconstructedimage by the pixel rearrange method

258   S. Irie et al.

4   Wide Distance-Range Imaging

4.1   Principle

One of the interesting features of compound-eye imaging is that it has a wide range of the in-focus zone for the object distance. From close to far positions, we can capture them without any mechanical adjustment. More exactly, each unit optics forms an in-focused image over a wide distance range, whereas the registration parameter varies according to the object distance. As a result, the object image can be retrieved with appropriate processing.

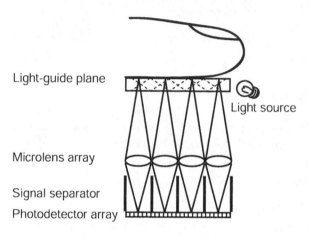

Light-guide plane

Light source

Microlens array

Signal separator

Photodetector array

Fig. 9. Optical setup for fingerprint capturing

As an extreme case, a close-up picture is taken as follows. In this case, each unit image holds information of the different part of the object. Therefore, the retrieval procedure is to trim the overlapped signals on the margins, to rotate the unit images by 180 degree, and to join the whole unit images.

4.2   Fingerpring Capturing

An application of close-up imaging, a fingerprint pattern is captured by the TOMBO system [9]. Fingerprint patterns can be used for biometrics authentification. Figure 9 shows an optical setup for fingerprint capturing. One problem in this implementation is the illumination method. Thus, a light guiding plate is set at the top of the system for the purpose.

Figure 10 is an experimental result of fingerprint capturing. In this experiment, a fingerprint picture printed on a transparent sheet was used as the target object. Figure 10(a) is the captured compound image and Fig. 10(b) is the reconstructed image. In addition to fingerprint imaging, the same configuration of the TOMBO system can capture an image of the object at a distant position. Using this feature of the system, we can embody a compact multi-modal authentification device capable of capturing images of fingerprint and face conveniently.

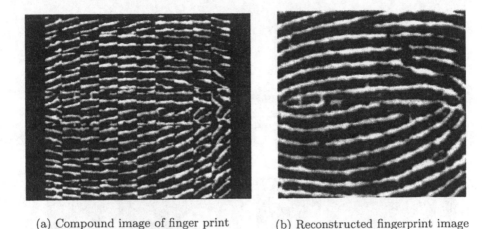

(a) Compound image of finger print   (b) Reconstructed fingerprint image

Fig. 10. Experimental result of fingerprint capturing

5 3-D Information Acquisition

5.1 Principle

The unit images on a compound image inherently contain parallax information of the target object. Thus 3-D information of the object can be retrieved from the compound image. Namely,the position of the object is determined by the triangulation technique using an arbitrary pair of unit images. Comparing to a binocular 3-D camera, the TOMBO system is inferior on the measurement resolution because of the short baseline for the triangulation. Instead this method is useful for 3-D measurement in a narrow space.

To retrieve 3-D information from a compound image, several methods are available. A convenient method is to presume a specific value for the distance of the target and to reconstruct the image at the plane. Then the same process is repeated with changing the distance value to obtain a set of the reconstructed images at different planes. Finally, 3-D mapping of the object points can be obtained as a set of sliced images.

5.2 Post-Focus Reconstruction

Figure 8 shows an experimental result of 3-D information acquisition. As shown in the figure, two craft balloons are set at different distance from the TOMBO system. Then the compound image was captured and processed to retrieve 3-D information. Figures 11(a) and (b) are the retrieved images using the distance values 62cm and 42cm, respectively. In both pictures, the central part of the posterior balloon is magnified to clarify the difference between the in-focus and the out-of-focus states. Note that these images are generated from the same compound image captured at a time. This procedure is considered as post-focussing on the object, which is expected to be useful for observation of high speed phenomena.

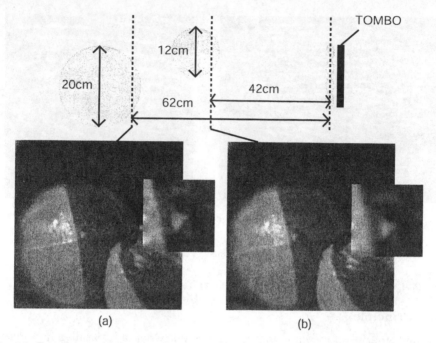

(a)   (b)

Fig. 11. Reconstracted images of objects in 3-D space: (a) focused at 620cm distance and (b) focused at 42cm distance

6   3-D Object Interface

6.1   Integral Photography

The compound imaging system can be applied to 3-D object reconstruction with slight modification. This technique is known as integral photography for 3-D object capturing and reconstruction[9][10]. Integral photography was invented by M. G. Lipmann in 1908 and various implementations have been presented[11][12]. Figure 12 shows the principle of integral photography. The object capturing process is the same as the TOMBO system where the obtained signal is nothing but a compound image. In the object reconstruction process, the captured compound image is displayed on the display device. Light rays emitted from the pixels of the display device are concentrated by the microlens array. Because of the reverse nature of light rays, the rays emitted from a point of the object are again focused on an identical point in the space by the reconstruction process. As a result, a 3-D object is reconstructed above the microlens array.

6.2   Concept and Implementation

As mentioned previously, the compound imaging system can be used for both 3-D object capturing and reconstruction. Utilizing compactness of the TOMBO system, the authors consider an application of the compound imaging system

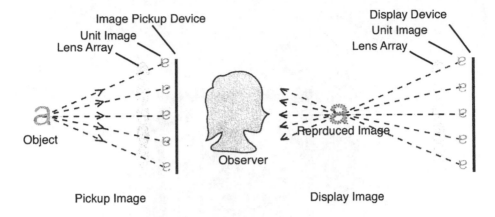

Fig. 12. 3-D object capturing and reconstruction by integral photography

to effective man/machine interface via 3-D objects. Figure 13 shows the concept of 3-D object interface. The device displays 3-D objects to the user and the user manipulates the 3-D objects. Then the device observes the motion of the user and makes an appropriate reaction on the object. Repeating the process, the user can interact to the machine via 3-D objects displayed by the device.

An important feature of 3-D object interface based on a compound imaging system is hardware compactness. Although a complex optical system may reconstruct realistic 3-D objects, usability of such a system is restricted. On the other hand, modification of the TOMBO system is expected to provide a quite compact interface device. Figure 14 shows a possible device implementation of 3-D object interface. Required functional extension of the imaging device is expected to be available according to progress in opto-electronic device technologies.

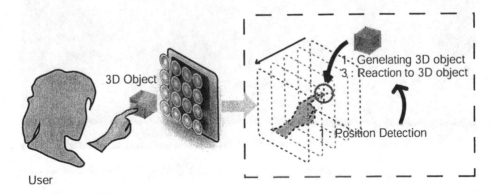

Fig. 13. Concept of 3-D object interface

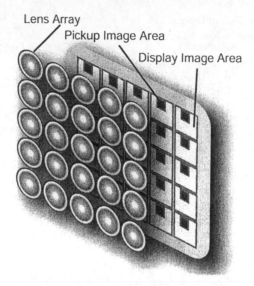

Fig. 14. Possible device implementation of 3-D object interface

6.3   Experiment Result

Button objects are generated and reconstructed in front of the lens array as a preliminary experiment. In the optical system, a liquid crystal display (pixel size 0.126 mm × 0.126 mm) was used as the display device. For the lens array, lenses (focal length 3.3 mm, aperture 1 mm) arranged in hexagonal were used.

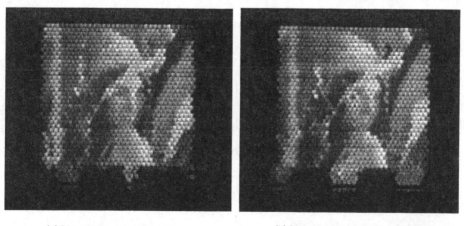

(a)Observation on left positon   (b)Observation on right posirion

Fig. 15. Button objects reconstructed by integral photography at different distance above the display

The objects displayed by the experimental system were three button objects and the Lena's photograph. The button objects were monochromatic planer circles. Figures 15 (a) and (b) are captured images of the reconstructed 3-D image from different positions. The distance of two observation positions is 10 cm parallel to the lens array; The heights of the observation positions are the same. We confirmed by the experiment that three button objects were reconstructed in front of the lens array where the distance from the lens is 19.8 mm and the Lena's photograph was displayed on the lens array. Figure 15 shows that the button has parallax and the position is in the space above the lens array, while the Lena's photograph has no parallax. It is confirmed that the button objects are properly reconstructed in the space and expected to be used as an agency for man/machine interaction.

7   Final Comments

A compound imaging system provides not only compactness and lightweight of the hardware but also functional features unable to be obtained by the conventional imaging system. Close-up imaging is a difficult task for the conventional imaging system whereas easy for the compound imaging system. This is a good example of the functional advantage of compound-eye imaging. 3-D information manipulation is also a promising application of the compound-eye imaging. From the anatomical point of view, insects and arthropods seem not to utilize the functional advantages of the compound-eye imaging conducting multiple unit images. However, combining the current information technologies, we can extend the application fields of this interesting hardware form. Design and optimization of postprocessing on the compound image are important issues of the photonic information systems based on compound-eye imaging.

8   Conclusion

In this paper, photonic information techniques based on compound-eye imaging have been presented. As a platform of the compound imaging system, the TOMBO system is useful, so that various applications can be implemented on the TOMBO system. Wide distance-range imaging, 3-D information acquisition, and 3-D object interface were introduced as promising applications of the compound imaging system. Hopefully, potential capabilities of the compound-eye imaging are explored, which contributes to progress of photonic information techniques.

Acknowledgments

This research was supported by 'Development of Basic Tera Optical Information Technologies,' Osaka Prefecture Collaboration of Regional Entities for the Advancement of Technological Excellence, Japan Science and Technology Agency, and 'Ultra-Thin Image Capturing Module,' at Innovation Plaza Osaka, Science and Technology Incubation Program in Advanced Region, Japan Science and Technology Agency. 3-D object interface is a part of a research in 21 Century COE Program, the Japan Ministry of Education, Culture, Sports, Science and Technology 'New Information Technologies for Building a Networked Symbiosis Environment' at Osaka University.

References

1. S. Ogata, J. Ishida, and T. Sasano: "Optical sensor array in an artificial compound eye," Opt. Eng. Vol. 33, pp. 3649–3655 (1994).
2. J. S. Sanders and C. E. Halford: "Design and annalysis of apposition compound eye optical sensors," Opt. Eng. Vol. 34, pp. 222–235 (1995).
3. K. Hamanaka and H. Koshi: "An artificial compound eye using a microlens array and its application to scale invariant processing," Opt. Rev. Vol. 3, pp. 264–268 (1996).
4. J. Tanida, et al.: "Thin Observation module by bound optics (TOMBO): concept and experimental verification," Appl. Opt., Vol. 40, pp. 1806–1813 (2001).
5. J. Tanida, Y. Kitamura, K. Yamada, S. Miyatake, M. Miyamoto, T. Morimoto, Y. Masaki, N. Kondou, D.Miyazaki, and Y. Ichioka: "Compact image capturing system based on compound imaging and digital reconstruction," in *Micro- and Nano-optics for Optical Interconnection and Information Processing*, Proc. SPIE, Vol. 4455, pp. 34–41 (2001).
6. K. Nitta, R. Shogenji, S. Miyatake, and J. Tanida: "Image reconstruction for thin observation module by bound optics using interative back projection method," Appl. Opt. (submitted).
7. J. Tanida, K. Nitta, and S. Miyatake: "compact image capturing system based on compound-eye optics and post digital processing," in Technical Digest of ICO04, pp. 59 - 60 (2004).
8. R. Shogenji, et al.: "Bimodal fingerprint capturing system based on compound-eye imaging module," Appl. Opt. Vol.43, No.6, pp. 1355–1359 (2004).
9. G. Lippmann: "La photographie integrale" Comptes-Rendus, Acad. Sci. Vol. 146, pp. 446–451 (1908).
10. C. B. Burckhardt: "Optimum parameters and resolution limitation of integral photography," J. Opt. Soc. Am. Vol. 58, pp. 71–76 (1968).
11. F. Okano, H. Hoshino, J. Arai, and I. Yuyama: "Real-time pickup method for a three-dimensional image based on integral photography," Appl. Opt. Vol. 36, 1598–1603 (1997).
12. M. Okui, J. Arai,M. Kobayashi,F. Okano: "Improvement of an integral three-dimensional television system through correction of geometrical position errors," Proceedings of SPIE, Vol. 5291, SPIE, San Jose, 5291-36, 321–328 (2004).

Attractor Memory with Self-organizing Input

Christopher Johansson and Anders Lansner

Department of Numerical Analysis and Computer Science,
Royal Institute of Technology, 100 44 Stockholm, Sweden
Fax: +46-8-7900930
{cjo, ala}@nada.kth.se

Abstract. We propose a neural network based autoassociative memory system for unsupervised learning. This system is intended to be an example of how a general information processing architecture, similar to that of neocortex, could be organized. The neural network has its units arranged into two separate groups called populations, one input and one hidden population. The units in the input population form receptive fields that sparsely projects onto the units of the hidden population. Competitive learning is used to train these forward projections. The hidden population implements an attractor memory. A back projection from the hidden to the input population is trained with a Hebbian learning rule. This system is capable of processing correlated and densely coded patterns, which regular attractor neural networks are very poor at. The system shows good performance on a number of typical attractor neural network tasks such as pattern completion, noise reduction, and prototype extraction.

1 Introduction

Autoassociative memory implemented with attractor neural networks works best with sparse activity, i.e. when each stored pattern only activates a small fraction of the network's units [1]. Further, this type of memory achieve a higher storage capacity with uncorrelated or weakly correlated, e.g. random, patterns than with highly correlated patterns. Real world data, e.g. sensor data, often consists of a large number of correlated measurements, resulting in densely coded and correlated input patterns. It has been suggested that for successful use of such raw data, the redundancies embedded in the data must be reduced and that this is done by the early sensory processing circuits, e.g. the primary visual cortex V1, in the mammalian brain [2]. At the same time as the redundancies in the sensory data are reduced, it is important to preserve the information in this data [3-6]. Linsker called this the Infomax principle. One way of assuring that the information present in the sensory data is maintained is to measure the reconstruction error of this data.

Barlow argues, based on arguments of computational efficiency, that preprocessing of sensory data should generate a factorial code, i.e. a code that can represent the input data by a limited number of components. Further, this factorial code should be sparse. A sparse activity is also supported by arguments of neural energy efficiency [7, 8]. Algorithms that generates such sparse codes from real world image data have been explored by several authors [7-13]. A cause commonly mentioned by these

A.J. Ijspeert et al. (Eds.): BioADIT 2006, LNCS 3853, pp. 265–280, 2006.
© Springer-Verlag Berlin Heidelberg 2006

investigators for recoding the sensory information with a sparse code is that it is better suited for use in an associative memory, which is demonstrated in several papers [14-17].

By extracting features from the input data a sparse and information preserving recoding is achieved. A powerful and commonly used approach to feature extraction is to use multiple layers of hierarchically arranged feed-forward networks that implements competitive learning [3-6, 18-25]. This type of structures can achieve accurate and invariant pattern recognition, e.g. with slow learning [21].

In this paper we investigate an attractor neural network that is paired with a self-organizing and competitive learning input network. The resulting system can by unsupervised learning store densely coded and correlated patterns, e.g. the images in Fig. 1. The purpose of the input network is to reduce redundancies and sparsify the input data, which is achieved by means of competitive learning [26].

An important aspect of the proposed system is that it is implemented with biologically plausible learning rules. These are learning rules that are local in at least space, i.e. weight updates that only depend on variables present in the pre- and postsynaptic junction. To this class of learning rules we count Hebbian and competitive learning. This type of local algorithms has the advantage that they parallelize well on cluster computers and in general are very fast.

Currently, few that work with biological models of the visual pathways have constructed larger systems that are capable of doing more than one step in the processing. Often, only a single specific component of the visual processing pathway is studied and modeled. A reason for this is that it is hard to get different models and neural network architectures to work properly together. One of the more interesting works that combines attractor neural networks with competitive learning is that by Bartlett and Sejnowski [16] who have built a neural system for viewpoint invariant face recognition. Here, we are not interested of building a system that can solve a particular task, although we use a selected problem for demonstration, but rather to build a general information processing system much like the brain like systems

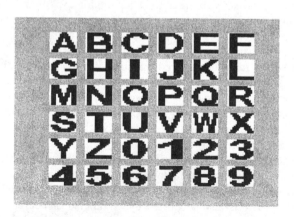

Fig. 1. The data set has 36 patterns representing both letters and digits that were derived from the font Arial. Each pattern is shown as a black and white 16×16-pixel image.

discussed by Hawkins [27]. We believe that attractor dynamics and distributed processing are important features of such system. The system that we propose in this paper can be used as a module in a larger hierarchal system, which is discussed in the end of this paper.

The experiments in this paper use the data set shown in Fig. 1. It consists of 36 black and white images of letters and digits, each represented by 16×16 pixels. These images were derived from the Arial font, and on average they have as many black as white pixels. Although the proposed system is evaluated on tasks involving image data, it should not be compared to state of the art image processing algorithms [28, 29] because it is not intended for image processing in particular.

The paper is organized as follows: In section 1.1 and 1.2 the learning rules, implemented in the system, are presented. In section 1.3, results on using the data set together with standard attractor neural networks is presented. In section 2, our system is described. In section 3 the results on applying the system to the image data are given. Section 4 contains a discussion of the results and future developments of the system. The conclusions are presented in section 5.

1.1 BCPNN

In the following we present the Bayesian Confidence Propagating Neural Network (BCPNN) with hypercolumns [30, 32]. This type of neural network can be used to implement both feed-forward classifiers and attractor memory. It has a Hebbian type of learning-rule, which means that it is local in both space and time (only the pre- and postsynaptic units activations' at one particular moment are needed to update the weights) and therefore it can be efficiently parallelized. Further, the network can be used with both unary-coded activity (spiking activity), $o \in \{0,1\}$, and real-valued activity, $o \in (0,1)$. The network has N units grouped into H hypercolumns with U_h units in each. Here, h is the index of a particular hypercolumn and Q_h is the set of all units belonging to hypercolumn h. When an attractor network is implemented, a symmetric weight matrix, $w_{ij} \in \mathbb{R}$, connects the units and there are no connections within a hypercolumn;

$$\{w_{ij} = 0 : i \in Q_h \wedge j \in Q_h\} \quad \text{for each } h = 1, 2, ..., H \tag{1}$$

The network is operated by initializing the activity and then run a process called relaxation in which the activity is updated. The relaxation process stops when a fixed-point is reached i.e. the activity is constant.   When using the network as an autoassociative memory the activity is initialized to a noisy or a partial version of one of the stored patterns. The relaxation process has two steps; first the potential, m, is updated (eq. (3)) with the current support, s (eq. (2)). Secondly, the new activity is computed from the potential by a softmax function as in eq. (4).

$$s_j = \log(\beta_j) + \sum_{h=1}^{H} \log\left(\sum_{k \in Q_h} w_{kj} o_k\right) \tag{2}$$

$$\tau_m \frac{dm_j}{dt} = s_j - m_j \tag{3}$$

$$o_j \leftarrow \frac{e^{Gm_j}}{\sum_{k \in Q_h} e^{Gm_k}} : j \in Q_h \quad \text{for each } h = \{1,...,H\} \tag{4}$$

The following values of the parameters were used throughout the paper; $\tau_m=10$ and $G=10$.

The biases, β_j, and weights, w_{ij}, are computed from probability estimates, p, of the activation and co-activation of units. Here, the presynaptic units are indexed with i and the postsynaptic units are indexed with j and we have used the relative frequency to compute the p estimates:

$$p_i = \frac{1}{P}\sum_{\mu=1}^{P} \xi_i^\mu$$

$$p_{ij} = \frac{1}{P}\sum_{\mu=1}^{P} \xi_i^\mu \xi_j^\mu \tag{5}$$

Here, ξ is a unary-coded pattern, P is the number of patterns, and μ is the index of a pattern. The estimates of p can be zero, and those cases must be treated separately when biases and weights are computed. The biases and weights are computed as:

$$w_{ij} = \begin{cases} 0 & \text{if } p_i = 0 \lor p_j = 0 \\ \dfrac{1}{P} & \text{else if } p_{ij} = 0 \\ \dfrac{p_{ij}}{p_i p_j} & \text{otherwise} \end{cases} \tag{6}$$

$$\beta_i = \begin{cases} \dfrac{1}{P^2} & \text{if } p_i = 0 \\ p_i & \text{otherwise} \end{cases}$$

1.2 Competitive Learning

Competitive selective learning (CL) [33] is here implemented by the units in the hidden population. The weights onto each of these units represent a code vector in the CL algorithm. The input to each of these units comes from the units in a few selected hypercolumns in the input population. These groups of hypercolumns in the input population are called the receptive fields. For each iteration of the training set, the code vectors (connections) of the winning units in the hidden population are updated. Dead units are avoided by constantly reinitializing the code vectors of these with values similar to units that are not dead. For a winning unit, j, the weights are updated as;

$$w_{ij} = w_{ij} + (i/U - w_{ij})/\tau_C \tag{7}$$

where i is the index of the input unit within its hypercolumn and U is the total number of units in this hypercolumn. Throughout the paper we use $\tau_C=10$.

1.3 Single Layer Networks

To establish the capabilities of single layered attractor neural networks we stored the patterns in Fig.1 in a BCPNN [30, 32] with $N=512$ units partitioned pair wise into $H=256$ hypercolumns. Here, each hypercolumn represented a pixel, and in each hypercolumn the two units represented the colors white and black. We also stored the patterns in a Hopfield network [1, 34] with 256 units. In the Hopfield network, the activity (-1 or 1) of each unit represented the color of a pixel. In these networks there are no hidden units and all units act as input units that are fully connected with each other. The stability of the trained patterns was tested by using each of these as a retrieval cue for itself and the resulting attractors are shown in Fig. 2. As seen in Fig. 2, both networks tend to cluster all patterns into a few particular attractors.

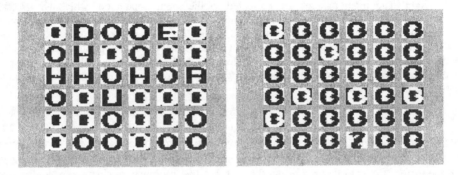

Fig. 2. The stable attractors in a 512 units BCPNN (left) and in a 256 units Hopfield network (right) after training with the data set in Fig. 1. On recall, a copy without noise of the stored pattern was used as retrieval cue.

2 Attractor Network with Self-organizing Input

In the previous section we demonstrated the poor performance of attractor memories on data consisting of densely coded and correlated patterns. To solve this problem we here propose a system where the input is fed through a preprocessing stage that serves to sparsify the data before it is stored in the attractor memory. This system has two populations of units, one input and one hidden population. The image data is presented to the input population and the hidden population implements an autoassociative memory (Fig. 3, right). In the experiments we also use a system without autoassociative memory as a reference (Fig. 3, left). The hidden population has 32 hypercolumns with 16 units in each and the input population consists of 256 hypercolumns with 2 units in each. Thus the average activity in the hidden population is 1/16 compared with 1/2 for the input population.

The recurrent projection of the hidden population, and the back projection from the hidden population to the input population, are trained with the BCPNN algorithm (section 2.1). These projections are *full*, meaning that all units in the sending population are connected to all units in the receiving population. The recurrent projection implements the autoassociative memory and the back projection enables accurate recons tructtion of the stored data.

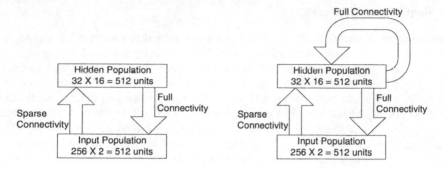

Fig. 3. A schematic diagram of the memory system without autoassociative memory, left, and with, right. The input patterns are presented to the input population, which has $H=256$ hypercolumns and $U=2$ units. Each hypercolumn represents a pixel and the two units in a hypercolumn represents the colors white and black. The hidden population has $H=32$ and $U=16$. The activity is propagated from the input to the hidden population through a set of sparse connections that are trained with competitive learning. The activity in the hidden population is back projected onto the input population through a set of connections that are trained with the associative BCPNN learning-rule.

The connections from the input to the hidden population are trained with a CL algorithm (section 2.2). These connections are sparse because every hidden unit receives afferent connections only from a small fraction of the input units. How these connections are setup has a great impact on the memory performance and noise tolerance of the system and hence this is thoroughly investigated by experiments in section 3. Here, we refer to this setup process as partitioning of the input-space and formation of receptive fields. In section 2.3 we present four different methods for setting up these connections.

The unsupervised training of this system consists of four phases: First, the input-space is partitioned, i.e. the feed-forward connections from the input to the hidden population are setup. This can be done either by domain knowledge such that the correlation decreases symmetrically around a pixel in an image with distance or it can be done in a data dependent way based on the statistics of the training data. In the experiments, 3 data independent and 1 data dependent methods for partitioning the input-space are explored. Secondly, the weights of the forward projection from the input to the hidden population are trained with CL. This is the most computationally intensive part for a system of the size in Fig. 3. Thirdly, the recurrent projection of the hidden population is trained. Fourthly, back projection from the hidden to the input population is trained. The last three steps could in principle be done all at the same time.

The retrieval or restoration of an image (pattern) is done in three steps: First, the retrieval cue, which can be a noisy version of a stored image, is applied to the input population and the activity is propagated to the units in the hidden population. Secondly, the attractor neural network is activated and the input from the input population is turned off. The activity in the attractor network is allowed to settle into a fix-point. Thirdly, the activity is propagated from the hidden population back to the input population in order to reconstruct or recall the image.

In the current implementation, unary coded activity is propagated between the populations, i.e. both populations have spiking units.

2.1 Receptive Fields

As is seen in the experiments, an important issue for the function and performance of the system is how the receptive fields are formed. Here we discuss four different ways of partitioning the input-space into regions (called receptive fields), three data independent and one data dependant methods. The data dependant method performs the partitioning based on the data's statistics. When the receptive fields have been formed, features from each field are extracted by CL. Each of these features are then represented by a specific unit in the hidden population.

The first data independent method partitions the input-space into lines (Fig. 4 upper left). This method assures that all input units have an equal number of outgoing connections and also that each hidden unit receives an equal number of incoming connections. We call this partitioning scheme *heuristic*.

The two other data independent methods partitions the input-space such that either all input units have an equal number of outgoing connections (called *random fan-out*) or such that all hidden unit receives an equal number of incoming connections (called *random fan-in*) (Fig. 4, lower row). In both of the methods, the difference in usage between any two units is not allowed to be greater than one. Apart from the above constraints the connections from the input to the hidden population are randomly setup.

The fourth and data dependant method, called *informed*, partitions the input-space such that hypercolumns with large mutual information are clustered together. Further, the receptive fields are constructed so that they all have an equal entropy. This means that a receptive field, consisting of hypercolumns with small entropies, will contain a large number of hypercolumns and vice versa. Additional to these two objective functions, it is assured that the number of outgoing connections from units in the input population does not differ by more than 1. In Fig. 4 we see that this method tend to construct receptive fields of spatially neighboring pixels. By organizing the input into

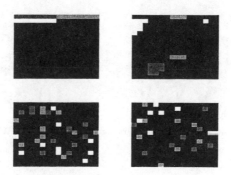

Fig. 4. Three different receptive fields, each coded in a shade of gray, plotted for each of the four partitioning schemes; *heuristic* (upper left), *informed* (upper right), *random fan-out* (lower left), *random fan-in* (lower right)

receptive fields with high mutual information the CL should be able to extract good features that accurately describes the input-space. In information theoretic terms, this type of partitioning schemes assures that the Infomax principle [6] is followed.

The mutual information between two hypercolumns x and y can easily be computed if the BCPNN weight matrix, with p_{ij} and w_{ij}, has been computed:

$$I(x; y) = \sum_{i \in Q_x} \sum_{j \in Q_y} p_{ij} \log_2 w_{ij} \qquad (8)$$

3 Results

Three different tasks were used to evaluate the performance of the memory system described in section 2. The first task tests pattern completion; the second task tests noise reduction; and the third task tests prototype extraction. These are three typical tasks that are used to evaluate the performance of an attractor neural network.

All experiments were done for the two different systems (with and without autoassociative memory) and for each of the four different partitioning methods used to form the receptive fields. The y-axis in the plots measures the total number of differing pixels between all of the 36 reconstructed images and the original images in Fig. 1. The total number of pixel errors in the retrieval cues used for testing pattern completion is 883 (Fig. 5, left) and in the retrieval cues used for testing noise reduction the average number of pixel errors is 849 (Fig. 5, right).

In all experiments, the CL procedure was run 20 times. In each run the code vectors were updated for 30 iterations and then relocated if necessary. Unused code vectors were relocated as well as the code vector with the smallest variance. The attractor neural network was run until a stable fix-point was reached or more than 500 iterations had passed.

The results were averaged over 30 runs, each in which the system was set up from scratch and the connections trained. In each such run, the performance of the system was evaluated on 20 different sets of noisy retrieval cues.

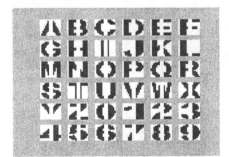 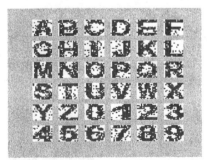

Fig. 5. The images used as retrieval cues in the experiments. Left, 20% of the pixels in the center of each image have been removed (set to white). These images have a total of 883 pixels flipped compared with the original ones. Right, 20% salt and pepper noise, which on the average resulted in a total of 849 flipped pixels in all of the images.

All of the following figures are arranged in the same manner, the left plot shows the results for the system without autoassociative memory and the right plot shows the results for the system with autoassociative memory. Further, each plot contains the results for each of the four receptive-field partitioning schemes.

3.1 Pattern Completion

The pattern completion experiment tested the memory system's capability to fill in a missing part of a stored pattern (Fig. 5). The images used as retrieval cues in this test had 20% of their pixels in the center set to white. A reconstruction error of less than 883 pixel errors meant that the system had partly succeeded in the image completion of the retrieval cues.

As seen in Fig. 6, large receptive fields gave the best result. It should be noted that there was a large variance in the performance between different runs and in some runs the reconstruction error was close to zero, in particular for the system with informed partitioning of the receptive fields. On this task, the best way of setting up the receptive fields was by a random method. By comparing the left and right plots in Fig. 6, it can be concluded that the auto associative memory function improves the reconstruction performance. It should be noted that this task, occlusion, is considered to be a hard problem in machine learning, because the system is tested with data that has a different distribution than the training data.

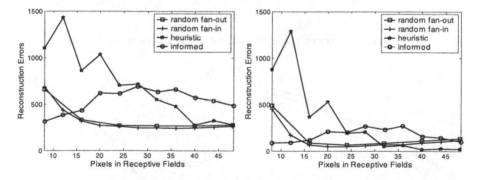

Fig. 6. The reconstruction error plotted as a function of the size of the receptive fields for each of the for input-space partitioning schemes; a constant number of connections from each unit in the input population (random fan-out), a constant number of incoming connections to each unit in the hidden population (random fan-in), the receptive fields are formed from line elements of pixels (heuristic), and receptive fields that are formed by a data driven process based on the mutual information between pixels (informed). Here, the retrieval cues were copies of the stored patterns that had 20% of their area occluded. The left plot shows the performance of the system with only feed-forward and feed-back connections and the right plot shows the performance of the system that also has a recurrent projection.

3.2 Noise Reduction

In the noise reduction experiment the memory system's capability to remove salt and pepper noise was tested. Retrieval cues with 20% salt and pepper noise were used

(Fig. 5, right). A reconstruction error of less than 849 meant that noise had been removed from the retrieval cues. In Fig. 7 the system's performance is plotted as a function of receptive field size. In Fig. 8, the ability to remove salt and pepper noise is plotted as a function of the noise level in the retrieval cues.

Again, it can be seen in Fig. 7, by comparing the left and right plots that the autoassociative memory contributes to an improved noise reduction capability. In Fig. 8, right, the effect of the autoassociative memory is seen as the S-shaped form of the curve showing the reconstruction errors. At first, all patterns are perfectly restored. Then, when more noise is added, the autoassociative memory begins to recall erroneous patterns and as a result the number of reconstruction errors increases drastically.

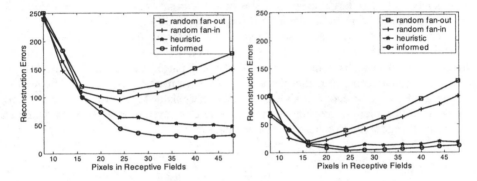

Fig. 7. Here, retrieval cues with 20% salt and pepper noise were used

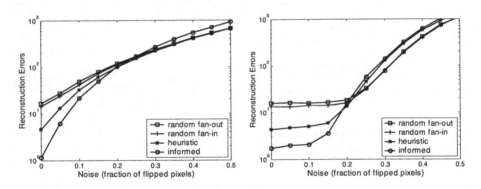

Fig. 8. The reconstruction error plotted as a function of the noise in the retrieval cues

3.3 Noise Reduction and Principal Components

Here, we experimented with a closed form learning algorithm to contrast the incremental CL. The forward weights, from the input to the hidden units, were set up according to the eigen vectors of the 16 largest eigen values. These eigen vectors, sometimes called principal components, were computed over all training patterns in each receptive field. The results in Fig. 9 show that this way of setting up the forward connections was not better than using CL. This result is not surprising since only the eigen vector that best describes the data is set active in the hidden population, and usually this is the one with the largest eigen value. Therefore, a few units in the hidden population are used all of the time, which affects the performance of both the attractor memory and the associative back projection in a negative way.

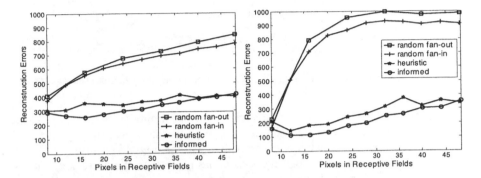

Fig. 9. Here, the forward weights were set up according to the principal components, of the training patterns, computed in each of the receptive fields. Retrieval cues with 20% salt and pepper noise were used.

3.4 Prototype Extraction

The prototype extraction experiment tested the system's ability to extract a prototype from noisy training data, i.e. remove noise from the training data (Fig. 10, Fig. 11). The training data was composed of twenty copies, with 20% salt and pepper noise, of the original images in Fig. 1. The retrieval cues used to test the system were the same as in section 3.2, also with 20% salt and pepper noise. The reconstruction error was measured against the patterns in Fig. 1 and not against the actual prototype means of

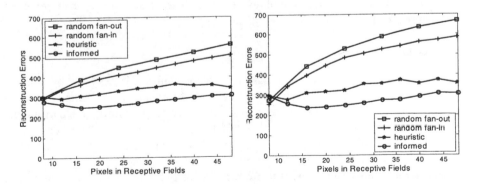

Fig. 10. Here, retrieval cues with 20% salt and pepper noise were used. The system was trained with twenty sets of images, each having 20% salt and pepper noise.

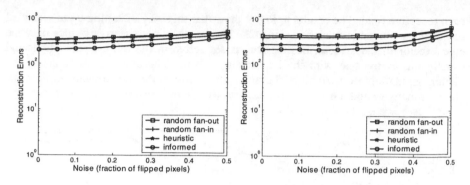

Fig. 11. The reconstruction error plotted as a function of the noise in the retrieval cues

the training set. The results of this experiment would improve slightly if a larger training set with more copies of each image is used, because the prototype mean of the training set would then better coincide with that of the original patterns.

It should be noted that although the system has never seen the noise free images, but only noisy versions of them with on average 849 pixel errors, it can reduce the noise in all of the retrieval cues to a value less than 849 pixel errors. Here, the advantage of the autoassociative memory is less apparent.

4   Discussion

The work presented in this paper is a first step towards a general framework for processing of sensory data. The proposed system integrated several neural network technologies; such as competitive learning, feed-forward classifiers, and attractor memory. Further, new algorithms for forming receptive fields were explored. These techniques are discussed in section 4.1. The way in which these different technologies are best combined still needs to be studied and the results presented in this paper could probably be improved.

In section 4.2 the mapping to biology of the proposed system is discussed together with future directions of development.

4.1   Receptive Fields

Partitioning the input-space in a data dependent (informed) way or by domain knowledge (heuristic) improved the system's performance significantly over a random partitioning in most of the cases. As expected, the informed partitioning created circular receptive fields because of the local relationship between nearby pixels. The heuristic partitioning can only be used when the correlation structure of the input data is known beforehand, as in images, which usually not is the case. The informed partitioning can be used to from receptive fields from arbitrary input data. Further, the informed partitioning together with CL, is the partitioning scheme that best comply with Linsker's Infomax principle.

The preprocessing stage does not decorrelate the patterns completely, but preserves the metric of the input data. This is necessary in order for the system to generalize well and perform clustering of the stored memories. Of course, preserving correlations between input patterns reduces the storage capacity slightly.

The self-organized formation of the receptive fields is implemented by a neural mechanism in the proposed system. But in a biological system the formation of the receptive fields may very well be governed by evolutionary factors and coded genetically.

In a future study it would be interesting to investigate e.g. the system's generalization abilities by using input patterns from a different font as retrieval cues.

4.2 An Abstract Model of Neocortex

The proposed system was designed with the goal of creating an abstract generic model of neocortex. Here, we discuss one possible mapping of this model onto the mammalian neocortex. In the hierarchal model proposed, the population is the module that is repeatedly duplicated to form an hierarchy. The exact mapping of the model onto the neurons of neocortex is dependent on the species and maybe also the particular area of neocortex, e.g. visual, somatosensory, or prefrontal.

The starting point for the model is the columnar structure of neocortex. In the neocortex, about 100 neurons are grouped into minicolumns and approximately 100 minicolumns form hypercolumns [35]. Because the pyramidal cells in layer 2/3 and 5/6 are tightly connected by excitatory synapses [36] the minicolumn can be seen as the functional unit in cortex. Further, the hypercolumns implements a normalization of the activity in the minicolumns [37].

In the model, each unit in the network corresponds to a cortical minicolumn. Further, the layer 4 stellate cells project to the pyramidal cells in layer 3, but there are no projections within a minicolumn from either layer 2/3 and 5/6 back onto these neurons. This means that information can only be transmitted from layer 4 neurons to the rest of the excitatory neurons within a minicolumn. This circuitry makes it possible to separate bottom-up data from top-down predictions. Discrepancies between these two data streams can be used to trigger learning mechanisms.

On a larger scale minicolumns are grouped into hypercolumns. The purpose of the hypercolumn is to normalize the activity of the layer 2/3 and 5/6 pyramidal cells in the minicolumns and to facilitate the competitive learning among the afferents to layer 4 neurons. This normalization is implemented by an inhibitory basket cell that receives projections from all minicolumns within a hypercolumn and project with inhibitory synapses back onto these minicolumns.

Within a restricted area (e.g. cortical area) of cortex the minicolumns form an autoassociative memory. This autoassociative network is implemented by synaptic connections between the neurons in layer 2/3 and 5/6. These connections can both be excitatory and inhibitory. The inhibitory connections are formed by pyramidal cells that project onto inhibitory double bouquet and bipolar cells in the postsynaptic minicolumn.

The pyramidal neurons in a minicolumn also project onto layer 4 neurons in other cortical areas. These connections are defined as forward projections and take part in the competitive learning performed by layer 4 neurons. Further, these projections are convergent meaning that they only project on a small fraction of the hypercolumns in the receiving cortical area.

The pyramidal neurons in a minicolumn also project backwards to pyramidal neurons in other cortical areas. These backward projections are used to infer holistic top-down knowledge. These connections have a divergent nature, meaning that they project onto a large number of hypercolumns in the preceding cortical area.

As is seen in Fig. 12, groups of hypercolumns (populations) can be arranged in a hierarchal fashion. In each forward projection, invariant features of the inputs are extracted, e.g. by competitive and slow learning. The sensory bottom-up data is then matched with predictions generated by the recurrent and top-down projections. In this paper we have shown that a limited version of this type of hierarchical system is useful when dealing with correlated input data. In the future it will be interesting to investigate the capabilities of a hierarchical system with more than two levels.

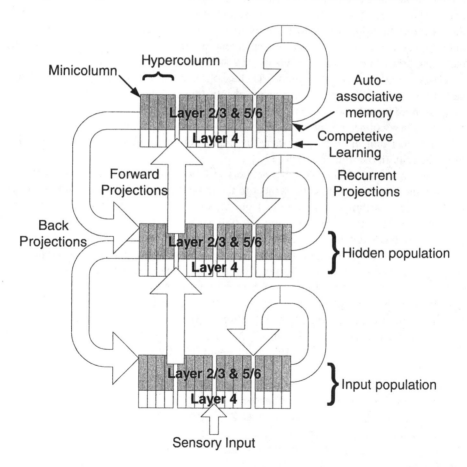

Fig. 12. The abstract generic and hierarchical model of neocortex

5 Conclusions

In this paper we have presented an integrated memory system that combines an attractor neural network with a decorrelating and sparsifying preprocessing stage. This memory system can work with correlated input as opposed to simpler autoassociative memories based on single layer networks. We demonstrated the system's capability on a number of tasks, involving a data set of images, which could not be handled by the single layered attractor networks.

References

1. Hertz, J., A. Krogh, and R.G. Palmer, *Introduction to the Theory of Neural Computation*. 1991: Addison-Wesely.
2. Barlow, H.B., *Unsupervised Learning*. Neural Computation, 1989. **1**(3): p. 295-311.
3. Linsker, R., *From basic network principles to neural architecture: Emergence of orientation columns*. Proc. Natl. Acad. Sci., 1986. **83**: p. 8779-8783.
4. Linsker, R., *From basic network principles to neural architecture: Emergence of orientation-selective cells*. Proc. Natl. Acad. Sci., 1986. **83**: p. 8390-8394.
5. Linsker, R., *From basic network principles to neural architecture: Emergence of spatial-opponent cells*. Proc. Natl. Acad. Sci., 1986. **83**: p. 7508-7512.
6. Linsker, R., *Self-organization in a perceptual network*. IEEE Computer, 1988. **21**: p. 105-117.
7. Olshausen, B.A. and D.J. Field, *Sparse Coding with an Overcomplete Basis Set: A Strategy Employed by V1*. Vision Research, 1997. **37**(23): p. 3311-3325.
8. Olshausen, B.A. and D.J. Field, *Sparse coding of sensory inputs*. Current Opinion in Neurobiology, 2004. **14**: p. 481-487.
9. Bell, A.J. and T.J. Sejnowski, *The Independent Components of Natural Scenes are Edge Filters*. Vision Research, 1997. **37**(23): p. 3327-3338.
10. Földiak, P., *Forming sparse representations by local anti-Hebbian learning*. Biol. Cybern., 1990. **64**: p. 165-170.
11. Olshausen, B.A. and D.J. Field, *Emergence of simple-cell receptive field properties by learning a sparse code for natural images*. Nature, 1996. **381**(6583): p. 607-609.
12. Schraudolph, N.N. and T.J. Sejnowski, *Competitive Anti-Hebbian Learning of Invariants*. Advances of Information Processing Systems, 1992. **4**: p. 1017-1024.
13. Yuille, Smirnakis, and Xu, *Bayesian Self-Organization Driven by Prior Probability Distributions*. Neural Computation, 1995. **7**: p. 580-593.
14. Peper, F. and M.N. Shirazi, *A Categorizing Associative Memory Using an Adaptive Classifier and Sparse Coding*. IEEE Trans. on Neural Networks, 1996. **7**(3): p. 669-675.
15. Michaels, R., *Associative Memory with Uncorrelated Inputs*. Neural Computation, 1996. **8**: p. 256-259.
16. Bartlett, M.S. and T.J. Sejnowski, *Learning viewpoint-invariant face representations from visual experience in an attractor network*. Network: Comp. in Neur. Sys., 1998. **9**(3): p. 399-417.
17. Amit, Y. and M. Mascaro, *Attractor Networks for Shape Recognition*. Neural Computation, 2001. **13**(6): p. 1415-1442.
18. Fukushima, K., *A Neural Network for Visual Pattern Recognition*. Computer, 1988. **21**(3): p. 65-75.

19. Fukushima, K., *Analysis of the Process of Visual Pattern Recognition by the Neocognitron.* Neural Networks, 1989. **2**(6): p. 413-420.
20. Fukushima, K. and N. Wake, *Handwritten Alphanumeric Character Recognition by the Neocognitron.* IEEE Trans. on Neural Networks, 1991. **2**(3): p. 355-365.
21. Földiák, P., *Learning Invariance from Transformation Sequences.* Neural Computation, 1991. **3**: p. 194-200.
22. Grossberg, S., *Competetive Learning: From Interactive Activation to Adaptive Resonance.* Cognitive Science, 1987. **11**: p. 23-63.
23. Rolls, E.T. and A. Treves, *Neural Networks and Brain Function.* 1998, New York: Oxford University Press.
24. Togawa, F., et al. *Receptive field neural network with shift tolerant capability for Kanji character recognition.* in *IEEE International Joint Conference on Neural Networks.* 1991. Singapore.
25. Wallis, G. and E.T. Rolls, *Invariant Face and Object Recognition in the Visual System.* Progress in Neurobiology, 1997. **51**: p. 167-194.
26. Rumelhart, D.E. and D. Zipser, *Feature Discovery by Competetive Learning.* Cognitive Science, 1985. **9**: p. 75-112.
27. Hawkins, J., ed. *On Intelligence.* 2004, Times Books.
28. Edelman, S. and T. Poggio, *Models of object recognition.* Current Opinion in Neurobiology, 1991. **1**: p. 270-273.
29. Moses, Y. and S. Ullman, *Generalization to Novel Views: Universal, Class-based, and Model-based Processing.* Int. J. Computer Vision, 1998. **29**: p. 233-253.
30. Sandberg, A., et al., *A Bayesian attractor network with incremental learning.* Network: Comp. in Neur. Sys., 2002. **13**(2): p. 179-194.
31. Lansner, A. and Ö. Ekeberg, *A one-layer feedback artificial neural network with a Bayesian learning rule.* Int. J. Neural Systems, 1989. **1**(1): p. 77-87.
32. Lansner, A. and A. Holst, *A higher order Bayesian neural network with spiking units.* Int. J. Neural Systems, 1996. **7**(2): p. 115-128.
33. Ueda, N. and R. Nakano, *A New Competitive Learning Approach Based on an Equidistortion Principle for Designing Optimal Vector Quantizers.* Neural Network, 1994. **7**(8): p. 1211-1227.
34. Hopfield, J.J., *Neural networks and physical systems with emergent collective computational abilities.* PNAS, 1982. **79**: p. 2554-2558.
35. Buxhoeveden, D.P. and M.F. Casanova, *The minicolumn hypothesis in neuroscience.* Brain, 2002. **125**(5): p. 935-951.
36. Thomson, A.M. and A.P. Bannister, *Interlaminar Connections in the Neocortex.* Cerebral Cortex, 2003. **13**(1): p. 5-14.
37. Hubel, D.H. and T.N. Wiesel, *Functional architecture of macaque monkey visual cortex.* Proc. R. Soc. Lond. B., 1977. **198**: p. 1-59.

Bio-inspired Replica Density Control in Dynamic Networks

Tomoko Suzuki, Taisuke Izumi, Fukuhito Ooshita,
Hirotsugu Kakugawa, and Toshimitsu Masuzawa

Graduate School of Information Science and Technology, Osaka University,
1-3 Machikaneyama, Toyonaka, 560-8531, Japan
Fax: +8-6-6850-6582
{t-suzuki, t-izumi, f-oosita, kakugawa, masuzawa}@ist.osaka-u.ac.jp

Abstract. Resource replication is a crucial technique for improving system performance of distributed applications with shared resources. A larger number of replicas require shorter time to reach a replica of the requested resource, but consume more storage of hosts. Therefore, it is indispensable to adjust the number of replicas appropriately for its application.

This paper considers the problem for controlling the density of replicas adaptively in dynamic networks. The goal of the problem is to adjust the number of replicas to a constant fraction of the current network size. This paper proposes algorithm inspired by the single species population model, which is a well-known population ecology model. The simulation results show that the proposed algorithm realize self-adaptation of the replica density in dynamic networks.

1   Introduction

One of the most important advantages distributed applications inherently have is resource sharing. A well-known example is file sharing on peer-to-peer networks [7, 6]. In such applications, each resource is accessed frequently by a significant number of users distributed over the whole network.

For such applications with shared resources, resource replication is a crucial technique for improving system performance and availability: replicas of an original resource are distributed over the network so that each user can get the requested resource by accessing a nearby replica. Resource replication can reduce communication latency and consumption of network bandwidth, and can also improve availability of the resources even when some of the replicas are unavailable.

In systems using resource replication, generally, a larger number of replicas require shorter time to reach a replica of the requested resource, but consume more storage of hosts. Therefore, it is indispensable to adjust the number of replicas appropriately for its application. For example, resource searching protocol PWQS has tradeoff between the reach time and the number of replicas, and

A.J. Ijspeert et al. (Eds.): BioADIT 2006, LNCS 3853, pp. 281–293, 2006.

requires replicas of each resource in numbers proportional to the network size (i.e., the number of hosts) to attain good performance [9].

However, in dynamic networks such as peer-to-peer networks, the appropriate number of replicas for its application changes with time, since network size varies with time. In addition, it is unrealistic to assume that each node knows the network size and the number of replicas on the network. Therefore, adjustment of the number of replicas for dynamical change of network size is not an easy task and requires investigation.

Biological systems inherently have self-* properties , such as self-adaptation, self-configuration, self-optimization and self-healing, to realize environmental adaptation. Thus, several biologically-inspired approaches have succeeded in realizing highly adaptive distributed systems. Successful projects include Bio-Networking project [2] and Anthill project [1]. These projects adopt biologically-inspired approaches to provide highly adaptive platform for mobile-agent-based computing [4, 12]. In our precedence work, we also focus on the biological system to control mobile agent population in dynamic networks [13]. Our algorithms are inspired by the well-known *the single species population model* and can adequately adjust the agent population in dynamic networks.

Contribution of this Paper. In this paper, we first formulate *the replica density control problem* in dynamic networks, and present a biologically-inspired solution for the problem. The replica density control problem requires to adapt the number of replicas to a given constant fraction of the current network size.

We propose a distributed solution for the problem using mobile agents. Mobile-agent-based distributed computing is one of the most promising paradigms to support autonomic computing in a large scale of distributed system with dynamics and diversity [10, 11]. Mobile agents are autonomous programs that can migrate from one node to another on the network, and traverse the distributed system to carry out a sophisticated task at each node.

To realize self-adaptation of the replica density, we borrow an idea from *the single species population model*, which is a well-known population ecology model. This model considers population of a single species in an environment such that individuals of the species can survive by consuming food supplied by the environment. The model is formulated by *the logistic equation* and shows that the population automatically converges to and stabilizes at some number depending on the amount of supplied food.

In the proposed algorithm, replicas of a resource are regarded as individuals of a single species, and agents created by nodes supply food for replicas. The algorithm try to adjust the number of replicas to a constant fraction of the network size by controlling the amount of food supplied by agents. The simulation results of the algorithm show that the proposed strategy can adequately adjust the replica density.

The rest of this paper is organized as follows. In Section 2, we present the model of distributed systems, and define the replica density control problem. In Sections 3 and 4, we propose the distributed solution for the problem and show its simulation results. Section 5 concludes the paper.

2 Preliminaries

2.1 System Models

Dynamic Networks. In this paper, we consider *dynamic networks* such that its node set and its link set vary with time. To define dynamic networks, we introduce discrete time and assume that each time is denoted by a non-negative integer in a natural way: time 0 denotes the initial time, time 1 denotes the time immediately following time 0 and so on.

Formally, a dynamic network at time t is denoted by $N(t) = (V(t), E(t))$ where $V(t)$ and $E(t)$ are respectively the node set and the link set at time t. A link in $E(t)$ connects two distinct nodes in $V(t)$ and a link between nodes u and v is denoted by e_{uv} or e_{vu}. We also use the following notations to represent the numbers of nodes and edges at time t: $n(t) = |V(t)|$ and $e(t) = |E(t)|$.

Mobile Agent Systems. A *mobile agent* is an autonomous program that can migrate from one node to another on the network. In dynamic networks, agents on node $u \in V(t)$ at time t can start migrating to node $v \in V(t)$ only when link e_{uv} is contained in $E(t)$. The agent reaches v at time $t + \Delta$ only when the link e_{uv} remains existing during the period from t to $t + \Delta$, where Δ is an integer representing *migration delay* between the nodes. The agent migrating from u to v is removed from the network when the link e_{uv} disappears during the period from t to $t + \Delta$.

Each of nodes and agents has a *local clock* that runs at the same rate as the global time. However, we make no assumption on the local clock values: the difference between the local clock values in the system is unbounded.

An agent and a node can interact with each other by executing operations: agent p on node u can change its state and the state of u depending on the current states of p and u, and node u can change its state and the states of the agents residing on u depending on the current states of u and the agents. Besides the above operations, each agent can execute operations to create new agents and to kill itself and each node can also execute operations to create new agents.

When agents reside on a node, the agents and the node have operations they can execute. For execution semantics, we assume that the agents and the node execute their operations sequentially in an arbitrary order. We also assume that the time required to execute the operations can be ignored, that is, we consider all the operations are executed sequentially but at an instant time.

2.2 Replica Density Control

For an application with shared resource, resource replication is crucial technique for improving system performance. Resources are items shared by the nodes on the network; files, documents, and so on. Replicas are copy of an original resource. In such systems, generally, a larger number of replicas lead to better performance, but consume more storage of hosts. Thus, it is required to control the number of replicas appropriately for its application.

In this paper, we consider the *replica density control problem*. Each node has zero or more replicas. We consider a original resource as its replica. Each node v can make same replicas from a replica on node v and delete replicas on node v. The goal of the problem is to control the number of replicas of a resource so that the ratio between the number of replicas and the number of nodes (called *network size* hereinafter) is kept to be a given constant. Let $r(t)$ be the number of replicas on the network $N(t)$ at time t: $r(t)$ is sum of the number of original resources and the number of its replicas. The problem is defined as follows.

Definition 2.1
The goal of **the replica density control problem** *is to adjust the number of replica $r(t)$ at time t to satisfy the following equality for a given constant δ $(0 < \delta \leq 1)$.*

$$r(t) = \delta \cdot n(t)$$

In this paper, we propose distributed solution for the replica density control problem. In the distributed solution, we assume that the constant δ is initially given to every node.

We consider distributed systems such that replicas are distributed over the networks and nodes can leave or join the networks. In such environment, it is obviously impossible to keep satisfying the above equation all the time. Thus, our goal is to propose distributed solution that realize quick convergence to and stability at the target number.

3   Replica Density Control Algorithm

In this section, we present a distributed solution for the replica density control problem. This algorithm is inspired by the single species population model (the logistic model), which is well-known in the field of the population ecology.

3.1   Single Species Population Model

In this subsection, we introduce the *single species population model* in the population ecology as the basis of our algorithm. This model considers an environment with a single species such that individuals of the species can survive by consuming food supplied by the environment. The model formulates the population growth of the species in the environment, and shows that the population (i.e., the number of individuals) in the environment automatically converges to and stabilizes at some number depending on the amount of food supplied by the environment.

We present more details of the single species population model. Each individual of the species periodically needs to take a specific amount of food to survive. That is, if an individual can take the specific amount of food then it can survive. Conversely, if an individual cannot take the specific amount of food then it dies. Moreover, in the case that an individual can take a sufficient amount of extra

food, then it generates progeny. Consequently, the followings hold: The shortage
of supplied food results in decrease in the population. Conversely, the excessive
amount of food results in increase in the population.

The single species population model formulates the above phenomena as follows: Let $p(t)$ be the population at time t. The single species population model
indicates that the *population growth rate* at time t is represented by the following
nonlinear first-order differential equation known as the *logistic equation* [8]:

$$\frac{\Delta p(t)}{\Delta t} = p(t) \cdot g(t) = p(t)(k \cdot f_a(t) - k \cdot f \cdot p(t)),$$

where $f_a(t)$ is the amount of food supplied by the environment at time t, f is the
amount of food consumed by one individual to survive and k is greater than 0.

The *per capita growth rate* $g(t)$ at time t is represented by

$$g(t) = k(f_a(t) - f \cdot p(t)).$$

The expression $f_a(t) - f \cdot p(t)$ represents the difference between the amounts
of supplied food and consumed food. When the supplied food exceeds the consumed food, $g(t)$ takes a positive value proportional to the difference, that is, the
positive per capita growth rate $g(t)$ is proportional to the amount of the surplus
food. A scarcity of the supplied food causes a negative value of $g(t)$ proportional
to the difference, that is, the negative per capita growth rate $g(t)$ is proportional
to the shortage of the supplied food.

The logistic equation has two equilibrium points of the population size $p(t)$:
$p(t) = 0$ and $p(t) = f_a(t)/f$. That is, the population remains unchanged, when
the population size is at the equilibrium points. The equilibrium point $p(t) =
f_a(t)/f$ represents the maximum population that the environment can keep, and
is called the *carrying capacity* of the environment.

If the population is larger (resp. smaller) than the carrying capacity then the
population decreases (resp. increases). Once the population reaches the carrying
capacity, then it remains unchanged (see Fig.1). Consequently, the single species
population model implies that the population eventually converges to and stabilizes at the carrying capacity. Notice that the carrying capacity depends on the
amount of food supplied by the environment.

3.2   Algorithm for Replica Density Control

In this subsection, we present an algorithm for the replica density control problem. The algorithm is inspired by the single species population model: replicas
regarded as individuals of a single species, and a network is regarded as an environment. That is, replicas need to consume food to survive and the food is
supplied by nodes of the network. These food are delivered to replicas by mobile
agents.

In the algorithm, we introduce time interval of some constant length denoted
by *CYCLE*. Behavior of each node and each replica can be divided into series of
the time interval: each node supplies food every the time interval and each replica

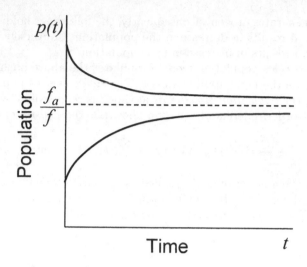

Fig. 1. Convergence to the equilibrium point in logistic equation

is decided its next state individually every the time interval. It should be noticed that the start time of the intervals at different nodes need not be synchronized and that next states of different replicas can be decided at different times.

Figure 2 shows the detailed behavior of nodes and agents in the replica density control algorithm.

The behavior of nodes and agents is simple: each node creates a new agent every $CYCLE$ time units (i.e., at the beginning of each time interval). Each agent has a specific amount of food on the initial state and traverses the network with the food. Each agent makes a *random walk* independently: an agent migrates from one node to one of its neighboring nodes with equal probability. When an agent visits node v, node v feeds replicas on node v with food the agent has. The replica can exist during the next time interval if it can be fed a specific amount of food, denoted by RF, during the current time interval. The replica is deleted if it cannot be fed food of amount RF during the time interval.

In addition, each node makes a new replica of replica i if the replica i is fed surplus food of amount RF. This idea derives from the fact that the positive per capita growth $g(t)$ in the single species population model is proportional to the amount of surplus food. This scheme is realized in the following way: each agent stores the surplus food into variable *surplus_food* and continues a random walk after $CYCLE$ time units from its creation time. When an agent that has surplus food visits node v, node v feeds replicas on node v with the surplus food the agent has. If the total amount of surplus food the replica on node v is fed is RF, node v makes one new replica of the replica by consuming the surplus food. If the agent has no food and no surplus food, it kills itself (i.e., removes itself from the network).

Now, we consider the amount of food F that each agent should supply. Since each node creates one agent every $CYCLE$ time units, the amount $F \cdot n(t)$ of

---

Behavior of node v
$time_v$: local clock time
/* its value automatically increases at the same rate as the global time */
eat_food_{vi} : the amount of food that replica i has consumed from *food* of agents
$eat\_surplus\_food_{vi}$: the amount of food that replica i has consumed from *surplus_food* of agents
$create\_time_{vi}$: creation time of replica i
/* the time at which i is made */
RF : the amount of food consumed by a resource to survive

  - at the beginning of each time interval (i.e., then $time_v$ **mod** $CYCLE$ =0 holds)
      create one agent
  - **for** each replica i on node v
      • on agent p's arrival at node v
          if ($eat\_food_{vi} < RF$) **then**
              $y := \min\{RF - eat\_food_{vi}, food_p\}$
              $eat\_food_{vi} := eat\_food_{vi} + y$
              $food_p := food_p - y$
          if ($surplus\_food_p > 0$) **then**
              $y' := \min\{RF - eat\_surplus\_food_{vi}, surplus\_food_p\}$
              $eat\_surplus\_food_{vi} := eat\_surplus\_food_{vi} + y'$
              $surplus\_food_p := surplus\_food_p - y'$
              if ($eat\_surplus\_food_{vi} = RF$) **then**
                  make a new replica of i ($create\_time$ of the replica is $time_v$)
                  $eat\_surplus\_food_{vi} := 0$
      • at the end of each time interval (i.e., when $time_v + create\_time_{vi}$ **mod** $CYCLE$ =0
        holds)
          if ($eat\_food_{vi} < RF$) **then** delete i
          else $eat\_food_{vi} := 0$ /*i survives into the next time interval */

Behavior of agent p
$food_p$: the amount of food that p supplies to replicas
$surplus\_food_p$: the amount of surplus food
$time_p$: local clock time
/* its value automatically increases at the same rate as the global time */
RF : the amount of food consumed by a resource to survive

  /*p makes a random walk on the network */
  - when p is created
      $food_p := \delta \cdot RF$
      $surplus\_food_p := 0.0$
      $time_p := 0$
  - at the end of time interval (i.e., when $time_p = CYCLE$ holds)
      $surplus\_food_p := food_p$
      $food_p := 0.0$
  - when all food are consumed (i.e., when ($food_p = 0.0 \wedge surplus\_food_p = 0.0$) holds)
      kill itself

Fig. 2. Behavior of node v and agent p

food are supplied on the whole network. The goal of the replica density control problem is to adjust the number $r(t)$ of replicas to $\delta \cdot n(t)$. Remind that the single species population model shows that the number of individuals converges and stabilizes at the carrying capacity $f_a(t)/f$. Thus, the algorithm tries to adjust $r(t)$ to $\delta \cdot n(t)$ by adjusting the carrying capacity to $\delta \cdot n(t)$. Since $f_a(t)$ corresponds to the total amount of supplied food on the whole network $n(t) \cdot F$ and f corresponds to the amount of food RF, the following equation should be satisfied:

$$\frac{f_a(t)}{f} = \frac{n(t) \cdot F}{RF} = \delta \cdot n(t).$$

From this equation, each agent should supply food of amount $F = \delta \cdot RF$.

4 Simulation Results

In this section, we present simulation results to show that the proposed algorithm can adjust the replica density.

In the simulation, we assume that each agent repeatedly executes the following actions: each agent stays at a node for one time unit, and then migrates to one of its neighboring nodes by a random walk. We also assume that the migration delay between any pair of neighboring nodes is two time units. The following values are initialized randomly:

- the initial locations of agents
- the initial values of the local clocks(i.e., $time_v$, $time_p$)
- the creation time of replicas on each node v (i.e., $create\_time_i(< time_v)$)
- the initial amounts of food that agents have (i.e., $food_p$)
- the initial amounts of food that replicas have fed on in the current time interval (i.e., eat_food_i).

The initial amounts of surplus food that agents have (i.e., $surplus\_food_p$) and the initial amounts of surplus food that replicas have fed (i.e., $eat\_surplus\_food_i$)are set to 0.

In the simulation, a new replica created by a node is allocated to th1e node selected randomly with probability proportional to their degrees. In real systems, replica allocation is very important to get good performance. In this paper, however, we focus on control of replica density rather than how to allocate replicas effectively on the network. The above allocation can be realized as follows: an agent picks up a new replica on a node, and drops the replica on the visited node after it traverses the network by a random walk during random time units.

We present the simulation results for *random networks* and *scale-free networks*. Scale-free networks are a specific kind of networks such that some nodes have a tremendous number of connections to other nodes, whereas most nodes have just a handful. The degree distribution follows a power law of k: the number of nodes with degree k is proportional to k^{-r}, where r is a positive constant. A scale-free network is said to be a realistic model of actual network structures [3, 5].

Simulation Results for Static Networks. Figure 3 shows experimental results for "static" random networks and "static" scale-free networks where nodes and links of the networks remain unchanged. In the simulation, the number $n(t)$ of nodes is fixed at 500 during the simulation. Random graphs with n nodes are generated as follows: each pair of nodes is connected with probability of $5.0/(n - 1)$. Scale-free networks are generated using the incremental method proposed by Balabasi and Albert [3]. More precisely, starting with 3 nodes, we add new nodes one by one. When a new node is added, three links are also added to connect the node to three other nodes, which are randomly selected with probability proportional to their degrees.

Figure 3 shows transition of the number $r(t)$ of replicas with time t. It shows the simulation results for four combinations of two values of δ (0.2 and 0.1),

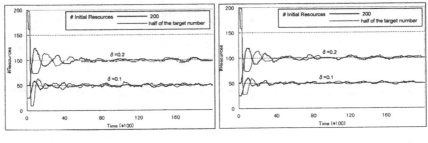

a. random networks ($n(t) = 500$)   b. scale-free networks ($n(t) = 500$)

Fig. 3. Simulation results on static networks

and two initial number $r(0)$ of replicas (200 and the half of the target number). The length $CYCLE$ of the time interval is set to 200 time units, and the initial number of agents is set to 100. These simulation results show that the number of replicas quickly converges to the equilibrium point, and has small perturbation after the convergence.

Simulation Results for Dynamic Networks. Figure 4 and Figure 5 show the experimental results for "dynamic" random networks and "dynamic" scale-free networks where nodes and links of networks vary with time. When a new node joins in the network, the new node is connected to other nodes with probability $5.0/n(t)$ for each other node on random networks, and the new node is connected to three other nodes randomly selected with probability proportional to their degrees on scale-free networks. When a node v leaves from the network, the links connecting to v are also removed from the network, and replicas the node v has and agents on node v or these links are also removed from the network. To show the adaptiveness of the proposed algorithm, Figure 4 and Figure 5 also show the difference ratio of the number of replicas: the ratio is defined by $|\delta \cdot n(t) - r(t)|/(\delta \cdot n(t))$ and represents the ratio of difference between the adjusted and the target numbers of replicas to the target number. (In static networks, the average of the difference ratio is about 0.02.)

Figure 4 shows simulation results for dynamic networks with continuous and gradual changes: some nodes join in the network and some nodes leave from the network constantly. In this simulation, the initial network size $n(0)$ is 500, and the following dynamical changes occur every 200 time units. In the first half (from time 0 to time 10,000) of the simulation, a single new node joins in the network with probability 0.05 and each node leaves from the network with probability 0.005. In the second half (from time 10,000 to time 20,000), one new node joins in the network with probability 1.0 and each node leaves from the network with probability 0.001.

In the simulation results of Figure 4, the length $CYCLE$ is set to 200 time units, the value of δ is set to 0.2, the initial number of agents is set to 100 and the initial number $r(0)$ of replicas is set to 100. Since the difference ratio is kept to be less than 0.08 and does not widely diverge from 0, the simulation results

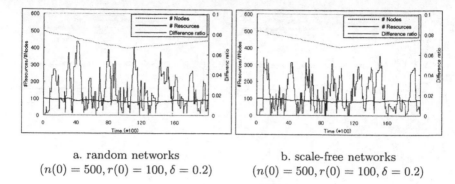

a. random networks
$(n(0) = 500, r(0) = 100, \delta = 0.2)$

b. scale-free networks
$(n(0) = 500, r(0) = 100, \delta = 0.2)$

Fig. 4. Simulation results on dynamic networks with gradual changes

show that the number of replica is adaptively adjusted in response to changes in the network size.

Figure 5 shows the simulation results for dynamic networks with drastic changes: in a short term, a large number of nodes leave from the network or join in the network. In this simulation, the initial network size $n(0)$ is 500, and 200 nodes leave from the network at time 6,000 of the simulation, and 400 nodes join in the network at time 13,000 of the simulation. The leaving nodes are chosen randomly.

In the simulation results of Figure 5, the length $CYCLE$ is set to 200 time units, the value of δ is set to 0.2, the initial number of agents is set to 100 and the initial number $r(0)$ of replicas is set to 100. While the difference ratio widely diverges from 0 immediately after drastic changes of the network, it quickly converges to the target number. The difference ratio is kept to be less than 0.07 after the convergence.

Simulation Results on Lifetime of Replicas. The goal of the replica density control problem is to adjust the number of replicas to a given ratio of the network size. However, from the point of application view, locations of each replica should

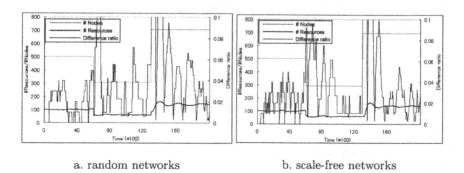

a. random networks
$(n(0) = 500, r(0) = 100, \delta = 0.2)$

b. scale-free networks
$(n(0) = 500, r(0) = 100, \delta = 0.2)$

Fig. 5. Simulation results on dynamic networks with drastic changes

Table 1. Average existence time of replicas

		CYCLE		
		100	200	400
	200	2772	16977	63528
n	500	2858	21797	104218
	1000	2915	23347	132340

a. random networks

		CYCLE		
		100	200	400
	200	3757	18230	62470
n	500	4505	27456	97399
	1000	4359	32442	123737

b. scale-free networks

not be change frequently. In real applications, if there is almost no change of locations of each replica, the searching performance of applications can improve. In our algorithm, each replica stays on the same node while the replica exists on the network. Thus, we can say the stability of locations is high by showing that lifetime of replicas is sufficiently long.

Lifetime lt_i of replica i is defined to be the time length from its creation to its elimination, i.e., $lt_i = td_i - tc_i$, where td_i is the time when i is deleted and tc_p is the time when i is created. Table 1 shows the average lifetime of replicas of ten trials. To focus on the lifetime of replicas after convergence of the number of replicas to the target number, the initial number $r(0)$ of replicas is set to the equilibrium point. In the simulation results of Table 1, the value of δ is set to 0.2 and the initial number of agents is set to the same number as the initial number of replicas. The simulation results show that lifetime quickly becomes longer when the length of the time interval $CYCLE$ becomes longer. Therefore, by setting an appropriate value to $CYCLE$, it is strongly expected that lifetime of each replica becomes sufficiently long.

Simulation Results Using Smaller Number of Agents. In the algorithm presented in Section 3.2, $n(t)$ agents are created and traverse the network every $CYCLE$ time units. Although the size of the agent is so small since the agent has only information of food, the number $n(t)$ of agents may be large for the system. To reduce network traffic, we try to reduce the number of agents by increasing the amount of food one agent has; that is, $1/c \cdot n(t)$ nodes create new agents with food of amount $c \cdot \delta \cdot RF$ every $CYCLE$ time units ($c > 1$). Each node picks a number from 0 to c-1 randomly on its initial state and decrements the value every $CYCLE$ time units. When the value becomes 0, the node create a new agent that has the amount $c \cdot \delta \cdot RF$ of food and the value is set to $c - 1$. In this regard, however, the length of the time interval $CYCLE$ needs to become longer depending on the value of c. The reason is that agents with larger amount of food must visit more nodes to supply food to more replicas. This method reduces by $1/c$ network traffic of agents.

Figure 6 shows the simulation results with small number of agents for "dynamic" random networks and "dynamic" scale-free networks. The value of c is set to 5; about $1/5 \cdot n(t)$ agents are created every $CYCLE$ time units. Networks change in the same way as the above simulation of Figure 4. In the simulation, the length $CYCLE$ is set to 400 time units, the value of δ is set to 0.2, the initial number of agents is set to 20 and the initial number $r(0)$ of replicas is set to 100.

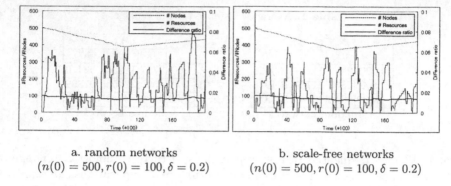

a. random networks
$(n(0) = 500, r(0) = 100, \delta = 0.2)$

b. scale-free networks
$(n(0) = 500, r(0) = 100, \delta = 0.2)$

Fig. 6. Simulation results on dynamic networks using small number of agents

The simulation results in Figure 6 show that the number of replica can be sufficiently adjusted in response to changes in the network size using only small number of agents. Without sacrificing accuracy, the network traffic of agents are reduced to $1/c \cdot n(t)$.

The algorithm we proposed can adjust the replica density even in the case that the value of δ is very small. However, the length of the time interval *CYCLE* needs to become longer when the value of δ is smaller. The reason is that the small value of δ indicates the low density replica and thus, agents must visit more nodes to supply food. We did simulations in small δ and obtained similar results to results in this paper.

Besides the simulations on random networks and scale-free networks presented in this section, we did simulations on several other networks such as complete networks, lollipop networks and star networks, and obtained similar results on these networks.

5   Conclusions

In this paper, we have proposed a distributed algorithm for the replica density control problem that requires to adapt the number of original resource and its replicas to a given constant fraction of the current number of nodes in a dynamic network. The algorithm is inspired by the single species population model, which is well-known in the field of the population ecology. The simulation results show that the proposed algorithm can adequately adjust the number of replicas in dynamic networks. In addition, from the simulation results, the lifetime of each replica becomes sufficiently long by setting an appropriate value to algorithm parameter *CYCLE*.

In this paper, we focus on only the number of replicas. In real systems that provide resource replication, allocation of replicas is also very important. Our future work is to develop the replica allocation algorithm for improving system performance: agents determine allocations of new replicas from network conditions that agents can learn by traversing over the network.

Acknowledgment

This work is supported in part by a Grant-in-Aid for Scientific Research ((B)(2)15300017) of JSPS, Grant-in-Aid for Scientific Research on Priority Areas(16092215), Grant-in-Aid for JSPS Fellows(2005, 50673), and "The 21st Century Center of Excellence Program" of the Ministry of Education, Culture, Sports, Science and Technology, Japan.

References

1. The anthill project. http://www.cs.unibo.it/projects/anthill/.
2. The bio-networking architecture. http://netresearch.ics.uci.edu/bionet/.
3. R. Albert and A. L. Barabasi. Statistical mechanics of complex networks. *Reviews of Modern Physics*, 74(1):47–97, January 2002.
4. O. Babaoglu, H. Meling, and A. Montresor. Anthill: A framework for the development of agent-based peer-to-peer systems. In *Proceedings of the 22th International Conference on Distributed Computing Systems*, pages 15–22, 2002.
5. A. L. Barabasi and E. Bonabeau. Scale-free networks. *Scientific American*, 288:50–59, May 2003.
6. I. Clarke, O. Sandberg, B. Wiley, and T. W. Hong. Freenet: A distributed anonymous information storage and retrieval system. In *Proceedings of the Workshop on Design Issues in Anonymity and Unobservability*, pages 46–66, July 2000.
7. Gnutella.com. http://www.gnutella.com.
8. R. Haberman. *Mathematical Model : Population Dynamics*. PRENTICE HALL, 1977.
9. K. Miura, T. Tagawa, and H. Kakugawa. A quorum-based protocol for searching objects in peer-to-peer networks. *IEEE Transactions on Parallel and Distributed Systems*. to appear.
10. V. A. Pham and A. Karmouch. Mobile software agents : An overview. *IEEE Communications*, 36(7):26–36, July 1998.
11. A. R. Silva, A. Romao, D. Deugo, and M. Mira. Towards a reference model for surveying mobile agent systems. *Autonomous Agents and Multi-Agent System*, 4(3):187–231, 2001.
12. J. Suzuki and T. Suda. Design and implementation of a scalable infrastructure for autonomous adaptive agents. In *Proceedings of the 15th IASTED International Conference on Parallel and Distributed Computing and Systems*, pages 594–603, November 2003.
13. T. Suzuki, T. Izumi, F. Ooshita, and T. Masuzawa. Biologically inspired self-adaptation of mobile agent population. In *Proceedings of 3rd International Workshop on Self-Adaptive and Autonomic Computing Systems*, August 2005. to appear.

Improving the Robustness of Epidemic Communication in Scale-Free Networks

Takuya Okuyama, Tatsuhiro Tsuchiya, and Tohru Kikuno

Graduate School of Information Science
and Technology, Osaka University, Osaka 567-0851, Japan
{t-okuyama, t-tutiya, kikuno}@ist.osaka-u.ac.jp

Abstract. As the name suggests, epidemic protocols mimic spread of virus to implement broadcasting with high reliability and low communication cost in peer-to-peer (P2P) overlay networks. In this paper, we study the reliability of epidemic protocols in scale-free networks, an important class of P2P overlay network topologies. In order to improve the robustness of epidemic protocols, we optimize the basic epidemic protocol in the following two ways. One optimization is to introduce an adaptive mechanism that allows each node to retransmit a broadcast message adaptively to the environment. The other optimization is to modify the protocol such that nodes will forward broadcast messages preferentially to neighbor nodes of small degree. The usefulness of these optimizations is demonstrated through simulation results.

1   Introduction

Epidemic protocols has recently gained popularity as a potentially effective solution for disseminating information in peer-to-peer (P2P) overlay networks [1, 2, 3, 4, 5]. As the name suggests, epidemic protocols mimic the spread of a contagious disease. Just as infected individuals pass on a virus to those with whom they come into contact, each node in a distributed system relays the broadcast message it has received to randomly chosen neighbors. Information is disseminated throughout the network by multiple rounds of such communication.

This proactive use of redundant messages provides a means to ensure reliability in the face of failures. Also, it is shown that the load on each node increases only logarithmically with the size of the network; so epidemic protocols are scalable.

In this paper we study optimization of epidemic protocols, aimed at further improving robustness to failures in *scale-free networks* [6]. Over the last few years, it has been suggested that many technological, social, and biological networks can be characterized as scale-free [6, 7], and so can P2P overlay networks [8, 9]. The majority of nodes in scale-free networks have only a few connections to other nodes, whereas some nodes are connected to many other nodes in the network.

In order to achieve improved resiliency of epidemic protocols in such networks, we first propose an adaptive message retransmission mechanism. The idea of

A.J. Ijspeert et al. (Eds.): BioADIT 2006, LNCS 3853, pp. 294–305, 2006.

this mechanism is to have each node retransmit a broadcast message when the node determines that the message has not been sufficiently disseminated. Each node autonomously makes the decision of retransmission by counting how many neighbors it sent/received the same message to/from. A conceptually similar approach can be found in broadcasting protocols for ad hoc networks [10, 11]. In ad hoc networks, a node can receive every message sent by its neighbors due to the nature of wireless communications; thus the node can easily sense the status of message dissemination. Clearly this is not the case with wired networks. To our knowledge, no attempt to apply this idea to wired networks has been published, except for our preliminary report [12].

We then combine this mechanism to another optimization technique, which was proposed by Portmann and Seneviratne [13]. A typical characteristic of scale-free networks is a power-law distribution of the node degrees. In [13] Portmann and Seneviratne presented a variant of an epidemic protocol, *deterministic rumor mongering*, which makes use of this information to make a more intelligent decision as to what set of neighbors to forward messages to. Specifically, in their protocol, the neighbors of lowest degree are preferentially chosen as receiver nodes. We present an epidemic protocol that integrates deterministic rumor mongering and our adaptive message retransmission mechanism.

Though simulation studies, we compare these variants of epidemic protocols and show that the one that incorporates these two optimization techniques achieves the highest robustness.

2   Preliminaries

2.1   Overlay Networks and Epidemic-Style Broadcast

An *P2P overlay network* is a logical network constructed on top of an underlying physical network for each P2P application. We can view a P2P overlay network as an undirected graph, where the vertices correspond to nodes in the network, and the edges correspond to open connections maintained between the nodes. A node i is said to be a *neighbor* of another node j iff they maintain a connection between themselves. The *node degree* of a node i is the number of i's neighbors. Messages may be transferred along the edges.

Epidemic-style broadcast is a reliable and effective method of broadcasting in P2P overlay networks. The most basic form of an epidemic broadcast protocol is depicted in Fig. 1 [14]. In this basic protocol when a node initiates broadcast, the node sends the message to f randomly selected neighbors. Message dissemination is carried out as follows: upon receiving a broadcast message for the first time, the node i randomly selects f neighbors as receiver nodes and forwards copies of the message to all these selected nodes. In turn, these receiver nodes forward the message in the same way. The broadcast message is thus eventually disseminated throughout the network.

The value f is usually referred to as a *fanout*. It should be noted that if i knows that a neighbor has already received m, then that neighbor will never be selected. In this paper we assume that when receiving m, the node can tell the

initiate broadcast of m:
    send m to f randomly chosen neighbors;

when a node i receives a message m:
    if (i has received m for the first time)
        i sends m to f uniformly randomly chosen neighbors
        that i knows who have not yet seen m;

Fig. 1. The basic epidemic protocol

sender node's address; thus the sender node is never chosen by i as a receiver node.

2.2   Scale-Free Networks

A *scale-free network* is a network with the property that the number of neighbors of a given node exhibits a power law distribution; that is, $P(k) \propto k^{-\gamma}$ where $P(k)$ is the probability of having k neighbors. Hence most nodes have only a few links to other nodes and a tiny number of hubs have a large number of links. Due to this property, scale-free networks are highly robust when facing random node failures, but vulnerable to well-planned attacks.

Scale-free networks occur in many areas of science and engineering. Examples include metabolic networks, the topology of web pages, and the power grid of the western United States [6, 7].

One of the particular attractions of such scale-free networks is that they can be generated by the following simple and plausible model: Networks that grow by new nodes preferentially forming connections with nodes that are already highly connected give rise to scale-free networks.

Barabási and Albert formalized this model as follows [6]: The evolution of a system starts with a small number (m_0) of nodes with no edges. At every time step a new node is added to the system with $m(\leq m_0)$ edges that link the new node to m different nodes already present in the system. The probability that a given existing node i will have a link with the new node is proportional to the degree of i. After t steps, the model leads to a network with $t + m_0$ nodes and mt edges, and the network asymptotically evolves towards a state where the node degree distribution follows a power law with an exponent $\gamma \approx 2.9$.

Recent approaches to building efficient overlay networks often employ the abstraction of a distributed hash table (DHT) [15, 16, 17]. These DHT schemes use a global naming scheme based on hashing to assign keys to data items and organize the nodes into an overlay network that maps each key to a responsible node. The network is hierarchically structured to enable efficient routing with the DHT.

However there are still many good reasons to consider scale-free networks to be an important class of topologies for P2P overlay networks. First of all, it was observed that GNUTELLA, one of the best known P2P systems, formed overlay networks of this type [8]. It seems that the Barabási-Albert model, based on preferential attachment and incremental growth, can well explain this observation, since apparently GNUTELLA has both these features.

Recently Chun et al. proposed a completely different explanation for the power law degree distribution observed in P2P overlay networks [9]. In [9] they modeled the evolution of selfishly constructed overlay networks as a non-cooperative game. They showed that in a wide range of parameter values, a network evolves towards a stable network which coincides with a Nash equilibrium of the game. Although the game can produce widely different networks, power law degree distributions are often observed in realistic settings.

An important property of scale-free networks is that they are low diameter networks. In [18], a P2P system called PHENIX is proposed which takes advantage of this property to achieve efficient performance. PHENIX constructs an overlay network of a scale-free type but at the same time provides means to hide the identity of highly connected nodes. PHENIX can thus exploit the low-diameter property and the robustness of scale-free networks, without exposing itself to the vulnerability to attacks.

It should be noted that the problem of searching in scale-free networks has been well-studied in the context of random walk [19, 20, 21]. Much of the research suggests that query messages should be directed towards nodes of high degree to reduce the hitting time and the cover time. Interestingly, this strategy is completely opposite to the one used in deterministic rumor mongering (and thus in ours), in spite of apparent similarities between epidemic and random walk.

3   Adaptive Message Retransmission

In this section, we propose a mechanism that adaptively retransmits broadcast messages depending on the status of message dissemination. The challenge in devising this mechanism is how to perceive the status of the system without explicit failure detection or aggregation.[1]

To this end, we introduce the following idea: Each node keeps track of both the nodes to which it forwarded each broadcast message and those from which it received the same message. Nodes thus can perceive the status of the system indirectly; if the same message has been received many times, it is likely that many other nodes also have successfully received the message. On the other hand, if a broadcast message has arrived only a few times, it can be inferred with a high probability that there are other nodes that have failed to receive the message. Thus in the latter case, retransmission of the message would probably promote the message dissemination process.

Fig. 2 shows the epidemic protocol that incorporates this mechanism. The protocol consists of three parts: initiation, forwarding, and retransmission.

---

[1] *Aggregation* refers to a set of functions that provide global information about a distributed system [22, 23].

N := the set of neighbors;
$buff$:= $\emptyset$;

initiate broadcast of m:
   $receivers$:= a set of $\min\{f, |N|\}$ nodes uniformly randomly chosen
     from N;
   send m to the nodes in $receivers$;
   $buff$:= $buff \cup \{m\}$;
   $known_m$:= $receivers$;

upon receiving broadcast message m from j:
   if $(m \notin buff)$
     $buff$:= $buff \cup \{m\}$;
     $receivers$:= a set of $\min\{f, |N\backslash\{j\}|\}$ nodes uniformly randomly
      chosen from $N\backslash\{j\}$;
     send m to the nodes in $receivers$;
     $known_m$:= $receivers \cup \{j\}$;
   else
     $known_m$:= $known_m \cup \{j\}$;

at time T after $m \in buff$ was received for the first time:
   if $(|known_m|/|N| < \theta)$
     send m to $\min\{f, |N\backslash known_m|\}$ nodes uniformly randomly chosen
      from $N\backslash known_m$;
   $buff$:= $buff\backslash\{m\}$;

Fig. 2. An epidemic protocol with adaptive message retransmission

To control the retransmission process, the protocol has two additional parameters: T and θ. T is the time in which a node waits to start retransmission, while θ is used to determine whether or not to perform retransmission. At time T after the first arrival of a message to a node i, i performs retransmission if the ratio of its neighbors who sent/received the message to/from i is below the threshold θ.

In Fig. 2 N and $buff$ are used to maintain the neighbors and the messages currently being handled, respectively. Variable $known_m$ is used to record both the nodes from which m was received and those to which m was forwarded. The nodes in $known_m$ will never be selected as the receiver nodes when retransmission is performed because they already received m.

4   Preferential Receiver Selection

4.1   Deterministic Rumor Mongering

An epidemic protocol that is optimized for scale-free networks was already proposed by Portmann and Seneviratne [13]. The protocol, which they call *deterministic rumor mongering*, makes use of the power-law characteristic of node

$N :=$ the set of neighbors;
$N_1 :=$ the set of neighbors of degree one;

initiate broadcast of m:
    send m to the nodes in N_1;
    $receivers := \min\{f, |N\backslash N_1|\}$ nodes in $N\backslash N_1$ of lowest degrees;
    send m to the nodes in $receivers$;

upon receiving a message m from j:
    if (m has been received for the first time)
        send m to the nodes in $N_1\backslash\{j\}$;
        $receivers := \min\{f, |N\backslash(N_1 \cup \{j\})|\}$ nodes in $N\backslash(N_1 \cup \{j\})$
            of lowest degrees;
        send m to the nodes in $receivers$;

Fig. 3. Deterministic rumor mongering

degrees by allowing message-forwarding nodes to preferentially select receiver nodes.

In the epidemic protocols we have discussed so far, the subset of neighbors to which messages are forwarded are chosen uniformly at random. Under the assumption that the nodes have no knowledge about the global topology of the overlay network, this uniformly random selection seems the best possible strategy.

Deterministic rumor mongering, on the other hand, uses a preferential receiver selection strategy, assuming that the overlay network topology is scale-free. Specifically, the selection of receiver neighbors is not performed randomly but is based on their node degree; i.e., the nodes of lowest degree are chosen first.

Fig. 3 shows this protocol. In this protocol, pendant nodes, i.e., nodes of degree one are treated not only as the first priority but also differently from the other neighbors. Every broadcast message is forwarded to all the pendant neighbors, since these nodes have no other chance of receiving the message. In Fig. 3, N_1 is used to maintain the pendant neighbors.

Obviously in this protocol, each node has to know the node degrees of its neighbors. To meet this requirement, the nodes need to exchange their node degree information. In [13], it is claimed that this can easily be implemented with a slight modification of P2P applications with only a slight increase of the minimum message size.

4.2   Combining the Two Optimization Techniques

Here we present another variant of an epidemic protocol which combines the deterministic rumor mongering and the adaptive retransmission mechanism

N := the set of neighbors;
N_1 := the set of neighbors of degree one;
$buff$:= $\emptyset$;

initiate broadcast of m:
    send m to the nodes in N_1;
    $known_m$:= N_1;
    $receivers$:= $\min\{f, |N\backslash known_m|\}$ nodes in $N\backslash known_m$ of lowest degrees;
    send m to the nodes in $receivers$;
    $buff$:= $buff \cup \{m\}$;
    $known_m$:= $known_m \cup receivers$;

upon receiving broadcast message m from j:
    if $(m \notin buff)$
        $buff$:= $buff \cup \{m\}$;
        $known_m$:= $\{j\}$;
        send m to the nodes in $N_1\backslash known_m$;
        $known_m$:= $known_m \cup N_1$;
        $receivers$:= $\min\{f, |N\backslash known_m|\}$ nodes in $N\backslash known_m$ of lowest degrees;
        send m to the nodes in $receivers$;
        $known_m$:= $known_m \cup receivers$;
    else
        $known_m$:= $known_m \cup \{j\}$;

at time T after $m \in buff$ was received for the first time:
    if $(|known_m|/|N| < \theta)$
        send m to $\min\{f, |N\backslash known_m|\}$ nodes uniformly randomly chosen
            from $N\backslash known_m$;
    $buff$:= $buff\backslash\{m\}$;

Fig. 4. An epidemic protocol with the two optimization techniques

described in the previous section. Fig. 4 shows the detailed description of this protocol.

Note that in Fig. 4 there are no particular steps that perform message retransmission to pendant neighbors. This is because when a node received a broadcast message for the first time, the node always forwarded the message to these pendant nodes.

5   Simulation

In this section we present the results of a performed simulation analysis. The simulation compares the following four epidemic protocols.

Protocol 0 The basic epidemic protocol
Protocol 1 The optimized version with adaptive message retransmission

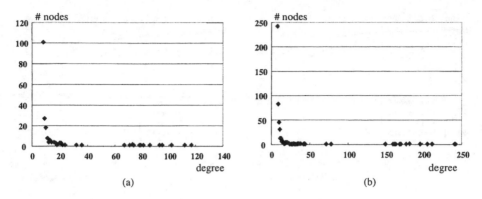

Fig. 5. Node degree distributions. (a) $N = 200$, (b) $N = 500$.

Protocol 2 Deterministic rumor mongering
Protocol 3 The optimized version integrating deterministic rumor mongering
and adaptive message retransmission

5.1 Settings

We created two scale-free networks based on the Barabási-Albert model which
is described in 2.2. In doing so, we set both m_0 and m to 8. The sizes (the
numbers of nodes) N of the two networks are 200 and 500. Figure 5(a) and
Figure 5(b) show the degree distributions of these networks. These distributions
clearly exhibit the characteristics of the power law.

We assume that a message delay between two nodes follows an Erlang distribution with mean one time unit. The timeout value T and the retransmit
threshold θ are set to 4.0 and 0.6, respectively.

We consider seven different percentages of failed nodes ranging from 0% to
60%. For each of the non-zero values, 10 failure patterns are randomly generated.
The broadcast is initiated 10 times by every node for each failure pattern.

5.2 Results

Resiliency. The experimental results depicted in Figure 6 show the resilience of
the epidemic protocols to node failures. Figures 6(a) and 6(b) display the results
for the networks of size $N = 200$ and 500, respectively. In the simulation we set
fanout $f = 8$.

In these graphs, the x-axes represent the percentage of failed nodes, while the
y-axes denote the mean percentage of correct nodes reached by each broadcast.
Different curves represent the results obtained for different protocols.

As clearly seen in these graphs, the resiliency to node failures is considerably improved by incorporating the optimization techniques. For example, in
the case $N = 500$, the basic epidemic protocol (Protocol 0) achieves only around
65 percent of reached nodes when half the nodes have failed. However this value
reaches near 80 percent when either of the optimization techniques is employed

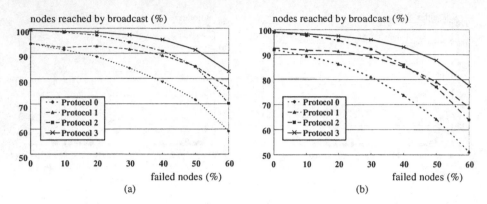

Fig. 6. Resilience to node failures (a) $N = 200$, (b) $N = 500$

(Protocol 1, Protocol 2) and near 90 percent when both are employed (Protocol 3).

One can also see that especially when failed nodes are not many, Protocol 2 and Protocol 3 achieve very high node coverage, thanks to the preferential receiver selection scheme which exploits the power-law degree distribution. In contrast, Protocol 0 and Protocol 1, in which nodes forward a message to uniformly randomly selected neighbors, achieve no more than 95% coverage even in the case of no node failure.

It can also be observed that Protocol 1 and Protocol 3 are much more robust to the increase of failed nodes than the other two protocols, from their slowly decreasing curves. Clearly this property is due to the use of the adaptive message retransmission mechanism. As a result, Protocol 3 which incorporates these two optimization techniques achieves the highest resiliency in the whole range of failed node percentage.

Message Overhead vs. Resiliency. The graphs in Fig. 7 show the relationship between communication cost and resiliency. The x-axes represent the total number of messages sent, while the y-axes represent the ratio of correct nodes reached by the broadcast. Thus the dots in these graphs indicates the message overhead required for achieving a given resiliency level.

We examined two node failure percentages: 0% and 30%. Fig. 7(a) and Fig. 7(b) display the results for the network of size $N = 200$ with the two different failure percentages, while Fig. 7(c) and Fig. 7(d) show those for the network of size $N = 500$.

Different types of dots in the graphs correspond to different protocols and different dots of each type represent the results obtained by using the corresponding protocol with different fanout values $f = 4, 6, 8, 10, 12, 14$.

From these graphs one can see that the dots for each protocol lie on a smooth curve and such imaginary curves are located from the bottom in the following order: Protocol 0, Protocol 1, Protocol 2, Protocol 3. This order coincides with the order of increasing cost-effectiveness. In Protocol 2 and Protocol 3, nodes attempt to avoid to forward messages to neighbors of high degree. This feature

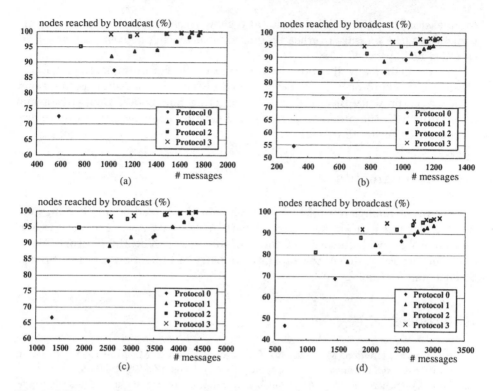

Fig. 7. Message overhead vs. resiliency (a) $N = 200$, failed nodes 0%, (b) $N = 200$, failed nodes 30%, (c) $N = 500$, failed nodes 0%, (d) $N = 500$, failed nodes 30%

reduces redundant messages, thus resulting in a good messaging cost-resiliency relationship of these protocols.

6 Conclusions

In this paper we studied two optimization techniques with the aim of improving the robustness of epidemic-style broadcast in scale-free networks. We first proposed an adaptive message retransmission mechanism. The basic idea of the proposed technique is to have each node retransmit a broadcast message when the node determines that the message has not been sufficiently disseminated. This decision is made in a fully autonomous fashion, simply by counting how many neighbors it sent/received the same message to/from.

Then we proposed to integrate this mechanism and deterministic rumor mongering, a variant of an epidemic protocol which makes use of the characteristics of scale-free networks to forward messages in an efficient manner.

We conducted a simulation analysis to examine the effects of these optimization techniques. The results obtained suggest that the epidemic protocol that incorporates both optimizations can significantly improve the robustness of broadcasting to failures. The results also show that by incorporating these optimizations, the message overhead required for achieving a given resiliency level can also be improved.

There remain many directions for future research. For example, the reliability of the proposed protocol should be evaluated under different failure assumptions, such as the presence of direct attacks targeting hub nodes. Comparison and integration with the proposed protocol and existing epidemic protocols are also an important future direction.

Acknowledgments

We thank the anonymous referees for their thoughtful reading and helpful comments. This research was supported in part by "Priority Assistance for the Formation of Worldwide Renowned Centers of Research — The 21st Century Center of Excellence Program" of the Japanese Ministry of Education, Culture, Sports, Science and Technology.

References

1. Birman, K., Hayden, M., Ozkasap, O., Xiao, Z., Budiu, M., Minsky, Y.: Bimodal multicast. ACM Transactions on Computer Systems **17** (1999) 41–88
2. Sun, Q., Sturman, D.: A gossip-based reliable multicast for large-scale high-throughput applications. In: Proceedings of the International Conference on Dependable Systems and Networks (DSN 2000), New York, NY (2000) 347–358
3. Eugster, P.T., Guerraoui, R., Handurukande, S.B., Kouznetsov, P., Kermarrec, A.M.: Lightweight probabilistic broadcast. ACM Trans. Comput. Syst. **21** (2003) 341–374
4. Eugster, P.T., Guerraoui, R., Kermarrec, A.M., Massoulié, L.: Epidemic information dissemination in distributed systems. IEEE Computer **37** (2004) 60–67
5. Pereira, J., Rodrigues, L., Monteiro, M., Oliveira, R., Kermarrec, A.: Neem: Network-friendly epidemic multicast. In: Proceedings of the 22nd IEEE Symposium on Reliable Distributed Systems (SRDS '03). (2003) 15–24
6. Barabási, A.L., Albert, R.: Emergence of scaling in random networks. Science **286** (1999) 509–512
7. Jeong, H., Tombor, B., Albert, R., Oltvai, Z.N., Barabási, A.L.: The large-scale organization of metabolic networks. Nature **407** (2000) 651–654
8. Ripeanu, M., Foster, I., Iamnitchi, A.: Mapping the gnutella network: Properties of large-scale peer-to-peer systems and implications for system design. IEEE Internet Computing Journal **6** (2002)
9. Chun, B.G., Fonseca, R., Stoica, I., Kubiatowicz, J.: Characterizing selfishly constructed overlay networks. In: Proceedings of Infocom 2004, Hong Kong (2004)
10. Ni, S.Y., Tseng, Y.C., Chen, Y.S., Sheu, J.P.: The broadcast storm problem in a mobile ad hoc network. In: Proceedings of the 5th annual ACM/IEEE international conference on Mobile computing and networking, ACM Press (1999) 151–162
11. Haas, Z.J., Halpern, J.Y., Li, L.: Gossip-Based Ad Hoc Routing. In: Proceedings of IEEE Infocom 2002, New York, NY (2002) 1707–1716

12. Tsuchiya, T., Kikuno, T.: On improving the reliability of probabilistic broadcast with an adaptive technique. IEICE Technical Report DC-346 (2004)
13. Portmann, M., Seneviratne, A.: Cost-effective broadcast for fully decentralized peer-to-peer networks. Computer Communications **26** (2003) 1159–1167
14. Lin, M.J., Marzullo, K., Masini, S.: Gossip versus deterministically constrained flooding on small networks. In: Proceedings of 14th International Conference on Distributed Computing, (DISC 2000). Volume 1914 of Lecture Notes in Computer Science., Toledo, Spain (2000) 253–267
15. Ratnasamy, S., Francis, P., Handley, M., Karp, R., Schenker, S.: A scalable content-addressable network. In: SIGCOMM '01: Proceedings of the 2001 conference on Applications, technologies, architectures, and protocols for computer communications, New York, NY, USA (2001) 161–172
16. Stoica, I., Morris, R., Karger, D., Kaashoek, F., Balakrishnan, H.: Chord: A scalable Peer-To-Peer lookup service for internet applications. In: Proceedings of the 2001 ACM SIGCOMM Conference. (2001) 149–160
17. Rowstron, A., Druschel, P.: Pastry: Scalable, distributed object location and routing for large-scale peer-to-peer systems. In: Proceedings of the 18th IFIP/ACM International Conference on Distributed Systems Platforms (Middleware 2001), Heidelberg, Germany (2001)
18. Wouhaybi, R.H., Campbell, A.T.: Phenix: Supporting resilient low-diameter peer-to-peer topologies. In: Proceedings of IEEE Infocom. (2004)
19. Adamic, L.A., Lukose, R., Puniyani, A., Huberman, B.: Search in power-law networks. Physical Review E **64** (2001) 046135-1–046135-8
20. Kim, B.J., Yoon, C.N., Han, S.K., Jeong, H.: Path finding strategies in scale free networks. Physical Review E **65** (2002) 027103-1–027103-4
21. Cooper, C., Frieze, A.: The cover time of two classes of random graphs. In: Proceedings of 16th ACM-SIAM Symposium on Discrete Algorithms (SODA 2005). (2005) 961–970
22. Gupta, I., van Renesse, R., Birman, K.P.: Scalable fault-tolerant aggregation in large process groups. In: Proceedings of the 2001 International Conference on Dependable Systems and Networks, IEEE Computer Society (2001) 433–442
23. Montresor, A., Jelasity, M., Babaoglu, O.: Robust aggregation protocols for large-scale overlay networks. In: Proceedings of the 2004 International Conference on Dependable Systems and Networks, IEEE Computer Society (2004) 19–28

On Updated Data Dissemination Exploiting an Epidemic Model in Ad Hoc Networks

Hideki Hayashi, Takahiro Hara, and Shojiro Nishio

Dept. of Multimedia Eng., Grad. Sch. of Information Science and Tech.,
Osaka Univ., 1-5 Yamadaoka, Suita, Osaka 565-0871, Japan
{hideki, hara, nishio}@ist.osaka-u.ac.jp
http://www-nishio.ist.osaka-u.ac.jp/

Abstract. In ad hoc networks, it is effective that each mobile host creates replicas of data items held by other mobile hosts for improving data accessibility. In our previous work, we assumed an environment where data items are updated and proposed two updated data dissemination methods which efficiently update old replicas. In these methods, the communication traffic is large since every mobile host necessarily requests updated data items when it knows that its own replicas are old. In this paper, we propose an updated data dissemination method exploiting an epidemic model, which is a popular bio-inspired approach, for reducing the communication traffic. In our proposed method, mobile hosts disseminate invalidation reports and discard old replicas when a mobile host updates a data item or when two mobile hosts are connected with each other. Each mobile host which discards an old replica requests the updated data item with a certain probability. We also present simulation results to evaluate the performance of our proposed method.

1 Introduction

Recently, there has been increasing interest in *ad hoc networks* constructed by only mobile hosts that play the role of a router [8, 11]. In ad hoc networks, disconnections frequently occur due to the free movement of mobile hosts and cause frequent network partitions. If a network partition occurs, mobile hosts in one of the two partitioned networks cannot access data items held by mobile hosts in the other network. In Fig. 1, if the central radio link is disconnected, the mobile hosts on the left-hand side and those on the right-hand side cannot access data items D_2 and D_1, respectively. To solve this problem, it is effective that each mobile host creates replicas of data items held by other mobile hosts. In ad hoc networks, there are many applications in which mobile hosts access data items held by other mobile hosts; a good example is rescue affairs at disaster sites and sensor networks. Therefore, the replica allocation for improving data accessibility is an important research issue. In [4], we assumed an environment where data items are not updated and proposed three replica allocation methods in ad hoc networks. These methods periodically relocate replicas to mobile hosts based on the access frequency to each data item and the network topology. This

A.J. Ijspeert et al. (Eds.): BioADIT 2006, LNCS 3853, pp. 306–321, 2006.

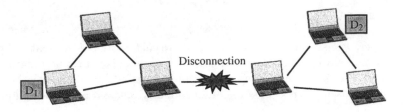

Fig. 1. Network partition in ad hoc networks

time period is called by *relocation period*. In [5], we assume an environment where correlation exists among data items and extended the methods proposed in [4].

In a real environment, it is more likely that data items are updated. In such a case, mobile hosts may access old replicas that have been updated. Accesses to old replicas are invalid and cause useless data accesses and rollbacks. This is a serious problem for mobile hosts that usually have poor resources. In [6], we proposed two cache invalidation methods for reducing the number of accesses to old replicas that have been updated. In these methods, mobile hosts broadcast invalidation reports and invalidate old replicas. Additionally, in [7], we proposed two updated data dissemination methods for improving the data accessibility. In these methods, the communication traffic for updated data dissemination is large since every mobile host necessarily requests updated data items when it knows that its own replicas are old.

In this paper, we propose an updated data dissemination method exploiting an epidemic model[3], which is a popular bio-inspired approach, for reducing the communication traffic. In an epidemic model, an infected person transmits the disease to a noninfected person with a certain probability when the infected person contacts the noninfected person. By repeating these processes, the infectious disease are widely spread. Therefore, it is effective to exploit an epidemic model for updated data dissemination in ad hoc networks because mobile hosts are frequently connected with each other. In our proposed method, mobile hosts disseminate invalidation reports when a mobile host updates a data item or when two mobile hosts are newly connected with each other. Each mobile host that receives the invalidation reports discards its own old replicas. Then, the mobile host requests the updated data item for the discarded replica with a certain probability. We also present simulation results to evaluate the performance of our proposed method.

The remainder of this paper is organized as follows. In Sect. 2, we describe our assumed environment. In Sect. 3, we describe updated data dissemination methods which we proposed in [7], then in Sect. 4 we propose an updated data dissemination method exploiting an epidemic model. In Sect. 5, we show simulation results to evaluate the performance of our proposed method. In Sect. 6, we show some works related to our research, and finally in Sect. 7, we summarize this paper.

2   Assumptions

In this paper, we assume an environment where each mobile host creates replicas of data items held by other mobile hosts in ad hoc networks where data items are updated. We do not place any restrictions on replica allocation methods because our proposed method behaves independently of the used replica allocation method.

A request for a data item succeeds only when the request-issuing host accesses the original data item or its replica with the same time stamp (version) as the original. When it accesses its replicas with a different time stamp from the original, the request fails. Therefore, the request immediately succeeds if the request-issuing host holds the original. Otherwise, if a connected mobile host holds the original, the request also immediately succeeds. In this paper, mobile hosts connected to each other by one-hop/multihop links are simply called *connected mobile hosts*. In doing so, the request-issuing host floods its connected mobile hosts with the query packet. If the request-issuing host or at least one connected mobile host holds the replica, the request-issuing host tentatively accesses the replica. After that, when the request-issuing host finds a connection to the mobile host holding the original, it asks the host holding the original whether the tentative access has either succeeded or failed. If the tentative access has failed, the rollback occurs as needed so that the request-issuing host recovers the state before it accessed the replica. If the request-issuing host and its connected mobile hosts do not hold the original/replicas, the request immediately fails.

In addition, we make the following assumptions:

- Each mobile host $(M_1, M_2, \cdots, M_m)$ moves freely. M_j $(1 \leq j \leq m)$ denotes a host identifier and m is the total number of mobile hosts.
- The original of each data item $(D_1, D_2, \cdots, D_n)$ is held by a particular mobile host. D_j $(1 \leq j \leq n)$ denotes a data identifier and n is the total number of data items.
- Each data item is updated by the mobile host holding the original. After a data item is updated, the replicas become invalid.

3   Conventional Updated Data Dissemination

In this section, we explain two updated data dissemination methods which we proposed in [7]. In these methods, each mobile host holds a *time stamp table* in which the latest update time (time stamp) of each data item is recorded. This table includes the data identifier and the time stamp as the attributes.

3.1   DU (Dissemination on Update) Method

In the DU method, when a mobile host updates an data item, it floods its connected mobile hosts with the invalidation report. This report includes the data identifier and the time stamp. When a mobile host receives the report, it

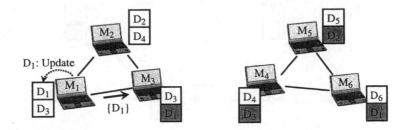

Fig. 2. Updated data dissemination in DU method

compares the time stamp in the report with that in its own time stamp table. If the former is larger, the host updates the time stamp in its own time stamp table to that in the report. Additionally, if the mobile host holds the replica, it discards the replica from its memory space and requests the updated data item to the mobile host which updates the data item. Then, the mobile host broadcasts the received report to its neighbors. Mobile hosts which receive the report behave in the same way.

Fig. 2 shows that M_1 transmits the updated data item D_1 to M_3 when M_1 updates D_1. In this figure, a rectangle denotes a data item and a gray rectangle denotes an invalidated replica.

In the DU method, the traffic is small because mobile hosts broadcast the invalidation report and disseminate the updated data item only when a mobile host updates the data item. When mobile hosts do not connect to the mobile host holding the original on the data update, they cannot receive the invalidation report nor the updated data item. Therefore, in an environment where the network topology frequently changes, connected mobile hosts may hold different time stamp tables and replicas with different versions of the same data item.

3.2 DC (Dissemination on Connection) Method

In the DC method, in addition to the updated data dissemination in the DU method, two newly connected mobile hosts disseminate updated data items.

Two newly connected mobile hosts compare each entry in their time stamp tables and update old time stamps with each other. Each of them floods its originally connected mobile hosts with invalidation reports of data items whose time stamps were old in its own time stamp table. When a mobile host receives the reports, it updates the time stamps in its own time stamp table. After that, each of the newly connected mobile host disseminates the updated data items. Here, the traffic for updated data dissemination may affect the system performance because the size of the updated data item is very large. Therefore we proposed the *DC/OO (One-to-One)* and *DC/GG (Group-to-Group)* methods. In the DC/OO method, two newly connected mobile hosts disseminate updated data items with each other. In the DC/GG method, two groups of mobile hosts that were originally connected to the two newly connected mobile hosts disseminate updated data items with each other.

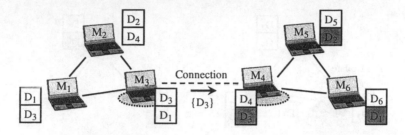

Fig. 3. Updated data dissemination in DC/OO method

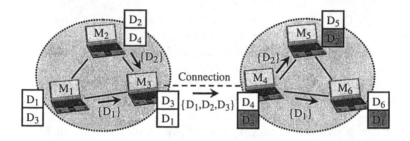

Fig. 4. Updated data dissemination in DC/GG method

Fig. 3 shows that, in the DC/OO method, M_3 transmits the updated data item D_3 to M_4 when M_3 and M_4 are newly connected. Fig. 4 shows that, in the DC/GG method, mobile hosts on the left-hand side $\{M_1, M_2, M_3\}$ transmits the updated data items $\{D_1, D_2, D_3\}$ to those on the right-hand side $\{M_4, M_5, M_6\}$.

In the DC method, connected mobile hosts hold the same time stamp table because invalidation reports are flooded every time two mobile hosts are newly connected. The data accessibility in the DC/OO method is larger than that in the DU method because two newly connected mobile hosts disseminates updated data items with each other. Furthermore, the data accessibility in the DC/GG method becomes larger than that in the DC/OO method because mobile hosts connected to the two newly connected mobile hosts can refresh old replicas. However, the traffic for updated data dissemination in the DC/GG method is much larger than that in the DC/OO method.

4   Updated Data Dissemination Exploiting an Epidemic Model

In this section, we propose an updated data dissemination method exploiting an epidemic model. First, we describe the epidemic model. Then, we describe the proposed method.

4.1   Epidemic Model

The propagation process of infectious diseases in the epidemic model is as follows.

A virus of an infectious disease breaks into a human body and infects the person with a certain probability. The infected person transmits the disease to a noninfected person with a certain probability when the infected person contacts the noninfected person. The noninfected person may be infected by absorbing the air including the cough and the sneeze of the infected person even if he/she does not directly contact the infected person. After the certain period (infection period), the infected person recovers and does not transmit the disease to noninfected persons. The recovered person has the immunity to the disease and are not infected with the disease.

4.2 Updated Data Dissemination

In our proposed method, mobile hosts disseminate updated data items with a certain probability when a mobile host updates a data item or when two mobile hosts are newly connected with each other. Tables 1 and 2 show the information managed by mobile hosts and the control packets, respectively. In these tables, "ID," "TS," "IR," and "UD" denote identifier, time stamp, invalidation report, and updated data, respectively. The path information in the invalidation report contains a list of pairs of the host identifier and the flag which represents whether the mobile host holds the data item (1) or not (0), where the order of the pairs corresponds to the order of the hosts to which the invalidation report was propagated.

When a mobile host updates a data item, it floods its connected mobile hosts with the invalidation report and they discard the old replicas. As mentioned in Sect. 1, if the mobile hosts that received the invalidation report necessarily request the updated data item, the traffic for the updated data dissemination becomes very large. Therefore, in this paper, we exploit an epidemic model. Specifically, each mobile host (noninfected person) that discards an old replica according to the invalidation report (virus) requests the updated data item to its nearby mobile host (infected person) with the *request probability* P_{req}. In Subsec. 4.3, we describe the definition of the request probability.

In order to widely spread the updated data items, we also exploit the epidemic model when two mobile hosts are newly connected with each other. Specifically,

Table 1. Information managed by mobile hosts

Table name	attributes
Time stamp table	data ID, TS, IR reception time, expiration time of IR/UD dissemination
Access status table	data ID, access frequency, number of access requests

Table 2. Control packets

Packet name	elements
Invalidation report	data ID, TS, path information (list of pairs of host ID and flag)
Updated data request	host ID, destination ID, data ID

when a mobile host that received an invalidation report (virus) newly connects to a mobile host, it disseminates the invalidation report and the updated data item (if holding the valid replica) to the newly connected mobile host just like an infected person. Additionally, it disseminates the invalidation report and the updated data item to mobile hosts which originally connect to the newly connected mobile host. Here, if mobile hosts permanently continue to disseminate the invalidation report and the updated data item, it produces a large amount of unnecessary traffic. The epidemic model can solve this problem since an infected person recovers and does not infect anyone after the infection period. That is, after the predetermined period (*dissemination period*) from the time when the mobile host received the invalidation report, it stops to disseminate the invalidation report and the updated data item.

In the followings, we describe the detailed behaviors when a mobile host, M_i, updates a data item, D_k, and when two mobile hosts, M_i and M_j, are newly connected.

[Behavior on data update]

The following is the behavior of our method when M_i updates D_k:

1. M_i updates D_k's information in its own time stamp table. Both TS and IR reception time are set as the updated time. The expiration time of IR/UD dissemination is set as the sum of the IR reception time and the dissemination period T_{snd} which is the predetermined constant.
2. M_i broadcasts the invalidation report to its neighbors, where the pair of the host identifier, M_i, and the flag, 1, is inserted into the path information.
3. When a mobile host, M_k, receives the invalidation report, it updates D_k's information just like M_i. If it holds the old replica, it discards the replica and requests the updated data item based on the request probability P_{req}. The request is sent to the nearest mobile host holding D_k, which can be determined from the path information in the received invalidation report. After that, M_k broadcasts the invalidation report to its neighbors, where the pair of the host identifier, M_k, and the flag, 1 if the host requested D_k or 0 otherwise, is added into the path information. Goes back to step 3.

Fig. 5 shows that M_4 and M_6 requests the updated data item of D_1 when M_1 updates D_1.

This method reduces the traffic for updated data dissemination because an appropriate number of mobile hosts refresh their old replicas by receiving the updated data items from their nearby mobile hosts.

[Behavior on connection]

The following is the behavior of our method when M_i and M_j are newly connected with each other:

1. $M_i(M_j)$ transmits an invalidation report for each data item whose expiration time is larger than the current time to $M_j(M_i)$.

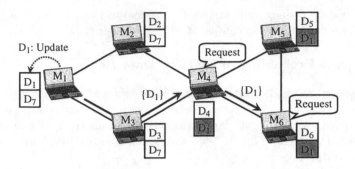

Fig. 5. Updated data dissemination on data update

2. $M_j(M_i)$ compares the time stamp for the data item in its own time stamp table with that in the received report. If the former is smaller, $M_j(M_i)$ updates the information in its own time stamp table. TS, IR reception time, and the expiration time of IR/UD are set as TS in the received report, the current time, and the sum of the IR reception time and T_{snd}, respectively. Additionally, if $M_j(M_i)$ holds the old replica, it discards the replica and requests the updated data item based on the request probability P_{req}. The request is sent to the nearest mobile host holding the data item, which can be determined from the path information in the received invalidation report. After that, $M_j(M_i)$ broadcasts the invalidation report to its neighbors, where the pair of the host identifier, $M_j(M_i)$, and the flag, 1 if the host requested the data item or 0 otherwise, is added into the path information.
3. Each mobile host that receives the invalidation report behaves in the same way as $M_j(M_i)$.

Fig. 6 shows that M_1 and M_2 request the updated data item of D_7 when M_6 and M_7 are newly connected and all mobile hosts except for M_7 receive the invalidation report for D_7.

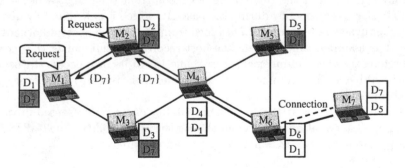

Fig. 6. Updated data dissemination on connection

The above processes can reduce the number of accesses to old replicas and improve the data accessibility because invalidation reports and updated data items are widely propagated. Moreover, our method can reduce the traffic for updated data dissemination compared with the original DC method.

4.3 Request Probability of Updated Data Items

In our proposed method, a mobile host requests an updated data item based on the request probability P_{req} when it receives the invalidation report and discards the old replica. As P_{req} gets larger, mobile hosts are more likely to request the updated data item. Thus, $1/P_{req}$ corresponds to the immunity against the infectious disease.

If a mobile host does not receive an invalidation report for a data item for a long time, it is likely that the host existed in a partitioned network in which the data item was inaccessible. Thus, it is effective to preferentially disseminate the updated data item to such mobile hosts. Additionally, it is also effective to preferentially disseminate updated data items that are frequently accessed. Based on these facts, we define the request probability, P_{req}, when the mobile host receives D_k's invalidation report by the following equation:

$$P_{req} = \alpha \cdot \frac{ET_k}{MAX\_ET} + (1 - \alpha) \cdot \frac{A_k}{MAX\_A}. \tag{1}$$

Here, $\alpha(0 \leq \alpha \leq 1)$, $MAX\_ET(> 0)$, and $MAX\_A(> 0)$ are predefined constants. ET_k denotes the elapsed time since the mobile host lastly received D_k's invalidation report and A_k denotes D_k's access frequency. ET_k is set as MAX_ET if $ET_k > MAX\_ET$ and A_k is set as MAX_A if $A_k > MAX\_A$. ET_k is calculated from the IR reception time in the time stamp table. A_k is calculated at every predetermined time, Δt, by the following equation:

$$A_k = \beta \cdot A_k' + (1 - \beta) \cdot A_{k(\Delta t)}. \tag{2}$$

Here, $\beta(0 \leq \beta \leq 1)$ is a predefined constant. A_k' denotes D_k's previous access frequency calculated at the time Δt before the current time. $A_{k(\Delta t)}$ denotes the actual D_k's access frequency during the past Δt, which is calculated by dividing the number of access requests for D_k issued from the mobile host and other hosts by Δt. It is assumed that each mobile host records the number of the received access requests as the "number of access requests" in its own access status table shown in Table 1. The number of access requests is reset to 0 at every A_k's calculation time.

It should be noted that the request probability can be represented in various ways except for equation (1). While the request probability much affects the system performance, we use equation (1) as an example.

5   Simulation Experiments

In this section, we present simulation results to evaluate the performance of our proposed method.

5.1 Simulation Model

The number of mobile hosts is 40 in the entire network. Each mobile host $(M_1, \ldots, M_{40})$ exists in a 500 [m] $\times$ 500 [m] flatland and moves according to the random waypoint model[1]. Specifically, each host randomly determines a destination in the flatland and moves toward the destination at a velocity randomly determined from 0.01 to 1 [m/sec]. When the host arrives at the destination, it pauses for the duration randomly determined from 0 to 1,000 [sec]. After the duration, it determines a next destination and moves toward the destination. The radio communication range of each mobile host is 70 [m].

The number of kinds of data items is 40 in the entire network and the size of each data item $(D_1, \ldots, D_{40})$ is 1 [MB]. M_i holds D_i $(i = 1, \cdots, 40)$ as the original. The access frequency of M_i to D_j is $p_{ij} = 0.0005 \times (1 + 0.001 \times j)[1/\text{sec}]$. Each mobile host updates its own original with intervals based on the exponential distribution with mean U (average update period) [sec].

Each mobile host creates up to 10 replicas in its memory space with the DCG (Dynamic Connectivity based Grouping) method that we proposed in [4]. The DCG method periodically (relocation period: T[sec]) creates stable groups (biconnected components) of mobile hosts and allocate many kinds of replicas in the groups.

Table 3. Parameter configuration

Parameter	value		
U	500	(100~3,000)	[sec]
T	1,000		[sec]
T_{snd}	1,000		[sec]
α	0.5		
MAX_ET	1,000	(100~2,000)	[sec]
MAX_A	0.005		[1/sec]
β	0.5		
Δt	1,000		[sec]

Table 3 shows parameters and their values in this experiments. The parameters are basically fixed to constant values, but some parameters are changed, indicated by values in parentheses shown in Table 3. We compare our proposed method in this paper with the DU and DC methods proposed in [7].

In the above simulation environments, we randomly determine the initial position of each mobile host and evaluate the following three criteria during 500,000 [sec].

– *Data accessibility*:
   The ratio of the number of successful access requests to the number of all access requests issued during the simulation period.
– *Rate of accesses to old replicas*:
   The rate of the number of tentative accesses that resulted in failure to the number of all access requests issued during the simulation period.

– *Traffic for updated data dissemination*:
   The product of the total hop count for transmitting updated data items and their sizes, which are performed during the simulation period.

5.2   Effects of Average Update Period U

First, we examine the effects of the average update period U on our proposed method. Figs. 7, 8, and 9 show the simulation results. In these graphs, the horizontal axis indicates the average update period U. The vertical axes indicate the data accessibility, the rate of accesses to old replicas, and the traffic for updated data dissemination, respectively. The performance of the method which we proposed in this paper is shown as "Epidemic" in these graphs. For comparison, we also show the performance when the dissemination of invalidation reports and updated data items are not performed as "NO."

Fig. 7 shows that as the average update period gets larger, the data accessibility in each method gets higher because the replicas held by each mobile host are valid for a longer time. When the average update period is very small, the data accessibility in our proposed method is lower than that in the DU method. However, when the average update period is high, the data accessibility in our proposed method is higher than that in the DU method and is approximately as high as that in the DC/OO method. In our proposed method, the reception intervals of invalidation reports get smaller as the average update period gets smaller, and thus, the request probability gets smaller because MAX_ET is a constant. In our method, lower request probability gives lower data accessibility. This can also be confirmed by the result in Subsec. 5.3, where the data accessibility in our method gets higher as MAX_ET gets smaller. The DC/GG method always gives the highest data accessibility because updated data items can be spread to the widest ranges.

Fig. 8 shows that as the average update period gets larger, the rate of accesses to old replicas in each method gets lower because the replicas held by each mobile

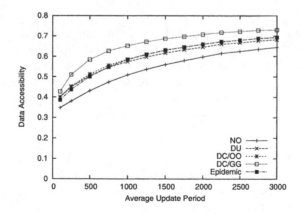

Fig. 7. Average update period and data accessibility

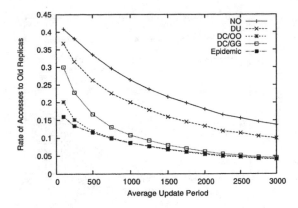

Fig. 8. Average update period and rate of accesses to old replicas

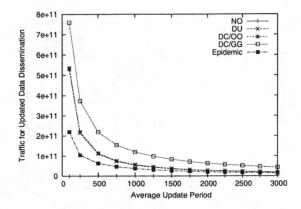

Fig. 9. Average update period and traffic for updated data dissemination

host are valid for a longer time. When the average update period is small, our proposed method gives the lowest rate of accesses to old replicas. This result shows that mobile hosts effectively disseminate invalidation reports and discard old replicas.

Fig. 9 shows that as the average update period gets larger, the traffic for updated data dissemination in each method gets smaller. This is because the frequency of updated data dissemination gets lower as the update frequency of each data item gets lower. Our method gives the lowest traffic for updated data dissemination. This is because each mobile host requests updated data items to its nearby mobile hosts with a certain probability.

5.3   Effects of MAX_ET

We examine the effects of MAX_ET on our proposed method. Figs. 10, 11, and 12 show the simulation results. In these graphs, the horizontal axis indicates

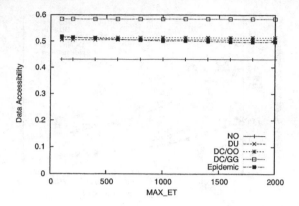

Fig. 10. *MAX_ET* and data accessibility

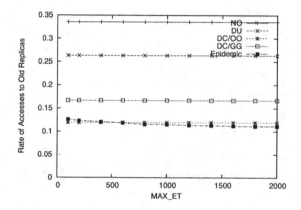

Fig. 11. *MAX_ET* and rate of accesses to old replicas

MAX_ET. The vertical axes indicate the data accessibility, the rate of accesses to old replicas, and the traffic for updated data dissemination, respectively. Although the change in *MAX_ET* does not affect the performances of the three methods in [7] and "NO," we show their results for comparison purpose.

Fig. 10 shows that as *MAX_ET* gets larger, the data accessibility in our proposed method gets lower. This is because the request probability gets lower and the frequency of updated data dissemination gets lower. When *MAX_ET* is small, the data accessibility in our proposed method is larger than that in the DC/OO method.

Fig. 11 shows that as *MAX_ET* gets larger, i.e., the request probability gets lower, the rate of accesses to old replicas in our proposed method gets lower. In our method, as the request probability gets lower, mobile hosts disseminate fewer updated data items. These disseminated items include old replicas whose versions are different with that of the originals, i.e., invalid replicas. This is the reason why fewer data dissemination gives lower rate of accesses to old replicas.

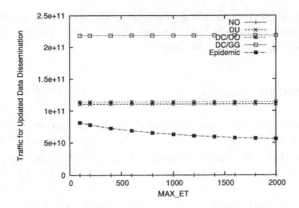

Fig. 12. MAX_ET and traffic for updated data dissemination

Fig. 12 shows that as MAX_ET gets larger, the traffic for updated data dissemination in our proposed method gets lower. This is due to the similar reason as that in Fig. 10. Our method always gives the lowest traffic for updated data dissemination.

From the above results, it is shown that our method is affected by MAX_ET. Therefore, when we apply our proposed method in a real environment, we should choose an appropriate value of MAX_ET according to the update frequencies of data items and the system characteristic, e.g., computational and buttery capacities of each mobile host. We should also choose appropriate values of MAX_A and β in the same way.

6 Related Works

In the research field of ad hoc networks, some studies on information dissemination exploiting epidemic model have been made.

In [2], the authors proposed an autonomous gossiping method which utilizes the opportunity of connecting with new mobile nodes for efficient data dissemination. In this method, each mobile host moves or replicates its own data items to another mobile host based on the host profile and the data item profile. This method aims to disseminate data items to users who are interested in these items, and thus, is different from our method that aims to efficiently refresh old replicas.

In [9], the authors proposed an epidemic model for a simple information diffusion algorithm and analytically investigated the spreading ratio of the information. However, they did not propose a concrete algorithm for information dissemination.

In [10], the authors introduced a distributed lookup service denoted as Passive Distributed Indexing (PDI) and proposed cache invalidation methods for reducing inconsistency among PDI index caches. This approach is similar to our method because a mobile host disseminates an invalidation report when the mobile host connects to another mobile host. However, this approach is different from ours because mobile hosts do not disseminate updated data items, and thus, data accessibility cannot be improved.

7 Conclusions

In this paper, we proposed an updated data dissemination method exploiting an epidemic model, which is a popular bio-inspired approach, for reducing the communication traffic for updated data dissemination. In our proposed method, mobile hosts disseminate invalidation reports and discard old replicas when a mobile host updates a data item or when two mobile hosts are newly connected with each other. A mobile host which discards an old replica requests the updated data item with a certain probability.

The simulation results showed that, compared with three methods in [7], our proposed method gives the lowest traffic for updated data dissemination while the data accessibility is approximately same as that in the DU and DC/OO methods.

In our proposed method, users need to determine the values of several system parameters such as T_{snd}, α, MAX_ET, MAX_A, β, and Δt. As part of our future work, we plan to consider a method for adaptively choosing appropriate values of these system parameters based on the system environment.

Acknowledgments. This research was partially supported by The 21st Century Center of Excellence Program "New Information Technologies for Building a Networked Symbiotic Environment" and Grant-in-Aid for Young Scientists (A)(16680005) and for Scientific Research (A)(17200006) of the Ministry of Education, Culture, Sports, Science and Technology, Japan.

References

1. J. Broch, D.A. Maltz, D.B. Johnson, Y.C. Hu, and J. Jetcheva, "A Performance Comparison of Multi-Hop Wireless Ad Hoc Network Routing Protocols," *Proc. of MobiCom'98*, pp. 85–97, 1998.
2. A. Datta, S. Quarteroni, and K. Aberer, "Autonomous Gossiping: A Self-Organizing Epidemic Algorithm for Selective Information Dissemination in Wireless Mobile Ad-Hoc Networks," *Proc. of Int'l Conf. on Semantics of a Networked World (ICSNW'04)*, pp. 126–143, 2004.
3. O. Diekmann, and J.A.P. Heesterbeek, "Mathematical Epidemiology of Infectious Diseases: Model Building, Analysis and Interpretation," *Wiley Series in Mathematical and Computational Biology*, 2000.
4. T. Hara, "Effective Replica Allocation in Ad Hoc Networks for Improving Data Accessibility," *Proc. of IEEE Infocom'01*, pp. 1568–1576, 2001.
5. T. Hara, N. Murakami, and S. Nishio, "Replica Allocation for Correlated Data Items in Ad-Hoc Sensor Networks," *ACM SIGMOD Record*, Vol. 33, No. 1, pp. 38–43, 2004.

6. H. Hayashi, T. Hara, and S. Nishio, "Cache Invalidation for Updated Data in Ad Hoc Networks," *Proc. of Int'l Conf. on Cooperative Information Systems (CoopIS'03)*, pp. 516-535, 2003.

7. H. Hayashi, T. Hara, and S. Nishio, "Updated Data Dissemination in Ad Hoc Networks," *Proc. of Int'l Workshop on Ubiquitous Mobile Information and Collaboration Systems (UMICS'04)*, pp. 29–43, 2004.

8. D.B. Johnson, "Routing in Ad Hoc Networks of Mobile Hosts," *Proc. of Int'l Workshop on Mobile Computing Systems and Applications (WMCSA'94)*, pp. 158–163, 1994.

9. A. Khelil, C. Becker, J. Tian, and K. Rothermel, "An Epidemic Model for Information Diffusion in MANETs," *Proc. of Int'l Workshop on Modeling, Analysis and Simulation of Wireless and Mobile Systems (MSWiM'02)*, pp. 54–60, 2002.

10. C. Lindemann, and O.P. Waldhorst, "Consistency Mechanisms for A Distributed Lookup Service Supporting Mobile Applications," *Proc. of ACM Int'l Workshop on Data Engineering for Wireless and Mobile Access (MobiDE'03)*, pp. 61–68, 2003.

11. C.E. Perkins, and E.M. Royer, "Ad Hoc on Demand Distance Vector Routing," *Proc. of IEEE Int'l Workshop on Mobile Computing Systems and Applications (WMCSA'99)*, pp. 90–100, 1999.

Modeling of Epidemic Diffusion in Peer-to-Peer File-Sharing Networks

Kenji Leibnitz[1], Tobias Hoßfeld[2], Naoki Wakamiya[1], and Masayuki Murata[1]

[1] Graduate School of Information Science and Technology,
Osaka University, 1-5 Yamadaoka, Suita, Osaka 565-0871, Japan
{leibnitz, wakamiya, murata}@ist.osaka-u.ac.jp
[2] Deptartment of Distributed Systems, University of Würzburg,
Am Hubland, 97074 Würzburg, Germany
hossfeld@informatik.uni-wuerzburg.de

Abstract. In this paper we propose an analytical model for file diffusion in a peer-to-peer (P2P) file-sharing network based on biological epidemics. During the downloading process, the peer shares the downloaded parts of the file and, thus, contributes to distributing it in the network. This behavior is similar to the spreading of epidemic diseases which is a well researched subject in mathematical biology. Unlike other P2P models based on epidemics, we show that steady state assumptions are not sufficient and that the granularity of the diffusion model may be appropriately selected.

1 Introduction

The volume of traffic transmitted over the Internet has enormously increased recently due to the upcoming of peer-to-peer (P2P) file sharing applications. The most popular applications, such as Gnutella [1], eDonkey [2], or BitTorrent [3], are often abused for illegally sharing copyrighted content over the Internet. In P2P technology, each participant (*peer*) serves simultaneously as client and server which makes the system more scalable and robust and distinguishes it from conventional client-server architectures. However, this also comes at a slight drawback when considering content distribution. Since now, no longer a single trusted server distributes the file, malicious peers (*pollution/poisoning*) [4] can offer fake or corrupted files and disrupt the file dissemination process. On the other hand, this can be also used as a method for the rightful owners of the files to protect their copyrighted property from being illegally distributed.

P2P networks can be briefly classified into *pure* and *hybrid* types [5]. Unlike pure P2P networks, e.g. Gnutella, hybrid networks have additional entities which have special functions. In the eDonkey network, each peer connects to an index server which indexes all shared files and over which the search for a certain file is performed. In a similar manner, BitTorrent uses trackers accessed over WWW pages to provide the information about other peers sharing the file. *Seeders* are peers that offer the complete file for other peers to download. After a file has

A.J. Ijspeert et al. (Eds.): BioADIT 2006, LNCS 3853, pp. 322–329, 2006.
© Springer-Verlag Berlin Heidelberg 2006

been downloaded, the peer may itself become a seeder or a *leecher* who does not participate in the file sharing after downloading it.

The file diffusion process itself is comparable to the spreading of a disease in a limited population. There exist many models for population dynamics in mathematical biology [6] dealing with predicting if a disease will become an epidemic outbreak or what vaccination strategy [7] is most appropriate. Epidemic models are also well suited to model the diffusion behavior of specific information in a network, see [8]. In this paper we will use modeling techniques from biological epidemics to predict the diffusion characteristics of single files shared in a P2P network. While in most papers, e.g. [9, 10], the steady-state network performance is investigated, we emphasize on the time-dynamics of the system which requires us to consider a non-stationary process, e.g. caused by flash crowd arrivals of file requests. Additionally, our model takes the distinction between leechers and seeders into account and we show the influence of selfish peers on the file dissemination process.

2   The eDonkey P2P File-Sharing Application

In the following we will consider a file sharing application similar to eDonkey which belongs to the class of hybrid P2P architectures and comprises two separate applications: the *eDonkey client* (or *peer*) and the *eDonkey server*, see [11]. The eDonkey client shares and downloads files. The eDonkey server operates as an index server for file locations and distributes addresses of other servers.

A main feature of P2P file sharing applications like BitTorrent, Kazaa, and eDonkey is the ability to perform *multiple source downloads*, i.e., peers can issue two or more download requests for the same file to multiple providing peers in parallel and the providing peers can serve the requesting peer simultaneously. Before an eDonkey client can download a file, it first gathers a list of all potential file providers. To accomplish this, the client connects to one of the eDonkey servers. Each server keeps a list of all files shared by the clients connected to it. When a client searches for a file, it sends the query to its main server which may return a list of matching files and their locations. In [12], we showed from measurements that about 50% of the total number of eDonkey users are connected to the seven largest index servers with population sizes N of up to 500,000 peers. This large number allows us to assume a Poisson process for the arrival of file requests. More details on the file sharing process itself can be found in [12].

The general structure of an arbitrary file f that is shared in the eDonkey network is depicted in Fig. 1. The file with a size of f_s kB comprises a number of $c_{max} = \lceil \frac{f_s}{c_s} \rceil$ chunks, each with a constant size of $c_s - 9500$ kB with exception of the final chunk c_{max} which may be smaller in size. A full chunk is not exchanged between the peers in whole, but is transmitted in blocks of size $b_s = 180$ kB.

A block is requested from a peer who shares the whole chunk containing this block. After all blocks of a chunk have been downloaded by a requesting peer, an error detection mechanism is performed. In eDonkey, this is done via comparing the hash value of the received chunk with the sender's hash value of the chunk.

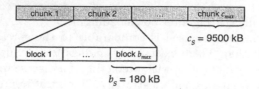

Fig. 1. Structure of a file on eDonkey application layer

In case of an error, i.e., at least one block is corrupted, the complete chunk is discarded and has to be requested and downloaded again.

After a peer has successfully downloaded all blocks of chunk i, he immediately acts as a sharing peer for this chunk and the number of sharing peers is incremented by one. Thus, all users in an eDonkey network may act simultaneously as sharing peers and downloading peers. Although, the user cannot influence that each chunk is shared during downloading, he can show a different behavior after the file has been entirely downloaded. We take this into account in our model by introducing p as the probability that a user shares the file for an exponentially distributed period B. All users in the system use the identical values of p and B. Hence, $p = 0$ indicates a system consisting entirely of *leechers*, i.e., users who only share the file during the download and immediately stop sharing it once the download has been completed.

3   Epidemic Model of File Diffusion

In the following, let us consider a basic epidemic model for P2P file sharing. In general, epidemic models categorize the population into groups depending on their state. A commonly used approach is the SIR model [6]. SIR is an abbreviation for the states that are taken during the course of the spread of the disease. At first, there are *susceptibles*, which are users that can be possibly infected with a certain rate. When they are contacted with the disease, they move to the state of *infectives* and can pass the disease on to other members of the susceptible population. Finally, there is the *removed* population, consisting of users who have either fatally suffered from the disease or have recovered and become immune to it. In either case, they can not get infected by the disease again. An important issue is that the total population N remains constant.

3.1   Analogy of P2P to Biological SIR Model

In this section we will describe the basic underlying biological model and show the commonalities with P2P file sharing. Although there are various analogies between both models, we will see that simply applying an SIR model is insufficient due to the complexity of the P2P applications. However, the principle time-dynamic modeling technique from biology will be maintained and unlike [9] we are able to consider cases that are not in steady state.

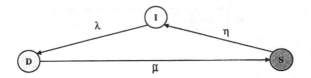

Fig. 2. Simple IDS state space

We denote the number of susceptibles as *idle peers* I at a certain time t. From this set, the file requests are generated with a rate of λ, which can be a time dependent function or a constant reflecting the popularity of the file over time, see [12]. Once the peer starts to download the file, he is attributed to the set of *downloading* peers D. The download rate $\tilde{\mu}$ depends on the number of peers sharing the file and the other downloading peers, which all compete for the download bandwidth. Once downloading of the complete file with size f_s is finished, the peer joins the *sharing* peers S, that offer the file to the other users. The peer shares the file only for a limited time after which he returns with rate η to the idle peers, see Fig. 2. This is a rather simplified view for a generic file sharing application, as the detailed mechanism in eDonkey involves downloading and sharing chunks of the file. Note that all of the above quantities are functions of time, but we will drop the time index in the notation for simplification.

Thus, the dynamic system of the sharing process can be expressed by the equation system given in (1). In analogy to the SIR model, we will refer to it as the IDS model.

$$\frac{dI}{dt} = \eta S - \lambda I \qquad \frac{dD}{dt} = \lambda I - \tilde{\mu} D \qquad \frac{dS}{dt} = \tilde{\mu} D - \eta S \qquad (1)$$

The initial values at time $t = 0$ are I_0, S_0, and $D_0 = N - I_0 - S_0$, respectively.

In Eqn. (1) we can at first assume a constant request arrival rate λ which is adapted to match a Poisson arrival process and the main problem lies in the determination of the download rate $\tilde{\mu}$. Let us define the upload and download rates as r_u and r_d, respectively. We assume homogeneous users with ADSL connections, resulting in rates of $r_u = 128$ kbps and $r_d = 768$ kbps. Since eDonkey employs a fair share mechanism for the upload rates, there are on average S/D peers sharing to a single downloading peer and we multiply this value with r_u which gives us the bandwidth on the uplink. However, since the download bandwidth could be the limiting factors, the effective transition rate μ consists of the minimum of both terms divided by the file size f_s, see Eqn. (2).

$$\tilde{\mu} = \frac{1}{f_s} \min \left\{ \frac{r_u S}{D}, r_d \right\} \qquad (2)$$

The dynamics of the populations of D and S are shown in Fig. 3 and compared to the mean population sizes, i.e., mean number of peers, obtained from the average over 5000 simulation runs. We selected $S_0 = 5000$, $I_0 = 100$ and a constant λ of 1300 requests per hour. For the sake of simplicity we consider at this point $\eta = 0$, i.e., all peers remain sharing peers after a completed download

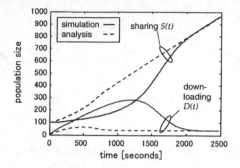

Fig. 3. Comparison of simulation results with basic IDS model

and do not leave the system. The shape of the I curves is not very interesting to us in this scenario, since it just linearly decreases due to the Poisson assumption.

When comparing the simulation with the analytical model, we can see that the same general shape matches for $t > 2000$, whereas a problem arises w.r.t. the accuracy of the model for smaller values of time t. This can be explained as follows. The transition from D to S is performed only after the complete file with fixed size f_s has been downloaded. The current model using the states I, D, and S, however, is memoryless and does not take into account the number of bits that have already been downloaded. The transitions between these states are given here as rates indicating the "average" number of transitions per time unit. In reality, the average download rate changes during the downloading process of an individual peer and it is insufficient to consider it a priori as constant for the complete file. While this assumption is generally applied in epidemic modeling of diseases, we wish to provide an enhanced mathematical model by considering a finer granularity. In the following we will, therefore, minimize the error by splitting the macro state D into M smaller states corresponding to the number of bits downloaded. We expect that when M approaches infinity, the error will be reduced to zero.

3.2   Detailed File Sharing Model

We consider in the following the last downloaded chunk of a file which is the most interesting case, as its completion results in the completion of the entire file. The user can then decide whether the whole file is shared or not, i.e., whether the peer becomes a leecher or a seeder. In the following the terms file and last downloaded chunk will be used interchangeably.

Let us split the file with size f_s into M logical units which we will consider individually. Our model thus increases by the states $D_0, \ldots, D_M$. We can interpret the states D_i as the state where i logical units have been successfully downloaded, i.e., D_0 means that the download is initiated and D_M indicates a complete download. After reception of each block, the queue mechanism of eDonkey determines the sharing peers from which the next block will be downloaded. This involves an update of the download rate μ after each logical unit. If we

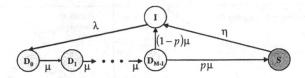

Fig. 4. Detailed IDS state space

choose the logical unit as blocks, our model is exact and the obtained numerical error is acceptably small, cf. Fig. 5(a). The transitions from the states D_i use a rate μ similar to the one described in Eqn. (2).

$$\mu = \frac{M}{f_s} \min \left\{ \frac{r_u S}{\sum_{i=0}^{M-1} D_i}, r_d \right\} \tag{3}$$

A further enhancement of the simple model is the introduction of p as the probability of sharing a file. The updated state space with transitions is illustrated in Fig. 4. After the M-th logical unit has been downloaded, the peer enters the sharing peers with probability p and returns to the idle state with $1 - p$. This corresponds to the user leaving the system after downloading (leecher) or downloading it another time again at a later time.

The new equation system is summarized below. The original model given in Section 3.1 corresponds to a value of $M = 1$. Obviously, the larger M is, the more accurate is the model, but the computational requirements for solving the equation system increase as well. Finding a good value of M involves a tradeoff between accuracy and computation speed.

$$\frac{dI}{dt} = (1 - p)\mu D_{M-1} - \lambda I + \eta S \qquad \frac{dS}{dt} = p\mu D_{M-1} - \eta S \tag{4}$$

$$\frac{dD_0}{dt} = \lambda I - \mu D_0 \qquad \frac{dD_i}{dt} = \mu (D_{i-1} - D_i) \quad \forall_{1 \le i < M} \tag{5}$$

Again, we must include the condition to keep the total population at the index server constant at $N = I + \sum_{i=1}^{M} D_i + S$.

However, since the equation system is a closed system, it is sufficient to ensure that the initial values obey this constraint. Hence, we assume that $N = I_0 + S_0$ and $D_i = 0$ for all i. The considered values for M are 1, 2, 18, and 53, corresponding to the download units of a chunk. Thus, the largest number of equations is when $M = 53$ and the units are blocks as described in Section 2.

The extended model is compared to simulation results in Fig. 5(a). We can recognize that using a large value of M greatly improves the accuracy of the model. Note that the task of comparing results averaged from simulation runs to the mathematical model is not fully appropriate. The differential equations describe the general behavior of a single evolution over time, depending on the initial values and boundary values. We can easily match the initial values, but the boundary conditions in the simulation depend for example also on the realization of each random variable. Each individual simulation run matches exactly the

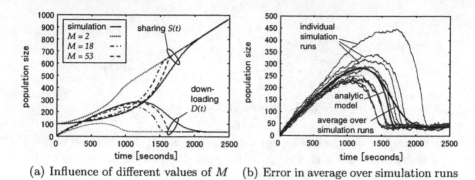

(a) Influence of different values of M (b) Error in average over simulation runs

Fig. 5. Extended IDS model

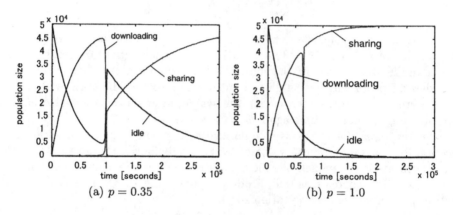

(a) $p = 0.35$ (b) $p = 1.0$

Fig. 6. Influence of sharing probability p

shape of the analytical model, however, depending on the random variables can be different in scale, see Fig. 5(b). When we average over the series of simulation runs, this leads to the different decreasing slope at about 1700 s in Fig. 5(a).

With our model, we can evaluate the influence of the parameters on the system behavior. In this paper, we focus on the sharing probability p. Two values of p are shown in Fig. 6. In Fig. 6(a), $p = 0.35$ and this percentage of peers becomes seeders right after downloading. The others return to the idle state and download the file again at a later time, only then there are more seeders available which makes the download time very short. The idle users decrease exponentially, since $\eta = 0$ and the sharing users increase accordingly. Finally, all peers will become seeders in spite of p being less than 1. The higher p is, the faster the file is distributed among all peers, see Fig. 6(b).

4   Conclusion and Outlook

We presented an analytical model for file diffusion in an eDonkey-like P2P file sharing network. It is based on an epidemic model like the well-known SIR model, but in our case corresponds to the populations of idle peers, peers currently downloading the file (or chunk), and those sharing it. We could see that using a simple SIR-like model is not very accurate, nor is the steady state assumption found in many publications. We, therefore, considered separate populations for peers having downloaded certain parts of the file and could improve the accuracy of the model when we compared the results to simulations.

The model provides the foundation to investigate many aspects of file diffusion properties. We are especially interested in the effects of pollution in P2P file sharing. Our main objective in the future will be to investigate the influence of peers sharing polluted data on the dissemination process.

Acknowledgement. This research was supported by "The 21st Century COE Program: *New Information Technologies for Building a Networked Symbiosis Environment*" and a Grant-in-Aid for Scientific Research (A)(2) 16200003 of the Ministry of Education, Culture, Sports, Science and Technology in Japan.

References

1. Gnutella Protocol Development Website. (http://rfc-gnutella.sourceforge.net/)
2. eDonkey2000 Home Page. (http://www.eDonkey2000.com/)
3. The Official BitTorrent Home Page. (http://www.bittorrent.com/)
4. Liang, J., Kumar, R., Xi, Y., Ross, K.: Pollution in P2P file sharing systems. In: IEEE INFOCOM, Miami, FL (2005)
5. Schollmeier, R.: A definition of peer-to-peer networking for the classification of peer-to-peer architectures and applications. In: IEEE 2001 International Conference on Peer-to-Peer Computing (P2P2001), Linköping, Sweden (2001)
6. Murray, J.: Mathematical Biology, I: An introduction. 3 edn. Springer (2002)
7. Verriest, E., Delmotte, F., Egerstedt, M.: Control of epidemics by vaccination. In: American Control Conference, Portland, OR (2005)
8. Khelil, A., Becker, C., Tian, J., Rothermel, K.: An epidemic model for information diffusion in MANETs. In: 5th ACM MSWiM, Atlanta, GA (2002) 54–60
9. Qiu, D., Srikant, R.: Modeling and performance analysis of BitTorrent-like peer-to-peer networks. In: ACM SIGCOMM'04, Portland, OR (2004)
10. Lo Piccolo, F., Neglia, G., Bianchi, G.: The effect of heterogeneous link capacities in BitTorrent-like file sharing systems. In: Intern. Workshop on Hot Topics in Peer-to-Peer Systems (HOT-P2P'04), Volendam, The Nederlands (2004) 40–47
11. Tutschku, K.: A measurement-based traffic profile of the eDonkey filesharing service. In: 5th Passive and Active Measurement Workshop (PAM2004), Antibes Juan-les-Pins, France (2004)
12. Hoßfeld, T., Loibnitz, K., Pries, R., Tutschku, K., Tran-Gia, P., Pawlikowski, K.: Information diffusion in eDonkey-like P2P networks. In: Australian Telecommun. Networks and Applications Conference (ATNAC), Bondi Beach, Australia (2004)

A High-Throughput Method to Quantify the Structural Properties of Individual Cell-Sized Liposomes by Flow Cytometry

Kanetomo Sato[1], Kei Obinata[1], Tadashi Sugawara[2],
Itaru Urabe[3], and Tetsuya Yomo[1,3,4,5]

[1] Department of Bioinformatic Engineering, Graduate School of Information Science
and Technology, Osaka University, 2-1, Yamadaoka, Suita, Osaka 565-0871, Japan
yomo@ist.osaka-u.ac.jp
http://www-symbio.ist.osaka-u.ac.jp/sbj.html
[2] Department of Pure and Applied Sciences, University of Tokyo, Komaba,
Meguro-ku, Tokyo 153-8902, Japan
[3] Department of Biotechnology, Graduate School of Engineering, Osaka University,
2-1, Yamadaoka, Suita, Osaka 565-0871, Japan
[4] Graduate School of Frontier Bioscience, Osaka University, 2-1, Yamadaoka, Suita,
Osaka 565-0871, Japan
[5] ERATO, JST, 2-1, Yamadaoka, Suita, Osaka 565-0871, Japan

Abstract. We describe a new high-throughput method to quantify the
structural properties of individual cell-sized liposomes. We labeled an
internal aqueous solution of liposomes with a green fluorescent protein
(GFP) and the membrane with a fatty acid conjugated with a red fluorescent probe. The internal aqueous volume and lipid membrane volume
of each liposome was measured, and double-labeled liposomes were analyzed by flow cytometry, a useful tool that enables us to estimate the
internal aqueous and lipid membrane volumes of individual cell-sized
liposomes independently of shape and structure. This method shows
promise in opening the way to understanding the characteristics of biochemical reactions occurring within a liposome, to optimizing the preparation method of liposomes, and to overcoming many of the difficulties
in realizing an artificial cell.

1   Introduction

The challenges of constructing an artificial cell may provide clues for understanding the essence of complex biosystems and their origin, [1-4] and the approaches
should be simple yet complex enough to include the essence of living biosystems.
Liposomes have already been used as compartments for artificial cells, and various types of biochemical reactions have been carried out within those liposomes.
[1-13] The essence of biochemical reactions within living organisms is RNA synthesis [6-7] and protein synthesis, [6,8-10,13] which have been achieved within
liposomes. It may be possible that constructing a functional cell-free genetic
network[14] in liposomes will lead to achievement of a higher degree of genetic

A.J. Ijspeert et al. (Eds.): BioADIT 2006, LNCS 3853, pp. 330–337, 2006.

complexity. We previously constructed a two-stage cascade genetic network in a liposome, and Ishikawa *et al.* demonstrated that the T7 RNA polymerase gene for an RNA polymerase was expressed at first, then the translated T7 RNA polymerase transcripted the mRNA for GFP translation by a T7 promoter.[13] To advance the prospects for realizing such a system, as a first step it is necessary to understand the relationship between the structural properties and the characteristics of the biochemical reactions occurring within the liposomes. This is because the structural properties of liposomes, including particle size, internal aqueous volume, composition of lipid mixture, and number of lamellae, promise to become important parameters affecting the properties of biochemical reactions. Considering that cell-sized liposomes used in constructing an artficial cell are often a highly heterogeneous mixture in size, shape, and membrane structure[15], it is desirable to measure quantitatively both the number of lamellae and the internal volume of individual liposomes simultaneously. Although various methods have been proposed for determining particle size and distribution [16,17] and the average internal volume [18,19] of liposomes, these methods are not applicable to the above aim. Furthermore, although microscopic methods have been used extensively in the characterization of individual particles, quantitation of images is difficult and tedious, especially for a large number of particles.

In this paper, we present a high-throughput method to measure simultaneously the internal aqueous volume and lipid membrane volume of individual cell-sized liposomes by flow cytometry. Flow cytometry is an extremely useful method that employs the principle of light scattering to analyze particles with a fluorescent marker suspended in a fluid stream. [20] Each individual particle is measured in a continuous flow system; in a way, a flow cytometer can be considered as a high-throughput fluorescence microscope able to detect and read multiple signals of a specific intensity range. The powerful analysis functions of flow cytometry make this technology ideal for reliable and accurate quantitative evaluation of structual properties of liposomes. In this research, the internal solution and membrane lipid were labeled with green and red fluorescent markers, [9,21] respectively. Fluorescence intensity data collected with a fluorescence-activated cell sorter (FACS) were corrected for the background, compensated for the overlapping fluorescence, converted to the number of marker molecules, and then to the volume of the internal solution or lipid membrane. This study promises to open a new avenue toward the realization of an artificial cell.

2   Material and Method

2.1   Materials

1-Palmitoyl-2-oleoyl-*sn*-phosphatidylcholine (POPC), 1-palmitoyl-2-linoleoyl-*sn*-phosphatidylcholine (PLPC), 1-stearoyl-2-oleoyl-*sn*-phosphatidylcholine (SOPC), and 1-stearoyl-2-linoleoyl-*sn*-phosphatidylcholine (SLPC) were purchased from Avanti Polar Lipids, Inc. Cholesterol was from Nacarai Tesque, Inc., and distearoyl phosphatidyl ethanolamine-poly(ethylene glycol) 5000 (DSPE-PEG5000) was kindly supplied by NOF Corporation. R-phycoerythrin

(PE) was purchased from Molecular Probes, Inc., and 11-{3",5"-bis(4"'-methoxy phenyl)-4", 4"-difluoro-4"-bora-3a,4a-diaza-s-indacenyl}-3',5'-dimethylphenoxy undecanoic acid (BODIP Y-RED-UA) was synthesized according to the literature. [21] Enhanced green fluorescent protein (EGFP) was purchased from BD Biosciences Clontech. The molar absorption coefficient of the EGFP was described as 55,000 $M^{-1}cm^{-1}$ at 488nm accoding to the BD Living Colors™User Manual. A purified mutant green fluorescent protein with a His-tag (GFPmut2-His6) was prepared as described previously. [9] (We found the mistake in the sequence of mutant GFP previously described [9,13]: the sequence should not be GFPmut1 but GFPmut2.) The molar absorption coefficient of the protein at 280 nm was determined to be 31,800 $M^{-1}cm^{-1}$ from the value of absorbance at 280 nm and the amino acid composition of the purified protein solution, as described previously. [22]

2.2   Liposome Preparation

Liposomes were prepared based on the freeze-dried empty liposomes method, [23] and the procedures were the same as those reported previously, [13] except that the experiments were carried out at room temperature unless otherwise stated. The lipid mixture (1.2 μmol; molar ratio of POPC:PLPC:SOPC: SLPC:cholesterol: DSPE-PEG5000:BODIPY-RED-UA = 129:67:48:24:180:14:1) dissolved in dichlor omethane/diethyl ether (1:1, v/v) was rotary-evaporated in a pear-shaped flask under vacuum to yield a thin lipid film. The lipid composition was almost the same as that reported previously, [9,13] except that BODIPY-RED-UA was added and egg yolk phosphatidyl choline (eggPC) was replaced with a mixture of POPC, PLPC, SOPC, and SLPC, of which the molar ratio was adjusted to that of eggPC (the analytical data were kindly provided by NOF Corporation).

2.3   Flow Cytometry

The liposomes were analyzed with an EPICS®ALTRA™HyPerSort FACS (Beckman Coulter, Inc.) equipped with a 488-nm water-cooled argon ion laser (Coherent Japan, Inc.) at 20 mW. Before the analysis, the liposome dispersion prepared above was diluted about 200 times with the isotonic buffer of 125 mM Tris-HCl (pH 7.8) to allow a rate of analysis below 2,000 events/s. The Flow-check™Fluorospheres 10-μm beads (Beckman Coulter, Inc.) were introduced prior to measuring the samples for alignment of the laser source, in order to set the half-peak coefficient of variation (CV) to less than 2 %. To calibrate the daily variance, fluorescence-labeled latex beads of 0.5, 0.75, 1, 3, and 6-μm diameter (Polyscience, Inc.) and non-fluorescent 1.5-μm latex beads were used. A discriminator of 10 channels out of 1,024 was set on forward-scatter (FS) to eliminate the influence of machine noise. Side-scatter (SS) signals were measured using in succession a 488-nm dichroic lens and a bandpass filter at 488 nm. GFP fluorescence signals were measured employing in succession a 488-nm band-block filter, a 550-nm dichroic lens, and a band-pass filter at 525±20nm. BODIPY fluorescence signals were measured successively by a 488-nm band-block filter, a

550-nm dichroic lens, a 600-nm dichroic lens, and a band-pass filter at 610 ± 10nm. FS, SS, and fluorescence data were collected with a logarithmic amplifier. The liposome count number was set to be 2.0×10^5.

2.4   Estimation of Internal Aqueous Volume and Lipid Membrane Volume

The data on fluorescence intensity collected with FACS were changed from the log channel number to the relative intensity number according to the EPICS™Hy PerSort system manual. For background correction, we used the data obtained for blank liposomes prepared by the same procedures as described above, except for omitting GFPmut2-His6 and BODIPY-RED-UA. The blank liposomes were scattered across the log(FS) and log(SS) plane according to their FS and SS values, the plane was divided into small blocks (32x32 channels), and then fluorescence intensity values of the blank liposomes in each small block were averaged. The average value was used as the blank value included in the fluorescence intensity values of individual GFP- and BODIPY-double-labeled liposomes contained in the same block on the plane. It was confirmed that the omission of GFPmut2-His6 and BODIPY-RED-UA does not change the scattering pattern of liposomes on the log(FS) and log(SS) plane. Since two types of fluorescence signal, green and red, were used to simultaneously quantify the internal and membrane volumes of individual liposomes, the fluorescence signals obtained by FACS need to be compensated for overlapping fluorescence. [24] Befor compensation, it was confirmed that two types of the fluorescent spectrums, EGFP and GFPmut2-His6, overlapping to the band-pass filter at 610 ± 10nm were almost the same. FACS analysis of EGFP calibration beads (BD Living Colors™EGFP Calibration Beads, BD Clontech), where EGFP is covalently bound, showed that the intensity of EGFP fluorescence overlapping the BODIPY fluorescence value is 0.057 % of the EGFP fluorescence intensity. On the other hand, FACS analysis of BODIPY-labeled liposomes, which were prepared

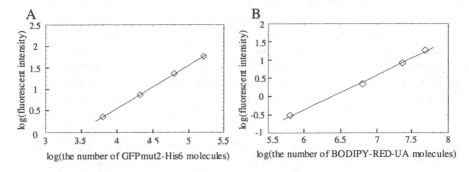

Fig. 1. The standard curves for GFPmut2-His6 (A) and BODIPY-RED-UA (B).The equation in A is [log(GFPmut2-His6 fluorescent intensity) = 1.0·log(the number of GFPmut2 molecules) —3.4] , and that in B is [log(BODIPY-RED-UA fluorescent intensity) = 0.94·log(the number of BODIPY-RED-UA molecules) — 6.0]. The values of the R^2 for these lines exceed 0.99.

by the same procedures as above except for omitting GFPmut2-His6, showed that the intensity of BODIPY fluorescence overlapping the GFP fluorescence value is 3.6 % of the BODIPY intensity. Using these data, the effects of over-lapping fluorescence were eliminated by calculation [24] from the background-corrected GFP and BODIPY fluorescence intensities obtained by FACS. We have confirmed that the concentrations of fluorescent probes, GFPmut2-His6 (3 μM) and the BODIPY-RED-UA (0.22 mol%), used in this work lie in a lin-ear range between the concentration of fluorescent molecules and fluorescence intensities.

The corrected values of the GFP and BODIPY fluorescence intensities were converted to the numbers of GFPmut2-His6 and BODIPY-RED-UA molecules, respectively, contained in each liposome by using standard curves (Fig. 1), which were constructed from the FACS analysis of the EGFP calibration beads (see above) and the QuantiBRITE^{TM}PE Quantitation kit (BD Bioscience), respec-tively. Before the conversion, since the former kit uses EGFP as a green flu-orescence marker, the EGFP fluorescence intensity was changed to the corre-sponding intensity of GFPmut2-His6 fluorescence using a coefficient for which the EGFP fluorescence is 1.4 times as intense as that of the GFPmut2-His6 flu-orescence. The coefficient was determined using 83, 167, and 250 nM EGFP and 100, 150, and 250 nM GFPmut2-His6 in 10mM Tris-HCl(pH 7.8). Their fluores-cence signals exited at 488 nm and, through a band-pass filter at 525±20nm, were recorded by a Hitachi F-2000 spectrofluorometer. Each fluorescence signal was integrated, and the values were plotted for each GFP against GFP concen-tration. The value of the coefficient was calculated from the slopes of the two regression lines. On the other hand, since the latter kit uses R-phycoerythrin (PE) as a red fluorescence marker, the PE fluorescence intensity was changed to the corresponding intensity of BODIPY fluorescence using a coefficient for which the PE fluorescence is 731 times as intense as that of the BODIPY fluorescence. The coefficient was determined using 4.7, 9.4, and 18.7 μM BODIPY-RED-UA in dichloromethane and 83, 125, and 167 nM PE in phosphate-buffered saline (pH 7.4). Their fluorescence signals exited at 488 nm and, through a band-pass filter at 610±10nm, were recorded by a Hitachi F-2000 spectrofluorometer. Each fluorescence signal was integrated, and the values were plotted for each dye against dye concentration. The value of the coefficient was calculated from the slopes of the two regression lines. The internal aqueous volume of a liposome was determined from the number of GFPmut2-His6 molecules in the liposome using a GFPmut2-His6 concentration of 3 μM. The lipid membrane volume of a liposome was determined from the number of BODIPY-RED-UA molecules in the liposome and the volume of lipid bilayer per BODIPY-RED-UA molecule estimated as follows. From the lipid composition of liposomes prepared in this work, the volume of lipid bilayer per BODIPY-RED-UA molecule was estimated to be 5.87×10^{-7} μm^3 using the value for the thickness of a 4.51 nm [25] lipid bilayer and the values of the surface areas of phosphatidyl cholines, cholesterol, and DSPE-PEG5000 of 0.694 nm^2, [25] 0.38 nm^2, [26,27] and 0.413 nm^2, [28] respectively.

3   Distribution of the Internal Aqueous Volume and Lipid Membrane Volume of Each Individual Liposome

Based on FACS data, Fig. 2 shows the double-labeled liposomes scattered as dots on the plane of the internal aqueous vomule (V_I) and the lipid membrane volume (V_M) calculated from the GFP and BODIPY fluorescence, respectively, as described above. Assuming that liposomes are simple spherical, multilamellar vesicles, the number of lamellae, L, in each liposome is related to V_I and V_M by the following equation:

$$V_M = (4\pi/3)\{(3V_I/4\pi)^{1/3} + d\cdot L\}^3 - V_I, \tag{1}$$

where d is the thickness of a lipid bilayer. The black lines in Fig. 2 are drawn using Eq. (1) with the indicated L values and a d value [25] of 4.51 nm. The results reveal that 80 % of the liposomes detected by FACS have 10 to 100 membranes, 19 % have more than 100 membranes, and only 0.6 % have fewer than 10 membranes. The contours of particle density are drawn in white lines in Fig. 2. A high-density region forms an elliptic shape with the long axis parallel to the lines with constant L values (10 < L < 100), and a short ridge from that region is seen to jut out in the same direction. On the other hand, a long main ridge extends toward the upper-right direction. This distribution pattern suggests that the liposome preparation consists of at least two components: Liposomes in one group have thinner membranes with a narrow range of the number of lamellae and a wide variety in their internal volume, whereas the number of lamellae of liposomes in another group grows with an increase in the liposomes' internal volume.

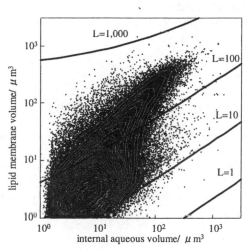

Fig. 2. Dot plot and contour-density plot of GFP- and BODIPY-double-labeled liposomes on the internal aqueous volume and lipid membrane volume plane

4   Discussion

Cell-sized liposomes are useful for constructing an artificial cell, which may provide clues for understanding the essence of life and its origin. [1-4] Because the preparation for the cell-sized liposome is a highly heterogeneous mixture, [15] it is crucial to measure the properties of individual liposomes in the as-prepared condition, and to correlate the structural parameters to the biochemical properties of each liposome.

Through conducting this research, we have established a new, high-throughput method to quantify the structural properties of individual cell-sized liposomes by using flow cytometry. This method of determining both the internal aqueous volume and the lipid membrane volume of individual liposomes requires no special assumptions about the shape and structure of liposomes. The fact that the structural and biochemical properties of individual liposomes can be analyzed opens the way to understanding the characteristics of biochemical reactions occurring within a liposome, to optimizing the preparation method of liposomes, and to overcoming many of the difficulties in realizing an artificial cell.

The system of biochemical network reactions in the living cell is robust, adaptable, and able to evolve against environmental perturbations. In constructing an experimental approach that uses a model system of artificial cells, it is important to comprehend the difference of the properties of the network system between living cells and artificial ones. Such an understanding will provide clues for elucidating the essence of life and for controlling the man-made network system robustly just as living cells do. The knowledge acquired from these efforts will lead to further ideas for developing applications to control bio-inspired information technology and architecture. Our results in this work are a most basic but important step toward achieving above aim, and we are now analyzing and attempting to understand the difference of the biochemical reactions between the artificial cell and the living one.

References

1. Szostak, J.W., Bartel, D.P., Luisi, P.L.: Synthesizing life. Nature **409** (2001) 387-390
2. Luisi, P.L.: Toward the engineering of minimal living cells. Anat. Rec. **268** (2002) 208-214
3. Luisi, P.L.: Autopoiesis: a review and a reappraisal. Naturwissenschaften **90** (2003) 49-59
4. Deamer, D.: A giant step towards artificial life? Trends Biotechnol. **23** (2005) 336-338
5. Pohorille, A., Deamer, D.: Artificial cells: prospects for biotechnology. Trends Biotechnol. **20** (2002) 123-128
6. Monnard, P.-A.: Liposome-entrapped polymerases as models for microscale/nanoscale bioreactors. J. Membrane Biol. **191** (2003) 87-97
7. Oberholzer, T., Wick, R., Luisi, P.L., Biebricher, C.K.: Enzymatic RNA replication in self-reproducing vesicles: an approach to a minimal cell. Biochem. Biophys. Res. Commun. **207** (1995) 250-257

8. Oberholzer, T., Nierhaus, K.H., Luisi, P.L.: Protein expression in liposomes. Biochem. Biophys. Res. Commun. **261** (1999) 238-241
9. Yu, W., Sato, K., Wakabayashi, M., Nakaishi, T., Ko-Mitamura, E.P., Shima, Y., Urabe, I., Yomo, T.: Synthesis of functional protein in liposome. J.Biosci. Bioeng. **92** (2001) 590-593
10. Nomura, S.M., Tsumoto, K., Hamada, T., Akiyoshi, K., Nakatani, Y., Yoshikawa, K.: Gene expression within cell-sized lipid vesicles. ChemBioChem 4 (2003) 1172-1175
11. Hanczyc, M.M., Fujikawa, S.M., Szostak, J.W.: Experimental models of primitive cellular compartments: encapsulation, growth, and division. Science **302** (2003) 618-622
12. Chen, I.A., Roberts, R.W., Szostak, J.W.: The Emergence of Competition Between Model Protocells. Science **305** (2004) 1474-1476
13. Ishikawa, K., Sato, K., Shima, Y., Urabe, I., Yomo, T.: Expression of a cascading genetic network within liposomes. FEBS Lett. **576** (2004) 387-390
14. Noireaux, V., Bar-Ziv, R., Libchaber, A.: Principles of cell-free genetic circuit assembly. Proc. Natl. Acad. Sci. USA **100** (2003) 12672-12677
15. Svetina, S., Žekš, B.: Shape behavior of lipid vesicles as the basis of some cellular processes. Anat. Rec. **268** (2002) 215-225
16. Woodle, M.C., Papahadjopoulos, D.: Liposome preparation and size characterization. Methods Enzymol. **171** (1989) 193-217
17. Lesieur, S., Grabielle-Madelmont, C., Paternostre, M.-T., Ollivon, M.: Size analysis and stability study of lipid vesicles by high-performance gel exclusion chromatography, turbidity, and dynamic light scattering. Anal. Biochem. **192** (1991) 334-343
18. Oku, N., Kendall, D.A., MacDonald, R.C.: A simple procedure for the determination of the trapped volume of liposomes. Biochim. Biophys. Acta **691** (1982) 332-340
19. Perkins, W.R., Minchey, S.R., Ahl, P.L., Janoff, A.S.: The determination of liposome captured volume. Chem. Phys. Lipids **64** (1993) 197-217
20. Shapiro, H.M.: Practical Flow Cytometry, 3rd ed.; John Wiley & Sons; New York, (1995)
21. Yamada, K., Toyota, T., Takakura, K., Ishimaru, M., Sugawara, T.: Preparation of BODIPY probes for multicolor fluorescence imaging studies of membrane dynamics. New J. Chem. **25** (2001) 667-669
22. Suga, Y., Yomo, T., Urabe, I.: Heme content of catalase I from *Bacillus stearothermophilus* J. Ferment. Bioeng. **81** (1996) 259-261
23. Kikuchi, H., Suzuki, N., Ebihara, K., Morita, H., Ishii, Y., Kikuchi, A., Sugaya, S., Serikawa, T., Tanaka, K.: Gene delivery using liposome technology. J. Control. Release **62** (1999) 269-277
24. Bagwell, C.B., Adams, E.G.: Fluorescence spectral overlap compensation for any number of flow cytometry parameters. Ann. NY Acad. Sci.**677** (1993) 167-184
25. Nagle, J.F., Tristram-Nagle, S.: Structure of lipid bilayers. Biochim. Biophys. Acta **1409** (2000) 159-195
26. Hofsäß, C., Lindahl, E., Edholm, O.:Molecular dynamics simulations of phospholipid bilayers with cholesterol. Biophys. J.**84** (2003) 2192-2206
27. Craven, B. M.: Pseudosymmetry in cholesterol monohydrate. Acta Cryst. **B35** (1979) 1123-1128
28. Israelachvili, J.N., Mitchell, D.J.: A model for the packing of lipids in bilayer membranes. Biochim. Biophys. Acta **389** (1975) 13-19

A User Authentication System Using Schema of Visual Memory

Atsushi Harada, Takeo Isarida, Tadanori Mizuno, and Masakatsu Nishigaki

Shizuoka University, 3-5-1 Johoku, Hamamatsu 432-8011, Japan
isarida@ia.inf.shizuoka.ac.jp
{cs7072, mizuno, nisigaki}@cs.inf.shizuoka.ac.jp

Abstract. On many image-based user authentication systems, they have to present a user's pass-image on their display at each authentication trial, so they can be vulnerable against an observing attack. This paper proposes a user authentication system using "unclear images" as pass-images, in which only the legitimate users are allowed to see the original images corresponding to the unclear pass-images in the enrollment phase. The legitimate users can easily remember their unclear pass-images by using the original images as clues, while illegal users without the clues have difficulties to find out and remember the other user's unclear pass-images.

1 Introduction

Although password-based systems are now widely used in all kinds of authentication, they have some shortcomings in its neglecting of a human limitation. On the password-based systems, if a user chooses a short or a meaningful password, it can easily be guessed by a password crack program. To avoid this, users must choose secure passwords (long and random strings). However, most of users prefer to use simple passwords or hesitate to change them frequently since it is not easy for humans to remember a long and random string. In fact, it is known that many users tend to use their names or birthdays as their passwords, to write down their passwords in pocket notebooks, or to reuse the same password in different cases of authentication. These humans' behaviors degrade the security of the authentication system. Further information about the shortcomings of password-based systems is described in [1].

To cope with these shortcomings, image-based user authentication systems using "pass-images" instead of passwords have been studied for reducing the burden of memorizing passwords. The authentication based on recognition of pass-images [1, 3, 4, 5] is especially effective since humans are significantly more efficient about recognition of previously seen images than precise recall of passwords. However, on such systems, there is another problem that it is needed to present a user's pass-image on their display at each authentication trial, so they can be vulnerable against an observing attack (shoulder surfing). An observing attack can be a serious problem for image-based authentication systems since the

A.J. Ijspeert et al. (Eds.): BioADIT 2006, LNCS 3853, pp. 338–345, 2006.

use of the images makes it easier not only for the legitimate users to remember their pass-images, but also for an attacker to peep and remember them.

Moreover, attention needs to be paid to illegal acts by the legitimate users; a legitimate user could intentionally leak his/her own authentication information to the others, e.g. for illegal sharing of a content. Pass-images are still easy to be shared since users could tell the meanings of their pass-images to the others even if we use "random-art" images (abstract images consisted of some geometric patterns produced by random computation [2]) as pass-images [1].

To solve this problems mentioned above, this paper proposes a user authentication system using "unclear images" as pass-images. An unclear image is created from an original meaningful image by image processing such as grayscaling, mosaicing, and noise adding to the spatial frequency domain. An unclear image still has some meanings of the original image, but it looks like a meaningless image for the users who have never seen the original image. Even for humans it is hard to remember a meaningless image.

Only the legitimate users are allowed to see the original images corresponding to their unclear pass-images in the enrollment phase. By seeing the original images, the legitimate users can recognize the meaning in the unclear pass-images and can easily remember them by using the original images as clues. In other words, our scheme gives only the legitimate users a kind of knowledge of their unclear pass-images by showing the corresponding original images. This kind of knowledge is called as "schema" in cognitive psychology [6]. Schema means a structure of knowledge that is unconsciously organized in humans' mind when humans memorize any incoming information. If once a legitimate user forms the schema of his/her unclear pass-images which is associated with the corresponding original image, he/she can easily recognize the meaning of the unclear pass-image. Therefore, the legitimate users can remember their unclear image as if it is a meaningful image, so the burden of memorizing their pass-images is small.

Usually, users cannot learn the appropriate schema without seeing the corresponding original image. Therefore, it is expected to be difficult for illegal users to remember the legitimate user's unclear pass-image, even if the illegal users are allowed to freely observe the legitimate users' authentication trial. In addition, it is also expected to be difficult for a legitimate user to leak his/her unclear pass-image precisely to anyone with words via e-mail or telephone.

2   Authentication System Using Unclear Images

2.1   Unclear Images

Unclear images $O(x, y)$ are produced from the meaningful color images $I(x, y)$ (original images) such as photographs.

1. The original image is a 256-color 300 × 300 pixel image $I(x, y)$.
2. The system creates $I'(x, y)$ by converting $I(x, y)$ to grayscale image and applying histogram equalization.

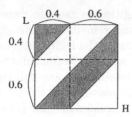

Fig. 1. Noise range for creation of an unclear image

Fig. 2. An example of the original image and the corresponding unclear image

3. The system creates $I''(x,y)$ by mosaicing $I'(x,y)$, where the size of mosaic block is 6×6 pixel each. That is, each mosaic block of $I''(x,y)$ is painted in the averaged color of the 6×6 pixels.

4. The system can contract $I''(x,y)$ by viewing each mosaic block (6×6 pixels) of $I''(x,y)$ as a pixel. By doing so, the system obtains $M(k,l)$ with 50×50 pixels.

5. The system applies 2-D DCT (discrete cosign transform) to $M(k,l)$, where in this system DCT block size is 50×50 for simplicity.

6. The system adds some noise to the DCT coefficients obtained at step 5. In this system, the DCT coefficients at the gray area depicted in Fig. 1 are changed to values from -100 to 100 randomly, and the DC (direct current) coefficient is set to 0. Then the system gets $M'(k,l)$ by applying IDCT (inverse DCT) to $M(k,l)$ with the modified DCT coefficients.

7. The system extends each pixel of $M'(k,l)$ to 6×6 mosaic blocks and applies histogram equalization again, then gets $I'''(x,y)$ with 300×300 pixels.

8. The system finally outputs $O(x,y)$ by overlaying $I''(x,y)$ on $I'''(x,y)$ with the following calculation, where $w = 0.3$ in this system.

$$O(x,y) = wI''(x,y) + (1-w)I'''(x,y), \quad \forall(x,y). \tag{1}$$

The left image in Fig. 2 shows an example of the original image. Using the above procedure, the right image in Fig. 2 is created. Although the unclear image loses its color and resolution considerably, it still holds a certain degree of information of the original image.

2.2   Authentication Procedure

Enrollment Phase

1. The system shows a certain numbers of the original images to the user.
2. The user chooses one original image which he/she would like to use as a source of his/her pass-image.
3. The system creates the unclear image from the original image chosen by the user.

4. The user remembers the unclear image as his/her pass-image. Note that since the user has seen the original image at step 1, the user can easily remember the unclear image.

Authentication Phase

1. The system presents the user's unclear pass-image along with some randomly chosen decoy unclear images. (The decoy images could be defferent in every authentication trial.)
2. The user should find out his/her unclear pass-image among the images.
3. If the user can answer the correct pass-image, the user is authenticated.

According to the required security level, the number of pass-images, the number of decoy images and the number of repetition (rounds) of authentication phases are decided. Note that this authentication procedure is hardly different from the procedure employed in the conventional image-based authentication systems [1, 3, 4, 5] except using unclear images.

3   Comparative Experiments

This section carries out experiments for confirming that our scheme has robustness against an observing attack and leakage of pass-images with words, compared to the conventional schemes.

3.1   Observing Attacks

System for the Experiment

a) Photograph authentication system. This system uses 90 photographs of well-known animals as pass-images.
b) Color random-art authentication system. This system uses 90 color random-art images [2] as the pass-images.
c) Grayscale random-art authentication system. This system uses 90 grayscale random-art images as the pass-images, where the images are generated by grayscaling the color random-art images of system b).
d) Unclear image authentication system (our scheme). This system uses 90 unclear images as the pass-images, where the images are created from the photographs of system a) by the procedure in Sect. 2.1.

The authentication of system d) is done by the procedure described in Sect. 2.2. Systems a), b) and c) employ the same authentication procedure as system d) except using their own types of pass-images respectively. System a) is an equivalent system of the conventional schemes based on photographic images [3, 4, 5], and systems b) and c) are the system based on random-art images [1].

In all the systems, the number of pass-images that a user should remember is one, and the number of the decoy images that are presented along with

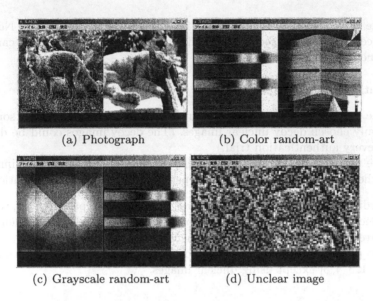

(a) Photograph   (b) Color random-art

(c) Grayscale random-art   (d) Unclear image

Fig. 3. The systems for the comparative experiment

the pass-image in each authentication phase is one. That is, the authentication in this experiments is a kind of "multiple choice question with 2-alternatives", where user authentication is completed by choosing one image from two (left or right). In this paper, let us refer to the system as "2-alternative-typed authentication". Figs. 3(a)–3(d) show the views of authentication windows of the systems a)–d).

Method. The examinees in the experiment are 10 male volunteers of college students. At first, each examinee is allowed to observe a legitimate user's authentication once; the examiner (a legitimate user) chooses the correct pass-image with a mouse click just in front of the examinee (an attacker). Then, the examinee is immediately required to impersonate the legitimate user. Here, the examiner always waits for 5 seconds then chooses the pass-image, i.e. the observation time for examinees is 5 seconds. The case of 1 second waiting is examined, too. The experiment is repeated five times with different pass-images for each examinee. The attack success rate and the time for each authentication are recorded.

Results. The upper part of Table 1 shows the results of the experiment. On systems a), b) and c), even if the observation time was only 1 second, the attackers (examinees) could perfectly remember the legitimate user's pass-image. On the other hand, our scheme d) could decrease the attack success rate by about 10 percent. We know that this experiment is considerably advantageous to attackers since the number of decoy images is only one (the 2-alternative-typed authentication). Therefore, "decreasing of the attack success rate by 10 percent" is a big improvement.

3.2   Leakage of Pass-Images with Words

Systems for the Experiment. The same systems as those used in Sect. 3.1 are used again. However, system a) is excluded in this experiment, since it is obvious that users can easily leak their photographic pass-images to anyone with words.

Method. The examinees in the experiment are 10 male volunteers of college students. At first, each examinee is allowed to get information of a legitimate user's pass-image; the examiner (a legitimate user) tells the characteristics of the pass-image to the examinee (an attacker) with words. Then, the examinee is immediately required to impersonate the legitimate user; the examinee tries the authentication for the examiner. The experiment is repeated five times with different pass-images for each examinee. The attack success rate and the time for each authentication are recorded.

The information that the examiner gave to the examinees is as follows respectively; for systems b) and c): "main geometric patterns in the pass-image (line, circle, etc.)", "its color and layout", and "simple or complex", for system d): "the category of the animal (dog, cat, etc.)", "which direction the animal is facing to", "whole body or a part", and "standing or sitting".

Results. The middle part of Table 1 shows the results of the experiment. On systems b) and c), the examinees could perfectly succeed in impersonating the

Table 1. Results of the experiments

		Observing attack	
System	Observation time	Attack success rate	Average time per round
a)	5 sec.	50/50 (100%)	1.332 sec.
	1 sec.	50/50 (100%)	1.364 sec.
b)	5 sec.	50/50 (100%)	1.599 sec.
	1 sec.	50/50 (100%)	1.397 sec.
c)	5 sec.	50/50 (100%)	1.671 sec.
	1 sec.	50/50 (100%)	1.469 sec.
d)	5 sec.	46/50 (92%)	2.655 sec.
	1 sec.	45/50 (90%)	3.133 sec.
e)	15 sec.	13/50 (26%)	18.382 sec.
		Leakage of pass-images with words	
System	-	Attack success rate	Average time per round
b)	-	50/50 (100%)	3.705 sec.
c)	-	50/50 (100%)	2.881 sec.
d)	-	37/50 (74%)	10.910 sec.
e)	-	0/50 (0%)	29.049 sec.
		Authentication by the legitimate users	
System	Authentication day	Success rate	Average time per round
e)	1 day later	50/50 (100%)	8.194 sec.
	8 days later	49/50 (98%)	7.104 sec.

legitimate user with the information that the legitimate user told them. On the other hand, our scheme d) could decrease the attack success rate to 74 percent. We know that this experiment is considerably advantageous to attackers since the number of decoy images is only one. Therefore, "decreasing of the attack success rate to 74 percent" is a big improvement.

3.3 Consideration

From the results of experiments in Sects. 3.1 and 3.2, it is confirmed that our scheme has a higher robustness against an observing attack and leakage of the pass-images compared to the systems based on photographic and random-art pass-images. It should be noted that our scheme could reduce the attack success rate even in an advantageous experiment for attackers (2-alternative-typed authentication). It is expected that our scheme can further reduce the attack success rate in N-alternative-typed authentication. However, the number of alternatives might also affect the recognition capability of the legitimate user, since the legitimate user would be more confused as the decoy images increase. Consequently, we will conduct more practical experiments in the following section.

4   Experiments on 9-Alternative-Typed System

4.1   Authentication by the Legitimate Users

In this section, the experiments with a 9-alternative-typed authentication system are carried out.

System for the Experiments. At first, the system d) in Sect. 3 is modified to 9-alternative-typed authentication system, in which the user has to choose his/her pass-images from 9 unclear images. Then, we set the number of rounds in an authentication of the system as four. That is, users are required to remember 4 of unclear pass-images and to repeat 4 rounds of the 9-alternative-typed authentication. In each round, the system chooses one pass-image randomly and presents it along with 8 decoy unclear images to the user. The system never chooses any pass-image that has been already chosen during the previous rounds. Only when the user can answer all the pass-images correctly in each of four rounds, the user is authenticated. Thus the probability that a brute-force attack will be successful is $1/9^4$, which is nearly comparable to 4-digit PIN system $(1/10^4)$. Let us refer to this system as system e).

Method. The examinees in the experiment are 10 male volunteers of college students. Firstly, each examinee registers 4 distinct unclear pass-images. Then, on the following day and 8 days later, every examinee is required to try the authentication (4 rounds of 9-alternative-typed authentication). The experiment is repeated five times with the same set of pass-images. The authentication success rate and the time taken to find out the pass-images among 9 alternatives for each round of authentications are recorded.

Results. The lower part of Table 1 shows the results of the experiment. All examinees have succeeded in the authentication of 8 days later as well as on the following day. The examinee who has failed once in authentication of 8 days later told us that he had not forgotten any of his pass-images, but just incautiously chosen a wrong image that resembles to one of his pass-images.

4.2 Observing Attack and Leakage of Pass-Image

As in the case of Sect. 3, the experiments for observing attack and leakage of pass-images on 9-alternative-typed system have also been conducted. These experiments use the same system as that of Sect. 4.1 (system e)). The results of these experiments are shown in the last rows of the upper and middle part of Table 1. The success rate of an observing attack has decreased to 26 percent, and the attack success rate of the leakage of the pass-images with words has achieved 0 percent.

5 Conclusions and Future Work

In this paper, we proposed a user authentication system using unclear images as pass-images. From the experiments in Sects. 3 and 4, the effect of using unclear images as pass-images has been basically confirmed. In the future, we would like to examine the relationship between security and usability of our scheme with more experiments in different settings. The security and usability could be affected by the unclearness of the pass-images. So we are to pursue an appropriate way of creating unclear images, too. Moreover, since the observing attacks in this paper were done just by peeping the display of the authentication system, we have to devise a countermeasure against observation with cameras.

References

1. R. Dhamija, A. Perring: Deja Vu: A User Study Using Images for Authentication, 9th USENIX Security Symposium, pp. 45–58, 2002.
2. A. Bauer: Gallery of random art, http://www.cs.cmu.edu/~andrej/art/, (Jul 2005)
3. T. Pering, M. Sundar, J. Light, R. Want: Photographic Authentication through Untrusted Terminals, IEEE Pervasive Computing, Vol. 2, No. 1, pp. 30–36, (Jan 2003).
4. T. Takada, H. Koike: Awase-E: Image-Based Authentication for Mobile Phones Using User's Favorite Images, LNCS 2795, Human-Computer Interaction with Mobile Devices and Services, pp. 347–351, Springer, 2003.
5. Real User Corporation: PassFaces, http://www.realuser.com/cgi-bin/ru.exe/_/homepages/index.htm (Jul 2005).
6. W. F. Brewer: Schemata., In R. A. Wilson and F. C. Keil (Eds.), MIT Encyclopedia of the Cognitive Sciences, pp. 729–730, 1999.

A Consideration of Application of Attractor Selection to a Real-Time Production Scheduling

Hiroaki Chujo, Hironori Oka, Yoshitomo Ikkai, and Norihisa Komoda

Graduate School of Information Science and Technology Osaka University,
2-1 Yamadaoka, Suita, Osaka 565-0871, Japan
{chujo.hiroaki, oka, ikkai, komoda}@ist.osaka-u.ac.jp

Abstract. In this research, "attractor selection," which adopts the concept of "attractor" chiefly defined in biological and physical fields, is applied to a scheduling problem. An attractor is an attraction area that an orbit in space converges on asymptotically, and this area denotes a stable state. The attractor to which an orbit from a certain state of an initial condition is attracted is statistically determined. Attractor selection is an algorithm that searches for a stable state flexibly under changing environments.

To apply attractor selection to a scheduling field, a scheduling framework based on scheduling strategy using a dispatching rule is introduced. A scheduling problem solution is scheduled by repeated applications of a prepared dispatching rule with plural strategies. The rule has a parameter that controls scheduling strategies based on the current "environment," which means kinds, amounts, and remaining to due of jobs, machine conditions, etc. Attracter selection controls the parameters under changing environments.

The proposed framework was applied to a real-time production scheduling problem, and the optimality of the parameters of the strategy and followup ability were considerd when environmental changes occur.

1 Introduction

In this research, "attractor selections[1]," which adopts the concept of "attractor[2]" chiefly defined in biological and physical fields, is applied to a scheduling problem. An attractor is an attraction area that an orbit in space converges on asymptotically, and this area denotes a stable state. The attractor to which an orbit from a certain state of an initial condition is attracted is statistically determined. When an environment change occurs, an orbit is attracted to a new attractor following the environmental change. Attractor selection is an algorithm that searches for a stable state flexibly under changing environments.

In this research, we concentrate on the autonomous adjustment ability of attractor selection to environmental changes. Attractor selection is applied to a real-time production scheduling problem of environments such as tendencies of jobs and situations of production sites that change constantly. First, a scheduling framework in which to apply attractor selection is proposed. In this framework, scheduling is created by using various strategies responding the current environment. To adjust to environmental changes,

A.J. Ijspeert et al. (Eds.): BioADIT 2006, LNCS 3853, pp. 346–354, 2006.

the strategy is applied by parameters controlled by attractor selection. Thus, it is possible to create scheduling based on the environment. The optimality of the parameters and followup to environmental changes are considered.

2   Outline of Attractor Selection

Attractor selection[1] is an algorithm that flexibly adjusts to environments by using the attractor concept while selecting the attractors, that is, the stable state. Here "parameter x," which controls the system and determines the "system activation degree" in a certain state is assumed to explain the concept the attractor selection. When the relation between parameter x and system activation degree is shown as Fig. 1, the shadowed areas where system activation degree is high are attractors.

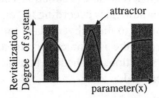

Fig. 1. Attractor selection

In attractor selection, an attractor with high system activation degree is selected autonomous to an environmental change by transitting parameter x using a general transition formula, shown as formula (1)[1],

$$\frac{d}{dt}x = f(x) \times activity + \eta \tag{1}$$

where *activity* is a given function that calculates the system activation degree, for example, the evaluation function of the system. *Activity* achieves a mechanism that enhances the transition speed of parameter x when system activation degree is high. Function $f(x)$ is a rule to transit parameter x in the direction increasing system activation degree. η is noise. In the area where system activation degree is low, x transits randomly by η. This is the mechanism to escape from the area where system activation degree is low. When parameter x is transitted repeatedly by using this general transiting formula (1), parameter x reaches a stable state at which system activation degree is high, an attractor. In this algorithm, the transition amount of parameter x by the general transitting formula depends on the system activation degree of the present parameter x, so this algorithm can only be applied by observation of the current system activation degree without investigating all values of system activation degree against parameter x.

Now this algorithm is used in the network symbiotic environment field[1][3]. In this field, attractor selection is applied to path metrics, available bandwidth, and automatically selects appropriate bandwidths for each path.

3   Application of Attractor Selection to a Real-Time Production Scheduling

In a production field, efficient production schedules are important. The loads of equipment and production time greatly differ depending on the processing order of jobs, etc. The real-time production scheduling problem treated in this research includes such environmental problems, as the tendencies of jobs and constant production site situations changes. Metaheuristic[4] is a remarkable scheduling method paradigm where Genetic Algorithm (GA), Simulated Annealing (SA), Tabu Search (TS), etc. are chiefly applied. However, these methods have weak points, it is difficult to create schedules rapidly to match environmental changes because too much calculation time is required.

In this research, attractor selection with its autonomous adjustment feature to environmental changes is applied to a real-time production scheduling problem. A schedule is created according to various strategies according to "environments": the amount and kinds of jobs, the days remaining to the delivery date, the situation and demand of the site, etc. Strategies are desided by the assignment parameter. By controlling this assignment parameter by attractor selection, a schedule that flexibly adjusts to environment changes in real-time can be created.

3.1   Framework of Application of Attractor Selection to Scheduling

In this research, attractor selection is a method that searches autonomously for the area where the assignment parameter is effective under a certain environment.

Generally, a schedule is created by switching several strategies by the "environment" of the amount and kind of job, the days remaining until delivery date, the situation and demand of the site, etc. For example:

- Many jobs with an early delivery date
  Jobs are assigned to the empty processing machine by priority.
- Demands at the site to reduce processing costs
  Jobs are processed with the low-cost processing machine by priority.

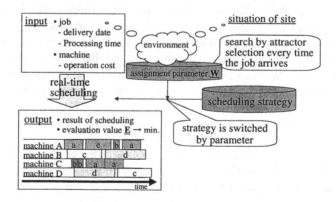

Fig. 2. Framework of application of attractor selection to scheduling

Therefore a scheduling framework is proposed that introduces assignment parameter W to control these strategies, and attractor selection adjusts W based on the current environment when new jobs arrive. The generated schedule is evaluated by evaluation value E, which is decided by W and differs based on the targeting problem. It also indicates the effectiveness of the assignment parameter, that is, the system activation degree. The purpose of this problem is the minimization of E because evaluation value E is defined by the weighted sum of processing costs and the sum of delays, etc. Fig. 2 shows the framework.

3.2   Transition Formula of the Assignment Parameter in a Scheduling Framework

The transition of attractor selection in this research is defined as follows:

$$\frac{d}{dt}W = \varepsilon(E_- - E_+)W \times \frac{1}{E_-} + \eta \qquad (2)$$

where E_- and E_+ indicate evaluation values of the schedules at previous and current transitions. "$\varepsilon(E_- - E_+)W$" corresponds to $f(x)$ of formula(1). It is a rule that judges whether evaluation value E improved it by the previous transition. This means the mechanism that transits assignment parameter W to reduce the evaluation value. "$\frac{1}{E_-}$" corresponds to $activity$ of formula(1). This means the mechanism by which transition speed is enhanced to the parameter area where evaluation value becomes small.

Assignment parameter (W) is transitted by formula (2) to the parameter area where a schedule with small evaluation value is obtained only by observing the evaluation value at the previous and current transitions without calculating the evaluation values of the schedules to all Ws.

3.3   Issues to be Considered

Issues when attractor selection is applied to a real-time scheduling problem are shown below:

1. Analysis of optimality and stability of assignment parameter W
   (a) Sensitivity analysis of parameter (ε, η) of transition formula (2)
       - Frequency distribution of assignment parameter W
       - Transition times to a stable state
   (b) Analysis of followup ability to environmental changes
   (c) Analysis of optimality transition ability to optimal area by avoiding local minimum
2. Expansion to two or more assignment parameters
   Plural assignment parameters ($W_1, W_2, ...$) are concurrently transitted.
3. Multi-point search for attractor selection
4. Evaluation comparisons with other metaheuristics
   Comparison of calculation time, environmental changes, and number of tuning parameters to Genetic Algorithm (GA) and Simulated Annealing (SA)

In this research, 1(a) and 1(b) are analyzed in the following sections.

4   Problem for Application

4.1   A Real-Time Production Scheduling Problem

In this section, the details of a target real-time production scheduling problem are explained. The sequential jobs ($a \times 7$, $b \times 7$, $c \times 3$, $d \times 3$, and $e \times 3$) are assigned to five processing machines in real times.

Since the processing time of each job type is different, each processing machine has different processing costs against the same job type, as shown in Table 1.

Table 1. Processing time, cost

job	processing time	cost M_1	M_2	M_3	M_4	M_5
a	1	10	15	20	25	30
b	0.5	6	9	12	15	18
c	2	10	15	20	25	30
d	2	2	3	4	5	6
e	1.5	10	15	20	25	30

The due date of each job is given depending on its arrival time.

4.2   Evaluation

Scheduling results are evaluated by the following two evaluation factors:

– Processing costs (C)
  This is the sum of the required costs when all jobs are processed.
– Sum of delays (D)
  Delays show how the processing completion time of each job is delayed from the deadline.

Evaluation function (E) is defined as the following weighted sum of those 2 factors:

$$E = R \times C + 1 \times D \qquad (3)$$

where R indicates weight. The purpose of this problem is the minimization.

4.3   Job Allocation by Assignment Parameter

In this research, the following two strategies are applied to job allocation.

1. Preferential allocation to a low-cost processing machine (reduction of processing costs)
2. Preferential allocation to the processing machine with less processing time of jobs to be processed (reduction of the sum of delays)

To achieve allocation, assignment parameter W and allocation score (A_{ki}) are introduced. W indicates which strategy receives priority. The allocation score of each processing machine is calculated for the first job k of the current sequence of jobs, and job k is assigned to the machine that has the minimum allocation score. When the processing cost of job k in machine i is assumed to be p_{ki}, and processing waiting time is assumed to be q_{ki}, allocation score (A_{ki}), which achieves two kinds of strategies, is defined as formula (4).

$$A_{ki} = W \times p_{ki} + 1 \times q_{ki} \tag{4}$$

5 Result of Considerations

Transition formula (2) of attractor selection was applied to a real-time production scheduling problem and developed on a computer: OS: WindowsXP, CPU: Pentium IV Processor 900 MHz, memory: 512 MB.

The weight of evaluation function (R), an initial value of the assignment parameter of allocation score (W_{ini}), ε and η (uniform distribution) is shown in Table 2.

Table 2. The value of the parameters

The kind of parameter	value
R	0.5
W_{ini}	2
ε	12
η	-0.25~0.25(uniform distribution)

In this condition, an example of assignment parameter (W) transition and evaluation value (E) with no environmental change is shown in Fig. 3.

After 98 transitions, the transition in the vicinity of the optimal value ($E = 116.5$) is repeated, so it can be regarded as a stable state. The calculation time required for 500 transitions is about one second.

In subsection 5.1, frequency distribution of the solution from the optimal value of the evaluation value and transition times to a stable state are analyzed, that is, a consideration of 1(a) in subsection 3.3. In subsection 5.2, the transitions of W and E when an environment change occur by changing the weight of evaluation function (R) is analyzed, that is, a consideration of 1(b) in subsection 3.3.

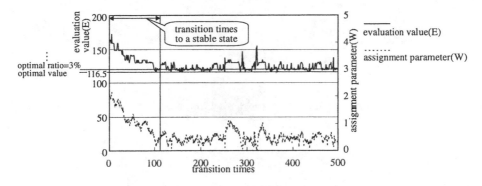

Fig. 3. Transition of W and E (no environmental changes)

5.1   Sensitivity Analysis of Parameter (ε, η) of the Transition Formula

Sensitivity analysis of the width of transition (ε) and the width of random numbers (η) was investigated. Here, "optimal ratio," which shows the percentage away from the optimal value of E, is defined as follows.

$$Optimal\ ratio = \frac{E - optimal\ value}{optimal\ value}(\%) \tag{5}$$

The left graph of Fig. 4 shows that the frequency distribution of solutions, whose optimal ratio approaches within 3% in a stable state. ε was changed with 8, 10, and 12, and η was assumed to be a uniform random number of $-0.125 \sim 0.125$, $-0.25 \sim 0.25$, and $-0.5 \sim 0.5$. The center and right graphs of Fig. 4 shows that the frequency of solutions are within 5% and 10%, respectively.

Next, the average transition time to stable state is analyzed against changes of parameters ε and η. The result is shown in Fig. 5.

If the width of η is small, the frequency distribution of solutions becomes high. Moreover, if η is small, the transition times until stabilization increases, as shown in Fig. 5. There is a trade-off between obtaining solutions with high accuracy and shortening transition times until stabilization. Considering these balances, with parameters

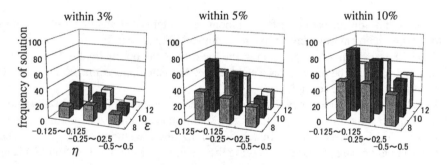

Fig. 4. Frequency distribution against optimal ratios in a stable state

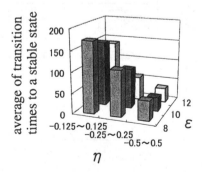

Fig. 5. Average of transition times to a stable state

of $\varepsilon = 10$ and $\eta = -0.25 \sim 0.25$ or $\varepsilon = 12$ and $\eta = -0.25 \sim 0.25$, assignment parameters with high accuracy are quickly obtained.

5.2 Analysis of Followup Ability to Environmental Changes

With $\varepsilon = 12$ and $\eta = -0.25 \sim 0.25$, transitions of E and W are verified when environmental changes occur.

When a transition is begun, the weight of evaluation function $R = 0.5$ and assignment parameter $W = 2$. The weight of evaluation function (R) was increased linearly (0.01 increases of R per transition) after a frequency of 200 transitions (environmental changes). In this condition, the transition results of W and E are shown in Fig. 6. The time required for 500 transitions is also about one second.

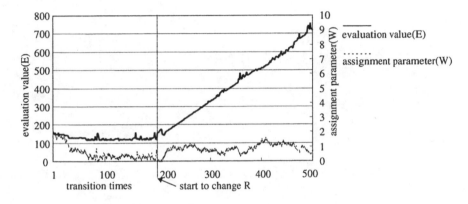

Fig. 6. Transition of E and W (environmental changes)

Fig. 6 suggests that attractor selection can adjust W smoothly following environmental changes. Therefore, it will be possible to search for assignment parameter corresponding to the environment in a short time. However, the assignment parameter is not completely stabilized. Assignment parameters that exist in the stable states vary. As described in subsection 3.3, when using this method for real problems, it is necessary to search for the multi-point based on the accuracy needs of the assignment parameter.

6 Summary

In this research, a framework was proposed that applied attractor selection, which is an algorithm using the attractor concept chiefly defined in biological and physical fields, to a real-time scheduling problem. The mechanism of a real-time production schedule problem and a scheduling framework by attractor selection was developed, and accuracy, transition speed, and followup to environmental changes were considered.

In addition, in the future, it will be necessary to consider the issues described in subsection 3.3 in the future.

References

1. S. Nishio:"New Information Technologies for Building a Networked Symbiotic Environment," IPSJ MAGAZINE, Vol.46(4), pp.385-390(2005-4)(in Japanese).
2. H. Haken:"SYNERGETICS," Springer-Verlag Berlin Heidelberg(1978).
3. K. Leibnitz, N Wakamiya, and M Murata:"Biologically Inspired Adaptive Multi-Path Routing in Overlay Networks" IFIP/IEE,E INTERNATIONAL WORKSHOP ON SELF-MANAGED SYSTEM AND SERVICES(SELFMAN 2005).
4. S. M. Sait, H. Youssef:"Iterative Computer Algorithms with Applications in Engineering," THE IEEE COMPUTER SOCIETY(1999).

Bio-inspired Organization for Multi-agents on Distributed Systems

Ichiro Satoh

National Institute of Informatics,
2-1-2 Hitotsubashi, Chiyoda-ku, Tokyo 101-8430, Japan
ichiro@nii.ac.jp

Abstract. This paper presents a middleware system for multi-agents on a distributed system as a general test-bed for bio-inspired approaches. The middleware is unique to other approaches, including distributed object systems, because it can maintain and migrate a dynamic federation of multiple agents on different computers. It enables each agent to explicitly define its own deployment policy as a relocation between the agent and another agent. This paper describes a prototype implementation of the middleware built on a Java-based mobile agent system and its practical applications that illustrates the utility and effectiveness of the approach in real distributed systems.

1 Introduction

Distributed computing systems are composed of a number of computers. The scale and complexity of distributed modern systems are beyond centralized and hierarchical management techniques. Distributed systems are dynamic in the sense that, computers may be added to or removed from it and channels between computers may be disconnected or changed. Software components, which an application consists of, are required to be adapted and deployed at computers in a distributed system according to changes in the requirements of applications and the structure and computational resources of the system.

This paper addresses the deployment of partitioned applications over a distributed system, because it is one of the most important issues regarding where and what software will be deployed at computers. It presents a framework to adapt a federation of software components. The framework is based on two key ideas. The first is to enable each component to specify its own deployment policy instead of any global policies. The second is to facilitate the dynamic federation of multiple components as more than one virtual distributed system over a real distributed system, instead of any simulation-based environments. The framework enables such a federation to be transformed and made mobile through bio-inspired self-organization, such as that undertaken by cells in their transforming and crawling locomotion. Furthermore, the framework can be used as a general test-bed for providing various bio-inspired approaches in distributed systems, as well as a middleware system for adaptive distributed systems.

A.J. Ijspeert et al. (Eds.): BioADIT 2006, LNCS 3853, pp. 355–362, 2006.

Several researchers have attempted to introduce biological metaphors into distributed systems. Most of this work has been based on simulation-based approaches. For example, Swarm [6] and MASS [3] are general simulators for multi-agent models. However, real systems are complex and varied. Unfortunately, most existing simulation-based results seem to have been based on arbitrary hypotheses in the sense that various parameters in their simulations have lacked any technical grounds. Unfortunately, such unrealistic simulations have often only provided non-sensical or impractical results. We still lack a great deal of data that are essential to simulating the approaches accurately. Therefore, real experiments in distributed systems must have priority over simulation-based experiments for us to accumulate actual experience.

2   Approach

A distributed application consists of partitioned applications that may run on different computers. This paper assumes that each partitioned application, called an agent, can be autonomous and mobile. To adapt an application to changes in a distributed system, partitioned applications, i.e., agents, partitioned applications must not be bound to particular computers. They should be dynamically deployed at appropriate computers without any centralized management system.

This can be supported by an metaphors drawn from biological process. When a computer is removed from the system or it shuts down, agents running on it should escape. Lamellipodia are flattened and protrusive projections that periodically expand from the surface of a cell. Effective movement requires a motile cell to be polarized, so that its protoplasm membrane is relatively quiescent everywhere else except its leading edge where lamellipodia periodically project outward in all directions. As they pull on one another they create intervening regions in which the cortex is stretched. This tug-of-war continues until one lamellipodium aligns in a dominant direction and becomes unipolar, then migrates in that direction. Lamellipodia can be viewed in terms of speculative migration or expansion.

Each agent should be able to explicitly specify its own constraints to migrate agents. For example, if an agent has a migration constraint dependent on another agent, when the other agent moves to another location, the former agent decides its destination according to its own migration constraints, i.e., the source or destination of the other agent. Such constraints are defined as policies within agents and allow us to specify physical structures and mechanisms in motile cells, such as membrane and cytoplasmic streaming. We provide several policies for agents to support bio-inspired deployments of agents.

3   Design and Implementation

The framework presented in this paper is a middleware for deploying and executing general-purpose software components. It can be used as a general test-bed for providing various bio-inspired approaches, in particular bio-inspired deployment of software, in distributed systems. It was implemented in Java (J2SE version 1.4 or later versions) and agents are implemented as a set of Java objects.

3.1 Runtime System

Figure 1 outlines the basic structure of a runtime system. Each establishes at most one TCP connection to each of its neighboring hosts and exchanges control messages, agents, and inter-agent communications with the other runtime systems through the connection. Since it is constructed on the Java virtual machine, it can conceal differences between the platform architecture of the source and destination computers. All runtime systems can exchange agents with others through the use of mobile agent technology.

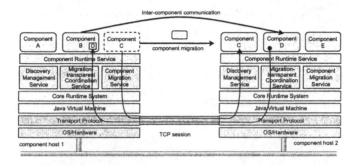

Fig. 1. Architecture of agent runtime system

Each agent can itinerate between multiple computers under their own control [7, 8, 9]. After arriving at its destination or being duplicated, each agent can continue working without losing accumulated work, such as the content of instance variables in the agent's program, at the source computers. It is also equipped with its own identifier and that of the federation that it should belong to. It can explicitly specify the computational capability that its destination hosts must offer in CC/PP [12] form as we will discuss later. If an agent is on a computer that cannot satisfy its requirements, its intent is to leave computer. While each agent is running, it can declare at most one deployment policy and one or more message policies by invoking a built-in method of the class that every agent must inherit. Although policies are open for developers to define their own policies, the current implementation provides the following deployment policies.

- If an agent declares a *follow* policy for another agent, when the latter migrates to another computer, the former migrates to the latter's destination computer.
- If an agent declares a *dispatch* policy for another agent, when the latter migrates to another computer, a copy of the former is created and deployed at the latter's destination computer.
- If an agent declares a *shift* policy for another agent, when the latter migrates to another computer, the former migrates to the latter's source computer.
- If an agent declares a *fill* policy for another agent, when the latter migrates to another computer, a copy of the former is created and deployed at the latter's source computer.

Figure 2 outlines four deployment policies. These policies are related to phenomena in biological processes. For example, a `follow` policy enables an agent to come near

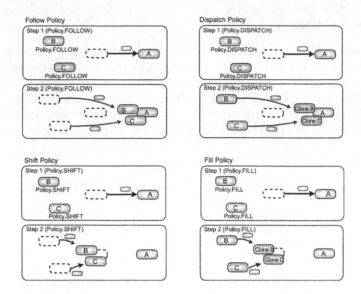

Fig. 2. Basic migration policies

another agent. For example, when multiple agents declare a policy for a leader agent, they can swarm around it. A *shift* policy enables an agent to follow the movement of another agent. The former agent can track the latter as it moves. The policy thus corresponds to the phenomenon of cytoplasmic streaming. A dispatch) policy enables an agent to stay in the current location and then deploy its clone at the destination of another moving agent. It can model the footprint of a motile cell. We have assumed that an agent can declare the policy for another agent and specify the TTLs of its clones as their life-spans. As the latter agent moves, cloned former agents are deployed at its footmark and these clones are automatically volatilized after their life-spans are over. Therefore, the clone agents can be viewed as a pheromone that is left behind after the latter agent has moved on. A *fill* policy corresponds to the phenomenon of cell division.

When an agent is created, the dispatch and fill policies can explicitly control whether the newly created agent can inherit the state of its original agent. The following message policies forward messages to agents when messages are specified in the policies.

- If an agent declares a *forward* policy for another agent, when specified messages are sent to other agents, the messages are forwarded to the latter as well as the former.
- If an agent declares a *delegate* policy for another agent, when specified messages are send to the former, the messages are forwarded to the latter but not to the former.

A *forward* policy is useful when two agents share the same information and *delegate* policy provides a master-slave relation between agents.

3.2 Current Status

A prototype system of this framework was implemented with J2SE version 1.4.2 and although it was not built for performance, we measured the cost of agent migration.

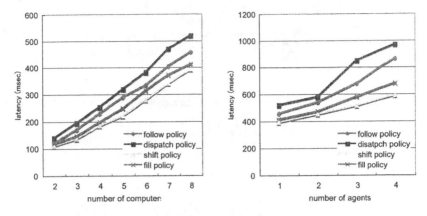

Fig. 3. Cost of multiple-hops for two agents between two to eight computers (left) and Costs of multiple-hops of multiple agents between eight computers (right)

The left of Figure 3 illustrates the cost of multiple-hops for two agents between two to eight computers (Pentium-M 1.4-MHz with Windows XP Professional and J2SE 1.4.2) through a fast ethernet, where the first agent declares a follow, dispatch, shift, or fill policy for the second and the second migrates between these computers sequentially without synchronizing the migration of the first.[1] Each cost in the left of Figure 3 is the latency of the first agent arriving after the second has begun to migrate to another computer. The cost of agent migration according to dispatch (or fill) policy is larger than the the follow (or shift) policy, because the former policy needs to create a copy of the first agent that has the policy. The cost of agent migration according to follow (or dispatch) is larger than that for dispatch (or shift), because the former and latter agents are deployed at different computers.

The right of Figure 3 shows the costs of multiple-hops of multiple agents between eight computers, when agents (from one to four) have follow, dispatch, shift, or fill policies for a moving agent. Unfortunately, with many hops is large, the follow and dispatch policies vary due to congestion at several computers. That is, two or more agents may attempt to have their own active threads in a single processor and to simultaneously transmit themselves to the destinations of their target agent in a TCP network connection. Once agents experience congestion at a computer, they tend to migrate as a chunk of agents rather than as individual agents to further destinations and the chunk often engulfs other newly arrival agents. The congestion does not always reappear, since computers are not synchronized and congestion often causes larger congestion in the routes of agents. We expect that fluctuations in the cost of agent migration will be large in a large-scale, heterogenous, distributed system.

---

[1] The latency between two computers is measured as the half-time of round-trip time between the source and destination computers. To measure latency between more than three computers exactly, these computers are connected through a ring topology. That is, the start and and goal of the second agent are assigned to the same computer and we measure difference between the timings of the first agent's starting and the second's arriving at the computer.

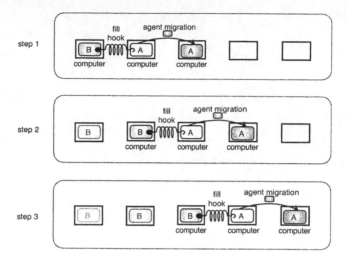

Fig. 4. Implementation of ant-based routing mechanism

4   Initial Experience

This section presents several examples that illustrate how the framework works.

4.1   Ants-Based Routing Mechanisms

Ants are able to locate a path to a food source using trails of chemical substances called pheromones that are deposited by other ants. Several researchers have attempted to use the notion of ant pheromones for network-routing mechanisms [2, 11]. Our framework allows moving agents to leave themselves on their trails and to become automatically volatilized after their life-spans are over. A mobile agent corresponding to an ant, A, corresponding to a pheromone is attached to another mobile agent corresponding to an ant according to the *fill* policy. When the latter agent randomly selects its destination and migrates to the selected destination, the former agent creates a clone and migrates to the source host of the latter. Since each of the cloned agents defines its life-span, they are active for a specified duration after being created. If there are other agents corresponding to pheromones in the host, the visiting agent adds their time spans to its own time span. When another agent corresponding to another ant migrates over the network, it can select a host that has the agents corresponding to pheromones whose time-spans are the longest from the neighboring hosts. We experimented on ant-based routing for mobile agents using this prototype implementation with more than eight computers. However, we knew that it would be difficult to quickly converge a short-path to the destination in real distributed systems, because routing mechanisms tend to be diverging.

4.2   Agent Diffusion in Sensor Networks

The second example is the speculative deployment of agents as is done with cell-lamellipodia. This provides a mechanism that dynamically and speculatively deploys agents at sensor nodes when there are environmental changes. This mechanism was inspired by lamellipodia in cells. It assumes that the sensor field is a two-dimensional surface composed of sensor nodes and it monitors environmental changes, such as motion in objects and variations in temperature. It is a well known fact that after a sensor node detects environmental changes in its area of coverage, some of its geographically neighboring nodes tend to detect similar changes after a short time. Diffusion occurs as follows. When an agent on a sensor node finds changes in its environment, the agent duplicates itself and deploys the copy at neighboring nodes as long as the nodes have the same kinds of agents. Each agent is associated with a resource limit that functions as a generalized Time-To-Live (TTL) field. Although a node can monitor changes in interesting environments, it sets the TTLs of its agents as their own initial value. It otherwise decrements TTLs as the passage of time. When the TTL of an agent becomes zero, the agent automatically removes itself.

5   Related Work

The section discusses several bio-inspired approaches to distributed and multi-agents systems. A few attempts have provided infrastructures for real distributed systems, like ours. The Anthill project [1] by the University of Bologna developed a bio-inspired middleware for peer-to-peer systems, which is composed of a collection of interconnected nests. Autonomous agents, called ants can travel across the network trying to satisfy user requests, like ours. The main difference between Anthill, including its applications, and our framework is that it introduces agents as independent entities and ours permits components to be organized in a self-organized manner. The Co-Field project [5] by the University di Modena e Reggio Emilia proposed the notion of a computational force-field model for coordinating the movements of a group of agents, including mobile devices, mobile robots, and sensors. However, the model only seems to be available within the limits of simulation and not within a real distributed system. Our deployment policies may be similar to the dynamic layout of distributed applications in the FarGo system [4]. However, FarGo's policies aim at allowing an agent to control other agents, whereas our policies aim at allowing an agent to describe its own migration, because our framework always treats agents as autonomous entities that travel from computer to computer under their own control. FarGo's policies may conflict when two agents can declare different relocation policies for a single agent. However, our framework is free of any conflict because each agent can only declare a policy to relocate itself instead of other agents. The author presented a bio-inspired deployment of software components [10]. The previous approach is an early implementation of the framework presented in this paper. It supported some of the deployment policies but not any message policies.

6   Conclusion

This paper presented a middleware system for dynamically deploying agents at different computers, instead of any simulation-based systems. We designed and implemented a prototype system of them middleware and demonstrated its effectiveness in several applications. Since the middleware enabled each agent to specify its own policy as a relocation between the agent and another agent, it cannot only move individual agents but also a federation of agents over a distributed system in a self-organized manner.

We would like to point out further issues that need to be resolved. We need various evaluations on real distributed systems. Although the current implementation focuses on the deployment of agents, we plan to extend it so that it can be used to modify the behavior of each agent, while they are running.

References

1. O. Babaoglu and H. Meling and A. Montresor, Anthill: A Framework for the Development of Agent-Based Peer-to-Peer Systems, Proceeding of 22th IEEE International Conference on Distributed Computing Systems, July 2002.
2. G. Di Caro and M. Dorigo, AntNet: Distributed Stigmergetic Control for Communications Networks, Journal of Artificial Intelligence Research, vol.9, pp. 317-365, 1998.
3. B. Horling, and V. Lesser, and R. Vincent, Multi-Agent System Simulation Framework Proceeding of IMACS World Congress 2000 on Scientific Computation, Applied Mathematics and Simulation, August 2000.
4. O. Holder, I. Ben-Shaul, and H. Gazit, System Support for Dynamic Layout of Distributed Applications, Proceedings of International Conference on Distributed Computing Systems (ICDCS'99), pp 403-411, IEEE Computer Society, 1999.
5. M. Mamei, L. Leonardi, F. Zambonelli, Co-Fields: A Unifying Approach to Swarm Intelligence, International Workshop on Engineering Societies in the Agents World (ESAW 2002), Lecture Notes in Computer Science, vol. 2577, Springer Verlag 2003.
6. N. Minar, R. Burkhart, C. Langton, and M. Askenazi. The Swarm Simulation System, A Toolkit for Building Multi-Agent Simulations, Technical report, Swarm Development Group, June 1996.
7. I. Satoh, Building Reusable Mobile Agents for Network Management, IEEE Transactions on Systems, Man and Cybernetics, vol.33, no. 3, part-C, pp.350-357, August 2003.
8. I. Satoh, Configurable Network Processing for Mobile Agents on the Internet Cluster Computing (The Journal of Networks, Software Tools and Applications), vol. 7, no.1, pp.73-83, Kluwer, January 2004.
9. I. Satoh, Selection of Mobile Agents, Proceedings of IEEE International Conference on Distributed Computing Systems (ICDCS'2004), pp.484-493, IEEE Computer Society, March 2004.
10. I. Satoh, Bio-inspired Deployment of Distributed Applications, Proceedings of International Workshop on Multi-Agents (PRIMA2004), Lecture Notes in Computer Science (LNCS), vol.3371,pp.243-258, Springer, August 2004.
11. R. Schoonderwoerd, O. Holland, and J. Bruten, Ant-like agents for load balancing in telecommunications networks, Proceedings of Conference on Autonomous Agents, pages 209-216. ACM Press, 1997.
12. World Wide Web Consortium (W3C), Composite Capability/Preference Profiles (CC/PP), http://www.w3.org/TR/NOTE-CCPP, 1999.

m-ActiveCube; Multimedia Extension of Spatial Tangible User Interface

Kyoko Ueda, Atsushi Kosaka, Ryoichi Watanabe, Yoshinori Takeuchi,
Takao Onoye, Yuichi Itoh, Yoshifumi Kitamura, and Fumio Kishino

Graduate School of Information Science and Technology, Osaka University,
Yamada-Oka, Suita, Osaka 565-0871, Japan
coe-ac@hi-mail.ise.eng.osaka-u.ac.jp

Abstract. A new Tangible User Interface (TUI) device, *m*-ActiveCube, is proposed as a multimedia extension of ActiveCube, which is a TUI device that enables more efficient human computer interaction than conventional devices. First, fundamental specifications of *m*-ActiveCube are determined to remove the processing performance and functionality limitation of the original ActiveCube. By utilizing improved performance, *m*-ActiveCube offers such novel functionalities as speech recognition with which more impressive applications can be constructed at any level of human living system.

1 Introduction

Recently, Tangible User Interfaces (TUIs) are being explored aggressively as a new breed of human computer interface. Among them, a spatial TUI is believed to be practical for resolving meaningful real-life problems owing to direct and interactive manipulation of 3D objects [1]. A key facet of human computer interface research is directed at the exploitation of our innate tactile and spatial abilities. The notion of a TUI emerged in [2], suggesting more elaborated uses of physical objects as computer interfaces. Ullmer and Ishii defined TUIs as *devices that give physical form to digital information, employing physical artifacts as representations and controls of computational data* [2]. TUIs make sense by engaging our natural talents for handling everyday objects in the physical world. One most important feature of TUIs lies in their spatiality, and thus spatial TUIs can be used to mediate interaction with shape, space, and structure in virtual domains. These spatial TUIs have three common characteristics: spatial mapping, I/O unifications, and support of "trial-and-error" actions [1].

As a flexible multimodal 3D spatial TUI, ActiveCube was developed [3], with a number of distinctive features dedicated to intuitive interaction with virtual 3D environments using physical cubes as bidirectional user interfaces. ActiveCube offers various kinds of I/O functionalities including motor, buzzer, vibrator, LED matrix, and ultrasonic, tactile, and gyroscopic sensors. However, due to the limited processing performance of the Neuron Chip [4] used in ActiveCube, there still remains room to enhance each device's functionality, especially in the processing capability of the multimedia aspects. Motivated by this tendency, the present paper constructs *m*-ActiveCube architecture that can offer novel media-processing functionalities.

A.J. Ijspeert et al. (Eds.): BioADIT 2006, LNCS 3853, pp. 363–370, 2006.
© Springer-Verlag Berlin Heidelberg 2006

First, we analyze the performance of the original version of ActiveCube and extend its fundamental specifications to achieve a more sophisticated human computer interface. Specifically, m-ActiveCube includes a high performance processor for realizing multimedia capability and utilizes module expandability of the characteristics of blocks. In addition, a high speed wireless link is supported for realtime speech and visual communication. Furthermore, m-ActiveCube expands flexibility of block connection of conventional ActiveCube and realizes novel system applications.

2 m-ActiveCube Architecture

2.1   ActiveCube

ActiveCube is comprised of plastic 5 cm cubes that can be connected to one another. Each cube is comprised of a Neuron Chip[4] microprocessor to be controlled in real time. Each cube and cube face have a unique ID. When cubes are connected or disconnected, their IDs are sent to a host PC so that it can recognize the physical shape of all of the cubes. Power is supplied through two hooks while shape recognition data is transferred through the others (Fig. 1(a)). The host PC is connected to a base cube (Fig. 1(b)) and communicates by broadcasting through networks #1 and #2 in Fig. 1(a). The base cube consists of a H8S/2633 processor as well as the Neuron Chip. Intercube communication is accomplished via RS-485 network while the base cube and the host PC communicate through the RS-232C network. Various input devices (i.e. gyroscope sensor) and output devices (i.e. motor actuators) are attached to the cubes.

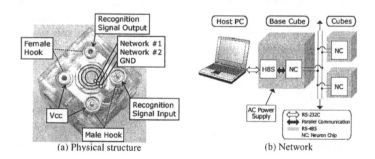

(a) Physical structure   (b) Network

Fig. 1. Physical structure and network of ActiveCube

2.2   Demands for m-ActiveCube

To realize more a sophisticated TUI, the following novel functionalities are examined.

Inter-cube communication - In ActiveCube, cubes must communicate with the host PC through the base cube. To avoid this inconvenience, wireless data link is preferable.

Flexible connection - Cubes are connected with male-female connectors, thus connectable direction is limited. A more flexible connection is needed.

Power supply - In ActiveCube, power is supplied from the host via the base cube. Freed from the base cube, the power supply problem should be resolved.

Higher performance - In ActiveCube, a host PC executes almost all data operations due to the limited performance and memory capacity of the cube's CPU. Therefore, a more powerful CPU is needed for *m*-ActiveCube, which can execute data operation locally.

2.3   Organization of *m*-ActiveCube

Associated with the above demands, *m*-ActiveCube is constructed. In *m*-ActiveCube, each cube face has eight magnets (Fig. 2(a)). Four face notrh and the remaining four face south so that any pair of cubes can be connected in any direction. Moreover, magnets are coated by metal, and thus shape recognition data are transferred between cubes. A rechargeable battery is embedded in each cube. Therefore, a base cube that supplies power to all cubes is no longer required.

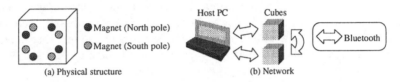

(a) Physical structure   (b) Network

Fig. 2. Physical structure and network of *m*-ActiveCube

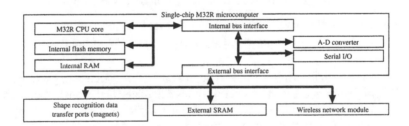

Fig. 3. Block diagram of *m*-ActiveCube

Fig. 3 shows the block diagram of *m*-ActiveCube. A single-chip M32R micropro-cessor (M32176F4TFP [7]) is comprised of an M32R core CPU, internal flash memory, and RAM, which offers higher performance and facilitates various functionalities. Since the chip also includes an A/D converter and a serial I/O, media input/output devices and sensing devices can be connected through them. To enable more complex data operation such as voice recognition, an external SRAM is connected to the M32R chip. A wire-less network module enables data transfer among cubes and the host PC (Fig. 2.(b)) without any physical contact. Abundant data such as images or audio are transferred through the wireless link. Cubes communicate through shape recognition data transfer ports and create the shape information, which is transferred to a host PC.

Table 1 summarizes the comparisons between ActiveCube and *m*-ActiveCube.

Table 1. Comparisons between original ActiveCube and *m*-ActiveCube

	ActiveCube	*m*-ActiveCube
CPU frequency [MHz]	NC:20, H8S:25	40
Memory size [KB]	NC: 2(RAM), 16(ROM), 2(EEPROM) H8S: 256(Flash), 16(RAM)	512(Flash) 24(RAM)
External memory	Not available	Available
Data transfer	Wired communication	Bluetooth
Power supply	Supplied through cubes	Rechargeable battery
Connectable direction	Limited by male-female connectors	All direction

3   Example of Basic Functionalities

Data transfer between cubes is accomplished via wireless networks, and *m*-ActiveCube has a higher performance embedded processor than the original ActiveCube. Thus, using distributed processing techniques, the *m*-ActiveCube system enables users to implement more valuable applications requesting high computational load, for which original ActiveCube can hardly be used. In this section, as an example of basic functionalities newly introduced by *m*-ActiveCube, methods for performing realtime speech recognition process using multiple *m*-ActiveCubes are described in detail.

3.1   Speech Recognition Overview

In our system, Julian[5] is employed as a speech recognition engine. The speech recognition process consists of feature extraction and search processes, as illustrated in Fig. 4.

Feature Extraction Process: As shown in Fig. 5, Mel Frequency Cepstrum Coefficient (MFCC) and energy of log-compressed signal are calculated in the feature extraction process.

Search Process: Julian performs frame synchronous beam search using Viterbi search. In this Viterbi search, score of each Viterbi path is calculated and evaluated to determine promising paths. Such promising path information is fed to search process in next frame and that of others is suppressed in order to reduce both of requested memory amount and computational complexity during search process. The maximum number of retained paths is called beam width.

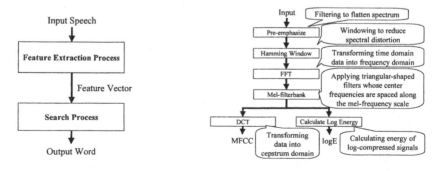

Fig. 4. Overview of Speech Recognition   **Fig. 5.** Feature Extraction Process

3.2   Computational Cost Analysis

To accomplish distributed computing by multiple *m*-ActiveCubes, total computational cost required for realtime speech recognition is estimated by using PD32RSIM, which is a simulator debugger for M32R processor. In this analysis 3217x processor is used as target processor. In order to estimate computational cost for performing a speech recognition task, 10 words for role-playing game (RPG) command (Table 2) are used, assuming that speech recognition function of *m*-ActiveCube system is applied in playing RPG application. Each word is uttered by one male and recorded five times respectively so as to make a test set consists of 50 speech data.

Table 2. 10 words for RPG Commands

"mae (forward)", "ushiro (backward)", "migi (right)", "hidari (left)", "hashire (run)","tomare (stop)", "dougu (tool)", "hanashikakeru (speak to someone)", "tatakau (fight)", and "mahou (spell)"

Table 3. Specification of Acoustic Model

Sampling	16kHz & 16bit
Framing	25ms long & 10ms shift
#Phones	43
#States per phone	5
#Gaussian/state	16
Features	MFCC(12), ΔMFCC(12), ΔLog Energy

The feature extraction process is implemented in fixed-point arithmetic to reduce computation load. The operation accuracy of fixed-point implementation in the feature extraction process is determined by performing evaluation using an RPG command test set. As a result, operation accuracy is resolved such that 32-bit for FFT and 64-bit for the other functions shown in Fig. 5. Execution cycles of original and fixed-point implementation, estimated through PD32RSIM, are 7,685,393 and 672,895, respectively. Consequently, to reduce execution cycles, a fixed-point arithmetic version is employed in our speech recognition system.

On the other hand, the search process consists of memory accesses and output probability computation by using an acousitc model, whose specification is shown in Table 3. Execution cycles for performing output probability computation, which is composed of Gaussian computation and addlog computation[6], are evaluated throught the use of PD32RSIM and `gprof` profiling tool. Execution cycles of Gaussian computation process and addlog computation process are estimated by using PD32RSIM, and then the number of calls per frame of each process is counted by using `gprof` profiling tool. As a result, estimated execution cycles per frame of Gaussian and addlog computations are 544,238 and 485,952, respectively. Consequently, total required operation frequency for realtime speech recognition is given by $(672, 895 + 544, 238 + 485, 952)$[cycles]/0.01[ms] = 171[MHz]. Each *m*-ActiveCube has only one M32R processor, which can be run up to 32 [MHz], and thus reduction of CPU load by distributed computing is needed to achieve speech recognition application by the *m*-ActiveCube system.

3.3   Load Balancing of the *m*-ActiveCube

To perform speech recognition task in realtime, feature extraction and search processes are executed by multiple *m*-ActiveCubes.

By using multiple m-ActiveCubes, a number of feature vector sets can be parallel calculated. If the number of assigned m-ActiveCubes for performing the feature extraction process is $M1$, each CPU has to perform the feature extraction process in $M1 \times 10$[ms], and thus the required operation frequency to perform the feature extraction process in realtime is given by $M1$ [cycles]$/(10$ [ms] $\times N1)$ [MHz], where $N1$ represents the total number of execution cycles.

As mentioned in section 3.1, beam search is adopted to prune search space in Viterbi search. The beam width has a constant value, and thus CPU load reduction can be achieved by using multiple m-ActiveCubes. Let $N2$ be the number of execution cycles per frame needed for performing the search process, $M2$ the number of allocated m-ActiveCubes to execute the search process, and the required operation frequency to fulfill realtime processing is given by $M2$ [cycles]$/(10$ [ms] $\times N2)$ [MHz].

Both feature extraction and search processes are performed frame by frame. Consequently, a two stage frame-level pipeline can be employed, where the pipeline boundary lays between the feature extraction and the search processes. As a result, the operation frequency required to perform speech recognition in realtime is given by $\max(M1$ [cycles]$/10$ [ms] $\times N1, M2$ [cycles]$/10$ [ms] $\times N2)$ [MHz]. Based on this equation, if seven m-ActiveCubes are available, required operation frequency is given by $\max(672, 896/10 \times 3, (544, 238 + 485, 952)/10 \times 4) = \max(23, 26) = 26$ [MHz]. As a result, CPU load is reduced by 85% and thus realtime speech recognition can be performed by using M32R processors.

3.4 Specification of Speech Recognition by m-ActiveCube

As a result, seven m-ActiveCubes running at 26MHz of clock rate enable the proposed speech recognition. Application size is 2,841 KBytes, which is mainly caused by about 2 MBytes table data for addlog computation. For facilitating practical applications, further development for efficient design of addlog computation is required.

4 System Applications

Multimedia extension of the ActiveCube system and its functionalities offer more impressive and interesting future applications in various fields, as shown Fig.6. In this section, the details of the proposed applications are described by referring to the benefits of speech recognition functionality.

Intuitive 3D Model Retrieval. We previously developed a 3D model retrieval system [8] by using the ActiveCube system without extension. In this system, users can retrieve a 3D shape model by simply combining physical cubes. As future works, we are planning to use additional voice keywords to decide the categories of retrieved results or to input additional features of objects such as animal calls or the sounds of musical instruments. Moreover, we can realize an application for a digital encyclopedia by expanding this system. m-ActiveCube system will facilitate these future works.

Educational Toys for Children. We have also developed educational toys for children called "TSU.MI.KI" [9]. First, children construct a shape by combining physical cubes. Second, the system transforms it into a virtual object that resembles the physical

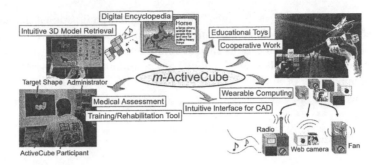

Fig. 6. Applications using *m*-ActiveCube

structure. After that, they interact with the virtual object by manipulating its physical structure. By using the *m*-ActiveCube system, we can utilize multiple sets of Active-Cube systems in the same cyberspace, allowing children to collaborate with each other in cyberspace. In addition, we can realize more intuitive interactions with cyberspace. For instance, a user can manipulate a virtual object by voice commands such as "migi (turn right)" or "tomare (stop)." If a user encounters a dangerous situation, output cubes flash warning messages. Thus, the *m*-ActiveCube system will allow TSU.MI.KI to provide more intuitive and collaborative edutainment experiences for children.

Assessment Training and Rehabilitation Tools for Medical Purposes. For medical purposes, we developed a system for the automated assessment of 3D spatial and constructional ability [10]. The system measures 3D spatial and constructional ability according to user attempts to construct physical cubes. The *m*-ActiveCube system can supply advice to users to construct a 3D structure by using I/O functionalities. For example, if a user needs help, she/he can request support by using the speech recognition function. When the system recognizes the request, it shows hints on the display and output cubes. We assume that this system would be useful for training and the rehabilitation of 3D spatial and constructional ability.

Wearable Computing. Because a battery is incorporated into each cube, it is possible to use the *m*-ActiveCube system outdoors. Therefore, users can utilize the *m*-ActiveCube as a wearable I/O device and create a variety of tools by combining several cubes. The constructed structures become various tools according to shape and I/O functionalities. The function of each cube can be flexibly and dynamically changed with connected positions/orientations or the assembled object shape. Moreover, users can easily add functions by simply connecting I/O cubes.

Consequently, with the *m*-ActiveCube system, various useful applications are available because spatial, temporal, and functional consistency is always maintained between the physical object and its corresponding virtual representation.

5   Conclusion

The present paper described a new TUI device as a multimedia extension of Active-Cube. According to the analysis of the original version of ActiveCube, the fundamental specifications of ActiveCube with high performance and high functionalities are examined, which enhance the benefits of human computer interfaces. m-ActiveCube achieves more impressive system applications such as intuitive 3D model retrieval, a digital encyclopedia, and so on. Further developments are continuing on the System-on-a-chip (SoC) implementation of m ActiveCube chip and the realization of the proposed system applications.

Acknowledgments

The authors are grateful to Hideo Kikuchi of System Watt Co., Ltd. for his helpful comments and suggestions. This research was supported in part by "The 21st Century Center of Excellence Program" of the Ministry of Education, Culture, Sports, Science and Technology, Japan.

References

1. E. Sharlin, B. Watson, Y. Kitamura, F. Kishino, and Y. Itoh, "On tangible user interfaces, human and spatiality," Personal and Ubiquitous Computing, Springer-Verlag, vol. 8, no. 5, pp. 338–346, Sept. 2004.
2. B. Ullmer and H. Ishii, "Emerging Frameworks for Tangible User Interfaces," in Human Computer Interaction in the New Millennium, J. M. Carroll Ed., Addison-Wesley, 2001, pp. 579-601.
3. R. Watanabe, Y. Itoh, Y. Kitamura, F. Kishino, and H. Kikuchi, "Distributed Autonomous Interface using ActiveCube for Interactive Multimedia Contents," Proc. of 15th Int'l Conf. Artificial Reality and Telexistence (ICAT '05), 2005. (to appear)
4. Toshiba Crop., http://www.semicon.toshiba.co.jp/prd/ics/neuron/neuron_top.html
5. Julian, http://julius.sourceforge.jp/
6. S. Yoshizawa, Y. Miyanaga, and N. Yoshida, "On a High-Speech HMM VLSI Module with Block Parallel Processing," IEICE Trans. on Fundamentals, vol. E88-A, no. 12, pp. 1440–1450, Dec. 2002.
7. RENESAS Technology, 32176 group data sheet, Jan. 2003.
8. H. Ichida, Y. Itoh, Y. Kitamura, and F. Kishino, "Interactive retrieval of 3D shape models using physical objects," Proc. of the 12th ACM Int'l Conf. on Multimedia 2004, pp. 692–699, 2004.
9. Y. Itoh, S. Akinobu, H. Ichida, R. Watanabe, Y. Kitamura, and F. Kishino, "TSU.MI.KI: stimulating children's creativity and imagination with interactive blocks," Proc. of the 2nd Int'l Conf on Creating, Connecting and Collaborating through Computing, IEEE Computer Society, pp. 62–70, 2004.
10. E. Sharlin, Y. Itoh, B. Watson, Y. Kitamura, S. Sutphen, and L. Liu, "Cognitive cubes: a tangible user interface for cognitive assessment," Proc. of Conference on Human Factors in Computing Systems (CHI '02), pp. 347–354, 2002.

Biologically Inspired Adaptive Routing by Mimicking Enzymic Feedback Control Mechanism in the Cell

Takashi Kawauchi, Tadasuke Nozoe, and Masahiro Okamoto

Dept. of Bioinformatics, Graduate School of Systems Life Sciences,
Kyushu University, Fukuoka 812-8581, Japan
{kawauchi, nozoe, okahon}@brs.kyushu-u.ac.jp
http://www.brs.kyushu-u.ac.jp/bioinfo/indexe.htm

Abstract. The routing algorithm of SPF (Shortest Path First) [1] is widely distributed in large scale network such as internet. Since this routing algorithm is designed in order to improve throughput of each packet which is sequentially generated at the nodes, it is not suitable for averaging load balance in the network. The enzymic feedback in the cell is the typical and basic control mechanism which can realize homeostasis of the value of every reactant in the metabolic pathway. The purpose of this study is to design an adaptive routing in which the packets generated at the nodes can be sent to the final destinations with avoiding the partial and time-variant congestions in the network, and the load balance in the network can be averaged. We have proposed here a new biologically inspired adaptive routing algorithm by introducing an enzymic feedback control mechanism in the cell.

1 Introduction

The metabolic pathway in the cell is so-called "a stream of water" and is composed of a lot of enzymic reaction steps in which reactant (substrate) is converted to the product by unique "enzyme" (catalyzed protein) and the produced product is converted to the product by enzyme at the subsequent reaction step and so on. Enzymes are proteins which catalyze the turnover of substrates without being consumed themselves and without changing the equilibrium point of the biochemical reaction. In metabolic pathways, the product of a late (or the last) step frequently acts as an inhibitor of the first committed step in this pathway (negative feedback control). This way, the end product of a pathway controls its own synthesis and prevents useless accumulation of intermediates and of end product. Enzymic feedback control can be considered to be a bandwidth control; rate velocity of consumption of substrate can be represented by the function of substrate (A) and feedback inhibitor (B). Under the steady-state assumption in the cell, many kinds of kinetic models of negative feedback control are well known such as competitive inhibition, uncompetitive inhibition, non-competitve inhibition and so on. For example, when the B is assumed

A.J. Ijspeert et al. (Eds.): BioADIT 2006, LNCS 3853, pp. 371–378, 2006.
© Springer-Verlag Berlin Heidelberg 2006

to control the rate velocity of A with a manner of competitive inhibition [2] (one of the negative feedback functions), the rate velocity of A (d[A]/dt, t represents time) can be mathematically written as follows:

$$d[A]/dt = -\frac{V\max[A]}{Km(1+[B]/Ki)+[A]} \qquad (1)$$

where *Vmax* represents maximum velocity (reaction rate) of enzyme activity, *Km* is the value of substrate giving 0.5*Vmax*, *Ki* is the feedback coefficient. Anyway, d[A]/dt is the function of the substrate A and the feedback inhibitor B. In the case of accumulation of B, the absolute value of the term in the right-side of eq.(1) become to be small. Since the B is the end product of the pathway, we can easily considered that the accumulation of B corresponds to be "congestion" of the pathway; the absolute value of the term in the right-side of eq.(1) represents new metric of "congestion" from the view point of network routing.

2 Proposed Routing Protocol

We define the following metric of routing by mimicking enzymic feedback control in the cell:

$$k = p/V\max \qquad (2)$$

$$p = \frac{V[a]}{Km(1+[b]/Ki)+[a]} \qquad (3)$$

where *V* represents the sending rate (Mbps) to the next-hop node ,[a] is the total of reserved sending packet size (Byte) to the next-hop node, [b] is the total accumulated packet size (Byte) at next-hop node, *Vmax* is maximum sending rate (Mbps) to all next-hop nodes , and *Km* and *Ki* are the arbitrary coefficients. The value of k in eq.(2) decreases with the increase in "congestion" of [b]. Furthermore, we define the following weighted multi-objective *f*:

$$f = (1-\alpha)k + \alpha(1/h) \quad 0 < \alpha < 1 \qquad (4)$$

where h is the number of hops to the final destination, α represents arbitrary coefficient; if α=1, the network routing will be performed according to the SPF (Shortest Path First) algorithm. The *h* value was calculated with using routing table created based on the Dikjstra method [1]. At the branching of node-pathways, the value of *f* at each branching pathway is calculated and it determines the node to be sent with having the larger value of *f*. In order to validate only the effect of feedback control [b] at the branching point, the value of [a] was defined by the total of the reserved sending packet size at the branching point; there is no difference in [a] between branching points, the value of *p* (eq.(3)) changes with only [b]. This is the outline of the proposed dynamic adaptive routing algorithm where most of the packets will be sent to the final destination with escaping from the congested nodes; the QoS (Quality of Service) of the proposed algorithm is expected to be "averaging the load within the network".

3   Case Study and Validation

The following node-network was used in order to evaluate our algorithm, where the numeral (0 to 5) represents the node-number, and the bold line is the connection pathway between nodes:

Suppose the three kinds of sequential packets to be sent randomly in the network (total number of packets is 300); one is the packets generated at the starting node 0 and sent to the destination node 3, second is those generated at the starting node 0 and sent to the destination node 2, and the last one is those generated at the starting node 0 and sent to the destination node 5. Each packet has 3072B size and is generated at every 150 μsec. The maximum sending rate between connection nodes is fixed at 100Mbps. The control packet (64B) is sending to the next-hop node at every 100 μsec. This control packet involves the information of the value of [b] (total accumulated packet size) in eq.(3). The time between the generating and arriving at the final destination (passage) of every packet and transient sending route of every packet were examined. The default route was supposed to be $0 \to 1 \to 2 \to 3$ for the packets sending to the node 3 and to be $0 \to 1 \to 2$ for the packets sending to the node 2 and to be $0 \to 4 \to 5$ for the packets sending to the node 5; the route $0 \to 1 \to 2$ is overlapped which will lead to the congestion of the packets at this route.

For comparison, the latency profile with packets to be sent was examined in the case of SPF algorithm; every packet is sent to the final destination according to the default route. The results can be summarized as follows: As shown in Fig. 2, the

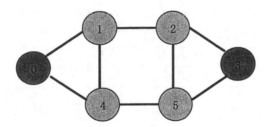

Fig. 1. 6 nodes-network

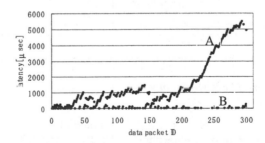

Fig. 2. Latency profile with data packet by using SPF algorithm. The abscissa and the ordinate represent data packet ID and latency (μsec), respectively. A, packet sending to the nodes 2 and 3; B, packet sending to the node 5.

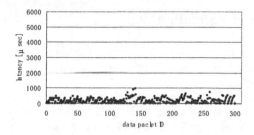

Fig. 3. Overwritten latency profile with data packet ID by using the proposed routing algorithm. The abscissa and the ordinate represent data packet ID and latency (μsec), respectively. The control packet is sending to the next-hop node at every 100μsec.

overwritten latency profile A(data packets sending from the node 0 to the nodes 2 and 3) increases with the data packet ID that means the congestion is occurred at the route between the nodes 0, 1 and 2. Since the maximum sending rate between all connection nodes is fixed at 100Mbps and the each data packet size is 3072B, the minimum required time sending to the next-hop node is 245.7 μsec (minimum required time sending from the node to the node 3 is 245.7 x 3 = 737.1 μsec).

Fixed the value of α in eq.(4) at 0.5, the latency profile with packets to be sent was examined by introducing our proposed routing algorithm. The overwritten latency profile with data packet ID is shown in Fig. 3. The average, minimum and maximum of latency in Figs. 2 and 3 are summarized in Tables 1 and 2, respectively.

Table 1. Summary of latency profile shown in Fig. 2

Total number of data packets	300
Average of latency (μsec)	1153.58
Standard deviation of latency	1498.64
Minimum latency (μsec)	0
Maximum latency (μsec)	5485.76

Table 2. Summary of latency profile shown in Fig. 3

Total number of data packets	300
Average of latency (μsec)	196.16
Standard deviation of latency	173.65
Minimum latency (μsec)	0
Maximum latency (μsec)	979.6

As shown in Fig. 3 and Table 2, most of the latency of data packets were averaged, which means that our proposed algorithm is effective for dynamic adaptive routing. According to Figs. 2 and 3, part of the transient latency profiles of packets and route sending to the final destination by using SPF algorithm and by using the proposed algorithm are summarized in Tables 3 and 4, respectively.

Table 3. Transient latency profiles of packets by using SPF algorithm

PacketID	generate	arrive	latency	route
250	37501	41546.84	3554.32	0>1>2
251	37651	42038.36	3650.08	0>1>2>3
252	37801	42038.36	3745.84	0>1>2
253	37951	42284.12	3841.6	0>1>2
254	38101	42780.76	3942.48	0>1>2>3
255	38251	38742.52	0	0>4>5
256	38401	42780.76	3888.24	0>1>2
257	38551	39042.52	0	0>4>5
258	38701	43272.28	3834	0>1>2>3
259	38851	43518.04	3929.76	0>1>2>3
260	39001	43768.92	4030.64	0>1>2>3
261	39151	43768.92	4126.4	0>1>2
262	39301	44260.44	4222.16	0>1>2>3
263	39451	44506.2	4317.92	0>1>2>3
264	39601	44757.08	4418.8	0>1>2>3
265	39751	45002.84	4514.56	0>1>2>3
266	39901	45253.72	4615.44	0>1>2>3
267	40051	40542.52	0	0>4>5
268	40201	45248.6	4556.08	0>1>2
269	40351	45745.24	4656.96	0>1>2>3
270	40501	45745.24	4752.72	0>1>2
271	40651	46236.76	4848.48	0>1>2>3
272	40801	46236.76	4944.24	0>1>2
273	40951	41442.52	0	0>4>5
274	41101	41688.28	95.76	0>4>5
275	41251	46733.4	4745.12	0>1>2>3
276	41401	46979.16	4840.88	0>1>2>3
277	41551	46979.16	4936.64	0>1>2
278	41701	42192.52	0	0>4>5
279	41851	47224.92	4882.4	0>1>2
280	42001	47470.68	4978.16	0>1>2

In Table 4, the circle marked columns represent the packets which were sent by using the non-default routes (default routes are 0→1→2→3 for the packets sending to the node 3, 0→1→2 for those sending to the node 2, and 0→4→5 for those sending to the node 5). In Table 4, most of the packets sending to the node 2 were sent by using the default route, except for packet IDs 256 and 280; alternative routes is 0→4→1→2. The routes for the packets sending to the node 3 are most flexible; the route 0→4→5→3 is another short-cut route and the route 0→1→0→1→2→3 (packet ID=260) took a timing for a while because the default route 0→1→2→3 was occupied by packet IDs 258 and 259. Furthermore by assigning the route 0→1→0 →1→2→3 for packet ID 260, the packet ID 262 can select "non-traffic" 0→4→5→3; latency is 0. This result shows the proposed algorithm can find alternative non-traffic routes with considering the smaller number of hops to the destination.

These results showed in the case where the control packet is sending to the next-hop node at every 100μsec. Next we examined the effect of sending time interval of control packets on the average of latency. The other conditions except for sending

Table 4. Transient latency profiles of packets and the route sent to the final destination by using the proposed algorithm

	PacketID	generate	arrive	latency	route
	250	37401	38003.64	111.12	0>1>2
O	251	37551	38288.28	0	0>4>5>3
	252	37701	38259.64	67.12	0>1>2
	253	37851	38520.76	178.24	0>1>2
O	254	38001	38738.28	0	0>4>5>3
	255	38151	38748.52	106	0>4>5
O	256	38301	39343.4	550.88	0>4>1>2
	257	38451	39229.8	287.28	0>4>5
	258	38601	39338.28	0	0>1>2>3
	259	38751	39840.04	351.76	0>1>2>3
O	260	38901	40372.52	734.24	0>1>0>1>2>3
	261	39051	39865.64	323.12	0>1>2
O	262	39201	39938.28	0	0>4>5>3
O	263	39351	40199.4	111.12	0>4>5>3
O	264	39501	40460.52	222.24	0>4>5>3
	265	39651	40628.52	240.24	0>1>2>3
O	266	39801	40716.52	178.24	0>4>5>3
	267	39951	40726.76	284.24	0>4>5
	268	40101	40643.88	51.36	0>1>2
O	269	40251	41228.52	240.24	0>4>5>3
	270	40401	40905	12.48	0>1>2
O	271	40551	41489.64	201.36	0>4>5>3
	272	40701	41192.52	0	0>1>2
	273	40851	41499.88	157.36	0>4>5
	274	41001	41761	268.48	0>4>5
	275	41151	41888.28	0	0>1>2>3
	276	41301	42150.88	112.6	0>1>2>3
	277	41451	42159.64	217.12	0>1>2
	278	41601	42092.52	0	0>4>5
	279	41751	42420.76	178.24	0>1>2
O	280	41901	42922.52	530	0>4>1>2

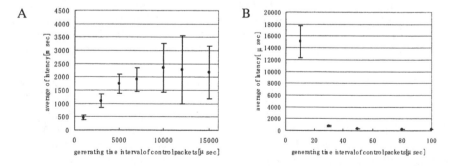

Fig. 4. Effects of generation time interval of control packet on the average of. latency A shows in the case where time interval varies between 0 and 15000 μsec, and B is the magnifying profile between 0 and 100μsec.

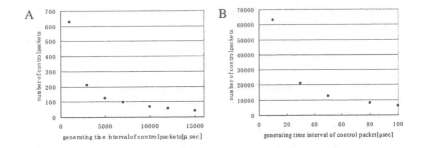

Fig. 5. Profile of the total number of sending control packets with sending time interval. B shows the magnifying profile when the time interval varies between 0 and 100.

time interval of control packets were the same as before. The results were summarized in Fig. 4. The average of latency took the minimum around time interval = 100μsec, and rapidly increased when the time interval is less than 30μsec. Fig. 5 represents profile of total number of generated control packets with changing the time interval of control packets. In Fig. 5(B), the total number of sending control packets rapidly increased when the time interval is less than 100μsec.

As shown in Figs. 4(B) and 5(B), the smaller time interval becomes, the less the time-delay of feedback information is, however, which leads to the generation of large amount of control packets causing the additional "congestion" in the network.. Thus in our proposed algorithm we should set up the optimal time interval for sending control packets to the next-hop nodes; 100μsec in this case.

4 Discussion

The OSPF (Open Shortest Pass First) [3] is the routing protocol by using various cost parameters as metrics; the followings are considered to be cost parameter: reliability,

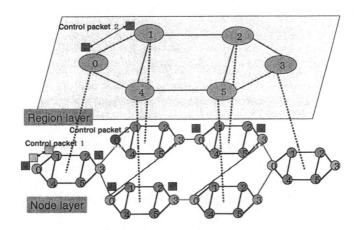

Fig. 6. Concept of hierarchical adaptive routing

delay, bandwidth, load, maximum transfer unit, communication cost. In this study, we proposed here eqs. (2), (3) and (4) by mimicking the mechanism of enzymic feedback function in the cell. As shown in eq. (3), the p is the integrated parameter considering both the current congestion status between the self-node and the next-hop node([a] in eq. (3) numerically reflects this information) and the most recent congestion status between the next-hop node and the next-next-hop nodes (the [b] in eq. (3) numerically reflects this information). The Km represents the [a] value giving the half speed of maximum sending rate ($Vmax$); the smaller Km value gives the steeper decrease of p-value. The Ki determines steepness of the p-value $vs.$ [a]-value; the smaller Ki value represents the stronger negative feedback control. In metabolic pathways in the cell we can observe various kinds of feedback function mechanisms eq. (1) in addition to [2, 4]. These functions including eq. (3) have high possibility to be acceptable as new metrics in OSPF.

For adaptive routing in large size of network, based on the results in this study we are now developing hierarchical adaptive routing or overlay routing shown in Fig. 6.

In Fig. 6, regarded the compact small network in Node layer as one node in Region layer, select the non-traffic route with the smaller number of hops in Region layer by using the biologically inspired routing algorithm (eqs. (2)-(4)) and this selection reflects the route searching in Node layer. This procedure is repeated time by time according to the traffic condition in the network.

References

[1] Dikjstra, E.W.: A note on two problem in connection with graphs, Numerische Mathematik, 1, pp269-271(1959)
[2] Okamoto, M., Takeda, Y., Aso, Y., Hayashi, K.: Steady-state approximation of enzyme activation and inhibition, Biotechnol. and Bioengineer., 25, pp1453-1463 (1983)
[3] Thomas M. Thomas II: OSPF Network Design Solutions 2nd. ed., Cisco Press (2003)
[4] Segel I.H: Enzyme Kinetics, Wiley-Interscience, New York (1975)

An Interest-Based Peer Clustering Algorithm Using Ant Paradigm

Taisuke Izumi and Toshimitsu Masuzawa

Graduate School of Information Science and Technology,
Osaka University 1-3 Machikaneyama, Toyonaka, 560-8531, Japan
{t-izumi, masuzawa}@ist.osaka-u.ac.jp

Abstract. The interest-based clustering is one of promising approaches
to achieve low-cost search in peer-to-peer file sharing. It organizes the
logical overlay network where peers having similar interests are closely
located. In this paper, we propose an interest-based peer clustering algorithm using ant paradigm. Our algorithm is inspired by the ant-based
clustering algorithm, which is one of heuristic methods to categorize
many data items. We also evaluate this algorithm by simulations.

1 Introduction

Recently, *peer-to-peer* (P2P) systems have been occupying an important position
of distributed computing. In contrast to the traditional server-client architecture,
all participants in peer-to-peer networks (called *peer*) are connected with each
other through a logical network overlaying on existing infrastructures such as
the Internet, and cooperatively provides a certain type of services. A typical one
of such services is *file sharing*, where each peer shares a large amount of files by
providing a part of its storage area. Boosted by the recent growth of network
bandwidth, several peer-to-peer file sharing systems, such as Napster[1], achieve
success, and the file sharing becomes most popular application of peer-to-peer
computing.

One of most important issues in peer-to-peer file sharing is *lookup*, that is,
finding the peer that stores searching files. In general, since peer-to-peer systems
consists of huge number of peers, it is almost impossible that each peer acquires
the whole information about the location of files. Hence, lookup algorithms must
be realized in some decentralized manner. This fact causes the implementation
of lookup to be a challenging task and to attract many researchers' interests.
Actually, many approaches for efficient lookup have been studied before now [7].
In such approaches, *flooding* is one of most popular schemes. In this scheme,
the searcher sends its query to all neighbors, and if a process receives a query
that is not forwarded yet, it forwards the query to all neighbors. The peer that
has the file matching the query, it replies its location to the searcher. This
approach is relatively simple and easy to implement. However, if the searching
file is located at one far from the searcher, the flooding-based search consumes
too many messages (the number of messages rapidly grows as the function of the

A.J. Ijspeert et al. (Eds.): BioADIT 2006, LNCS 3853, pp. 379–386, 2006.
© Springer-Verlag Berlin Heidelberg 2006

distance between the searcher and the file holder). An alternative of the flooding-based search is the k-random walker search, where searchers inject k queries that randomly walk on the network [7]. This scheme requires less number of messages than the flooding-based search. However, in contrast, it consume too many times to find faraway files. Thus, as the number of peers increases, both approach faces the scalability problem.

The *interest-based clustering* is one of promising approaches to avoid this problem. The underlying principle of this approach is that users usually have some specific interest, and that the behavior of each peer is based on the interest of its user. For example, in sharing music files, some like rock music, some like classical music, some like jazz, and so on. Then, it is natural that the peer whose user likes rock music sends the query to find the rock music. Thus, if we can gather the peers which have same interest in the network, it is expected that the overall search performance is improved. In the interest-based clustering, it is assumed that each peer has some information representing user's interest, and that for two different kinds of interests, their similarity is defined by some metrics. Then, the objective of interest-based clustering is to organize the logical overlay network where peers having similar interests are closely located.

In this paper, we propose an interest-based peer clustering algorithm. For construction of the algorithm, we adopt an bio-inspired approach, called *ant-based clustering*[3, 4, 5, 6]. An ant-based clustering is one of techniques to categorize several kinds of items distributed in some field. This approach uses a number of agents whose behavior is inspired by ants in real world. In general, the ant-based clustering algorithm works as follows: each ant-like agent walks around the field. If an agent encounters an item, it probabilistically picks up the item. Then, the pickup probability depends on the density of similar items around the pickup target. That is, if there are many similar items around the target, its pickup probability becomes low, and vise versa. By the same way, each agent with an item probabilistically put the item. Its probability also depends on the density of similar items. With high probability, the item is put at the place around which many similar items are located. Repeating pickup and drop of items, the locations of items are eventually clustered according to their similarity, that is, similar items are closely located. Based on this idea, we construct an interest-based peer clustering algorithm. In our algorithm, each peer provides *token* which is labeled by the provider's interest. Each agent walks around the network, picks up tokens, and drops tokens. When a token is put on a peer, the token holder is logically linked with the token provider. If, same as the ant-based clustering algorithm, the token is gathered in some place, peers with similar interests are connected with each other via the place where their tokens are gathered.

To our knowledge, this algorithm is the first one to apply the ant-based algorithm to the clustering of peer-to-peer networks. We also evaluate our algorithm by simulations, and show that our algorithm is slightly better than another straightforward algorithm.

This paper is organized as follows. First, we define peer-to-peer systems and introduce the ant-based clustering in Section 2, and briefly explain the notion of the ant-based clustering technique in Section 3. Our clustering algorithm is presented in Section 4. The evaluation of this scheme is given by simulations in Section 4.1. Finally, we conclude this paper and state the future research issues in Section 5.

2 Preliminaries

2.1 Peer-to-Peer Systems

We consider a *peer-to-peer system* consisting n processes $\{p_0, p_1, p_2, \ldots, p_{n-1}\}$[1]. Two peers can directly communicate with each other by exchanging messages if they are connected by a link. The network we consider in this paper is *overlay networks* consisting of *logical links*. The logical link between two peers does not imply that they are physically connected. It rather implies that two peers know their physical address (e.g. IP address) with each other. When a peer sends a message to one of its (logical) neighbors, it actually sends the message with the physical address of the destination. This message is transferred through some physical path. The translation from logical links to physical paths is handled by the underlying protocol (e.g. TCP/IP). In this sense, the link set connecting to a peer p can be regarded as the connection list, which is the list of peers whose physical addresses are known to p. We allow the network topology to be arbitrary as long as any two peers are connected with each other. However, by the nature of overlay networks, we also allow each peer to change the network topology by removing or creating links connected to itself. Actually, this is done by adding a physical address to the connection list or removing the physical address from the connection list. We assume that the system is synchronous. More precisely, an execution of the system follow discrete time, which is represented by nonnegative integer $0, 1, 2, \ldots$. In one time unit, each peer can communicate with its neighbors and execute local operation. Notice that this synchrony assumption is introduced only to simplify the argument. Actually, our algorithm correctly works even if no such synchronization mechanism exists.

We also assume that each peer has an *interest*, which is some kind of information (such as keywords) representing its user's interest. In addition, for any two kind of interests, their similarity is defined. The similarity is represented by a single real value with range $[0, 1]$.

2.2 Mobile Agents

The system can use a number of *mobile agents* (in what follows, we simply call "agent"). A mobile agent is a autonomous program that can migrate from node to node in the network. A agent can interact to the peer on which it visits by executing operations. In one time unit, each agent can execute local operation, and can migrate to a neighbor of the peer at which it currently stays.

---

[1] Usually, in peer-to-peer systems, the set of peers varies with time by join or leave of peers. However, the main objective of this paper is to present the possibility of interest-based cluster organization using ant paradigm. Thus, for simplicity, we does not consider join or leave of peers.

3   Ant-Based Clustering Algorithm

In this section, we briefly explain the ant-based clustering algorithm (ABC), which is the basis of our algorithm. The ABC algorithm is an nature-inspired heuristic approach for cluster analysis of data items. In this approach, each item is distributed in a field (typically 2D-grid). The objective of ABC is to design the map of those items. More precisely, the map is an arrangement of items in the field that represents their relationship. That is, in the map, closely related items are closely placed in the field. The ABC algorithm is inspired by a real ant behavior of cemetery organization (i.e. the clustering of dead corpses). The study of ABC is originated by Deneubourg et al. [4]. In their paper, the model for such cemetery organization behavior is proposed. Subsequently, Lumer and Faieta [6] applied this model to the data analysis. This result is the basis of our algorithm. Thus, in the followings, we introduce the ABC algorithm of Lumer and Faieta (in what follows we simply call this algorithm "the ABC algorithm").

In the ABC, we consider a two dimensional grid. In a unit area of the field, one item can be placed. The ABC algorithm begins with randomly distributing the items we want to analyze into the field. Then, for any two data items, their similarity is defined with the range $[0,1]$. The field also has a number of agents. An execution of the ABC algorithm proceeds in steps. In one step, each agent random walks to one of neighbor areas. After the walk, if the agent already has an item, it probabilistically decides whether it drops the item or not. In the same way, if the agent encounter the item at the area to which it moves, it probabilistically decides whether it picks up the item or not. Then, the probability with which the item i is picked up or dropped is determined by the *neighborhood function* defined by:

$$f(i) = \max\left(0.0, \frac{1}{|L|}\sum_{j \in L}\left(1 - \frac{(1 - \delta(j,i))}{\alpha}\right)\right),$$

where $\delta(j,i)$ is the similarity between the item i and j, L is the set of areas which adjacent to the area where the item i is placed ($j \in L$ means "for any item existing in L"), and α is a data-dependent scaling parameter.

Using this neighborhood function, the pickup probability is given by:

$$p_{pick}(i) = \left(\frac{k^+}{k^+ + f(i)}\right)^2,$$

and, the drop probability is given by:

$$p_{drop}(i) = \left(\frac{f(i)}{k^+ + f(i)}\right)^2,$$

where the k^+ and k^- is threshold constants.

The ABC algorithm repeats this step until some termination condition holds (typically, the number of repeat times reaches to some predefined value). The resultant map is the field when the termination condition holds.

4 Interest-Based Peer Clustering Inspired by ABC

This section presents our interest-based peer clustering algorithm based on the ABC algorithm. In our algorithm, the whole network and each peer respectively corresponds to the field and an unit area. Each peer provides *token*, which is corresponds to data items in the ABC. Each token is labeled by the interest of its provider. Same as ABC, an agent randomly walks on the networks, and probabilistically picks up or drops tokens. Then, if a token provided by a peer p_1 is placed at some other peer p_2, p_1 and p_2 is logically connected. Since we can expect that tokens provided by peers with similar interests is clustered in the networks, peers with similar interest is connected with each other via the place where their tokens are gathered. In other words, the place where tokens with similar interests are clustered works as a hub. Thorough this hub, each peer is clustered based on its interest. In what follows, we explains the details of our algorithm.

Node Behavior. In our algorithm, each peer has two types of logical links, *static links* and *dynamic links*. The role of static links is to keep connectivity of the network. They are created at initialization process of each peer, and never removed or added. Dynamic links are ones that connects token holders and token providers. They are created when a token is placed, and removed when a token is taken. In our algorithm, each peer creates several static links at the initialization phase. We assume that static links are created such that any two peers are connected with each other. Each peer has some number of *token place*, which is a container to put the token. A token place can hold one token. At the initialization, each peer creates tokens, and put them to its token places. The aim of token places is to limit the degree of each peer. Except for static links, the degree of each peer can be bounded by the sum of the number of injected tokens and that of its token places. Our algorithm allows each peer to determine by itself how many number of token places is prepared. This implies that each peer can control the imposed load by itself because the load of each peer strongly depends on its degree.

Each peer changes the networks topology when a token changes its position. To explain the detail of the topology change, let us consider an situation that an agent agt is going to take a token tok at peer p_1. The provider of tok is denoted by p_2. In our algorithm, a token contains the physical address of its provider and the peer where it was placed last. In this situation, the token tok contains the information about the physical address of p_1 and p_2. Then, we explains the behavior when tok is actually taken: if tok is taken by agt, the logical link between p_1 and p_2 is not immediately removed. While tok is carried by agt, it is temporarily held by both agt and p. Thus, another token cannot be put on the place of p_1 where there had been tok until tok is put to another place. If tok is put on some node p_3, p_3 first add the address of p_1 and p_2 to its connection list (recall that the address of p_1 and p_2 is contained in the token tok). It sends the message with p_3's physical address to p_1 and p_2 to inform the new place of tok. When p_1 receives this message, it removes tok from the token place. The peer p_2 receiving the message from p_3 adds the address of p_3 to its connection list.

Agent Behavior. In one time unit, an agent agt first migrates a randomly chosen neighbor p. If agt have an item and the peer p have an empty token place, it decides whether it puts the carrying item to p or not. It also decides whether an item on p is taken or not if p have an item and agt have a room to take an item. Same as the ABC algorithm, these decision is done in probabilistic way. However, the probability function is quite different from the ABC. The neighborhood function in our algorithm is defined by:

$$f(i,p) = \frac{1}{\alpha N_{TP}(p) + \sum_{q \in N(p)} N_{TP}(q)} \left(\alpha \cdot \sum_{t \in T(p)} \delta(t,i) + \sum_{q \in N(p)} \sum_{t \in T(q)} \delta(t,i) \right),$$

where p is the peer that have the token i, the $T(p)$ is the set of token on peer p, $N(p)$ is the set of neighbors of peer p, $N_{TP}(p)$ is the number of token places at peer p, and α is a design parameter. In addition, our algorithm use the different drop probability function from the ABC.

$$p_{drop}(i) = \left(\frac{1}{f(i)} \right)^{\beta},$$

where β is a design parameter. This probability is inspired by an advanced result for ABC [5]. For the pickup probability function, the algorithm uses the same one as the ABC algorithm. In addition to this probabilistic decision, each agent has one exceptional pickup scheme: if an agent encounters the token tok at the peer which provides tok, it necessarily picks up the token tok.

Let an agent agt pick up a token tok on p. Then, the behavior of agt until dropping tok consists of there phases: In the first phase , the agent agt only walks around the network, and never drops the token tok. The aim of this phase is to carry the token far apart from p. The first stage begins when agt picks up the token tok, and continues until the migration times of agt reaches to some predefined value l_{1st}. In the second phase, the agent agt is allowed to drop the token tok. The second phase continues until the token tok is dropped or the migration times reaches to some value l_{2nd}. Then, only in the latter case, the agent proceeds to the next phase. The third phase is the release phase. In this phase, the agent agt drops the token tok on the peer where the value of the neighborhood function is relatively high. More precisely, when tok is picked up from p, agt stores the value of the neighborhood function $v(= f(tok))$. The agent agt drops the token tok on the peer where the value of neighborhood function for tok is not smaller than $f(tok)$. The third phase continues until the token tok is dropped.

Our algorithm allows an agent to have one or more tokens. There is a capacity cap for the number of tokens one agent can have. For each token that one agent has, the thread of the above phases independently executed.

4.1 Simulation Results

In this subsection, we evaluate the efficiency of our algorithm by the simulation. Whereas evaluation needs benchmarks and measure for efficiency, the interest-based clustering have neither of them. Thus, in this section, we first introduce our criterion to measure the efficiency of an algorithm and one of benchmarks.

Our criteria is called k-*coverage*. To define it, we first give the k-coverage $C_k(p)$ for a peer p by:

$$C_k(p) = \sum_{p' \in N_k(p)} \delta(p', p),$$

where $N_k(p)$ means the set of peers whose distances from p are within k. The k-coverage of the whole network is defined by the average of $c_k(p)$ for all p in the system. Since our objective for organizing the interest-based clusters is the better peer-to-peer search, this criterion is straightforward and reasonable.

As a benchmark, we use an algorithm based on greedy strategy. This algorithm works as follows: for each peer p, the algorithm chooses one non-neighbor peer p' whose interest is the most similar with that of p, and adds the edge connecting p to p'. This process is repeatedly done until the number of additional edges are equal to that of dynamic links in our algorithm. More precisely, if one peer creates two tokens in our algorithm, the greedy algorithm adds two edges for one peer.

Figure 1 shows the transition of 3-coverage in the simulation of our algorithm. The vertical axis is the value of 3-coverage and the horizontal axis is time. The instance of the network used in the simulation consists of 5000 peers. As the topology of static links, we consider d-random regular graphs, that is, the graph where degrees of all peers are d. The graph topology is constructed by the method of Bollobás [2], that is, repeatedly choosing a pair of peers whose degrees are lower than d at random until all peers have degree d. In the simulation, we create a 4-random regular graph, and use it as the topology of static link. The interest of each peer is represented by an real value in the interval $[0..1]$, and its similarity is simply defined by their difference. The parameter setting of our algorithm is as follows: $k^+ = 0.05$, $k^- = 0.1$, $\alpha = 5.0$, $\beta = 4.0$, $l_{1st} = 200$, $l_{2nd} = 400$, and $cap = 10$. The number of agents is 500. Each peer prepares 6 token places, and creates two tokens. In figure 1, the value of 3-coverage is plotted every 200 time

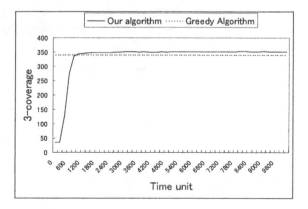

Fig. 1. The number of searches

units. The simulation result shows that our algorithm rapidly converges to the slightly better value than the greedy algorithm.

5   Conclusion

In this paper, we proposed an interest-based peer clustering algorithm. Our algorithm is inspired by the ant-based clustering (ABC) algorithm, which is one to categorize data items for data analysis. The key idea of our algorithm is to introduce tokens, and to indirectly organize peer cluster by clustering tokens. We also evaluated this algorithm by simulations, and showed our algorithm is slightly better than an simple greedy algorithm.

Acknowledgment. This work is supported in part by a JSPS, Grant-in-Aid for Scientific Research ((B)(2)15300017), and "The 21st Century Center of Excellence Program" of the Ministry of Education, Culture, Sports, Science and Technology, Japan.

References

1. Napster website. http://www.napster.com/.
2. B. Bollobás. *Random Graphs.* Academic Press, 1985.
3. E. Bonabeau, M. Dorigo, and G. Theraulaz. *Swarm Intelligence. From Natural to Artificial Systems.* Oxford University Press, 1999.
4. J.-L. Deneubourg, S.Goss, N. Franks, A. Sendova-Franks, C. Detrain, and L. Chretien. The dynamics of collective sorting: Robot-like ant and ant-like robot. In *Proc. of 1st Conference on Simulation of Adaptive Behavior: From Animals to Animats*, pages 356–365, 1991.
5. J. Handl, J.Knowles, and M. Dorigo. *Artificial Life*, 2005. To appear.
6. E. Lumer and B. Faieta. Diversity and adaptation in populations of clustering ants. In *Proc. of 3rd International Conference on Simulation of Adaptive Behavior: From Animalsto Animats 3*, pages 499–508, 1994.
7. Q. Lv, P. Cao, E. Cohen, and S. Shenker. Search and replication in unstructured peer-to-peer networks. In *Proc. of International Conference on Supercomputing(ICS)*, pages 84–95, 2002.

Author Index

Lecture Notes in Computer Science

For information about Vols. 1–3760

please contact your bookseller or Springer

Vol. 3806: A.H. H. Ngu, M. Kitsuregawa, E.J. Neuhold, J.-Y. Chung, Q.Z. Sheng (Eds.), Web Information Systems Engineering – WISE 2005. XXI, 771 pages. 2005.

Vol. 3805: G. Subsol (Ed.), Virtual Storytelling. XII, 289 pages. 2005.

Vol. 3804: G. Bebis, R. Boyle, D. Koracin, B. Parvin (Eds.), Advances in Visual Computing. XX, 755 pages. 2005.

Vol. 3803: S. Jajodia, C. Mazumdar (Eds.), Information Systems Security. XI, 342 pages. 2005.

Vol. 3802: Y. Hao, J. Liu, Y.-P. Wang, Y.-m. Cheung, H. Yin, L. Jiao, J. Ma, Y.-C. Jiao (Eds.), Computational Intelligence and Security, Part II. XLII, 1166 pages. 2005. (Sublibrary LNAI).

Vol. 3801: Y. Hao, J. Liu, Y.-P. Wang, Y.-m. Cheung, H. Yin, L. Jiao, J. Ma, Y.-C. Jiao (Eds.), Computational Intelligence and Security, Part I. XLI, 1122 pages. 2005. (Sublibrary LNAI).

Vol. 3799: M. A. Rodríguez, I.F. Cruz, S. Levashkin, M.J. Egenhofer (Eds.), GeoSpatial Semantics. X, 259 pages. 2005.

Vol. 3798: A. Dearle, S. Eisenbach (Eds.), Component Deployment. X, 197 pages. 2005.

Vol. 3797: S. Maitra, C. E. V. Madhavan, R. Venkatesan (Eds.), Progress in Cryptology - INDOCRYPT 2005. XIV, 417 pages. 2005.

Vol. 3796: N.P. Smart (Ed.), Cryptography and Coding. XI, 461 pages. 2005.

Vol. 3795: H. Zhuge, G.C. Fox (Eds.), Grid and Cooperative Computing - GCC 2005. XXI, 1203 pages. 2005.

Vol. 3794: X. Jia, J. Wu, Y. He (Eds.), Mobile Ad-hoc and Sensor Networks. XX, 1136 pages. 2005.

Vol. 3793: T. Conte, N. Navarro, W.-m.W. Hwu, M. Valero, T. Ungerer (Eds.), High Performance Embedded Architectures and Compilers. XIII, 317 pages. 2005.

Vol. 3792: I. Richardson, P. Abrahamsson, R. Messnarz (Eds.), Software Process Improvement. VIII, 215 pages. 2005.

Vol. 3791: A. Adi, S. Stoutenburg, S. Tabet (Eds.), Rules and Rule Markup Languages for the Semantic Web. X, 225 pages. 2005.

Vol. 3790: G. Alonso (Ed.), Middleware 2005. XIII, 443 pages. 2005.

Vol. 3789: A. Gelbukh, Á. de Albornoz, H. Terashima-Marín (Eds.), MICAI 2005: Advances in Artificial Intelligence. XXVI, 1198 pages. 2005. (Sublibrary LNAI).

Vol. 3788: B. Roy (Ed.), Advances in Cryptology - ASIACRYPT 2005. XIV, 703 pages. 2005.

Vol. 3787: D. Kratsch (Ed.), Graph-Theoretic Concepts in Computer Science. XIV, 470 pages. 2005.

Vol. 3785: K.-K. Lau, R. Banach (Eds.), Formal Methods and Software Engineering. XIV, 496 pages. 2005.

Vol. 3784: J. Tao, T. Tan, R.W. Picard (Eds.), Affective Computing and Intelligent Interaction. XIX, 1008 pages. 2005.

Vol. 3783: S. Qing, W. Mao, J. Lopez, G. Wang (Eds.), Information and Communications Security. XIV, 492 pages. 2005.

Vol. 3782: K.-D. Althoff, A. Dengel, R. Bergmann, M. Nick, T. Roth-Berghofer (Eds.), Professional Knowledge Management. XXIII, 739 pages. 2005. (Sublibrary LNAI).

Vol. 3781: S.Z. Li, Z. Sun, T. Tan, S. Pankanti, G. Chollet, D. Zhang (Eds.), Advances in Biometric Person Authentication. XI, 250 pages. 2005.

Vol. 3780: K. Yi (Ed.), Programming Languages and Systems. XI, 435 pages. 2005.

Vol. 3779: H. Jin, D. Reed, W. Jiang (Eds.), Network and Parallel Computing. XV, 513 pages. 2005.

Vol. 3778: C. Atkinson, C. Bunse, H.-G. Gross, C. Peper (Eds.), Component-Based Software Development for Embedded Systems. VIII, 345 pages. 2005.

Vol. 3777: O.B. Lupanov, O.M. Kasim-Zade, A.V. Chaskin, K. Steinhöfel (Eds.), Stochastic Algorithms: Foundations and Applications. VIII, 239 pages. 2005.

Vol. 3776: S.K. Pal, S. Bandyopadhyay, S. Biswas (Eds.), Pattern Recognition and Machine Intelligence. XXIV, 808 pages. 2005.

Vol. 3775: J. Schönwälder, J. Serrat (Eds.), Ambient Networks. XIII, 281 pages. 2005.

Vol. 3774: G. Bierman, C. Koch (Eds.), Database Programming Languages. X, 295 pages. 2005.

Vol. 3773: A. Sanfeliu, M.L. Cortés (Eds.), Progress in Pattern Recognition, Image Analysis and Applications. XX, 1094 pages. 2005.

Vol. 3772: M.P. Consens, G. Navarro (Eds.), String Processing and Information Retrieval. XIV, 406 pages. 2005.

Vol. 3771: J.M.T. Romijn, G.P. Smith, J. van de Pol (Eds.), Integrated Formal Methods. XI, 407 pages. 2005.

Vol. 3770: J. Akoka, S.W. Liddle, I.-Y. Song, M. Bertolotto, I. Comyn-Wattiau, W.-J. van den Heuvel, M. Kolp, J. Trujillo, C. Kop, H.C. Mayr (Eds.), Perspectives in Conceptual Modeling. XXII, 476 pages. 2005.

Vol. 3769: D.A. Bader, M. Parashar, V. Sridhar, V.K. Prasanna (Eds.), High Performance Computing – HiPC 2005. XXVIII, 550 pages. 2005.

Vol. 3768: Y.-S. Ho, H.J. Kim (Eds.), Advances in Multimedia Information Processing - PCM 2005, Part II. XXVIII, 1088 pages. 2005.

Vol. 3767: Y.-S. Ho, H.J. Kim (Eds.), Advances in Multimedia Information Processing - PCM 2005, Part I. XXVIII, 1022 pages. 2005.

Vol. 3766: N. Sebe, M.S. Lew, T.S. Huang (Eds.), Computer Vision in Human-Computer Interaction. X, 231 pages. 2005.

Vol. 3765: Y. Liu, T. Jiang, C. Zhang (Eds.), Computer Vision for Biomedical Image Applications. X, 563 pages. 2005.

Vol. 3764: S. Tixeuil, T. Herman (Eds.), Self-Stabilizing Systems. VIII, 229 pages. 2005.

Vol. 3762: R. Meersman, Z. Tari, P. Herrero (Eds.), On the Move to Meaningful Internet Systems 2005: OTM 2005 Workshops. XXXI, 1228 pages. 2005.

Vol. 3761: R. Meersman, Z. Tari (Eds.), On the Move to Meaningful Internet Systems 2005: CoopIS, DOA, and ODBASE, Part II. XXVII, 653 pages. 2005.